T0367866

THE EXCITING TRUTH ABOUT THE END-TIMES

~ *Why Christians shouldn't be Afraid of what Lies Ahead* ~

A Strictly Scriptural Understanding of John's Revelation and End-Time Prophecy

B. VINCENT SHELTON

WESTBOW PRESS®
A DIVISION OF THOMAS NELSON & ZONDERVAN

Copyright © 2014 B. Vincent Shelton.

All rights reserved. No part of this book may be used or reproduced by any means, graphic, electronic, or mechanical, including photocopying, recording, taping or by any information storage retrieval system without the written permission of the author except in the case of brief quotations embodied in critical articles and reviews.

WestBow Press books may be ordered through booksellers or by contacting:

WestBow Press
A Division of Thomas Nelson & Zondervan
1663 Liberty Drive
Bloomington, IN 47403
www.westbowpress.com
1 (866) 928-1240

Because of the dynamic nature of the Internet, any web addresses or links contained in this book may have changed since publication and may no longer be valid. The views expressed in this work are solely those of the author and do not necessarily reflect the views of the publisher, and the publisher hereby disclaims any responsibility for them.

Any people depicted in stock imagery provided by Thinkstock are models, and such images are being used for illustrative purposes only.
Certain stock imagery © Thinkstock.

ISBN: 978-1-4908-5759-6 (sc)
ISBN: 978-1-4908-5760-2 (hc)
ISBN: 978-1-4908-5758-9 (e)

Library of Congress Control Number: 2014919102

Print information available on the last page.

WestBow Press rev. date: 09/19/2016

Acknowledgments

My Creator, Father and closest Friend, knowing better than I my greatest needs and weakness, searched carefully among all his faithful daughters and selected just one perfect soul. He can give no greater gift to His children than a perfect companion, and my wife is just such a gift. Thanks "Honey" for always having a bright smile and positive outlook and for faithfully being my constant companion and best friend!

Jeanie and I wish to thank the following brothers and sisters in Christ for the great and lasting impact they've had on our lives.

~ Connie Shelton, Vondalee Frank, Sam and Kristin Minyard, Jack and Mary Duetsman and all our wonderful brothers and sisters at Havenhouse Church in Santa Clarita, Jon and Lena McDowell — all of whom have consistently been there with love, prayer and support when we've needed it most. Thank you so much!

Special thanks to Angelo and Maria Cusumano for their friendship, encouragement and love. And last but certainly not least, to my "study-buddy" and faithful prison ministry partner - Larry Wadley and his wife Georgia. Thanks partner for all the inspiring studies and travel time talks. Keep up the good work for the Lord!

Introduction

Over the years, hundreds of powerfully thought provoking books, films and docudramas have been written with the goal of bringing to life a rapidly approaching, extraordinarily horrific final seven-year period. That period is referred to, in Scripture, as a period of "GREAT TRIBULATION." Sadly, while some of those books and movies have made every effort to align themselves with what the Bible actually reveals, other (*mostly secular*) writers and producers, despite clear scriptural warnings, have often shown a complete lack of reverence for the sanctity of God's Holy Word.

And, while books and movies about "Armageddon" and the end of the world are often exciting and, to some degree, enlightening, the truth is many of those books and movies have been based on "traditional," widely taught, *"theoretic"* interpretations of end-time prophecies, some of which we now know cannot be properly supported by Scripture alone. That being said, we should not be ashamed or embarrassed of our former inability to fully and accurately interpret end-time prophecy, because our inability to do so was, in itself, a fulfillment of prophecy. That's right! Long ago, the very prophets who foretold of these end-time events were warned that the saints would not be able to properly interpret certain "**key**" end-time prophecies until "**the time of the end**."

Well I'm happy to announce that the time of the end has come! All those formerly mysterious, prophetic pieces of the end-time puzzle have fallen neatly into place. Christians no longer have to curiously wander through an endless wilderness of speculation and supposition, theorizing as to how all these end-time prophecies are going to be fulfilled. Instead, by allowing the Bible to interpret itself, Christians can now easily study and understand the end-times, including John's book of Revelation, and they can confidently support what they learn after doing so.

A House Of Cards

The Church's current edifice of "latter-day-knowledge" has been built like a house of cards, with the interpretation of each end-time prophecy representing a single card. Some of those cards are solid, having not been weakened by *"speculation"* or *"supposition."* Others, unfortunately, are hopelessly weak and never should have been laid upon that foundation. When those cards are removed — and we must remove them — much of our current end-time interpretation of prophecy quickly comes crashing down!

There is, however, a bright and encouraging light at the end of the tunnel. Since all evidence suggests that we've apparently reached "**the time of the end**," if we can resist our natural, prideful inclination toward *"supposi-*

tion," we'll find that God has designed His perfect Word to interpret itself. We don't have to guess! All we have to do is be willing to humbly reexamine our current views and honestly subject everything we *"believe we know to be true"* to the scrutiny of pure scripture. If we're willing to do this and, in doing so, are also willing to disregard all commonly accepted *terminologies, theories,* and *errant teachings* that cannot be clearly proven to have "self-emerged" from the text (*i.e., the whole of Scripture*), we will soon be able to see how miraculously God's infallible Word has been designed to "self-interpret." Thus, we'll finally know and be able to properly support, without *"supposition,"* the answers to questions that have baffled the Church for centuries, questions like:

- Will the "**Rapture**" (*the catching-away of the saints*) take place before, during, or at the end of the seven-year tribulation period?
- Will the "**Marriage Supper of the Lamb**" really take place immediately after the Rapture?
- How horrific will it be for our lost and still unrepentant loved ones if they get "**left-behind**?"
- What does "**the beast**" in John's Revelation vision actually represent? *(Can it really symbolize just a mere mortal being?)*
- What will the "**mark of the beast**" be, and how will it be enforced? *(The answer to that question may surprise you!)*
- Should we be teaching that the "**Door of Salvation**" will still be open during the Millennial Period?
- What does the Bible actually reveal about the "**Millennial Period**" kingdom of Christ and God's eternal heavenly kingdom?
- Could it be said that, today, end-time teaching is often based on an "**emotionally obscured**" view of prophecy, rather than an impartial and accurate interpretation of the text?

As we're about to see, the answers to these and many other end-time questions are scripturally provable. God certainly didn't give us this great wealth of end-time prophecy with the intent of creating confusion. On the contrary, our understanding of the "truth" (*God's infallible Word, which includes end-time prophecy*) should engender unity and singleness of mind among those who follow Christ (*the true Church*). And, as we're about to learn, powerful evidence does exist, suggesting that this generation may just be the first generation of believers to whom these amazing end-time scriptures are being fully revealed.

During this future period of "GREAT TRIBULATION," God will initiate His final call to repent to this progressively rebellious and obstinate world; thus, these important prophecies are intended to enable all true believers in Christ to have at least a basic understanding of what will happen during and immediately prior to the commencing of that dreadful period. This should be exciting news to every faithful follower of Christ! True Christians have absolutely no reason to fear the future. In fact, being able to clearly and confidently understand, teach and prove what the Bible actually reveals about our final days on earth, whether a novice student of Scripture or a seasoned Bible teacher, is a major faith booster and will greatly enhance one's ability to be a powerful witness for Christ. We should treat every day as though it were our last chance to share the Gospel, because we don't know how much time we have left. So, let's get to it! As our blessed Savior said:

"THE TIME IS AT HAND."

Table of Contents

Chapter 1

What Makes the Book of Revelation So Powerfully Unique?

Certainly no one who has dared to venture through its mysterious corridors of global destruction, angelic intervention, and eternal damnation has, afterward, referred to John's book of Revelation by saying: *"It's just another book of the Bible."* All by itself the name Revelation, with its disturbing images of underworld darkness, global anarchy, universal plagues, and countless other unfathomable events, evokes fear in the hearts of many non-Christians and Christians alike. From the beginning of time there has been no other truly prophetic book that has continually provoked the same measure of awe-inspiring reverence and fear, year after year, century after century, as has John's book of Revelation! *"Is this book unique?" — to say the least!*

Like a rusty caution sign nailed to an old, weathered fence, the first few verses of John's book post a stern warning to every curious soul that those who dare venture within must soon decide where to pitch their spiritual tents; in the camp of faith and trust in the Creator of all things or in that of continued rebellion and doubt. Straddling the fence in this spiritual battle between "**GOOD**" and "**EVIL**" is simply not an option; at least it's not an option for those who when the battle's over wish to abide in the good graces of the Lord.

From God's first communication with Adam in the Garden of Eden to this final interaction with the apostle John on the island of Patmos, faith and obedience have remained the only conduit to a right relationship and understanding of God and His eternal plan for the salvation of Man. It should not, therefore, surprise us to find that, in this last book of the Bible, nothing has changed.

'Blessed is he that readeth, and they that hear the words of this prophecy, ***and keep those things which are written therein****: for the time is at hand.'*

Rev. 1:3

Studying through the first few verses of John's vision, some have concluded that a heavenly blessing is promised to all who simply read or hear the words of this book. But is that correct? Is that really what we're promised? Unfortunately, I've heard it taught that way by countless well intentioned ministers. That, however, is not what a careful assessment of the scripture actually reveals.

Looking more closely, we find that the blessing is in the "**keeping**" of the words of John's book, not just in the reading and hearing of them. Keeping the words requires a faith motivated response on our part, a reverent acknowledgement that what we're reading will surely come to pass. Conversely, for those who choose to reject Christ's warning, that which was lovingly imparted by way of blessing sadly becomes a curse, a promise of unspeakable doom and eternal condemnation. Therefore, given the supreme accuracy of biblical prophecy, the choice of whether to heed and obey or to doubt and reject what is written should be a no-brainer.

What else makes the book of Revelation so powerfully unique?

More than with any other prophetic book, Christians, young and old, seem to quiver at the mere thought of studying John's end-time vision. Some have confessed that they become outright terrified at the thought of reading it! Others have said, *"I don't believe it's possible to understand, so why bother?"* And yet, like mystery novels, books written about the end-times and books attempting to explain John's Revelation vision seem to fly off bookstore shelves. Unfortunately, no two books explain John's end-time vision in precisely the same way. And, making matters worse, the movie industry is all too happy to help cloud our understanding by creating countless doomsday movies that freely and irreverently misinterpret true end-time Bible prophecies.

Understanding how God created the earth and understanding end-time events, while vastly different subjects, have at least one thing in common; no matter how many opinions there are about either subject, there is but one truth. God gave us the book of Genesis so we wouldn't be in the dark regarding His divine creation, and He has likewise given us the book of Revelation and other prophetic books so as to prevent us, unlike those without faith, from being surprised at His coming.

~ If that's true, why is the book of Revelation so hard to understand? ~

As a young Christian I read several end-time books, attempting to find the one book that could clearly explain John's Revelation vision of tribulation events, but to no avail. Each time I started a new book I got excited, thinking: *'Finally, I'm going to understand the book of Revelation!'* Unfortunately, book after book, the author's interpretation seemed to hit a brick wall, proving to be more opinion than fact. The authors obviously believed they were on the right track and boldly taught their opinions as if they could easily support them, just as I had. On the surface our perspectives appeared to be true, but when honestly subjected to the refining fire of God's infallible Word the teachings just didn't hold up. I knew God didn't give us these prophetic books to confuse us, so why did no one seem to have a real grasp of end-time events? These prophecies are meant to be understood, at least in part; aren't they?

Most will state that the book of Revelation is difficult to understand because the prophecies in it will only fully be revealed during their future occurrence. That happens to be at least partly true; however, from my perspective, the real problem is something more fundamental. Apparently, we (*the Church*) have collectively neglected to apply the simple, straight forward method of interpreting prophecy to John's end-time vision as has been consistently demonstrated throughout Scripture. Not one of the books I've read successfully interprets John's or Daniel's visions through the use of the simple biblical method to which I'm referring. Fortunately, there's a verse in the book of Daniel that I believe gives us a possible clue as to why so many of us have formerly failed in our attempts to interpret these scriptures, and we'll get to that enlightening verse very soon.

The key word here is "Allegory"

Our being able to properly interpret many of the Bible's prophetic passages is directly tied to our understanding of "**allegorical**" prophecy. By allegorical prophecy, I simply mean prophecies that use metaphorical figures to create images of future events through the use of dreams and visions. As we revisit these end-time scriptures and really begin to put our eschatological foundation to the test, we're going to find that many end-time passages are excellent examples of allegorical prophecy.

A few Examples

Starting in Genesis 37:5-10 (*the very first book of the Bible*), we read of the patriarch Joseph having two dreams. In those dreams, God revealed His plans for Joseph's future eminence in Egypt. In the first dream God used *bowing sheaves* to represent Joseph's older brothers and an *upright sheave* to represent Joseph. In the second dream, Joseph saw the *sun*, the *moon,* and *eleven stars* paying obeisance to him. By these simple allegorical dreams, Joseph understood that someday in the future he would rule over his father, mother, and his eleven brothers. What's more, because this allegorical method of revelation is so simple to interpret, when Joseph told his family the dreams, they not only understood them but scolded him for what they considered to be a blatant lack of humility on his part! We now know, of course, that both of Joseph's dreams were accurate revelations of the Lord's will and were fulfilled shortly thereafter.

Throughout the Bible we find this method of allegorical revelation being used repeatedly. Let's take a quick look at another dream experience in Joseph's life, also in Genesis, starting with Chapter 40:1. In that passage, while Joseph is serving as trustee for the keeper of the prison, we read that he was put in charge of two important prisoners, the king's butler and his baker. While awaiting Pharaoh's judgment, certainly fearful of their impending fate, the butler and baker each had an allegorical dream, much like the dreams Joseph experienced earlier.

The butler dreamt of three blossoming grape vines and of squeezing them into Pharaoh's cup. The baker dreamt of three baskets of bakemeats on his head and of birds eating out of the uppermost basket. God gave Joseph the interpretation of each of their dreams. The butler was to be restored to the service of the king within three days, while the baker was to be beheaded. And, as is to be expected, that's precisely what happened.

Two years later the Pharaoh also had a two-part dream in which he saw *seven fat-fleshed cows* and *seven lean-fleshed cows*. The *fat-fleshed cows* were eaten up by the *lean-fleshed cows*. Next, he saw *seven plump ears of corn*, then *seven thin ears*. The *plump ears of corn* were devoured by the *thin ears*. Once again, God gave Joseph the interpretation of the dream, which Joseph relayed to Pharaoh. The *seven fat cows* and *seven plump ears of corn* followed by *seven lean cows* and *seven thin ears of corn* was a warning that seven years of great plenty (*in Egypt*) would be followed by seven years of unimaginable famine.

We all know the story. God's giving Joseph the ability to relay this interpretation to Pharaoh not only saved Joseph's and his families' lives but also resulted in Joseph being placed in high esteem in Egypt, second only to Pharaoh. Thus, Joseph's earlier dreams of ruling over his father, mother and eleven brothers were fulfilled through his prominence in Egypt, which saved his entire family from probable starvation. In each of these examples, God first gave an allegorical dream or vision and followed it with the actual interpretation. Dreams and visions that follow this basic allegorical format can be found in many books of the Bible.[1]

While I don't want to overstress the importance of understanding the Bible's fluid use of allegorical prophecy, I do want to lay a solid foundation for our recognizing this type of prophecy as we progress through the Scriptures. Failing to do so will prevent us from understanding exciting passages, passages that reveal essential details about this end-time period

[1] Ez. 37, Dan. 2, 4, 5, 7, 8, Acts 10 and 16—just to list a few.

in which we live. Moreover, because we (*the Church*) have often neglected to follow God's simple allegorical method of interpreting prophetic scripture, we have consequently failed to properly interpret obvious scriptures that were intended to give us greater insight into important events, like the catching-away of the church (*commonly referred to as "the Rapture"*).[2]

Of course Jesus made it clear that it's not for us to know the actual day or hour when He will return to resurrect and/or "catch-away" (*rapture*) the saints.[3] Nonetheless, while this is clearly true, Jesus did intend for us to know, with certainty, whether the catching-away of the saints will happen—*before, during or after*—the great tribulation period. In fact, as we'll soon see, John's book of Revelation clearly reveals this mystery.

I realize that many probably think (*as I formerly did*) that there is no way of knowing for sure whether the Rapture will happen—*before, during or after*—the tribulation period, but I'll be surprised if you still hold that opinion after we've finished thoroughly examining John's remarkable Revelation vision. As we venture, verse by verse, through John's awesome prophetic book, we're going to see one mystery after another become a "**revelation**," just as God intended. What's more, as we do, John's vision will begin to paint a clear, scripturally supportable picture of the entire end-time period, including the millennial reign of Christ and the establishing of God's eternal kingdom on the new earth.

I'm not teaching something new!

Allegorical prophecies are an integral part of Scripture, so please don't misunderstand me. I'm not claiming to have had a private revelation. I'm simply trying to help those who want to understand the end-times recognize how truly simple it is to correctly interpret the many allegorical prophecies that are "**key**" to our end-time comprehension. As the apostle Paul wrote:

*'. . . God is **not** the author of confusion . . .'*

ꕤ 1Cor. 14:33 ꕤ

The truth is we **are** that fortunate, specific generation to whom end-time prophecy is being revealed. God certainly didn't give us these end-time prophecies with the intent of furthering our foundation for disagreement! We're expected to gain at least a basic, chronological understanding of current and future end-time events. Therefore, if your ambition is to confidently understand the end-times and to be able to scripturally support what you learn, you should be getting pretty excited about this. I've

[2] 1Th. 4:13 thru 5:1-1, 1Cor.15:50-54
[3] Mt.24:24-36

been studying this subject for decades, and I still get excited just thinking about what lies ahead! In the past, I've led studies through the book of Revelation with pastors, home fellowship groups, missionary students, even hardcore prison groups and had great success. If you join me and sincerely pray your way through this book, when we've finished we'll have a scripturally accurate and complete understanding of the end-times and all major corresponding events. However, we do need to keep in mind that many of the details of these prophecies will not be revealed until they're fulfilled. Therefore, if we don't want to be led astray from the straight and narrow "PATH OF TRUTH," we must be careful not to allow ourselves the freedom of unrestrained speculation.

The Goal:

Our goal is to understand the basic "**timeline**" of essential end-time events and to be able to confidently and clearly support our findings, while never forgetting that

> Scripture always gives meaning to Scripture.

The Bible is a divine system of scriptural *"checks and balances"* and is, therefore, perfectly designed to allow "truth" to self-emerge from the text. In other words, God has miraculously designed the Bible to reveal itself. We need only to filter out of the mix all *"opinions," "suppositions"* and *"traditionally held beliefs and terminologies"* that cannot be proven to have self-emerged from Scripture <u>alone</u>. There are many end-time *"terms and catchphrases"* that have become common to the Church, even though they really have no true scriptural foundation. So, while venturing through these exciting passages, our goal will be to identify these errant *"terms"* and *"interpretations"* and, when necessary, replace them with the correct biblical appellations.

Chapter 2

The Generation to Whom End-Time Prophecy Is Revealed

There are some extraordinarily important scriptures that I believe have been almost completely ignored by the Church as a whole, and it may be that their importance cannot be overstated. They're found in the book of **Daniel 12:4-9**. In those verses, Daniel recorded that after having finished delivering a message of future events, the angel Gabriel told him to: "*. . . **shut up the words, and seal the book, even to the time of the end: many shall run to and fro, and knowledge shall be increased.***" Gabriel's words may very well refer specifically to our current end-time generation; therefore, his words could quite possibly be essential, not only to our understanding of the end-times, but also to our understanding of all related tribulation period events. We now know that it's not possible to properly interpret John's Revelation vision without properly interpreting Daniel's corresponding visions. And yet, even though Gabriel clearly explained that we would not be able to understand some of Daniel's prophecies until ***'the time of the end,'*** we could build a mountain with the books of those who've unsuccessfully tried to interpret Gabriel's message.

If Gabriel's directive to Daniel is intended to describe the future generation to whom Daniel's end-time visions would be revealed, then Gabriel's words (*'many shall run to and fro, and knowledge shall be increased'*) perfectly describe the world today. His word would not, however, accurately characterize any generation that existed prior to today's global society.

Today, in our generation, we can board a plane in San Francisco after breakfast and be in New York in time for lunch. It's hard to believe, but roughly one hundred years ago the world's main mode of personal transportation was still the horse and buggy, which is not much different from that of Daniel's generation. Public mass-transportation, just a few generations back, was a choice between cruise or cargo ship and steam powered train — both of which took days or even weeks, not hours, to get you where you wanted to go.

In the early 1800's, if you wanted to move your family and belongings across the state or country, the most common method of travel was horse drawn wagon, which could take weeks or, more likely, months. Even in the late 1800's (*roughly 2,400 years after Daniel's generation*) it still took several days to do the same thing by steamship or train. If we were to take a look at any of the countless historical videos of the 1930's *Great Depression Era,* which was less than one hundred years ago, we would see many displaced families commuting by means of horse drawn wagon. The state and federal highway systems, which would eventually become the veins through which this nation's transportation blood-line would flow, were, at that time, only just beginning to form. Thus, we can safely say that past generations did not fulfill Gabriel's — ***'many shall go to and fro'*** — characterization of the future transportationally advanced generation that would be able to properly interpret the message God gave Daniel.

What about the second part of Gabriel's directive – ***'and knowledge will be increased'***? The key word here is "**knowledge**." On the surface it's difficult to know whether the verse is referring specifically to knowledge of God and His eternal plan of salvation or if it refers, more generally, to scientific, technological knowledge. If the latter is the case, then, once again, only our current generation could be characterized as being the technologically advanced generation to whom Daniel's prophecies are at least beginning to be revealed.

Today's technology is explosive! The technological progress of past generations pales in comparison to our current high-tech world. In the past two centuries we've gone from candle-light *to "fiber optics and laser surgery,"* from telegraph-wires to the *"world-wide-web and global satellite communication."* We even have space voyagers on route to destinations hundreds of millions of miles from earth. I don't know about you, but I can't keep up with it all. The computer or cell-phone I buy today will be out dated almost before I purchase it!

On the other hand, what if Gabriel's directive refers to knowledge of God's eternal plan rather than technological knowledge? That would be a difficult argument to support for one very simple reason. Gabriel's directive refers not just to *"knowledge"* but to *"knowledge"* and to *"many going to and fro,"* thus signifying mass-transportation. And, as we have already established, no generation prior to our generation has been capable of daily, global mass-transportation. Therefore, if Gabriel's having declared that ***'many shall run to and fro, and knowledge shall be increased'*** was not just a general statement (*which it doesn't seem to have been*), then it's possible that no prior generation of believers truly qualified to understand the full meaning of the critically important end-time prophecies to which Gabriel was referring. Hence, it would not be illogical to conclude that we might just be that fortunate, *"technologically"* and *"mass-transportationally"* advanced generation to whom Daniel's prophecies are now being more fully revealed. I realize that this is a bold perspective, and I don't propose its possibility lightly. The simple truth is I'm only stating the obvious. If we are not that unique, end-time generation to whom Gabriel was referring, then just what did Gabriel's message mean, and to which generation was Gabriel referring?

Even so, while that is a logical question and needs to be considered, we should note that it is still possible that Gabriel's message was just an acknowledgment that mankind will continue to traverse the world and gain insights into God's plan of salvation and science (*technology*). However, if that is the case, we still have Gabriel's warning that Daniel's visions would not be understood until — ***'the time of the end.'***

~ *Why is this so important?* ~

This is important because, for hundreds of years, the Church has struggled, having little success, to properly interpret important portions of Daniel's end-time visions. If the Church could have properly interpreted the specific end-time visions to which Gabriel was referring, despite Gabriel's statement to the contrary, Gabriel's statement would be incorrect, and that's just not possible. Moreover, since some of John's Revelation vision closely aligns with key portions of Daniel's visions regarding that same end-time period, it's logical to conclude that, since Gabriel told Daniel that some of his end-time visions wouldn't be revealed until ***'the time of the end,'*** then John's corresponding visions would likewise not be completely revealed until ***'the time of the end.'*** And that's not a stretch by any means; it's just plain and simple logic!

~ *Okay, so why'd the Church even bother attempting to interpret these visions?* ~

The Church had no choice but to endeavor to interpret Daniel's prophecies, because, like us, they had no way of knowing exactly what was and was not being revealed. The truth is we still don't know, with complete certainty, precisely what is being or has been revealed. This is particularly important for us to acknowledge, because as Christians we are commanded to study to show ourselves approved and to rightly divide the Word of God.[4] Therefore, it's understandable that the Church has been feverously trying, all these years, to interpret these exciting prophecies.

As we carefully examine the book of Revelation side by side with the parallel prophecies in the book of Daniel and other prophetic books, we'll uncover exactly how some of these visions have been and continue to be

---

[4] 2Tim. 2:15

misinterpreted. We'll also expose the most commonly used *"errant"* end-time terminologies, which, like huge stumbling-blocks, have continually caused the Church to trip and fall-short with respect to accurately interpreting and teaching end-time prophecy. Who am I to state that observation? Absolutely nobody! Being part of the body of Christ, however, I'm just acknowledging that, since there is only one true interpretation and most of us are interpreting many of these end-times scriptures differently, we must be falling short.

If we take Gabriel's message into consideration we have no choice but to consider the possibility that at least some of our commonly used terms and interpretations, regarding the seven-year tribulation period, may have actually been formulated before God began fully revealing the specific prophecies from which they originated. That may explain why some of today's end-time terminology is incorrect and cannot be properly supported by Scripture alone. This is where we separate the men from the boys, or — to put it more directly — we separate those who truly seek a right understanding of Scripture from those who merely want to continue believing they're right, regardless of what the Scriptures clearly reveal.

It's wise to keep in mind . . . .

A prideful hearted Christian searching the Scriptures is as likely to lay hold of the truth as is a blind man apt to paint the perfect portrait. The sad truth is that most of us believe we're basically humble, teachable Christians, and yet, the existence of multiple Christian denominations proves otherwise. If we're all as humble and teachable as we believe ourselves to be, our interpretations of Scripture, in general, should differ very little. Sadly, most experienced pastors will confirm that, while many Christians come to church with humble hearts, eager to learn, others go to church or Bible studies full of false humility, just waiting to see if the lesson being taught is what they already believe. If it's not, they either don't like the church or they don't like the teacher. I keep the following self-check in mind:

> We all have ministers and teachers with whom we almost always agree, yet in some areas we're usually confident their teaching is possibly "a little off." Only Christ is right all the time. Therefore, if our favorite teachers are sometimes wrong without knowing it, then the same applies to us. We too have beliefs that are possibly "a little off" or even "flat out wrong;" we just don't realize it.

Unfortunately, we don't usually know when we've gone off course, which is why humility is always in order, for the teacher as well as the student, in fact, for the teacher much more than the student! A teacher, above all, should be eager to learn and slow to argue.

As I earlier stated, I formerly taught about the end-times using the same *"ill-supported"* interpretations as most other ministers and teachers I knew. We all deviated a little in our teachings, but, for the most part, we basically taught the same improperly founded *theories*. That was the problem. Although we didn't realize it, what we were teaching was largely based on *theory*, not fact. And *theories* and *suppositions* are like a giant fog bank clouding the path of truth. Of course, I used several scriptures to support my teaching, just as did everyone else. I was convincing and sounded like I had it all figured out. I mean I believed I really knew that stuff! But I was wrong — "sincere" — but still very wrong. The fact was I just didn't have the solid, confident feeling that usually accompanies one's knowing that what he or she is teaching is truly in alignment with all of God's Word. Sadly, since everything I taught was tied to tons of scripture, I naively believed my teaching to be scripturally sound — *what a rookie!* Pointing to a boatload of Bible verses doesn't necessarily qualify what's being taught. When teaching is truly inspired and substantial it just emerges, all by itself, from the study of Scripture "AS A WHOLE;" it doesn't need our *theoretic* help. Thus, when we allow the proper interpretation to "**self-emerge**" from the text, every additional, relevant verse of Scripture will serve to further illuminate that inspired interpretation. This is the essence of true, divinely inspired teaching, and teaching of that nature and discipline is self-supporting.

The Challenge

Before studying the rest of this book, I encourage every reader, whether a novice or a seasoned eschatologist, to join me in spending however much time in prayer as is needed to humbly invite the Author of the Word (*the Holy Spirit*)[5] to open our hearts and minds to the understanding of these scriptures. If we sincerely surrender our personal opinions to the divine scrutiny of "only Scripture" (*sola Scriptura*), holding nothing back, the Holy Spirit will miraculously bring the truth to light from within the text, and when that happens there's no mistaking it!

---

[5] John 14:14-26, 1Jn. 2:27

Chapter 3

Using the Biblical Method of Interpretation

Most seasoned Christians have spent years reading books and listening to their favorite preachers teach about the end-times. Thus, many are proud of their knowledge of end-time prophecy, and are, therefore, frequently confident that their eschatological interpretations are, without a doubt, correct. Sadly, however, it's been my experience that most Christians are not nearly as humble and teachable as they believe themselves to be. In fact, many are defiantly rigid regarding their understanding of Scripture. In some cases it would be easier to sell them a smelly old pair of boots than to get them to sincerely, humbly reevaluate the actual origin of their supposedly *"scriptural"* foundation.

~ So, how can we be sure we're on the path of truth? ~

The Holy Spirit wrote the Bible through humble men of God. Consequently, it stands to reason that if we sincerely humble ourselves and pray before opening the Bible to study, the Holy Spirit will open to us its meaning. That's what the Scriptures teach;[6] therefore, we know we're on a track toward true understanding when the entirety of Scripture continues to support and further substantiate what we're learning.

~ Tunnel-vision to a Bible student is what wearing dark sunglasses would be to a Stargazer. ~

During the early days of my Christian life, I quickly learned to beware of the dreaded "Tunnel-vision Monster!" *OO--oo-oo, were you scared?* You should have been. If we're not prayerfully alert, during our daily forage through the Scriptures in search of truth, we can easily become ensnared by the terrifyingly relentless "Tunnel-vision Monster." And, if that happens, for many, there's virtually no escaping his evil grasp!

---

[6] 1Jn. 2:27, James 1:5, 1Cor 2:10-16, 1Ti 3:16

How Tunnel-vision Grabs Us

"Tunnel-vision" attacks happen very subtly. We'll just be meekly skipping along, from verse to verse, blissfully basking in the heavenly glow of God's infallible Word, when all of a sudden, without even realizing it, we'll have been ensnared! Our mind and vision will have become frozen to just one passage or verse. "REASON" and "LOGIC" — our only natural defenses — will become inaccessible, leaving us completely vulnerable and ensnared by just one passage. Thus, because a particular scripture will appear to be saying one specific thing, we'll have irrationally become fixated on just that passage.

Sadly, when "Tunnel-vision" grabs us it holds on tightly and can do so for years! Unfortunately, when that happens absolutely no one can reason with us. It becomes nearly impossible to broaden our vision and take in the complete "BIGGER—PICTURE" that the entirety of Scripture is actually presenting. What's more, if (*on our journey through the Scriptures*) we are defiantly harboring "PRIDE" in our backpack, we might as well forget it! Only prayer infused with sincere humility can help us break free of "Tunnel-vision's" grasp.

So, how do we defend ourselves?

Our best defense is remembering that no "single verse" or "group of verses" stands alone. Thus, when an individual passage or verse seems to be expressing a meaning that does not agree with the totality of Scripture, that passage must give way to what the preponderance of Scripture teaches. This, of course, does not mean that the scripture in question is contradictory or incorrect. It simply means that we're somehow failing to grasp the true meaning of that passage. When this happens, it's usually because we're missing a crucial piece of scriptural or historical information. With a little faith, patience, and prayerful study, if we just press on we'll eventually begin to understand the passage's proper interpretation. We should never let a single passage or verse so captivate our vision that it becomes impossible for us to see — "THE WHOLE OF SCRIPTURE."

It's also important for us to remember that not all scripture has, as of yet, been revealed, and some prophecies won't likely be revealed during our lifetime. For those of us who *"live to study,"* recognizing the boundaries of what has and has not been opened to our understanding requires our most reverent restraint and strictest discipline. To the Church the Word of God is no less than the Ark of the Covenant, and I certainly don't want to become another Uzza.[7] Thus, the study of God's infallible Word demands our most supreme respect.

---

[7] 1Chr. 13:9-10

The World's Largest Mural

Most of us have seen a large picture or portrait that caught our attention, and as we got closer we realized that the whole picture was created by the artist placing a variety of little photographs side by side to create one larger image. Like Bible verses, all the little images are different from the next, yet together they create one large, clear picture. In the same way, if we were to illustrate each chapter and verse of the Bible, using them like an artist, we could create one enormous, awe-inspiring mural, depicting the entire biblical record of God's eternal plan, from beginning to end.

Let's try for a minute to imagine this. For our illustration of the Bible to be accurate it would have to correctly depict all of the Bible's stories, prophecies, psalms, proverbs, parables, and historical events, from the creation of the first angel and dwelling place of God to the Second Coming of Christ and the establishment of His final, eternal kingdom. To get a clearer picture, we'll imagine that this mural is actually an enormous puzzle, mounted on the side of a massive building, with each verse of the Bible being just one piece of our colossal puzzle. A building large enough to display an image of this magnitude would have to be more than one hundred stories high and at least ten city blocks wide. You could easily skydive from the top of it!

Now, we'll pretend that, having never seen the immense puzzle's image, we're standing, blindfolded, directly in front of the puzzle, with our noses just a couple inches away from the gigantic image. Having our faces that close to the puzzle, if our blindfolds were to be removed, could we confidently describe everything the enormous image is depicting? Of course not! Even what we could see right in front of us would be unclear. The same would be true if we were to take a single "**verse**" or "**passage**" of Scripture out of context and begin to try and interpret its meaning.

Now let's imagine that we've moved a full step back and are standing a little more than arm's length away from the vast, building size puzzle. With our eyes adjusting and refocusing on an area about six feet in diameter, we're finally beginning to comprehend what we're seeing. From a foot and a half back we can clearly see the little images on each of the tiny puzzle pieces in front of us and the lines that indicate the boarders of each piece, but we can't see how all those little, individual pieces interact and relate to the massive, building-size image as a whole. Thus, we can't really understand what we're seeing.

In the same way, reading a verse or studying a single passage or chapter of Scripture can give us a great deal of insight into a particular subject but only when we see how that passage relates and interacts with Scripture "AS A WHOLE." Ascribing meaning to an individual passage or verse, from that limited perspective, would be irresponsible.

That's precisely what "Tunnel-vision" does to our understanding of Scripture. It keeps us pridefully focused on a single verse or passage and prevents us from seeing the much "BIGGER—PICTURE" that's being illustrated by the fullness of Scripture. This sounds obvious enough, but you'd be surprised how often "Tunnel-vision" prevents even seasoned Christians from recognizing what is or is not scripturally supportable while studying.

So, let's see what happens when we move - *way- ay - ay - back!* Alright, now that we've moved far enough back to see the whole puzzle all at once, it's finally become impossible for the dreaded "Tunnel-vision Monster" to strike.

~ *Wait! Why can't he strike?* ~

When we move far enough back to see the picture as a whole, something almost poetic happens. Those thin lines that border each individual puzzle piece are no longer visible. All the little pieces, the individual passages and verses, have collectively become "ONE GIANT IMAGE." Thus, the dreaded "Tunnel-vision Monster" can no longer strike! When we move far enough away to see the whole mural all at once, it becomes impossible to focus on just one piece of the puzzle. Likewise, when we study God's Word "AS A WHOLE" our own interpretations and opinions as to the significance of each individual verse of Scripture become irrelevant. Therefore, it's our ability to see God's entire plan as one complete image that enables us to understand the true meaning of all the individual chapters and verses that make up the Bible — not the other way around. And yet, even after we've seen the entire "BIGGER—PICTURE," having spent many years in prayerful study, we will still have only just begun to understand the entirely of God's Word.[8] The apostle Paul put it this way:

*'For now **we see through a glass**, **darkly**; but then face to face:*
*now **I know in part**; but then {when we've become immortal}*
shall I know even as also I am known.'

∞ 1Cor. 13:12 ∞

One final thought about the Puzzle

Now that we're far enough away to see the whole puzzle, if someone were to remove just one of its millions of tiny pieces, would we notice its absence? No way! We wouldn't notice without the use of a powerful telescope. What if a little cluster of pieces were to be removed; would it hinder our ability to see the "BIGGER–PICTURE?" It would make little difference,

[8] 1Cor. 13:9-10

if at all. Seeing the picture "AS A WHOLE" reveals the true meaning of all the little pieces, not the other way around. Therefore, we must never give more weight to a single verse or passage of Scripture than we give to Scripture "AS A WHOLE."

That's precisely why that 1,000 piece puzzle you gave poor old Aunt Bethany when she came home after having hip surgery last year had a big picture of the completed puzzle on the front of the box. Imagine how difficult it would be for your old Auntie if that huge puzzle came in a plain white box and she had to assemble it, having no idea what all those little pieces put together should illustrate!

The next time you get together with your home fellowship or study group try a little experiment. Bring a 500 or 1,000 piece puzzle. Then, without showing anyone in the group the completed puzzle's image, give each person their own private handful of puzzle pieces. Next, after giving each of them time alone to study only the handful of varied pieces they were given, have each individual draw a picture of what they would guess the much larger, completed puzzle's image actually depicts. If you had to predict the outcome, would you guess that all their pictures will look alike? More importantly, do you think any of their drawings will correctly portray the actual completed puzzle's image?

When we make the mistake of ascribing too much importance to an individual verse or passage, without first viewing it in the light of Scripture "AS A WHOLE," it's like trying to predict and describe the whole puzzle's image after having only looked at a few pieces. This, unfortunately, is the reason for the existence of so many contradictory Christian denominations. If we, during the early formation of the Church, would have humbly assessed the totality of Scripture, disallowing our personal, prideful inclinations, we could have continued as one unified body of believers, just as Paul admonished.[9] Sadly, however, many who presently teach the Bible are, themselves, standing with their noses only inches away from the giant puzzle's image. Thus, they're not seeing the much "BIGGER–PICTURE" that all the scriptures together — "AS ONE GIANT IMAGE" — are revealing.[10]

[9] 1Cor. 1:10-31, 3:1-23

[10] 1Cor. 8:2, 13:12

Chapter 4

A Little Background on Revelation's Author

The book of Revelation was written by John the beloved, late in the first century, near the end of his life. This particular John is the same disciple whose affection for Christ was so strong and uninhibited that he would often rest his head against Jesus' chest while they ate. What a neat guy!

Accredited with having written the most intimate of the four Gospels John also wrote three other inspiring letters of admonition and encouragement to the Church and, of course, the book of Revelation. In his Gospel, John referred to himself as being *"the disciple whom Jesus loved."* This gave credence to the recognition that John had a special relationship with the Savior. Certainly, we know that Jesus loves all of His children, but after reading John's Gospel it's easy to see that John had good reason to feel at least a little special about his relationship with Christ. Not only was he one of the three core disciples (*along with Peter and James*), which gave him special access to certain miraculous events in Jesus' life, but John also apparently felt comfortable approaching Jesus at times when the other disciples were apprehensive.[11]

Though Peter definitely had regular, direct communications with Jesus and was also one of Jesus' inner three disciples, his relationship with the Lord, at least on the surface, didn't seem to reach the same comfort level as did John's.[12] Perhaps that's why Peter apparently felt a little insecure and possibly even a little jealous of John. This becomes evident in the latter part of John's Gospel, where Peter is forewarned by Jesus that he, like Jesus, would die a martyr's death. Peter, obviously uncomfortable with that prophetic warning, turned and, seeing John, asked: *"Lord, and what shall this man do?"* [13] To which Jesus answered: *"If I will that he tarry till I come, what is that to thee? follow thou me."* From this admonition the rumor started that Jesus said John would not die. This obviously wasn't what Jesus had said, though, as usual, it's likely there was hidden meaning

---

[11] John 13:21-26, 21:20
[12] John 13:24
[13] John 21:15-24

in Christ's words. John eventually out-lived all the original disciples and, after recording his amazing Revelation vision, died a natural death.

Being spared a martyr's death, however, would only be considered a blessing to some. For a believer like John, ***'to live is Christ, and to die is gain.'***[14] But, during His final agonizing moments on the cross, Jesus had given John a very special commission. Looking at His mother (*Mary*), Jesus said: "***Woman, behold thy son***"[15] — referring her to John. Then, looking at John, Jesus said: "***Behold thy mother.***" John understood this to mean that Jesus wished him to adopt Mary as His mother. In spite of all Jesus' suffering, as always, His concern was for those for whom He was dying. There must have been something truly special about John, because Jesus had living brothers and sisters who (*as far as we know*) could have taken care of Mary. Why Christ commissioned John in this way we can only speculate. Nonetheless, whatever the reason, John adopted Mary as his mother and took her to his home, caring for her until her death.

While John was fulfilling his commitment to take care of Mary, he also labored with Peter and James laying the foundation of the early Jerusalem Church. It's commonly accepted among historians that John was an active participant at the AD 49 "Council of Jerusalem," where the basic doctrines of what would develop into present day Christianity were decided.

Some historical records state that after Mary's death John traveled to the city of Ephesus, in Asia Minor, where (*in approximately AD 95*) he was arrested for preaching the Gospel of Christ. Subsequently, during the reign of the Emperor Domitian, John was taken to Rome to stand trial. Apparently the emperor didn't like John's Gospel message, because he sentenced John to be boiled in oil! When it comes to our living or dying, however, God always has the last word, and God had been preserving John's life for a very special purpose. Thus, their malicious attempt to kill John failed, which must have been quite a sight. John was mercilessly lowered into a massive, red-hot caldron of boiling oil and yet emerged unscathed!

Hence, in an effort to save face, the Emperor Domitian had John exiled to a rocky penal island settlement called, *Patmos,* off the west coast of Asia Minor, southwest of Miletus in the *Aegean Sea*. It was there, in about AD 95,[16] that John experienced his historic vision, which has now become the most exhaustive compilation of end-time prophecy in all of Scripture, the last and most exciting book of the New Testament, John's incomparably illuminating — *"Book of Revelation."*

---

[14] Phil. 1:21

[15] John 19:26-27

[16] The actual date and period during which John recorded his vision is considered by many scholars to be questionable.

LET'S NOT FORGET OUR GOAL:

Before we begin our dissection of John's vision it's important to understand that our goal is to lay a solid foundation on which to build a clear, basic understanding of major end-time events. We don't want to just travel along the same old, heavily trodden (*though frequently unproven*) paths, creating new, unsupportable *"suppositions and theories."* Doing so would only throw more fuel on the already roaring fire of confusion. Our objective is to clear the storage bins of our minds of any pre-adopted *beliefs* and *terminologies* that have not truly "**self-emerged**" from the text.

Martin Luther formerly coined the great phrase, "Sola Scriptura" (*Bible Only*). As we study, this will be our absolute standard of purity. If it didn't originate "**solely**" from Scripture it will be considered our enemy (*supposition*); thus, we won't gather it into our backpacks. When it's absolutely necessary, we'll address some of the more prominent (*commonly adopted, though un-supportable*) *theories* and *terms* and replace them with solid, supportable, biblical truths and terminologies. To accomplish this, however, we must be disciplined and stay focused on the basic goal of our study. Remember, the paths of confusion are endless and run in every direction; hence, straying too far down those paths will only invite more *"confusion"* and *"supposition."* Conversely, the path of the "TRUTH" is straight and narrow and has but one origin, and that origin is found in the Word of God, which is Christ.[17]

Our Reward

In the future, when we share what we've learned with others, we won't have to fumble around trying to explain our views. Instead, we'll be ready and able to open our Bibles and read the passages that support what we're teaching. But, as I formerly stated, we must not forget that not all end-time prophecy has been revealed. Therefore, when we can't find the answers within the text, we won't simply embrace improperly founded conclusions. Along our journey if I feel it will be helpful to openly speculate I'll make it clear that what I'm saying is mere conjecture or opinion. Hey, I enjoy pondering the possibilities regarding the fulfillment of Bible prophecies just as much as the next guy. Frankly, I don't see how any intelligent student of eschatology can avoid wondering how some of these scriptures are going to come to pass. Nonetheless, we must never allow the line between what is "PURE SCRIPTURE" and what is *"mere conjecture"* to become blurred.

---

[17] John 1: 1-14, Rev. 19:13

Chapter 5

The Sixty Year Reunion

We're about to enter the first chapter of John's amazing Book of Revelation, and after all these years I still get excited. This is going to be one great ride! So, strap yourself in, warm up your finger muscles, and get ready to grow in exciting end-time knowledge, because the eternal Word of God is about to come alive as only it can!

John, on the Island of Patmos

Rev. 1:1-3

> ***'The Revelation of Jesus Christ, which God gave unto him, to shew unto his servants things which must shortly come to pass; and he sent and signified it by his angel unto his servant John: Who bare record of the word of God, and of the testimony of Jesus Christ, and of all things that he saw.***
>
> ***Blessed is he that readeth, and they that hear the words of this prophecy, and keep those things which are written therein: for the time is at hand.'***

We don't really know how many years had passed since John and the other disciples had witnessed Christ's ascension in Galilee,[18] but thanks to **Rev. 1:10** we know that our brother John was praying when he received his incredible end-time vision. Having no doubt inspired John to pray, the Lord responded to John's prayer by sending His angel to meet him and impart to him the greatest end-time revelation of all time. And, as the preceding scripture reveals, God the Father gave this revelation to Christ with the intent of revealing (*to the Church*) the things which must shortly[19] come to pass.

The first three verses of this chapter contain two important bits of information. First, the vision John saw was a revelation of Jesus Christ, and,

---

[18] Acts 1:1-11

[19] Let's not forget that *"a day is as a thousand years and a thousand years as one day"* to the Lord, which, metaphorically speaking, means that God exists beyond the parameters of chronological (*linear*) time — 2Pt. 3:8-9.

second, whosoever reads or hears the words of this prophecy *"and keeps them"* will be blessed. I don't believe it's possible to know for certain precisely how that blessing will impact each individual Christian, but I do believe it has to do with a cultivating of faith in the inspired nature of God's Word in the heart of the hearer.[20] We can be certain that everyone who reads John's Revelation vision doesn't have exactly the same faith building experience, but that promised blessing is as tangible today *"for all who <u>keep</u> the words of this prophecy"* as it was when John first penned this book.

John's Salutation to the Churches in Asia

Rev. 1:4 thru 2:22

John's salutation to the seven churches in Asia Minor (*commonly known today as Turkey*) begins in **Rev. 1:4** with a greeting from John on behalf of God the Father, Jesus Christ, and the Seven Spirits before God's throne. Although it would be easy to read right over these enigmatic verses, a careful look begs the question: *"Just what or, more respectfully, just who are the Seven Spirits of God?"* I hope you're not expecting me to answer this question, because I haven't the foggiest notion! I do know, however, that this is one subject that requires our most reverent exploration.

The Seven Spirits of God have been a mystery throughout the ages, and yet it's quite possible that some of Israel's most holy vessels have served to represent their significance. I've often wondered if the seven flames of the sacred candlestick in the Tabernacle were a representation of the Seven Spirits of God. There is certainly ample evidence to justify our at least considering that possibility. However, to ponder the relative significance of the Seven Spirits of God is to tread on extremely holy ground; thus, we must be wary of drawing conclusions that could lead to irreverent speculation.

In **Rev. 3:1**, when Jesus is dictating His letter to the church in Sardis, He states that He (*Jesus*) is the one who ***'hath the Seven Spirits of God and the seven stars.'*** Next, in **Rev. 4:1-5**, John is in the spirit, in Heaven, and sees the ***'seven lamps of fire burning before the throne,'*** which are said to be the Seven Spirits of God. Then, in **Rev. 5:6**, we see a representation of the Savior appearing in the midst of the throne, as a Lamb, having ***'seven horns and seven eyes,'*** which, we are told, ***'are the Seven Spirits of God sent forth into all the earth.'***

Notice the similarity between verses **2:1** and **3:1**. In those verses it seems as though Jesus uses *"the Seven Spirits of God"* interchangeably with the word, *"candlesticks,"* as though they mean the same thing. There's a

[20] Eph. 2:5

reason for pausing to address this scriptural mystery, and we'll discuss it later when we move further into John's vision.

Paul Apparently Had a Similar Experience

In **2 Cor. 12:2-11**, Paul seems to be relaying the general details of an extraordinary event, which a man he knew had experienced. I personally believe Paul was actually attempting to cloak himself with humility by speaking of himself in the third person, but whether that's true or not, that individual was taken up to the third heaven (*the dwelling place of God*). While he was there, he heard unspeakable words, which he learned were not lawful for a man to utter. This record of Paul's experience is particularly interesting in light of John's similar experience in **Rev. 10:1-4.** There, John writes that after hearing the ***'seven thunders utter their voices'*** he was about to write what he heard when a voice from Heaven told him to: ***"Seal up those things which the seven thunders uttered, and write them not."*** John was given no explanation as to why he was not permitted to record what he heard in his book; however, when we examine John's and Paul's experiences together, it seems apparent that they each heard words that were not to be recorded or repeated.

Perhaps what they heard was so holy that merely speaking of it while in their present carnal bodies would have been irreverent. Then again, it may have nothing to do with their carnal nature. It might simply be a matter of timing. Perhaps the words they heard would have revealed something God didn't want revealed at that particular time. Whatever ends up being the case, the truth of their experiences remains a mystery and so does the identity and significance of the Seven Spirits of God.

The Bottom Line

The only thing we know for sure about these Seven Spirits of God is that we know very little about them. We know even less about *"the seven thunders that utter their voices"* in **Rev. 10:4**, but that, unfortunately, hasn't prevented some teachers from voicing their wild theories and opinions regarding their mystique. We would all do well to remember that supposition without foundation equals "**CONFUSION**!" I'm comfortable accepting the fact that as long as we're in these mortal bodies there will always be questions we can't answer and scriptures we won't fully understand. This should be no cause for embarrassment or shame to any Christian. It's only when we start thinking we've got all the answers that we actually have good reason to be embarrassed.

Back to John's Salutation to the Churches

Rev. 1:5-6

> ***'And from Jesus Christ, who is the faithful witness, and the first begotten of the dead, and the prince of the kings of the earth. Unto him that loved us, and washed us from our sins in his own blood,***
>
> ***And hath made us kings and priests unto God and his Father; to him be glory and dominion for ever and ever. A'-men.'***

Reading from Peter's later writings, his first general epistle states that those who believe in Christ are *a holy priesthood, a royal priesthood*, and *a holy nation*.[21] This, of course, aligns perfectly with John's preceding declaration that Jesus ***'hath made us kings and priest unto God.'***

Every Eye shall see Him

Rev. 1:7

> ***'Behold, he cometh with clouds; and every eye shall see him, and they also which pierced him: and all kindreds of the earth shall wail because of him. Even so, A'-men.'***

In this verse the angel of the Lord just sort of bursts-out with a lively declaration of Christ's future triumphant return to judge the earth, as if his zeal for that glorious day could no-longer be restrained. But, unfortunately, even though his words clearly indicate a reference to Christ's eventual "Second Coming" (*which will occur at the end of the future seven-year tribulation period*), some have mistakenly concluded the angel to have been referring, instead, to the Rapture (*the future resurrection and "catching-away" of the saints, which, we will learn, will occur at the beginning of that seven-year period).*[22] Thus, we must be careful not to make the same mistake.

If we look carefully at the angel's words, we read that he is prophesying of an event during which ***'every eye shall see Him** (Christ)**, and they also which pierced Him.'*** This is an obvious declaration that every person who has ever lived, including those who physically participated in Jesus' crucifixion, will witness His spectacular return to judge the earth — *"the Second Coming of Christ."*[23] Every eye will definitely see that event, and it will occur at the end of the seven-year tribulation period. It's at that time that Christ will triumphantly return and establish His millennial (*1,000 year*)

---

[21] 1Pet. 2:5-10

[22] Luke 17:33-36, 1Th 4:13-5:9, 1Cor. 15:51-54

[23] Mt. 16:27, 24:27,30,36-39, 26:64

kingdom. Every eye will not, however, see the rapture of the Church. In fact, I know of no scriptural indication that those who crucified Christ will be able to see the instantaneous resurrection and rapture of the saints (*we'll get back to this and Christ's 1,000 year reign on earth later).*

As we recall, this is not the first time John and the other disciples were told that every eye shall see Christ's return to earth. On the day of Christ's glorious ascension into Heaven (*forty days after His resurrection*), two angels stood by the many witnesses[24] and proclaimed: ***"This same Jesus, which is taken up from you into Heaven, shall so come in like manner as you have seen Him go into Heaven."*** Jesus prophesied of His return to earth more than once, most notably in His famous end-time sermon (*Mt. 24:21-30*).

In **Rev. 1:7** John states that ***'all kindreds of the earth shall wail because of Him.'*** John's words clearly speak of Christ's taking vengeance on all those who will oppose Him at His coming (*His triumphant return to earth*).[25] Those who've died without Christ will not be resurrected to witness the catching-away (*rapture*) of the Church; therefore, John could not have been referring to them. The Rapture will be a time of great rejoicing for all its participants; it will not be a time of *"weeping"* and *"wailing,"* as will be the vengeful return of Christ. We'll cover this thoroughly at the proper time.

The Alpha and Omega

Rev 1:8

> ***'I am the Alpha and Omega, the beginning and the ending, saith the Lord, which is, and which was, and which is to come, the Almighty.'***

I don't know about all of you eschatological geniuses but I sometimes have a hard time figuring out just exactly what John was seeing or hearing when he wrote certain verses. I realize John didn't write in *chapter and verse*, but I think you know what I mean. **Rev. 1:8** is a good example. Did John directly see Jesus say these words or did John receive this declaration from Christ's angel and write it down? I doubt it matters much. Surely, understanding the message is more important than understanding exactly how it was delivered. I happen to use a *King James Version* Bible (*for various reasons, which will become evident later*), and in the *KJV* most of **Rev. 1:8** is printed in red. This, as you know, denotes the words of Christ, which is all we really need to know. Only Jesus is the "**Alpha**" and "**Omega**," the

---

[24] 1Cor.15:3-8, Act 1:9-11

[25] Luke 18:8, Jude 14-16, Rev. 19:11-21

beginning and the ending; therefore, we know these words at least originated in Christ.

A Very Important Lost Word

Rev 1:9

> ***'I John, who also am your brother, and companion in tribulation, and in the kingdom and patience of Jesus Christ, was in the isle** (island) **that is called Patmos, for the word of God, and for the testimony of Jesus Christ.'***

This instructive verse has been consistently neglected and overlooked, year after year, and, because of this neglect, we've repeatedly failed to recognize exactly when a critically pivotal event in the future of the Church will take place. I'm referring to the long-awaited resurrection and catching-away of the saints — *"the Rapture."* When the time is right, I'll explain this verse's significance in detail, and you'll see (*probably for the first time*) just how powerful a statement John is making in this verse. To briefly explain, the most important word in the verse is "**tribulation**." John is plainly declaring that he, along with all others who share in ***'the kingdom and patience of Jesus Christ,'*** are companions in ***'tribulation.'*** That's right! John is clearly stating that his experience on Earth, as a believer in Christ, qualified him as being a companion to all who endure ***'tribulation.'***

~ *Why is that so important?* ~

During His short time with the disciples, Jesus warned that following His teaching would mean a life of both anguish and affliction. Not to go off on a *Greek* word tangent, but the actual *Greek* word for *anguish, affliction, oppression, distress, trouble,* and *tribulation* is — ***thlipsis*** *([thlē'-psēs], tribulation).* This simple *Greek* word is used throughout the New Testament to denote the day to day suffering of those who follow Christ. As a matter of fact, Jesus warned that this future "**tribulation**" (*persecution*) would arise because of the Word (*the Gospel message*) in His famous *"Seed Parable."*[26] Moreover, Luke recorded Paul's and Barnabas' words to the Christians in Antioch as follows:

> *'. . . exhorting them to continue in the faith, and that we must* ***through much tribulation*** *enter into the kingdom of God.'*

Acts 14:22

[26] Mt. 13:21

The same *Greek* word for "**persecution**" is used (*in one form or another*) by the writers of the New Testament over forty times — all of which to describe the everyday patient endurance of Christians in the midst of persecution. Grant it, some champions of the faith suffer a great deal more than others, but if we're truly fulfilling the commission of Christ,[27] as Paul wrote, ***'all that will live Godly in Christ Jesus shall suffer persecution.'***[28] Later, we'll see how and why this is so essential to our understanding of John's vision. Remember, every little piece of the puzzle helps to create one "GIANT IMAGE." That image will give us a clear understanding and chronological time-line of the entire book of Revelation and all major end-time prophecy and events.

"I've wet myself for less . . ."

Rev 1:10-20 ♦ *please read these verses before continuing.*

When Christians receive a message from the Lord they often say something like: *"I heard the still, small voice of the Lord."* Well, if John had ever referred to the Lord's voice that way before he probably never did again after receiving this particular message. What a shock! This must have scared John out of his cloak or whatever he was wearing. Can you imagine being alone on an island, engaged in fervent prayer, and suddenly hearing a voice as loud as a trumpet-blast behind you? I think I'd have had to go change my shorts.

At any rate, the voice John heard told him to write in a book the things he was about to see and send it to the seven churches in Asia (*Asia Minor*). After hearing this, John turned and saw seven golden candlesticks and one ***'like unto the Son of man'*** standing in their midst, holding ***'seven stars'*** in His right hand. Apparently, this was more than just a vision of Christ in all His heavenly, resurrected splendor, because when John saw Jesus he fell at His feet as if he were dead. Then, with a reassuring touch, Jesus revived John and began explaining the meaning of the ***'seven golden candlesticks'*** and the ***'seven stars.'***

Jesus told John that the seven stars are the seven angels of the seven churches and that the seven candlesticks are the seven churches. Thus, these seven angels could actually be heavenly beings who've been assigned the task of caring for the seven churches. However, since the original *Greek* suggests the word *"angel"* would correctly be interpreted to mean *"messenger"* or *"one who is sent,"* it's also possible that Jesus is referring, instead, to the seven pastors of the seven churches. It wouldn't seem to make much sense for Jesus to be telling John to write a message and

---

[27] Mt. 28:18-20

[28] 2Tim 3:12

send it to seven angelic-beings, and yet, seven "specific" angels do suddenly appear before the throne directly following the rapture of the Church. Isn't that interesting? We'll dig into the significance of that fact a little further along our path.

We can take a closer look at the seven candlesticks that Jesus said are the seven churches when we get into Rev. Chapter 4. Right now I think we should take a moment and acknowledge the incredible declaration Jesus made in **Rev. 1:18.** In that verse, Jesus revealed to John that He (*Jesus*) holds ***'the keys of hell and of death.'*** I don't know about you, but it makes me feel incredibly secure knowing that my best friend and Savior holds the keys to my eternal destination. That's no little declaration! Let's not forget that ***'the prince of the power of the air'*** *(the devil, Satan)* formerly had possession of those keys, and he expected to be our eternal jailor. We, being imprisoned in these fleshly bodies of sin and death, were, by nature, helpless, ***'the children of wrath.'***[29] That's why Christ, through His willful death and triumphant resurrection, took possession of those allegorical keys of hell and death and, thereby, forever reclaimed authority over the eternal fate of our souls. If Jesus hadn't loved us enough to make that supreme sacrifice, we would all be lost, with no hope of ever being saved or resurrected.

Jesus willfully accepted the Pain of the Cross

I realize that I'm going off on sort of a tangent here, but I sometimes wonder if we fully appreciate the fact that our Savior could have redeemed us without dying such a violent death. That's right! Jesus could have fully atoned for all sin by suffering a quick and relatively painless death. There are several more humane and certainly less humiliating ways through which Jesus could have allowed Himself to be sacrificed, while still adequately fulfilling His ministry as both High Priest[30] and sacrificial Lamb of God.[31] I certainly don't remember the acting High Priests torturing the sacrificial lambs before offering them on the altar! A quick, relatively painless, death would have completely satisfied the Law and atoned for our sins, and the Lord could have chosen that path.

Of course, even if a more humane method of sacrifice had been sought, Jesus would have felt some discomfort, but He didn't have to endure the many agonizing hours of fearful prayer, the sleeplessness, the severe beatings, the scourgings, the degradingly merciless crown of thorns, or the naked humiliation He chose to endure as part of His horrifically excruciating death. Yet, God the Father, God the Son, and God the Holy Spirit chose

---

[29] Eph.2:1-10, Heb.2:14-15

[30] Heb.5:1-10

[31] John 1:29-36, Rev.5:6

this extreme redemptive method before the world began[32] for one very important reason:

> Mere words could never effectively express the depthless love God has for his children.

Love of that sort must be demonstrated in order to be understood. Thus, Jesus demonstrated God's love in spades. And the physical proof of Christ's extraordinary sacrifice will be evident throughout all eternity. For Jesus alone will bear scars in Heaven[33] — not as a shameful reminder of our former sinful nature but, rather, as a lasting declaration of His infinite love for those who've humbly surrendered their lives to God's will.

[32] Rev. 13:8

[33] Luke 24:39-40, John 20:24-29

Chapter 6

The Seven Church Ages

"Huh - what was that?"

What happened to: "Nothing but Sound Doctrine"?

Those of you who teach or study eschatology have probably stumbled upon the improperly founded teaching known as *"The Seven Church Age Theory."* I'm not going to explain the complex thinking behind that theory, because I believe that doing so will only cause more confusion. But, if studying it left you feeling a little unsure of its source, don't feel bad; there's good reason for your concern.

Some of my favorite Bible teachers regularly use this unsubstantiated theory when teaching about the end-times. I understand why they've accepted that theory and could easily argue their views for them. I could explain them clearly and reference scripture in an attempt to substantiate what I was saying, but would my doing so prove what I was saying to be true? Of course not! Referencing scriptures from which a theory or supposition was formulated does not validate that supposition, nor does it provide a true, solid foundation for the establishment of sound doctrine.

A good test for determining whether a particular interpretation is biblically sound or whether it is, instead, nothing more than mere conjecture is to completely forget that interpretation (*theory*), then, read the verse or passages to which the teacher or theory has referred. If the Bible is clearly rendering the same interpretation as is the teacher's theory, that theory "**may**" be true. I say it "**may**" be true, because, in order for us to be sure, the entirety of Scripture must support what's being put forth. The thought or theory shouldn't need our help or require interpretive supposition in order to be established.

I personally don't believe that we who study Scripture have the right to create theories that are derived solely from suppositions, especially when dealing with the book of Revelation. It's precisely because of this type of unfounded free thinking that the understanding of John's Revelation vision has eluded so many Christians for years.

> The truth is, if you had never heard *"The Seven Church Age Theory"* and you simply read Jesus' letters to the seven churches, that theory would never "**self-emerge**" from the text.

Although many knowledgeable brothers and sisters in Christ encouraged me to write this book, I still wrestled with the prospect of actually doing so for many years before setting out to write it, mostly because I have such a profound respect for the purity of God's Holy Word. Commenting on or attempting to interpret God's infallible Word should be a reverently fearful endeavor for all of us. We should be unnerved by the prospect of potentially being found guilty of having *"added-to"* or having *"taken-away"* from what the apostles and early Church leaders have determined to be the divinely inspired Word of God. God's Word is both perfect and holy, and, though God graciously allows us our occasional suppositions and opinions, His Word is not open to our personal interpretations. There is but one truth. When we casually teach our *theories, opinions* or *suppositions* as if they actually "**self-emerged**" from Scripture and are fact, we hinder others in their attempt to lay hold of that simple truth within the text that only the Holy Spirit can reveal.[34] Therefore, when we can't scripturally prove an interpretation, it's our responsibility to respectfully admit it and move on.

[34] John 14:15-26, 1 Cor. 2:10-16, James 1:5, 1Jn. 2:27

Chapter 7

Jesus' Letters to Ephesus, Smyrna and Pergamos

If you've been studying eschatology for any length of time, you've encountered endless commentaries that have attempted to explain John's Revelation vision. As I briefly explained, while it's virtually impossible to avoid leaving my literary fingerprints all over these end-time prophecies, my goal is not to create another commentary of John's end-time vision. We're going to study John's end-time vision in the same straight forward, orderly manner as God revealed it to John. We'll treat it like we're seeing it for the very first time. This will free our minds from all errant *"teachings"* and *"terminologies"* and allow the purity of Scripture to interpret John's vision for us.

Jesus' Message to the Church at Ephesus

Rev 2:1-5 ♦ *please read these verses before continuing.*

Jesus, being the fatherly King He is, started His letter to the Ephesians by lovingly acknowledging the good they had done in His name. They had worked hard and without fainting. They rejected false teaching and continually resisted evil. That sounds pretty good; doesn't it? That's a better report than many churches would receive today I'm sure! Unfortunately, years of relentless attacks from false teachers (*wolves in sheep's clothing who claimed to be true ambassadors of Christ*)[35] had left the Ephesians spiritually bankrupt and in need of constant shepherding; thus, it's no coincidence that Paul's *"Armor of God"* treatise is found in one of his letters to this church.[36]

In the early days of the Ephesian church's formation, both Paul and Timothy spent a great deal of time molding and shaping this church's doctrinal foundation and laboring to establish them firmly in the grace of God.[37] Nonetheless, by the time John received this message for the church at Ephesus, the Christians there were in need of serious spiritual rejuvenation. As Jesus plainly stated, ***'they had left their first love,'*** and if they

---

[35] Mt.7:15, 10:16, Acts 20:16-30

[36] Eph.6:12-17

[37] 1Tim.1:2-10

didn't ***'repent and do the first works'*** He (*Jesus*) would come quickly and ***'remove their candlestick out of his place.'***

Whenever I encounter the word "**candlestick**" in Scripture I immediately visualize the seven lamps of fire burning before the throne of God, which (*as Jesus' angel told John in Rev. 4:5*) are the Seven Spirits of God. We touched on this earlier, and, while doing so, I mentioned that in **Rev. 5:6** Jesus' angel told John that the Seven Spirits of God have been sent forth into all the earth. This seems relevant, because in this letter Jesus is warning the Ephesian church that He will come quickly and remove their ***'candlestick'*** from out of his place if they don't repent and regain their former zeal (*their first-love*). If, therefore, the candlestick is intended to represent the Seven Spirits of God, wouldn't the removal of that candlestick suggest the spiritual end of that church? That seems logical to me.

I - Too - Hate the Deeds of the Nicolaitanes

Rev 2:6-7 ♦ *please read these verses before continuing.*

I just love the subtle diplomacy of the Lord. He affectionately starts His message to the Ephesians with an encouraging commendation. Next, He firmly warns them to return to where they started or face going it alone. Then, finally, He mends any possible emotional wounds with some soothing words of praise. Like a tough but lovable coach at the end of a rough game, Jesus gives the Church in Ephesus an inspiring pat on the back by declaring that He too hates the detestable deeds of the Nicolaitanes. The Nicolaitanes were a stiff-necked people, who apparently put personal freedom ahead of their Christian witness by choosing to eat meat that had openly been sacrificed to idols. And, as if that wasn't enough, with complete disregard for the teachings of Jesus and the apostles, the Nicolaitanes reportedly practiced fornication and open polygamy.

As Jesus does in each of His seven letters, He closes this letter to the Ephesians with an encouraging promise: ***'To him that overcometh will I give to eat of the tree of life, which is in the midst of the paradise of God.'*** These words are significant, and we'll see why as we near the final chapters of John's vision.[38]

Jesus' Letter to the Persecuted Church at Smyrna

Rev 2:8-11 ♦ *please read these verses before continuing.*

If ever a church had a prophetic name, this was it. I've found many varied opinions as to the actual meaning of the name *Smyrna*, but the most common definition seems to be related to the plant derivative *myrrh*. Like the church at Smyrna, *myrrh* has at least two appropriate word associa-

[38] Rev.22:2-3

tions: "**bitter**" and "**sweet**." As a gum *myrrh* has a bitter taste, which is probably why the *Aramaic* word for *myrrh* is *"bitter."* But, if *myrrh* is subjected to extreme pressure and crushed, a beautifully sweet aroma is released. Throughout most of its existence, the church at Smyrna experienced just this sort of crushing pressure and relentless tribulation. Like the church at Ephesus, Smyrna was battling continual attacks from false teachers, who, as the Lord indicated, claimed to be Jews but, as Jesus put it, were actually ***'of the synagogue of Satan.'***

Smyrna's faithful, obedient service and persistent prayer, amidst such unyielding persecution, must have filled the throne room of God with an aroma that no apothecary could hope to equal. I say this because Jesus had no reproof for these faithful brothers and sisters in Christ, just tender words of encouragement and the promise of a *"crown of life"* for those who overcome.

There's tribulation, and then there's "**TRIBULATION**"!

It's important to acknowledge the Lord's use of the word "**tribulation**" in His letter to the church at Smyrna. Each time He used it He was referring to Smyrna's daily persecution. This is important to note, because in the last three hundred years or so the Church has significantly changed the biblical definition of the word tribulation by attaching a completely different meaning to the word. This began when today's modern church started referring to the seven-year period that will precede the Second Coming of Christ as "**the tribulation period**." By referring to that particular seven-year period in this manner, we've unwittingly cast a gigantic stumbling block in front of what should have been a relatively simple understanding of that end-time period.

I think we can all agree that that specific seven-year period is going to be, without a doubt, the most dreadful years of tribulation the earth will ever endure. That's precisely my point. During the early Church's development, when Christians spoke of suffering *"tribulation"* for the furtherance of the Gospel, they were simply referring to ordinary, everyday persecution, the same persecution to which all believers around the world were and are being subjected. They were not referring to a specific seven-year period of pre-apocalyptic terror.

Some of God's kids have it Easier than Others

Certainly some devout, frontline Christians experience a great deal more tribulation than those who skate casually along avoiding conflict. Nonetheless, tribulation is still scripturally considered to be endured by all who truly carry the torch of the Gospel of Christ. In fact, Jesus taught that standing firm in the midst of tribulation and persecution — along with brotherly love — would be the proof of our faith.[39] That's the reason for our being openly baptized into the body of Christ. *"How so, you ask?"* Our willful baptism is the very essence of our outward commitment; it's meant to be an observable, personal declaration of our intent to resiliently stand against all opposition for the Gospel of Christ. But repentance, baptism, and confession of our faith in Christ are just the beginning of that stand. This is why Jesus' disciples only baptized those who were old enough to choose to openly renounce their sin and commit their lives to serving God in the name of Christ. An infant can't, of its own freewill, make that lifelong commitment, and the child's parents can't make that commitment for the child. If we could, it stands to reason that every Christian offspring would be baptized at birth and, subsequently, grow up to serve the Lord.

Sometimes it's simply a matter of Longitude

Those who live in the western hemisphere experience very little daily, physical persecution for having placed their faith in the Gospel of Christ. In the eastern hemisphere, however, where far too often Christianity isn't tolerated, there are thousands of Christians being put to the test, daily, for their faith in Christ. Many are, in fact, being severely tortured and/or killed for their faith. In numerous parts of the world, Christians live under the threat of being publicly stoned just for having a Bible or for speaking openly about their faith. Even in Israel, our beloved country of origin (*the birthplace of our faith*), Christians are not free to openly practice their faith as many do, for example, in the United States.

No question about it, the word *"tribulation"* is as real and palpable today for many of our brothers and sisters in the east as it was for the founders of our faith, who were frequently martyred due to their commitment to the Gospel of Christ. We will see why this is so significant to acknowledge as we continue.

Jesus' Message to the Church at Pergamum

Rev 2:12-17 ♦ *please read these verses before continuing.*

The Lord's message to the church at Pergamos (*Pergamum*) is similar to His message to the church at Ephesus, with one important difference; the Pergamos Christians were not sufficiently resisting those who were practicing the doctrine of Balaam.[40] It's worth noting that Jesus separately mentioned the wicked deeds of the Nicolaitanes as if to indicate that those following the doctrine of Balaam were in some way different from the Nicolaitanes. The differences between the two groups are debatable, but

[39] Mt. 13:21
[40] Nu.31:16

the point Jesus was making was that the Pergamos church leaders were not putting a stop to the Nicolaitanes' evil witness and influence in the church. It seems that *compromise* and *rationalization*, rather than a strict adherence to sound doctrine, defined the spiritual walk of the first century Christians at Pergamos. And, sadly, if we're honest, we must admit that in many ways we're still struggling to overcome that problem today.

Pretty Impressive Cities Indeed

Historically speaking, the cities of Pergamum and Ephesus were architectural wonders in their day. Ephesus was the uncontested commercial hub of Asia (*modern day Turkey*), and Pergamum was its political equal. Unfortunately, Pergamum was as ungodly as it was architecturally impressive. It was, therefore, necessary for the Lord to continue demonstrating His Fatherly love and oversight over the churches' spiritual growth by warning the Christians in Pergamos not to tolerate those who follow Balaam's wicked example.

Bannering the Gospel message in a city renowned for housing a throne that aptly bore the name — *"Satan's Seat"* — must have been nearly as difficult a task as attempting to keep a match lit in a wind tunnel! Nevertheless, spreading the Gospel was their Christian commission just as it is ours today. Like many cities in ancient Asia, Pergamos was an open cesspool of immorality. We don't know for certain that Jesus wasn't just speaking metaphorically when He said that Pergamum is the place where Satan's seat is, but we know that both emperor and idol worship were rampant during that particular era. Thus, it's quite possible that a throne bearing the name — *"Satan's Seat"* — was actually being used by the citizens of Pergamos for the purpose of deifying emperors and facilitating their public worship. The citizens of Pergamum were certainly not immune to the political and social pressures one would face for choosing not to participate in civil rituals of that sort. Consequently, many first and second century Christians were martyred for their refusal to bow to the so called *"human-deities"* of their day.

Another possible explanation for Jesus having said that Satan's seat is in Pergamum is the archeological evidence indicating that, on a mountaintop in Pergamos (*sometime around the second century BC*), an altar was erected to the mythological father of the gods, *Zeus.* That altar was mysteriously named *"Satan's Seat,"* and it's likely that it was still standing at the time John recorded Jesus' letters to the churches. Incidentally, a scaled replica of that first century altar is currently on display in a Berlin museum.

Unlike the church at Smyrna, neither Pergamos nor Ephesus got clean bills of spiritual health. It was time for both churches to make some instant changes or be ready to face immediate consequences. Jesus warned the Ephesians to ***'repent, and do the first works'*** or He would come quickly and remove their ***'candlestick out of his place.'*** It seems that once the Lord reaches the end of His patience, He then moves quickly to affect change. The church at Pergamos got a similar warning, but this time Jesus said He would personally come and fight, ***'with the sword of His mouth,'*** those who were in opposition to His will. According to Jesus' reproof, it was time for Pergamos to initiate some serious corporate repentance.

Rev 2:17 ~ *shown below*

Jesus — forever striving to help us affix our gaze on the things of Heaven, not wishing to allow the slightest opening through which *"the accuser"* (*Satan*) can cast a dart of condemnation our way — sums up His reproof of Pergamos with an intimate promise of renewal:

> *'. . . he that hath an ear,*[41] *let him hear what the Spirit saith to the churches; To him that overcometh will I give to eat of* ***the hidden manna, and will give him a white stone, and in the stone a new name written, which no man knoweth saving he that receiveth it****.'*

Rev. 2:17

The last time Jesus explained about His being that true bread or *"manna from Heaven,"* almost all but His original twelve disciples deserted Him. They probably (*as did the rest of the crowd*) thought He was insane. Thankfully, John was inspired to include Jesus' *"Bread of Life"* message in his Gospel.[42] Today, through the Church, the Holy Spirit has revealed that Jesus is that ***'hidden manna,' 'the bread from Heaven,'*** the true ***'bread of life.'*** Therefore, he who has Christ has eternal-life. Before the day of Pentecost had come, this was still a mystery even to those who followed Christ. We'll examine the eternal significance of that mystery — "THE MYSTERY OF GOD" — later.

What about the White Stone?

Before we move on, this particular promise to the church at Pergamos from Christ Jesus is my absolute favorite. Jesus promises to give all those who overcome a ***'white stone.'*** His message indicates that in the white

[41] The ear to which Jesus is referring is that spiritual inner-ear, which only those who possess a willfully obedient heart toward God have. It's with that inner-ear that we hear Jesus' call to repent. And the hidden manna to which Jesus referred is "life-eternal," which begins the moment we're "born-again" in Christ—John 3:1-8.

[42] John 6:25-69

stone a new name will be written, which no man will know except he who receives it. I realize that some scholars have reason not to believe this to be a literal "white stone," but they could be wrong. And I sure hope they are, because I want that white stone and new name!

For a couple hundred years, both before and after Christ, white stones were used in a variety of ways. On occasion they were given to the accused at the end of a trial as a means of proclaiming his or her innocence. Conversely, if the accused was guilty, a black stone was presented. We all deserve black stones, but since Jesus so mercifully offered Himself as a means of purchasing white stones for each of us, after we've surrendered our lives to Christ, we can boldly[43] enter eternity as guiltless, sanctified recipients of white stones.

Probably the most common use for smooth white stones in Jesus' day was that of serving as an admittance ticket to a special social or political event. There again, the analogous white stone perfectly aligns with Scripture. We never could have earned admittance to the throne room of God,[44] so Christ purchased the right of entry for us. Now, having made us joint heirs of His infinite glory, Jesus promises all those who've suffered persecution with Him as part of the body of Christ a white stone of admittance, entitling each recipient admission into the eternal Kingdom of God.

'. . . And if children, then heirs; heirs of God, and joint heirs with Christ; if so be that we suffer with Him, that we may be also glorified together.'

Romans 8:17

It is possible that the promised white stone may be a simple analogy, intended to represent nothing more than our assurance of a future, guiltless admittance into Heaven, but couldn't the white stone represent all of this and still be a real stone — a necklace or bracelet-medallion perhaps? I don't see why not. It's not like it's hard for God to think-up new names or make white stones. When God changed *Abram's* name to *Abraham* and *Sarai's* name to *Sarah* that was certainly real, and when He later changed *Jacob's* name to *Israel* there was nothing allegorical about that. The truth is changing the names of His servants is not a new concept to God. As a matter of fact, upon first laying eyes on Peter, before even being introduced, Jesus said: "***Thou art Simon the son of Jona: thou shalt be called Cephas.***"[45] God's whole purpose in sending Christ to die for our redemp-

[43] Heb. 10:19-20
[44] Ro. 8:12-23
[45] John 1:42

tion is rooted in His final plan of making all things new.[46] Even Jesus, in His letter to the church at Philadelphia, revealed that He also will have a new name, which He will write upon all overcomers. And, while we won't know for sure about these white stones until we get to Heaven, prayerfully reading **Rev. 2:17** may help reveal why I think this verse might just be a prophetic diamond in the ruff. In that verse, Jesus doesn't speak as though the white stone is solely analogous. Instead, His words exude a suggestion of privacy, a certain intimate, *"one-on-one"* quality. Paul wrote to the Galatian church[47] and explained that, through Christ, God has made all who put their trust in Him His true sons and daughters, just as true as if by physical birth. Shouldn't the true parent (*which, in our case, is God*) name the child? That seems logical to me!

Certainly we're all on a pilgrimage home, but one glorious day, in the not too distant future, our pilgrimage will abruptly come to an end. Can't you just envision that euphoric moment, when you at long last will have suddenly been "caught-up" to Heaven?[48] Try and imagine that that miraculous event has just occurred, and right now, in this instant, you've been miraculously "caught-up" into the vary presence of God. The glorious day for which you've waited so long has finally arrived!

Face to Face at Last!

There He is! After years and years of hopeful longing and seemingly endless separation, you can clearly see Him. Your wearisome pilgrimage is finally over, and your glorious Savior is standing right in front of you! Earthly portraits didn't even come close to resembling His true likeness or radiant majesty, and, yet, you recognize Him. Immediately you're allured by the powerfully welcoming sensation that you know Him more intimately than you've ever known anyone before. Never had you imagined that His commandingly strong, yet tenderly affectionate eyes could speak, *"Welcome home!"* so reassuringly into your heart. It's as if He's been eagerly standing and waiting in that very spot all these years, with confident, eager anticipation of your successful arrival.

Observably comforted by the sight of you, His welcoming smile draws you near. From an internal depth of emotion you didn't even know existed, the overwhelming sensation that this is where you belong comforts you like a warm blanket. It's as though you've always been there, unified with the Savior, *"as one,"* but how? How could you have ever even imagined feeling anything quite like this? It's a little like the sudden surge of relief you used to feel when you saw the concerned, compassionate smile of a

---

[46] 2Cor.5:17, Rev.21:5

[47] Gal.3:26-4:7

[48] 1Th. 4:13-18

loved one looking down at you after having awakened you from a nightmare. But this time it's not a dream; you're really in Heaven. Instantly, it's all so clear; you're really home! You're finally exactly where you're supposed to be, and, best of all, you know you'll never be asked to leave.

It's obvious now that He who's smiling at you has loved you all your life; you just couldn't see Him. That dense cloud of *confusion* and *deception,* which Satan formerly used to obscure and shroud your daily perception of life, has given way to the clarity of pure holiness and truth; what an incredible difference! It's far too surreal to be true, but it is true! Overwhelmed by His glorious, holy presence, you can't help but collapse. Nearly instantly your eyes open and you begin to feel yourself being lifted. It's His steady hands you're feeling. You ask yourself, *'Can this be real?'* Feeling almost like a toddler in His loving grasp, how right helplessness feels when you're in His arms. You're His child, and in His sheltering embrace all your former worries and fears are instantly replaced with the heartwarming, euphoric sensation of truly divine peace and tranquility.

A twinge of anxiety tries to creep in as you begin to wonder: *'How, with all that's happening in Heaven, does He have time to stop and welcome me?'* But, before that earthly wisp of anxiety has a chance to completely formulate in your mind, His protectively captivating eyes again draw your gaze upward, and all your anxiety astonishingly dissipates. It's miraculous; He's not in a hurry at all! It's as if everything He's doing is just for you alone. His sweet, adoring smile grows wider, and you notice He looks eager and excited, as if He can't wait to show you something He's hiding behind His back. Meekly you return His smile as He raises His clenched hands and presents them before you, but, as He does, you can't help but to wince from within: *'Oh no; there they are!'* You can actually see them, His scars! Those dreadful scars! Until today you had only read about them, but now, there they are, right in front of you. It was difficult enough before, just picturing them in your mind, imagining the selfless agony He innocently endured because of your sin. How can you possibly hold it together? Are you actually expected to rejoice, while seeing with your own eyes His thorn-pitted forehead and nail-scarred hands?

Then, before grief and shame can break-in and overwhelm you, Jesus' mercifully protective love mightily rushes in! This is not a moment for sorrow or shame. The very last thing Jesus wants is to see you suffer the shame of past sins, sins He has already chosen to forget.[49] No, that's not why Jesus' hands are raised before you. His hands are raised because today your rebirth, at long last, is complete, and the Lord has been eagerly waiting your entire life for this very special moment. Now it's time for a

[49] Psalm 103:12-14, Isaiah 43:25

new, divinely chosen name, and something this significant and personal Jesus has not taken lightly.

Still staring warmly and adoringly into your eyes, Jesus turns over and opens His hands to reveal a glistening white, intricately engraved stone. As He gently places it in your hand, you're captivated by the stunning purity of the stone. Curiously admiring the beautiful word engraved on its surface, you look inquisitively up with a look of, *"What does this mean?"* Jesus places both hands on your shoulders and gently pulls Himself in close, as if to tell you a secret. You're so overwhelmed with love for Him that you feel you're going to just burst with uncontrollable emotion! Then you hear Him adoringly whisper the most charmingly mysterious word you've ever heard. Knowing that you don't understand, He pulls back, and, looking straight into your eyes, He tenderly says:

"My child, this is your true name. I've created it just for you. Never before has man or angel seen or heard it. It's an expression of my infinite love for you. From this day forward and throughout all eternity there will never be another child in all of My Kingdom, neither in Heaven nor on earth, who will bare this name I have given you. You are that special to Me. With this name you will always know how much I love you and how individually significant you are to Me. Welcome home child!"

Of course, we don't know if our arrival in Heaven will be anything like this, but we do know, without a doubt, that we will each receive a new name. And that name will be unlike any other throughout eternity. That's a direct promise from our King and Savior — **Rev. 2:17**.

A Word of Wisdom before Continuing To Thyatira

Now that we've begun examining Jesus' messages to the seven churches, it should be evident that every word of instruction or reproof, even those that give personal, direct instruction to a specific church, are inspired; thus, they're good for our instruction as Christians today. This is food for thought when considering the validity or, more importantly, the true origin of *"The Seven Church Age Theory."* Why am I readdressing this issue? A minister, under whom I formerly served, frequently quoted Solomon, saying: *"It's the little fox that spoils the vine."* [50] As ministers and students of God's perfect Word, we must be ever diligent to preserve the divine intent of the text (*Scripture*). Whenever we allow uninspired teach-

[50] Sgs. 2:15

ing or theorizing into our actual interpretation of God's Word, it acts as a smokescreen, misdirecting and, therefore, camouflaging the true meaning and/or intent of the text. Later, we'll examine how the incorrect addition of just a single three letter word has inadvertently blinded (*to some degree*) the Church, thus preventing us from clearly understanding and interpreting an extremely important end-time prophecy. Sometimes these misdirections seem harmless, and yet, however insignificant and seemingly harmless they may be, they always take us off and away from the divinely inspired path of truth.

Think of it this way:

Your plane lands late in the evening at a big international airport, in the middle of a huge foreign city. A little scared and definitely out of your comfort zone, you're situation brightens when the helpful, English speaking car rental clerk gives you written directions to the only hotel with a vacancy. As you gratefully review his written directions, you notice that the hotel is more than twenty miles outside of town! Definitely worried about finding it but eager to feel that soft, clean hotel pillow against your cheek, you express your gratitude with a generous tip, wearily collapse into the seat of your rental car, and drive away.

Sadly, unbeknownst to you, that wonderfully helpful clerk, for whom you were so grateful just moments earlier, has made a little mistake while writing down the directions. At the first intersection he accidently wrote *"left turn"* instead of *"right turn."* No big deal, right? Most of what he wrote is correct. It shouldn't matter if you start your trip by turning the wrong way. You'll probably still find the hotel, right?!

~ I Don't Think So! ~

Most likely, by the time you realize that the directions are no good, you'll be so lost that just finding your way back to where you started will take another tank of gas and a lot of help from people who know the city well! With that thought in mind, we must ask:

> Which of the Church's responsibilities is more important than the unadulterated preservation of God's holy Word?

Chapter 8

Jesus' Letters to Thyatira, Sardis and Philadelphia

Thyatira

Rev. 2:18-19 ♦ *please read these verses before continuing.*

As always, the Lord starts His reproof with kind words of encouragement, making the church at Thyatira sound like the kind of church of which you could be proud to be a part. That, of course, changes when Jesus begins to describe their short comings. The church at Thyatira: *did good-works, was kindhearted, was active in ministry, was faithful and patient in endurance, and was full of good-works.* I realize I listed *good-works* twice, but so did Jesus. And, since Jesus doesn't make mistakes, I figure there must be a good reason for His twice having referred to their good-works.

The first place to dig when seeking to understand Jesus' reference to good-works is the original *Greek* text. Unfortunately, that's a dead-end, because Jesus used the same *Greek* word for *"works"* both times in this passage. Therefore, we don't know (*with certainty*) why Jesus twice commended Thyatira for their works. If I had to guess (*which I detest doing*), I'd say Jesus most likely repeated Himself for effect. He probably just didn't want to break the spirit of the Christians at Thyatira, especially after they had so faithfully worked spreading the Gospel in the midst of such wicked opposition. That, however, is just a presumption based on historical evidence. It's not provable.

At the end of Thyatira's list of praises, Jesus adds: ***'. . . and the last to be more than the first.'*** We don't need to guess what Jesus meant by adding those words, because both Mark[51] and Luke[52] recorded discourses of times when Jesus used those precise words in His teachings. Formerly, when Jesus used those words, He was basically teaching His disciples two essential aspects of one important precept. Primarily, Jesus taught that many who expect access to Heaven will be denied; whereas, others, who were previously considered to be strangers and outcast, will be granted en-

---

[51] Mk.9:33-27

[52] Luke 13:29-30

trance. Furthermore, Jesus said: *"**If any man desires to be first, the same shall be last of all, and servant of all.**"* Thus, Jesus' use of these words in His characterization of the church at Thyatira was likely a commendation for their humility and ministry to both Gentiles and Jews.

Jezebel is back, or at least she was!

Rev 2:20-25 ♦ *please read these verses before continuing.*

Few ministers teach that Jesus is referring to a real woman named *"Jezebel"* in these verses. Given the inherently ill-reputed association of the name, the thought that any woman would knowingly refer to herself as Jezebel is understandably difficult to imagine. However, the specific words Jesus chose when referring to this wicked beast of a woman leaves me believing that she actually existed and that she was so abominable that she demanded (*in utter defiance to God*) to be referred to as *"Jezebel."*[53] Claiming to be a prophetess, she openly seduced the servants of God into eating things that had been sacrificed to idols. That blatant rebellion was a stench to the nostrils of God and a potentially terminal cancer in the body of Christ (*the Church*), which Jesus intended to quickly and violently cut out if the elders at Thyatira didn't move swiftly to do it for Him!

~ Sick sheep quickly spread disease if left grazing and breeding as they please! ~

I didn't intend for that to rhyme, but it's cute isn't it? As we learned from Jesus' letters to Ephesus and Pergamos, once Jesus gives His final warning, He moves swiftly to protect and preserve the purity of His fold. Whether this Jezebel was real or figurative, Jesus was finished waiting for Thyatira's rebellious children to obey and repent. Their eternal salvation was at stake. Thus, Jesus was not only going to severely punish those who participated in Jezebel's rebellion, but the consequence of their sin would be no less than eternal damnation. When Jesus said: *"I will kill her children with death,"* that's precisely what He meant! To be killed with death means to suffer eternal damnation, and, from that, there's no escaping!

When true Christians (*Christ's sheep*) hear Jesus' voice they respond.[54] Remember, not one of the *"Good Shepard's"* sheep will be lost.[55] But the hypocritical goats[56] in the fold, who cause confusion and conflict while making a pretense of knowing Christ, will take part in the "second death,"

[53] 1Kgs. 18:19 thru 21:25, 2Kgs.9:7-37
[54] John 6:39, 10:11-16
[55] John 17:10-12
[56] Mt. 25:32-33

a death from which there's no hope of restoration or forgiveness.[57] Moreover, when Jesus said: *"... **all the churches shall know that I am He which searcheth the reins and hearts: and I will give unto every one of you according to your works,**"* He made it perfectly clear that His words of admonition, encouragement, and instruction are not solely for the church at Thyatira. By instructing John to record his Revelation vision and take it to each of the seven churches in Asia, the Lord was intentionally making all seven letters accessible to the entire body of Christ. Hence, every word in John's book, like the rest of the Bible, is intended to reprove, encourage and guide the whole Church, from one generation to the next. And, given that this has always been the Lord's intent, Jesus gave us the following words of comfort and confirmation:

"Heaven and earth shall pass away: but my words shall not pass away."

Matthew 24:35

When Jesus made the preceding statement nobody was following Him around taking notes, and there were no printing presses. Knowing this, it seems impossible that, nearly two thousand years later, the Bible could still be the most printed document in the history of the world, and yet, it is. If that fact doesn't suggest a miraculous fulfillment of prophecy then I don't know what would!

A Solid Promise to the Overcomers

Rev 2:26-29 ♦ *please read these verses before continuing.*

I can't imagine how Jesus could have been more generous than He was in the close of His letter to Thyatira. In His usual paternal manner, Jesus extended an honor to all "overcomers" — an honor that was given exclusively to Him by God the Father.[58] Perhaps we can't rightly claim (*with absolute certainty*) to know who God used to write the second Psalm, but it's a beautiful declaration from God the Father to God the Son. In that Psalm, God the Father declares Jesus' complete power and authority over all the nations of the world. And yet, here, at the close of His letter to Thyatira, Jesus promises to relinquish that ***'power over the nations'*** to all those who ***'overcome'*** and remain faithful in ***'good works'*** until the end.

Topping it all off, Jesus also promises to give those of us who overcome the greatest gift of all — Himself! Jesus said: ***"He that taketh not his cross,***

[57] Rev. 20:11-15
[58] Ps. 2:1-12

and followeth after me, is not worthy of me.*"*[59] Jesus taught this because He agonizingly earned every ounce of our loyalty, not only as our Savior but also as our Creator and, therefore, has every right to demand our complete submission to His will. And yet, as if giving His all to pay the penalty for our multitude of sins wasn't enough, Jesus essentially *"gave His all"* so that He could *"give us His all again"* during the regeneration (*Christ's millennial kingdom*).[60] Simply put, Jesus gave all He could give *"on earth"* (*as the Son of man*) so that later (*as the Son of God*) He'll righteously be able to share all of His inheritance with the saints *"in Heaven."* This is, in part, what Jesus meant by promising[61] to give the ***'morning star'*** to every overcomer. Jesus is that Morning Star. Hence, during His earthly ministry, Jesus said the following: ***"He that hath the Son hath life; and he that hath not the Son hath not life."*** [62]

Jesus' Chilling Letter to the Church at Sardis

Rev. 3:1-6 ♦ *please read these verses before continuing.*

Of the seven letters written to the churches, this letter to Sardis is, in many ways, the most frightening. When I read John's record of the Lord's rebuke of this first century church, haunting visions of a dark, lifeless graveyard begin to creep into my mind's eye. Can't you just feel the eager clutch of Satan's fingertips straining to grab hold of these carefree, *"pseudo-Christians?"* Apparently they had received good teaching during their formation but had failed to truly repent and begin growing in Christ.

Absolutely no praise for this Church

I can't find a single word of praise or recognition in Jesus' letter to Sardis, at least not for the church of Sardis as a whole. Jesus' words, ***'thou hast a name that thou livest, and art dead,'*** say it all, while clearly pointing an accusatory finger at the obvious hypocrisy of this church. It should be a truly terrifying experience to be told by the Lord that your reputation for being a lively church is a lie! When Jesus said: ***". . . I have not found thy works perfect . . . ,"*** He was likely referring to their lack of sincere growth and true faith. Apparently, Sardis had the proverbial cart before the horse. Sardis had developed a reputation as being a working church, without actually experiencing repentance and true spiritual rebirth. It was time to hit the brakes, back up, and completely reevaluate their calling while there was still time to do so. Hence, Jesus made it clear that if they didn't experi-

---

[59] Mt. 10:38-39

[60] Mt. 19:28

[61] Rev. 2:28, 22:16

[62] 1Jn. 5:12

ence immediate and thorough revival, He would then, ***'as a thief,'*** come. Jesus didn't reveal exactly what He intended to do if He had to stealthily visit Sardis, but we can be relatively certain that whatever He intended to do would be severe!

To the Faithful Few

Refreshingly penetrating the lingering haze of Sardis' continual hypocrisy was the weary dim light of a few enduring souls. The only inspiring words in Sardis' letter were directed to this faithful remnant, who, unlike the others, had not defiled their heavenly garments. To those spiritually famished, though worthy individuals, Jesus' sweet words of encouragement must have been as nourishing as a tropical oasis would be to sojourners traversing a drought barren desert. And a spiritually barren desert it was! With a Bible always within reach, our spiritual oasis is never more than a prayer and a verse away. That wasn't true for the faithful few at Sardis. They desperately needed to hear the Lord's reassuring words of promise that, one glorious day, He would boldly confess their names before His Father, clothe them in white raiment, and allow them to freely walk with Him in His eternal kingdom. And, incidentally, that promise is for all those who overcome, in every generation, including ours!

Jesus' Refreshing Letter to the Church at Philadelphia

Rev. 3:7-9 ♦ *please read these verses before continuing.*

It's a relief to read the Lord's letter to these tried and still true battle-scarred saints[63] at Philadelphia. Unlike His letter to the church in Sardis, Jesus' letter to these saints doesn't contain a single word of reproof. These inspiring brothers and sisters of ours were apparently "Gumby-like" in their resilience. No matter what trial or opposition came their way, they just hung-on to their faith and sprung back into action!

As was the case in many first century cities during the formation of the Church, the city of Philadelphia was plagued by the influence of many

---

[63] Though some religions fail to acknowledge the true biblical definition of the word *"saint,"* the Lord considers every truly *"born-again"* believer in Christ to be a *"saint."* This is an absolute fact and is supported by all of Scripture, starting with Moses (*Deut. 33:2-3*) and ending with John's book of Revelation. The Biblical definition for the word *"saint"* (*both in Hebrew and Greek*) means: *"to be holy, sanctified, and set-apart."* In these mortal bodies we don't see ourselves as being *"holy,"* but, once we've surrendered our lives and wills to Christ and have become His servants, God does! That's what counts, God's holy Word, not unsupportable religious misinterpretations. In God's eyes we are instantly *"sanctified"* (*set-apart*) as soon as we repent and fully surrender our hearts and lives to Christ—Eph. 2:14-22, 1Cor. 1:2, 2Cor. 1:1.

prominent Jewish leaders, who believed that only a strict adherence to God's law could gain them approval before God. Thus, those religious leaders adamantly refused to recognize the Christian claim of being sanctified through faith in Christ Jesus without the works of the Law. Nevertheless, Jesus' words in the following passage make it perfectly clear that He alone holds the ***'the key of David,'*** the key that unlocks the Door of Salvation for all of us — Jews and Gentiles alike.

*'And to the angel of the church in Philadelphia write; These things saith he that is holy, he that is true, **he that hath the key of David**, he that openeth, and no man shutteth; and shutteth, and no man openeth . . . .'*

Rev. 3:7

Jesus' reference to this ***'key of David'*** in **Rev. 3:7** is the second of only two references I've found in Scripture. We don't want to digress into the history of the text, but the first mention of this allegorical key of David can be found in the following passage, where it seems at least possible that Isaiah was giving a twofold prophecy, referring both to *Eliakim* (*son of Hilkiah*) and to the Messiah, who (*at that time*) was still to come:

*'. . . And **the key of the house of David** will I {God the Father} lay upon his {the Messiah's} shoulder; and **he shall open**, **and none shall shut**; and he shall shut, and none shall open.'*

Isaiah 22:22

After reading Isaiah's words, it becomes pretty clear that Jesus' reference to ***'the key of David'*** in His message to the church at Philadelphia was an allusion to Isaiah's nearly eight hundred year old prophecy. Hence, regardless of what the antagonistic Jews of the day were saying, Jesus was declaring Himself to be the long awaited Messiah and, therefore, a fulfillment of Isaiah's prophecy. Thus, Jesus is the true possessor of the allegorical ***'key of David,'*** and only He can open and shut the Door of Salvation and grant access to eternal life. God the Father confirmed this truth on the day of Christ's crucifixion so convincingly that, after witnessing three hours of midday darkness, a mighty earthquake, and the soul-surrendering repentance of one of the two thieves who had been crucified next to Christ, even Jesus' executioners were forced to openly proclaim Him to be the true Son of God.[64]

---

[64] Mk. 15:39

What's more, while all of this was happening atop a little hill in Golgotha, God the Father was making another powerful statement of affirmation in the very heart of the Jerusalem Temple. With the ground still violently shaking and the rocks breaking in two, Jesus' death so completely atoned for all sin that, as a further declaration of that truth, at the very moment of Jesus death, God ripped that massive veil that separated the Holy Place from the Holy of Holies in the Temple right down the middle![65] That veil was there to serve as a perpetual reminder of the barrier that man's sin places between man and the holiness of His Creator.

For the record, this was no small affirmation!

We should note that only God could have torn that enormous, sixty to eighty feet tall veil in half! Matthew wrote: ***'behold, the veil of the temple was rent in twain from the top to the bottom.'*** I still get chills every time I think of how incredible that must have been. Some experts estimate the original veil (*the veil in the Tabernacle, not Herod's Temple*) to have been nearly four inches thick and heavily embroidered, but this veil (*the veil in Herod's Temple*) could have been as much as twelve inches thick! Nonetheless, it was ripped from top to bottom, which means only God could have done it. It certainly wasn't cut in half, though I suppose someone with an extremely tall ladder, a sharp knife, and a great deal of time could have done it — provided of course that they could have gotten past the Temple guards and all the Levites and priests without being dragged outside the city and stoned! Lacking God's help, it would take at least two very large teams of powerful work-horses, pulling against each other, to tear that veil in half, and, still, you'd have to make a starter cut for them to do it!

~ So what's the point? ~

The point of all this (*as the following passage declares*) is that, when God the Father tore that enormous veil in two, He was powerfully declaring that "**sin**," which had acted as a barrier between God and man, had been completely atoned for through Christ's death and resurrection. Consequently, man could now directly approach God through the veil of Jesus' sinless, broken body and be saved.

*'Having therefore, brethren, **boldness to enter into the holiest by the blood of Jesus**, By a new and living way, which he hath consecrated for us, **through the veil**, **that is to say**, **his flesh** . . . .'*

Heb. 10:19-20

[65] Mt. 27:50-54.

Therefore, because Jesus, after having lived a perfectly sinless life, willfully offered Himself as the eternal atonement for all sin, He alone is the rightful bearer of the symbolic ***'key of the house of David.'*** Thus, Jesus' reference to this term in His letter to the church of Philadelphia is analogous to His reference to ***'the keys of hell and death'*** in the following passage, which we read earlier, in the first chapter of John's vision:

> *". . . Fear not; I am the first and the last: I am he that liveth, and was dead; and, behold, I am alive for evermore, Amen;* ***and have the keys of hell and of death****."*

Rev. 1:17-18

Will it be a Pre, Mid, or Post-tribulation event?

Rev. 3:10-11 ♦ *please read these verses before continuing.*

Usually, one of the first questions people ask me when they learn that I study and teach eschatology is: *"So, do you believe in a pre, mid or post-tribulation period rapture of the Church?"*

~ Good question - huh? ~

Jesus knows our strengths and weaknesses better than we ourselves. He knows that feeding us a lot of sugar (*in the form of praise and encouragement*) will give us a quick refreshing boost, but it won't sustain us when the trials rush in. So, at the end of His letter to the Philadelphian church, Jesus tempers His promising words of praise with these cautionary words of advice: ***". . . hold that fast which thou hast, that no man take thy crown."*** Plainly stated, Jesus was telling the church to continue to keep the faith and to not let anything dissuade them from attaining their heavenly goal. Those are good words to live by for all saints.

~ Okay, but what has that to do with the question of a pre, mid or post-tribulation catching-away of the saints? ~

To answer that question, let's take a closer look at **Rev. 3:10.** Jesus told the church of Philadelphia that, since they had unwaveringly endured persecution for their faith, He was going to keep them ***'from the hour*** *(period)* ***of temptation, which shall come upon all the world, to try them that dwell upon the earth.'*** Given that Jesus was obviously referring to a specific, end-time period of global temptation (*trials and tribulations*), I think we can safely conclude that Jesus' assurance may have been intended for the whole body of Christ, not just the church at Philadelphia. Certainly none of the Philadelphian Christians will be alive to suffer through the seven-year tribulation period, so Jesus has already kept that promise. But by promising to keep the Philadelphian Christians from ***'the hour*** *(a specific period)* ***of temptation, which shall come upon all the world,'*** Jesus was definitely referring to the seven-year tribulation period, not just a general period of temptation or trials. Therefore, Jesus' words must also have been a promise to the Church in every subsequent generation. The question is: *"Can this be proven?"* I think it can.

Luke recorded another very similar message from Christ.[66] While foretelling of future world events, Jesus gave all of us the same promise He gave the church at Philadelphia. He essentially told us not to be overcome with the cares of this life (*drunkenness or surfeiting, i.e., overindulging*) and, thus, not be found worthy to be included in the Rapture. Jesus didn't actually use the word rapture; instead, He said "**that day**" in reference to the Rapture. If I seem to be reaching a bit in arriving at that conclusion, I don't believe I am. Let's take a careful look at Jesus' message and see if we can grasp its full meaning.

Speaking specifically about the end-times, Jesus said the following: ***". . . for these be the days of vengeance, that all things which are written may be fulfilled."***[67] Then, Jesus continued and explained about a specific day that we must be prayerful not to let take us unawares. Referring to that day, Jesus said: ***". . . as a snare shall it come on all them that dwell on the face of the whole earth."*** That means that that particular "**day**" of which Jesus spoke will unexpectedly affect every person on the planet (*just as will the day of the Rapture*). And notice how Jesus used the words, ***'. . . as a snare shall it come . . . .'*** That's very clear! The end-time events to which Jesus was referring, starting with the miraculous *"catching-away of the saints,"* [68] are going to "**shock**" every person who's left on earth, just as stepping into a ***'snare'*** shocks the hunter's prey. Jesus never exaggerates. Therefore, since Jesus warned that "**that day**" (*the day of the Rapture*) will come ***'as a snare,' — 'as a snare'*** it will come, and when it does, all who are left on earth will be terrifyingly "**shocked**" at its sudden occurrence! They'll not have anticipated the instantaneous disappearance of hundreds of millions of saints, nor the immeasurable devastation that will follow.

~ So what exactly does that tell us? ~

It tells us that, in order for the rapture of the saints to occur unexpectedly (*like the unexpected slamming-shut of a snare*), which Jesus clearly stated it will, the sudden catching-away of the saints will have to occur

[66] Luke 21:5-36
[67] Luke 21:22-36
[68] 1Th. 4:13 thru 5:3

before the start of the seven-year tribulation period. If that were not the case, as soon as the tribulation period began, Christians would know that, sometime during the next seven years, the resurrection and rapture of the saints will occur. Thus, when the Rapture eventually occurred, neither they nor those to whom they had been witnessing would be completely surprised *("shocked")* at its occurrence; instead, they will have anticipated it. That would mean that Jesus was wrong, which, of course, isn't possible.

*'Watch ye therefore, and pray always that ye may be accounted worthy to **escape all these things** that shall come to pass, and to **stand before the Son of man**.'*

Luke 21:36

The key words in the preceding verse are underlined. First, Jesus is telling the final generation of Christians that, if they pray and are found worthy, they can ***'escape all these things'*** (*the hour – or period – of temptation*) and ***'stand before the Son of man.'*** That sounds like a pretty good description of the Rapture to me. When Jesus said to pray to be accounted worthy to ***'escape all these things,'*** Jesus was referring to escaping **all** of the events that He had just explained (*Luke 21:5-33*) would be part of the seven-year tribulation period. Therefore, since Jesus is assuring us that a specific generation can "**escape**" those end-time events and, instead of having to endure them, be found worthy to ***'stand before the Son of man,'*** I don't see how Jesus could have been referring to anything other than the instantaneous and unexpected resurrection and rapture of the saints.

These are very exciting scriptures, and we're just scratching the surface here. All the really heavy pre-tribulation rapture evidence is still ahead, and when we get to those passages they will further clarify Jesus' words.

The Pillars of His Kingdom

Rev. 3:12-13

Him that overcometh will I make a pillar in the temple of my God, and he shall go no more out: and I will write upon him the name of my God, and the name of the city of my God, which is new Jerusalem, which cometh down out of heaven from my God: and I will write upon him my new name.

He that hath an ear, let him hear what the Spirit saith unto the churches.

As far as the Lord is concerned, we're not merely attendees in the Lord's heavenly Kingdom; we are the metaphorical pillars on which His heavenly Temple is built. Moreover, according to the preceding passage, we're going to have the Savior's name and the name of His City written on our foreheads. How's that for permanence? And, whether Jesus' words are meant to be taken literally or figuratively, they successfully convey one comforting thought:

> ~ Once we've been "born again"[69] as citizens of Christ's eternal kingdom, our citizenship in that kingdom will never be revoked! ~

[69] John 3:1-11, 5:24, 8:31-36

Chapter 9

Jesus' Final Letter to the Church at Laodicea

Rev. 3:14-18 ♦ *please read these verses before continuing.*

With the exception of possibly the church at Sardis, this final message to the Laodiceans was perhaps the saddest message John had to deliver. What an emotionally taxing letter to read, not a single word of praise is directed towards this wealthy, self-sustaining church. Jesus used the word *"lukewarm"* to critique the works of the Laodicean church, bringing to mind a day old, room temperature bowl of soup — "yum, yum!" When it comes to serving the Lord, tepidness just doesn't cut it. But what troubles me most about this message to Laodicea is the fact that I'm left seriously wondering if this soup was ever hot! There's room to doubt whether these people ever truly got saved. I certainly hope I'm wrong, but when we put all the letters of the Lord's appraisal of this church together they spell "LOST!"

Paul apparently wrote letters to both the church at Colossae[70] and the church at Laodicea and instructed both churches to exchange letters (*Col. 4:16*). But I don't know if it can be proven that Paul ever actually visited the church at Laodicea or that they actually followed through with his instruction and read the letter he sent to the church at Colossae. If Paul had actually visited the Laodiceans perhaps that would have made a difference in their spiritual growth. Paul had a meek, yet powerful[71] way of calling false teachers on the carpet, which might have been helpful in Laodicea.

Not personally knowing the inner workings of the Laodicean church and its leadership, we need to be careful about drawing any hard and fast conclusions. That being said, the words Jesus used in His analysis of their spiritual condition are disapprovingly harsh and severe in the extreme. Jesus starts by scolding the seemingly arrogant Laodiceans, saying: ***"because thou art lukewarm, and neither cold nor hot: I will spue thee out of my mouth."*** The Laodiceans needed to be reminded that it would be

---

[70] Col.2:1, 4:12-16

[71] 1Cor.2:1-4, 4:18-21

better for them to have never heard the Gospel than to, having heard it, fail to follow through and truly repent.

Jesus continues: ***". . . thou art wretched, and miserable, and poor, and blind, and naked . . . ."*** These are not the sort of words that our *"Good Shepherd"* uses when chastising sincerely repentant, young Christians, who are simply struggling in their walk with God. No, these words of reproach and admonition are more reminiscent of Jesus' former criticisms of the Pharisaical religious leaders, who were self-righteously unrepentant at His and John the Baptist's preaching. The Laodicean church should have been laying up for themselves incorruptible treasures in Heaven, but, instead, they chose to coast fatly along, comfortable in their continual impenitence.

Much of Laodicea's wealth had come from a medicinal eye ointment, which they had successfully marketed throughout Asia. Therefore, Jesus — always the wise, fatherly teacher and master of parables — used the following analogous admonition in His warning to these monetarily wealthy, though spiritually impoverished, Laodiceans:

*'I council thee to buy of me gold tried in the fire, that thou mayest be rich; and white raiment, that thou mayest be clothed, that **the shame of thy nakedness** do not appear; **and anoint thine eyes with eyesalve**, **that thou mayest see**.'*

Rev. 3:18

Do these words ring a bell? They should. The Lord was imploring the Laodiceans to repent and be "born-again." This is the same counsel Jesus once gave a wealthy young man,[72] who had asked:

"Good Master, what good thing shall I do, that I may have eternal life?"

After Jesus responded — *telling the young man to love his neighbor as himself, honor his parents, and keep all the commandments and the Sabbaths* — the young man proudly replied:

"All these things have I kept from my youth up: what lack I yet?"

We all know the sad story, but there's something in Jesus' encounter with that spiritually deprived young man that directly correlates to these so called Christians at Laodicea. When the young man told the Lord that he

[72] Mt. 19:16-24

had kept all the commandments from his youth up, he wasn't lying.[73] If he had been lying, Jesus would have called him on it. Instead, Jesus told the rich young man:

> *"If thou wilt be perfect, go and sell that thou hast, and give to the poor, and thou shalt have treasure in heaven: and come and follow me."*

In doing so, Jesus told the rich young man essentially the same thing He's now telling the Laodiceans in this letter. When Jesus used the word ***'perfect'*** *(in both his admonitions to Laodicea and the church at Sardis),* He meant "**complete**," "**spiritually whole**." If we haven't sincerely repented (*totally surrendering our hearts and lives to Christ*), all our so called *"good-works"* are, as Jesus put it, ***'lukewarm.'*** That means they're uninspired. Without the indwelling Holy Spirit's inspiration and direction in our lives, all our *"good-works"* are works of rebellion rather than submission. To be clear, once the Lord has revealed His will for our lives, from that moment on, if we do not totally and completely submit to His call and sincerely repent, everything we do is an act of rebellion and, therefore, vanity (*i.e., worthlessness*). I realize that this may seem somewhat cold and harsh, so let me put it in familiar terms. I've used the following parable countless times to explain the difference between true, fruitful works of righteousness and fruitless works of prideful rebellion.

God requires Obedience - Not Sacrifice!

In this parable, you're the father of fifteen year old identical-twin boys, **Ray** and **Jay**. First of all, I can't believe you actually named your twins Ray and Jay; what were you thinking?! Anyway, imagine that your wife (*Ray's and Jay's mother*) is finally returning home tonight after having been away, working hard, all week. Before she left on her business trip, several days ago, she sat **Ray** and **Jay** down and gave them the following firm warning:

> "Your rooms are an absolute mess! I've been telling you for three weeks to get them cleaned-up before you do any of your other chores, but neither of you have done what I asked. I'm not happy about it! When I get home at the end of the week, the first thing I'm going to do is check to see that each of you did a good job cleaning your rooms. If you love me, you won't disappoint me!"

---

[73] This in no way suggests that the young man had never sinned, but, rather, that, after having done so, he always offered the necessary sacrifice.

Now, it's Saturday morning, and your wife is returning in the afternoon. So, before you head off to work, you go in to wake the boys and notice that neither of them has done the one thing their mother told them to do while she was away. Knowing how sad and disappointed your hard working wife will be if she returns to find that **Ray** and **Jay** didn't clean their rooms as she demanded, you hold your temper and give them this firm, clear warning:

"Boys, you both remember what your mother said before she left. You've had all week to clean your rooms, but instead you chose to goof-off! Now I'm laying down the law. The only thing your mother wants is for you to clean your rooms before she gets home tonight. So, today, **that's all I care about**! If you fail to clean your rooms, **for any reason at all**, you will spend the rest of your summer vacation **grounded**, **doing chores**! I hope I've made myself clear! I'm very serious! **Before you do anything else, get your rooms clean**!"

After you head off to work, since **Ray** has always been much lazier than **Jay**, he grumbles and goes back to bed in a huff. Meanwhile, **Jay** (*always the energetic type*), proudly tells his father: *"Okay Dad, no problem,"* then heads off to the kitchen for some breakfast.

After about an hour, lazy **Ray** hears the lawnmower going in the front yard, so he goes to check **Jay's** room to see if he's already cleaned it. *"Nope, it's still a pigsty!"* Confused, **Ray** looks out the front window, and, sure enough, it's **Jay** out there mowing the front lawn instead of cleaning his room as he was told. **Ray** scratches his head and says to himself, *'What does Jay think he's doing?'* Then he heads back down the hall and crawls back into bed.

Another hour goes by, and a loud clanking sound from the garage awakens **Ray**. Realizing what the sound must have been, **Ray** sits up and, starting to feel a little guilty, says to himself: *"No way, Jay's cleaning the garage now too?"* **Ray** climbs out of bed and checks to see if **Jay** has cleaned his room: *'Just as I thought. It's still a mess. I don't believe this guy! What is he thinking? Didn't he hear what Dad said about getting our rooms cleaned?'* Completely perplexed about all the extra work **Jay's** doing, **Ray** shakes his head and, again, heads back off to bed. Outside, the neighbors up and down the street, who've been watching **Jay** work hard all morning, are saying to each other:

"First he mowed the lawn. Then he washed the car, and now he's cleaning the garage! What a great kid! What's up with his lazy brother Ray? Shouldn't he be out there helping?"

Over hearing the neighbors' compliments, **Jay** starts feeling pretty good about himself — that is until his father's words begin to haunt him:

"Getting your rooms clean is all I care about. If you fail to clean your rooms, **for any reason at all**, you'll spend the rest of your summer vacation grounded, doing chores! I'm very serious. **GET YOUR ROOMS CLEAN**!"

Definitely feeling guilty, **Jay** thinks to himself: *'But I hate cleaning my room! I'd rather wash the car. Plus, just look at all the other work I've done, and everybody thinks I'm a great kid!'* Shaking off the anxiety of his father's clear, direct admonition, **Jay** ignores his nagging conscience and just keeps washing the car.

Meanwhile, lazy **Ray** can't ignore his conscience any longer. Seeing his mother's tearfully disappointed face would be more than his little teenage heart could stand; not to mention, he'd have to face the eminent wrath and displeasure of his, soon-to-be-livid, father! So, after lazily sleeping half the day away, with just enough time to create a room that will put a gratifying smile on his mother's weary face, **Ray** springs into a room cleaning frenzy and gets the job done! *"What a relief!"* **Ray** says, as he finishes cleaning his now beautiful room, *"And I still have enough time left over to kick-back and watch a little TV; — how cool is that?!"*

Jay, on the other hand, after spending the whole day doing only what he felt like doing, while basking in the prideful glow of his neighbors approval and praise, no longer has time to even begin to clean his room. Knowing that his Mom and Dad will be home from the airport any minute, **Jay** tries to settle his restless conscience by telling himself: *"It'll be okay. Mom and Dad won't be mad. Just look at all the good-work I've done. Ray only did one thing - clean his room - big deal! He's such a loser! Surely Dad won't be upset with me for doing what I thought was best, especially after the neighbors tell him about all my hard work."* But, again, **Jay's** father's commanding words begin to rattle his conscience:

"Get your rooms clean! That's **all** I care about!"

What do you think?

If Jay's Dad is a good, righteous father, will Jay spend the summer doing chores, as his father warned he would? Salvation has never been about good-works. We simply could never do enough of them to earn it. Forgiveness of sin and admittance into God's eternal kingdom has always been about one thing, which is our humble ability to trust, not in our own righteousness (*of which we have none*)[74] or in good-works we believe we've done, but, rather, in God's merciful willingness to provide a way of righteousness for us. All we need to do is humbly obey and receive God's mercy and forgiveness.

*'Enter ye in at the strait gate: for wide is the gate, and broad is the way, that leadeth to destruction, and many there be which go in thereat: Because strait is the gate, and narrow is the way, which leadeth unto life, **and few there be that find it**.'*

Mt. 7:13-14

Those whom I love I rebuke . . .

Rev. 3:19-22 ♦ *please read these verses before continuing.*

Jesus tells the Laodiceans: ***"As many as I love, I rebuke and chasten."*** It's a miserably sad state of affairs when a reminder from the Lord that He rebukes all those He loves is the closest your church gets to a word of comfort from the Savior, but that's all Laodicea got. And, while it saddens us to think of the Lord having to chastise us, these words of Christ's are a beautiful testimony to the paternal love the Lord has for His kids, the Church.

Over the years I've met believers who've persistently tried to convince me that it's possible to walk perfectly, every day, without sinning in these mortal bodies. Oddly enough, some of those who told me this were doing life sentences in the prison where my partner Larry and I were teaching. It's too bad they didn't start their perfectly sinless lives before they committed the sins that put them there. The humble truth about our ability to live every day without sinning in the mind or in the flesh is that that notion is a "**TOTAL FARCE!**" What's more, when you meet that falsely humble, so called Christian, who claims to be living daily without sin, don't forget to duck. If you don't, when they turn around to reprove you, you're going to get brained by that huge beam sticking out of their eye.[75]

~ *Why did I bring this up?* ~

---

[74] Prov. 14:12, 16:25, Romans 3:10-20, Gen. 6:5-7, Is. 64:6-7, Mt. 19:17
[75] Mt. 7:3-5

I brought this up because Jesus said: ***"As many as I love, I rebuke and chasten."*** Are there any Christians whom Jesus doesn't love? Of course not! Therefore, there are no Christians whom Jesus does not rebuke and chasten. Hence, all Christians sin and need the Lord's chastisement regularly.[76]

'And ye have forgotten the exhortation which speaketh unto you as unto children, My son, despise not thou the chastening of the Lord, nor faint when thou art rebuked of him: For whom the Lord loveth he chasteneth, and scourgeth every son whom he receiveth.'

Heb. 12:5-6

It all seems pretty simple and straight forward to me. Since none of us are perfect, the Laodiceans, like us, needed correction. But Jesus' plea was for the Laodiceans to be zealous and repent. The word *"zealous"* in Jesus' plea means: *to be heated to a boil, to desire earnestly, to pursue.* In other words, Jesus is telling them to hunger and thirst after righteousness[77] — to be born-again into the kingdom of God. These final words from the Lord's invitation to the church at Laodicea reverberate even today, as the faithful in Christ continue echoing Jesus' global call to repent:

'Behold, I stand at the door, and knock; if any man hear my voice, and open the door, ***I will come in to him,***[78] *and will sup with him, and he with me.'*

Rev. 3:20

---

[76] Heb. 12:5-12

[77] Mt. 5:6

[78] This is the essence of being *"born-again"* into the Kingdom of God—John 3:1-21.

Chapter 10

Come up hither

John is called up to the Throne

Rev. 4:1

After receiving the last of Jesus' messages for the seven churches in Asia, John immediately saw a door open in Heaven. He didn't describe the door, but he heard the trumpet-like voice of the Lord's angel say: ***"Come up hither, and I will show thee things which must be hereafter."***

As eager as I am to get into the next few verses, which will whisk us directly into the throne room of God, we first need to grab a sledgehammer and knock a bad brick off the foundation of our end-time knowledge. To what am I referring exactly? I'm referring to the fact that John's having seen a door open in heaven immediately after he finished recording the seven letters to the seven churches in no way constitutes proof that the rapture[79] of the Church had just occurred. I know; some of you are scratching your heads and saying, *"Huh, what's he talking about?"* That's good! That's precisely what we should be asking when we hear that completely unsubstantiated notion suggested. The whole idea is an extreme reach and is completely unsupportable without employing reckless supposition.

~ But I've heard that taught for years and by some very prominent ministers! ~

The theory that the open door in **Rev. 4:1** suggests that John was seeing evidence that the church had just been caught-up to Heaven (*raptured*) is largely based on the proposition that the church no longer appears to be mentioned after Chapter 3 of John's vision. That, however, is not true. As we continue, we will see that, while the word — *"church"* — will not be found throughout the remainder of John's vision, a clear reference to the Church and the Rapture will clearly emerge from the text.

~ Why is this so important? ~

---

[79] 1Th. 4:13-18, 1Cor. 15:51-54

This is important because, if we teach or are taught that the open-door in **Rev. 4:1** was meant to indicate to John that the Church had just been raptured, then, later, when we read the scriptures in John's vision that actually teach about the Rapture, we'll fail to realize what we're reading. In fact, that's largely why the Church, as a whole, has misunderstood this amazingly straightforward prophetic book, and that's how one bad brick can make the whole building weak — especially when that brick is part of our foundation. As we learned earlier, if we start-off wrong, we certainly can't expect to finish right, so let's not allow ourselves the irreverent freedom of supposition without acknowledging that we're doing so. Let's keep our scriptural foundation pure and strong.

Whisked Up to the Throne

As soon as John heard the trumpet-like voice of Christ's angel, he was taken (*in the spirit*) up to the throne and dwelling place of God. Based on John's record of his Revelation experience, we can't tell whether he was physically taken into Heaven or simply shown a vision. Whichever was the case, John was *"in the spirit"* and recorded what he experienced as though he had physically been taken into the presence of God.

There was a Rainbow round about the Throne

Rev. 4:2-3

> ***'And immediately I was <u>in the spirit</u>: and, behold, a throne was set in heaven, and one sat on the throne. And he that sat was to look upon like a jasper and a sardine stone: and <u>there was a rainbow round about the throne</u>, in sight like unto an emerald.'***

John's description of God's throne only gives us a vague understanding of the brilliant colors he saw. The difficulty is in knowing just what colors the *jasper* and *sardine* stones actually represent. The *jasper* stone can, at times, look like *polished-brass*, or it can look *bluish-green* or even *purple*. And the *sardine* stone can have a *reddish-brown* appearance, almost the color of *flesh* (*which doesn't tell us much*). Let's face it, God is a Spirit. And Heaven, though very real, is a spiritual place, so it couldn't have been easy for John to relay his awesome experience with mere words. John did, however, make one thing pretty clear: ***'. . . there was a rainbow round about the throne, in sight like unto an emerald.'*** I'm no expert, but I think even in John's time emeralds were green. We must remember, however, that it's not uncommon for emeralds to have secondary hues of *blue* and even *yellow*. Thus, the rainbow around God's throne must have been absolutely breathtaking!

Twenty-Four Inexplicable Men

Rev. 4:4

> ***'And round about the throne were <u>four and twenty seats</u>: and upon the seats I saw <u>four and twenty elders sitting</u>, clothed in white raiment; and <u>they had on their heads crowns of gold</u>.'***

The actual *Greek* word for *throne* in this verse is the same word as is used for the word *seats*. That doesn't mean that the twenty-four elders' seats were anywhere near as magnificent as the Lord's throne, but they must have been fairly impressive, since in the original text John described them using the same word as he did when referring to God's throne.

I've heard it taught that these twenty-four elders consist of the twelve apostles, plus the major patriarchs — *like Abraham, Isaac, and Jacob. Oh, and hey; what about King David? He's got to be one of those elders; doesn't he? Oh yah – and Hezekiah, and Josiah, and - um -m – m - - Moses, - yah - Moses, and Joshua . . . . Oh no! We're still about four short. Who else is really important . . . ?* This kind of teaching isn't really teaching at all; is it? It's just irresponsibly filling gaps!

When I was new at teaching about the end-times, I pretty much taught the same thing, because that was basically what the books I was studying and the ministers, to whom I was listening, suggested. I didn't realize how damaging and irresponsible that type of unsubstantiated teaching was. I was just doing what others were doing — "filling-gaps" — and it was my irreverently filling-gaps that was actually blinding me and those with me to the otherwise obvious truth within the text. It took me awhile to learn that there is no shame in just saying: *"I don't know what this scripture means. Maybe it hasn't been revealed, or perhaps I just don't understand it!"* It's much easier to recognize what we **<u>do</u>** know and **<u>can</u>** scripturally support when we first learn to recognize and admit what we **<u>don't</u>** know and **<u>can't</u>** support.

But aren't the Apostles going to sit on thrones?

There's a scripture that on the surface seems to tie-in with John's seeing these twenty-four elders sitting on thrones. In **Mt. 19:27-30** it's recorded that Peter asked Jesus the following question:

> *"We have forsaken all, and followed thee;*
> *what shall we have therefore?"*

To which Jesus responded:

"Ye which have followed me, in the regeneration when the Son of man shall sit in the throne of His glory, ye also shall sit upon twelve thrones, judging the twelve tribes of Israel."

When we research the scriptural meaning of the word, *"regeneration,"* we find that Jesus was alluding to the Millennial Period — the thousand year period directly following Jesus' Second Coming (*at the end of the seven-year tribulation period*). During that thousand year period Satan will be bound in the bottomless pit, all the demons (*fallen-angels*) will have been cast into the *"lake of fire"* (*we'll see that proven*), and Jesus will rule the world from Jerusalem.[80] Also, during that period, the twelve apostles will sit on twelve thrones judging the twelve tribes of Israel, just as Jesus said. We'll cover all of this in detail as we continue. The point is, while it's true that twelve of the disciples will eventually sit on thrones during Christ's millennial reign, the fact that they will do so in no way suggests that they must also be twelve of the twenty-four elders John saw presently seated around the throne.

Possibly the Greatest Mystery in the Bible

Rev. 4:5

'And out of the throne proceeded lightnings and thunderings and voices . . .'

If we really imagine being John — seeing lightning and hearing thunder and mighty voices coming out of God's throne — it should almost make us feel like running for cover! God's throne is the center of all power, not only of this physical universe but also in the realm of that which is spiritual.

Rev. 4:5 ~ *continued*

As I shared earlier, while we made our way through Jesus' letters to the seven churches, John's following words speak of what I believe to be one of the greatest mysteries in the Bible:

'. . . and there were seven lamps of fire burning before the throne, which are the seven spirits of God.'

John doesn't try to explain the significance of the Seven Sprits of God, so, out of respect, we won't either. However, as I briefly touched on earlier, I do believe it's important to note that the candlestick (*which formerly illuminated the original Tabernacle—Ex. 25:1-37*) was likely symbolic of these Seven Spirits of God, which John is being shown burning as lamps of

---

[80] Isa. 2:1-5

fire before the throne. Like the seven lamps burning before the throne, the candlestick in the Hebrew Tabernacle also had seven pools of oil that continually burned.

Considering that the Old Testament {*the Law and the Tabernacle*} was just a shadow of the New Testament {*Grace and the Church*}, there must be a direct connection between the candlestick in the Tabernacle and the seven golden candlesticks that Jesus told John are the seven churches (*Rev. 1:20*). We don't completely understand how the Seven Spirits of God make that connection, but, fortunately for us, that doesn't hinder our quest to understand the rest of John's revelation. We can be comfortable just knowing that if God wanted us to understand the Seven Spirits of God He would have clearly revealed them to us, and, as of yet, He has not chosen to do so.

The Sea before the Throne

Rev. 4:6

Although John doesn't give us details about the actual seat part of God's throne, he does tell us that ***'a sea of glass like unto crystal'*** lies before it. Daniel saw something similar during his vision of the *"Ancient of Days,"*[81] but there's no reason for us to combine what Daniel saw in his vision with what John is seeing here. As I stated earlier, Daniel's vision was of the *"Ancient of Days"* (*God the Father*) and of His throne during a different period than that of John's Revelation vision. We should also acknowledge that John's description of God's throne in **Rev. 22:1-2** (*the end of his vision*) is a description of God's eternal kingdom and the new earth, not the same Heaven to which John is referring here in **Rev. 4:1-11**. Therefore, we can't combine information from Daniel's, Ezekiel's and John's descriptions of God's throne just because the visions they each had contained similarities. This becomes obvious as we continue reading.

In the second half of **Rev. 4:6**, John wrote: ***'. . . and in the midst of the throne, and round about the throne, were four beasts full of eyes before and behind.'*** The *Greek* word for *"beasts"* in this verse basically means, *"living creatures"* or *"living things."* This is very similar to Ezekiel's vision of God's throne.[82] However, while Ezekiel did see four, winged, living creatures (*just as did John*), Ezekiel's description of those creatures is not exactly the same as John's. Their similarities, however, are remarkably strong. In fact, I can appreciate the temptation to mentally simplify the matter and just assume that if the *beasts* in John's vision this closely resemble the *living creatures* in Ezekiel's vision then Ezekiel and John must

---

[81] Dan. 7:9-14

[82] Ez. 1:4-6

have seen the same heavenly beings. Nonetheless, actually making that assumption would be a mistake, and I'll explain why.

Although the *living creatures* in Ezekiel's and John's visions are surprisingly similar, they do have some very distinct differences. For example, the creatures Ezekiel saw each had *four-wings* and *four-faces*; whereas, the creatures (*or beasts*) John saw each had *six-wings* and *one-face*. Thus, the creatures are amazingly similar while still being very different. Another somewhat freakish similarity between Ezekiel's and John's *living creatures* is that they are apparently covered with eyes from head to toe — "WOW!" How strange that must be to look upon or, rather, to have look upon you! It's definitely going to be excitingly odd to one day behold these awesome heavenly beings.

A Man, a Lion, an Ox and an Eagle

Rev. 4:7-11 ♦ *please read these verses before continuing.*

In Ezekiel's vision (*Ez. 1:4-14*) each of the four living creatures had four wings and four different faces, and each face looked a different direction. Apparently, the face that looked forward was the likeness of a "**man**," and the face on the right-side was that of a "**lion**." On the left-side they each had the face of an "**ox**" (*a young calf or bull*), with the face of an "**eagle**" on the back.

Conversely, John's six winged beasts each had only one face. The first beast had the face of a "**lion**," the second a "**calf**," the third a "**man**," and the fourth had the face of a "**flying-eagle**." It's interesting that John describes the fourth face not just as that of an eagle but of a "**flying-eagle**." If we examine photographs of perched eagles as opposed to eagles in flight, we can begin to imagine the protuberant, naturally aggressive look of the fourth beast's *"flying-eagle-like"* face.

Holy, Holy, Holy . . . .

While John wrote that the four beasts never stop saying: ***"Holy, holy, holy, Lord God Almighty, which was, and is, and is to come,"*** the four beasts are not robotic. In addition to saying this, John wrote that they also give *glory*, *honor*, and *thanks* to God. Thus, in so doing, they evoke worshipful praise from the twenty-four elders, who then fall down, casting their golden crowns before God's throne, while saying:

> ***'. . . Thou art worthy, O Lord, to receive glory and honour and power: for thou hast created all things, and for thy pleasure they are and were created.'***

A Final Note about the Twenty-Four Elders

As I briefly mentioned when we first looked at **Rev. 4:4**, John didn't record having seen himself or any other apostle with whom he had formerly served seated as one of the twenty-four elders before the throne. Additionally, John didn't mention having recognized Elijah, Moses, Abraham, King David or any other prominent biblical figure. Of course, John had never seen Abraham or David, so he probably wouldn't have recognized them if he had seen them. That, however, doesn't hold true with regard to Moses and Elijah or the other eleven apostles.[83]

~ So where does that leave us? ~

While I suppose it is remotely possible that these twenty-four elders are actually familiar biblical characters, whom John was just unable to identify, since there's no record of twenty-four prominent elders having (*as of yet*) been resurrected, it's far more probable that the twenty-four elders John saw seated around the throne are simply special heavenly-beings who were created for the purpose of worshipping God, precisely as John witnessed them doing — just as do the *"four beasts"* around God's throne. We'll touch on this again later, in the next chapter of John's vision.

[83] John, Peter and James saw both Moses and Elijah during Jesus' miraculous transformation experience. How they were able to instantly recognize Moses and Elijah, having never seen them prior to that day, only the Lord knows. Perhaps (*and we can't know for sure*) the credit for their sudden knowledge can be attributed to the powerful presence of the Holy Spirit on that mountain top during Jesus' transformation—Mt. 17:1-9, 2Pt. 1:16-18.

Chapter 11

Who Is Worthy To Open The Book?

Rev. 5:1

After witnessing the four beasts and the twenty-four elders reverently worship God in **Rev. 4:8-11**, John saw a very special book appear in God's right hand. This special book (*or scroll*) had writing on both sides and was sealed with seven seals. Simply declaring this book to be very special, however, is almost as much of an understatement as saying: *"Jesus was a very special teacher!"*

~ So, what makes this book so special? ~

Only one scripturally accurate path leads all the way through John's end-time vision, and this book from God's right hand is the signpost pointing the way to that path. That makes this book "**key**" to our understanding of both Daniel's and John's end-time visions.

Only One is found Worthy

Rev. 5:2

'And I saw a strong angel proclaiming with a loud voice, Who is worthy to open the book, and to loose the seals thereof?'

In order to get a clearer picture of what John saw in his vision we have to think like a detective trying to solve a murder by recreating the crime scene in his mind. Like a detective, we have the statement that was given to us by John, the eye witness. In order to be completely accurate and true to the text, we won't assume anything. We'll imagine being John and seeing everything just as he described it, as though we are seeing Heaven through John's eyes.

~ Let's start recreating John's vision in our minds. ~

John saw a strong angel proclaiming with a loud voice (*As opposed to what, a weak angel with a soft voice?*). I don't think there is any such thing as a weak angel, at least not in Heaven, but if there is, I don't want to be the fool who tries to test his strength! It may seem like I'm being a little irreverent, but I'm not. I'm simply making the point that, since there are no weak angels (*especially in Heaven*), John must have found this particular angel uniquely impressive to behold.

After hearing the angel loudly ask: ***"Who is worthy to open the book and to loose the seven seals thereof?"*** John began to actually weep because no person (*who had ever lived*) was found worthy to open the book or even to look closely at it. For those of you who, like me, don't like to leave any stone unturned while studying Scripture, this raises the immediate question: "*Who, other than the angels and the twenty-four elder's, was in Heaven when John heard the mighty angel ask this question*?" That question opens up a huge can of worms for a lot of Christians, because there are so many different points of view regarding what happens to believers after their mortal bodies cease to function.

So what happens to our bodies when we die?

Throughout the history of the Church many thousands of books, study guides, and sermons have been written about this subject. Scholars continually hold conflicting opinions, with some insisting that at the moment of death we're immediately ushered into Heaven, where we instantly take on some form of *physical/spiritual* existence in the presence of God. Others hold that at the moment of death the souls of the faithful immediately ascend to Heaven, where they experience a timeless, sleep-like, unified existence with God, while awaiting the up and coming Rapture of the Church, when they'll finally be instantly united with a new, immortal, spiritual body, while being resurrected.[84]

I could continue laying out the many differing points of view concerning the afterlife for the faithful, but that would only cause some of us more confusion and doubt. When addressing an emotionally *"close to the heart"* topic of this nature — regarding which some feel there is no real, concrete scriptural answer — it's wise to humbly seek common ground. One aspect of the afterlife about which all reasonable Christians seem to agree is the belief that after death the soul returns to God who gave it.[85] It may also help us understand life after death from a purely biblical perspective if we remember that the God we serve is an eternal Spirit[86] and is, therefore, not bound by the same chronological time barriers as are we. Jesus has made it perfectly clear that He is the ***'Alpha and Omega, the beginning and the end.'***[87] In other words, Jesus is *"in the beginning"* and *"in the ending"* at the

---

[84] 1Th. 4:13-18, 1Cor. 15:51-54
[85] Ecc. 12:7
[86] John 4:24
[87] Rev.21:6, 22:13

same time. Unfortunately, for the time being there is no way we (*being mortals*) can truly hope to understand the spiritual concept of God's eternal existence. If I were to extremely simplify my personal opinion about whether or not we will be spiritually and/or physically conscious in Heaven immediately after death, I would say:

> "If we could grasp God's spiritual nature of existing outside of chronologically-linear time, we would recognize that many Christian perspectives regarding the afterlife of the faithful in Christ are, to some degree, consistent."

I know; you're probably thinking, *'Gee, thanks; what in the world does that mean?'* To put it in a nutshell, our souls (*i.e., the souls of God's faithful, not lost souls*) are in the spiritually eternal, omnipresent hands of God — both now and at the moment of death. Therefore, when our souls leave our lifeless bodies here on earth they instantly return to God in Heaven. About that most Christians are basically in agreement. To grasp a practical understanding of this we need to picture our current, earthly, chronologically-linear state of being, while at the same time broadening our perspective to picture God's eternal, timeless existence. When I say timeless, I'm referring to God's omnipresent, spiritual nature and existence in <u>all</u> points of time, at the <u>same</u> time! That's actually what it means to be omnipresent. I realize that if you haven't given this much thought, it may, at first, be a little difficult to conceptualize. But don't worry; we'll do it together.

~ *The idea is actually very simple.* ~

Let's start by picturing a horizontal escalator. Sometimes people call them moving sidewalks or moving walkways. You know what I'm talking about. They're long, flat, conveyor-like walkways on which people stand while being moved forward in one direction. They're commonly found in large public places, such as airports and zoos. Okay, now let's imagine that we're looking at a moving walkway that's running from left (*where it starts*) to right (*where it ends*). The moving walkway we are imagining represents a 6,000 year period on earth, moving from left (*the first day of creation*) to right (*the day of the Rapture*). So, to be clear, the left end of the moving walkway is the beginning (*about 6,000 years ago*), and the right end is the rapture of the Church[88] — when the souls of the faithful will be resurrected and/or ascend to meet the Lord in the air (*which, we're about to learn, will initiate the future seven-year tribulation period*).

---

[88] 1Th. 4:13-17

The first Man on the Walkway

Adam was the first person to be placed on our symbolic moving walkway, and God placed him there about 6,000 years ago, when he was created. Adam was instantly followed by *Eve, then Cain, then Abel and so on ....* Remember, our symbolic walkway ends at the Rapture, so, since we expect the Lord to return relatively soon, our walkway only represents about six thousand years. Therefore, on our walkway each year will equal one mile:

1 year = 1 mile; therefore, 6,000 years would = 6,000 miles.

That's simple, right? Good! Now, since moving walkways have handrails to keep people from getting off before they reach the end, a moving walkway will perfectly represent the chronologically-linear time constraints of our mortal, earthly lives. At the proper time, God metaphorically places each of us on this walkway. If we were able to watch the walkway from God's perspective, we would see God place *Adam* and *Eve* on the walkway the moment they were created, and, subsequently, *Cain* and *Abel* would appear behind them and immediately start arguing. Just kidding!

There's nobody in front of *Adam* and *Eve* on the walkway, but people are being placed on it behind them daily. Once someone steps onto the walkway they remain in that same position, moving forward, until they die. Thus, *Adam* will keep moving forward until his death, about 930 years (*miles*) later, when his soul (*not his body*) will instantly be freed from linear time and return to a peaceful unity with God. *Adam's* remains, however, will continue moving forward (*on earth*) for roughly another 5,070 years (*or miles*), until they reach the end, when the Lord will rapture the saints and unite Adam's soul with an eternal, spiritually revived body. Don't ask me how God will do that, but it's going to be awesome! That's how chronologically-linear time (*time as we know it here on earth*) works.

Now that we've got a simple picture of our physically time constrained life on earth, let's get a picture of our lives from God's omnipresent, non-chronologically-restricted perspective. The whole reason we're taking the time to envision this moving walkway is to enable us to better understand what may have happened to *Adam's* soul at the moment of his death, when his soul left his body deteriorating on our walkway, about 5,070 years ago. We know from Scripture that *Adam's* soul returned to God (*Ecc. 12:7*), but does that necessarily suggest that *Adam* has actually been conscious and fully aware in the presence of God all these years? Let's see.

Alright, we'll try to forget about Adam's deteriorating body for a just a minute and picture our 6,000 mile long moving walkway from up in the air. To do so, we're going to have to use the space shuttle, because, being 6,000 miles long, our walkway is about twice the length of the United

States. Okay, from way up here in space we can now see the whole walkway and — "WOW!" It's long! Well it may be long to you and to me, but it's not long to God. You see, we can't imagine God's spiritual nature of existing beyond our linear time barriers, so we'll need to substitute that divine characteristic with a like characteristic we can understand. We can easily imagine God being really big!

Seeing it as God does

If we envision the earth being right next to the sun it would resemble a pea being held up to a beach ball. In the same way, let's envision God being large enough to pick up our 6,000 mile long moving walkway, with two fingers, and place it on His dinner plate. For God that would be as simple as picking up a single french fry. Now, if we imagine that we're sitting on God's shoulder, looking down at our french fry size walkway on His plate, we can begin to understand God's perspective while being *"in the beginning"* and *"in the end"* at the same time. Just look, the 6,000 years and all those people are going by on a plate right in front of us, and yet, from God's timeless vantage point there is comparatively little difference between the "**beginning**" (*creation week*) and the "**end**" (*when God will resurrect and/or rapture the saints and the tribulation period will begin*). God can quickly respond to what's happening at one end of the walkway just as easily as the other. From God's omnipresent perspective, time on earth is a matter of our position on the walkway, which God can change instantly and at will. As the Scriptures declare, a day really is as a thousand years to God.[89]

In our allegorical scenario the walkway on God's plate represents the first 6,000 years of linear time on earth, and from God's perspective He can hear every prayer from every person on the walkway, in all points of time, instantly and at the same time. What's more, God can quickly send angels back and forth to answer those prayers. He can even send angels ahead on the walkway and begin answering our future prayers before we've even prayed them. From God's heavenly, timeless perspective, He can be telling Noah how to build the Ark while also changing water into wine for Jesus and rapturing the Church — and all at the same time! Thus, God can easily see and respond to every prayer and "point in time" in an instant. Therefore, when Adam died, all God needed to do was receive Adam's soul out of 3,070 BC (*sequential time*) into His protective omnipresent existence, so Adam's soul could later be resurrected in a new spiritual body, on the day of the Rapture. In which case to Adam it would

---

[89] To God, there really is no difference between a day and 1,000 years—2 Pt. 3:8. For that matter, to God, there is no difference between a millisecond and a trillion years!

seem like no time had passed at all. What's more, that's precisely how Paul described the future resurrection and catching-away of past and present saints.[90]

As I said, God can move our souls in and out of chronological time whenever He wishes, both now and after we die. In fact, that's probably exactly how God revealed this vision to John. Think about it! Thus, when Adam died, from his point of view, he may have closed his eyes and re-opened them to find himself among billions of other resurrected believers, clothed in a white robe, and standing right in front of the throne on the very day of the Rapture. That case scenario would leave no necessity for soul-sleep. Of course this is only one perspective, but in light of God's omnipresence, it's a very reasonable and certainly very logical perspective.

~ So, what have we learned? ~

The previous analogy will hopefully serve to help us comprehend God's ability to carry out His eternal plan, while having absolutely no physical time constraints or barriers. When a child of God dies their physical, chronological time-constraints give way; thus, they instantly become one with God and His omnipresent "**Alpha**" and "**Omega**" state of being. There are no time shackles on God's ankles, so when we die and are unified with God our mortal time shackles are instantly broken.

'But, beloved, be not ignorant of this one thing, that one day is with the Lord as a thousand years, and a thousand years as one day.'

℘ 2Pet 3:8 ℘

If you're having a difficult time grasping this it's probably because you're allowing yourself to think in terms of linear time. Think of it this way: God has the ability to remove us from *"time-on-earth,"* take us up into Heaven (*into His timeless existence*), and put us back into *"time-on-earth"* at the precise time He removed us (*just as He likely did to John, when revealing this vision*). If we can get that possibility straight in our minds we can begin to understand what Jesus may have meant when He said: ***"I am the Alpha and Omega, the beginning and the ending."***[91] Here are a few additional scriptures that may help shed light on the subject:

1Cor. 15:51-54, **1Th**. 4:13-18, **2Cor**. 5:8, **Phil**. 1:23-24, **Mk**. 5:39, **Jn**. 5:28-29 & 11:11, **Dan**. 12:2

[90] 1Th. 4:13-18
[91] Rev. 1:8

Seven Horns and Seven Eyes

Rev. 5:3-6

In **Rev. 5:4** we find our big brother John weeping, because:

> ***'. . . no man in heaven, nor in earth, neither under the earth, was able to open the book*** *(in God's right hand)*, ***neither to look thereon.'***

While John wept, one of the twenty-four elders directed his attention to the throne, where John witnessed:

> ***'. . . a Lamb as it had been slain, having seven horns and seven eyes, which are the seven Spirits of God sent forth into all the earth.'***

The scripture explains that the *seven eyes* are the *Seven Spirits of God*, but it doesn't explain the significance of the *seven horns*. To find biblical insight regarding these *seven horns*, we'll need to turn to the book of Daniel. In Daniel's visions, the *horns* represent kings and authority. The size, position and shape of each individual horn are meant to represent the strength or prominence of the corresponding king. Thus, Daniel wrote:

'Then I lifted up mine eyes, and saw, and, behold, there stood before the river ***a ram which had two horns****: and the two horns were high; but one was higher than the other, and the higher came up last.'*

Dan. 8:3

We now know that Daniel's preceding vision of a ram foretold of the soon to come *Median* and *Persian Empires. The Median Empire* had four successive kings from about 678-549 BC. Those kings were represented in Daniel's vision by the lower of the two high horns (*which came up first*). *"Cyrus the Great"* conquered the *Median Empire* in about 550 BC, and is, therefore, represented by the higher of the ram's two horns.

A complete and thorough study of Daniel's visions in Chapters 7 and 8 will reveal additional examples of *kings* and *kingdoms* being represented by *horns* on *beasts*. Understanding this will help us as we get deeper into John's Revelation vision, but I don't know if it will help us understand the significance of the *seven horns* on the Lamb, whom John saw in the midst of the throne.[92] One immediately obvious inconsistency that arises when comparing Daniel's visions with John's is the number of horns on the Lamb in John's vision. There are seven. Only Jesus is the *"Lion of the tribe of*

[92] Rev. 5:6

Judah," "the Root of David," just as the mighty angel in John's vision proclaimed.[93] So why are there *seven horns* when there is only one King? Does it have something to do with the *seven eyes* and the *Seven Spirits of God?* It probably does, but if we were to make that declaration we would be taking liberties that our reverence for the Scriptures will not allow. So let's just say: *"We're not sure,"* and move on.

God Saves our Prayers

Rev. 5:7-8

> ***'And he** (the Lamb) **came and took the book out of the right hand of him that sat upon the throne.'***
>
> ***'And when he had taken the book, the four beasts and four and twenty elders fell down before the Lamb, having every one of them harps, and golden vials full of odours, which are the prayers of saints.'***

What a sweet sentiment, God actually saves our prayers in vials of pure gold, just as though they were precious oils of incense. Our past pleas for divine intervention, even those we've forgotten and are sure have gone unanswered, have not been forgotten. On the contrary, God has lovingly preserved them, at arm's length, patiently awaiting the proper time for His just response and fulfillment. Hence, God hasn't forgotten a single distressing word. In fact, He has a very special use for those prayers, and we'll soon see what that is.

"Tunnel-Vision" – *what a drag!*

Look-out! The dreaded "Tunnel–vision Monster" usually jumps out somewhere before the end of this chapter! *OO – oo - be careful! Scary, – isn't it?* We learned earlier not to be too quick to draw conclusions based on suppositions or from information derived from individual passages or verses, and here's a good example why. After the Lamb took possession of the mysterious book from God's right hand, the *four beasts* and the *twenty-four elders* sang a new song.

Rev. 5:9-10

> ***'And they** (the beast and the twenty-four elders) **sung a new song, saying, Thou art worthy to take the book, and to open the seals thereof: for thou wast slain, and hast redeemed us to God by thy blood out of every kindred, and tongue, and people, and nation;***

[93] Rev. 5:1-7

And hast made us unto our God kings and priests: and we shall reign on earth.'

A slightly irresponsible Bible teacher might be tempted to grab these few verses and declare them to be proof that the *twenty-four elders* were once mortals, who've been redeemed by the blood of Christ. It's not hard to understand how a well-meaning eschatologist could make that mistake, if indeed it is a mistake. I mean, why else would the *twenty-four elders* be singing this new song of redemption and gratitude? They must have, at some point in time, lived on earth; right? Even a novice attorney could blow a hole right through that argument by simply directing our attention to the following few relevant words from within the text:

'. . . the four beasts and four and twenty elders fell down before the Lamb.'

Since the *four beasts* also fell down and started singing this song of gratitude and redemption, we have to ask: *"Can we apply the same logic to the four beasts as we were ready to apply to the twenty-four elders? Can we actually say that the four beasts also once lived on the earth and were redeemed by the blood of Christ?"* Since the answer to that question is obviously no, how then can we explain the participation of the *four beasts* in the singing of this song? That's the ultimate question, and whatever the answer to that question is will also explain why John saw the *twenty-four elders* singing this song of thanksgiving for all the saints.

If we look at this logically and without supposition, we know from Scripture that at this point in John's vision there are only a few saints in Heaven.[94] Thus, there are no saints in Heaven, ***'out of every kindred, and tongue, and people, and nation,'*** to sing this song for themselves. Therefore, if (*as some teach*) the open door John recorded seeing in **Rev. 4:1** is, in fact, proof that the Church was raptured during that earlier portion of John's vision, why (*in these verses*) didn't John record having seen all those billions of resurrected saints singing this celebratory song of praise for themselves? If at this point in John's vision all the faithful have already been resurrected and the Church has already been caught-up to God's throne (*where John happens to be witnessing this vision*), why is it necessary for the *four beasts* and the *twenty-four elders* to sing this song of praise and thanksgiving on their behalf? I can think of no logical, scripturally supportable answer for that question.

---

[94] Thus far, John has not recorded having seen a single resurrected being; however, we know from Scripture that at least a few individuals have been resurrected and/or caught-up to Heaven (*Enoch, Elijah, Moses and others—Mt. 27:52-53*). This will be thoroughly explained as we continue.

So, is it possible that John witnessed the *beasts* and the *elders* singing this song of praise to the Lamb of God for his benefit, on behalf of all *past, present* and *future* saints — since during this portion of John's vision the saints hadn't yet been raptured and were, therefore, not present to sing this song for themselves? That seems logical to me. What's more, that's precisely what the remainder of John's vision is about to reveal, so let's keep moving.

Before moving on, we should note the following:

We want to remember the words, ***'every nation, kindred, people and tongue'*** from this song of praise and thanksgiving, because that's exactly how the resurrected and raptured saints will be identified when John does actually witness their sudden appearance before the throne.

The Angel's Proclamation

Rev.5:11-12

After the *beasts* and *elders* finished singing their song of praise, John saw an innumerable sea of heavenly hosts (*angels, but not hundreds of millions of saints*) gloriously assembled around the throne. Then, with one mighty angelic crescendo, they made the following grand declaration:

> ***'. . . Worthy is the Lamb that was slain to receive power, and riches, and wisdom, and strength, and honour, and glory, and blessing.'***

Can you imagine how hard it must have been for John to finish out his life on earth after having witnessed such awe-inspiring sights and sounds as he had witnessed in Heaven? He probably fell asleep every night longingly wishing to return.

Every knee shall bow . . .

Rev. 5:13-14

Paul prophesied as follows:

> *'. . . That at the name of Jesus every knee should bow, of things* ***in heaven****, and things* ***in earth****, and things* ***under the earth****; And that every tongue should confess that Jesus Christ is Lord, to the glory of God the Father.'*

℘ **Phil. 2:10-11** ℘

The only time when every soul who ever will have lived will be assembled in front of Christ is at the "Great White Throne Judgment." [95] I bring this up because of what John wrote at the end of this chapter. In **Rev. 5:13** John wrote that he heard every creature in heaven, on the earth, and in the sea saying: ***'Blessing and honour, and glory, and power, be unto him that sitteth upon the throne, and unto the Lamb for ever and ever.'*** This essentially means that John heard every person who has ever lived or ever will live say those words. That's no little thing! And there is no explanation as to how or when this event will occur, but just as the scripture states, it's going to happen.

Hey — where are all the saints?

Before plunging into the always exciting Revelation Chapter 6 (*arguably the most important eschatological chapter in the Bible*), we first need to ask ourselves the following important question: *"Did John hold back critically vital information from us, or did he relay everything he saw the way he saw it?"* We all know the answer. John was directly instructed by Jesus to write everything he saw in a book and send it to the seven churches in Asia.[96] Therefore, while we certainly can't expect that John was able to clearly relay each and every detail of his end-time vision, I do think we can trust that John recorded every prophetically significant detail, which begs the question:

~ *If, as is frequently taught, millions of saints who went on before us are already in Heaven, where were they?* ~

If (*as some suggest*) the saints, at the moment of death, are immediately ushered into Heaven to begin some sort of *"spiritual/physical,"* conscious existence in the presence of God, why hasn't John, thus far, recorded seeing millions upon millions of saints anywhere in his vision of Heaven?[97] Was God hiding them from John for some reason? I doubt it. That wouldn't make sense. John recorded seeing thousands upon thousands of angels around the throne, so why didn't he also record seeing all the saints?

Quickly reviewing a couple of Paul's early letters will help answer this question.[98] John didn't record seeing any saints, because none of the saints (*with the possible exception of those who were resurrected immediately*

---

[95] Rev. 20:11-15

[96] Rev. 1:11

[97] Certainly our souls immediately return to God and His omnipresent (*timeless*) state of being as soon as we die (*Eccl. 12:7*), but according to Paul (*1Th. 4:13-18*), those who've gone on before us have not, as of yet, been resurrected.

[98] You might want to take another look at the following passages before continuing—1Cor. 15:48-57, 1Th. 4:13-18.

after Jesus rose from the dead—Mt. 27:52-53),[99] at this point in John's vision, had been resurrected and transformed.

There is no doubt that the *"souls"* (*not the bodies*) of the faithful who've gone on before us are — at this very moment — peacefully secure in God's spiritually-timeless loving care.[100] That being said, according to John's vision of future events, there is (*at present*) no scriptural justification for teaching that the saints are somehow in bodily form in Heaven. We just can't think in terms of earthly, mortal, chronological-time if we want to understand our being one with God after death. God is a Spirit; thus, if the departed souls of our loved ones have become one with God, they've become free from linear time constraints — just as is God. For those souls, "**time**" has become relative to God's omnipresent existence.

Simply put, when we die our mortal existence will instantly end; therefore, we will no longer be subject to chronological-time. But, according to Scripture, we will not take on immortal bodies until after the Lord returns to resurrect and "catch-away"[101] the saints (*the Rapture*). Hence, once that happens, we'll never again be mere mortals. Instead, we'll be similar to Christ after His resurrection. We'll be spiritual beings with physical characteristics and abilities. But the Scriptures do not indicate that this change will occur at the moment of death, though to us, having become one with God, it will likely seem as though it did.

If you're having difficulty understanding why John still hasn't seen millions of saints in Heaven, reviewing our earlier moving-walkway analogy may be helpful. We must acknowledge that, thus far, John has recorded nothing that could be "**clearly**" interpreted to indicate his having witnessed the resurrection and rapture of the saints or the actual start of the tribulation period. Therefore, at this point in John's vision there is no reason for John to have recorded having seen what will certainly be an innumerable gathering of both Old and New Testament saints, but when we get to that exciting portion of John's vision there will definitely be no mistaking it!

---

[99] This will be thoroughly addressed when we reach the pertinent portion of John's vision.

[100] That means that the saints who have gone on before us are not *"soul-sleeping."* They simply no longer exist in a state of chronologically linear time; but, rather, they peacefully coexist within God's omnipresent state of being.

[101] 1Th. 4:13-18, 1Cor. 15:42-54

Chapter 12

The Key to Understanding Eschatology

(Hey, that rhymes!)

> ☙ Understanding the meaning of this Chapter six portion of John's vision will enable us to more accurately interpret all end-time prophecy. ❧

If you haven't earnestly prayed before studying today it would be wise to stop and do so. The enemy doesn't want Christians to have a solid understanding of God's plan of salvation or end-time prophecy. What's more, it's impossible to understand scripture, especially prophetic scripture, unless we trust the Holy Spirit to reveal it, and understanding this specific chapter of John's exciting Revelation vision is vitally important when attempting to interpret end-time prophecy.

A note about the text:

I realize that even the meekest of Christians can sometimes become closed minded and defensive with regards to which particular version of the Bible they choose to study. It's a touchy subject, because people love their Bibles. They also love their pastors and teachers, so whichever version their pastor endorses is often the version they use and defend to the death. I personally believe, if any individual is sincerely seeking the truth, the Holy Spirit is able to reveal it through any complete Christian translation. That does not, however, mean that I believe all translations to be equal in purity, especially when studying eschatology, as we are here.

Having thoroughly examined nearly every major modern translation of the Bible, I've found that many passages in the book of Revelation can be at least partially understood while using most modern translations. And yet, while I believe that to be true, I've chosen to reference the *"King James Version"* of the Scriptures when directly quoting from the text.

~ Why have I chosen the King James Bible? ~

There are verses in all modern translations that have additional words that did not exist in the original manuscripts. These seemingly harmless additional words often dramatically change the significance of the entire verse or passage in which they are found. This is one of the reasons why the book of Revelation has, for the most part, been taught incorrectly year after year. Studying with a *King James Version* (*KJV*) Bible or at least having one on hand will allow you to see for yourself how the added words have changed the interpretation of John's vision, causing confusion rather than simple, straightforward clarification.

If access to a *KJV* Bible just isn't possible, don't worry. Throughout most of this book you will find that I have displayed the actual *King James Version* of the text and have thoroughly explained the content of each verse.

A quick refresher before diving in:

Thinking back to what we learned earlier about "**allegorical**" prophecy, when the Lord enabled Joseph to experience prophetic dreams and visions, Joseph would first dream of symbolic objects (*like, e.g., lean and fat fleshed cows, bowing sheaves and blossoming grapevines*). Then, when the allegorical portion of Joseph's vision was over, the Lord would conclude by revealing the interpretation of those allegorical figures, thereby enabling Joseph to understand what those symbolic figures represented.

Because the use of allegorical prophecies is so effective, Jesus continued using that divine method of revelation throughout His earthly ministry. In fact, Jesus taught almost exclusively through the masterful use of a more familiar form of allegorical teaching, commonly referred to as "**the parable.**" Following Jesus' example, we still use parables to help students envision the lessons we teach today; we just call them "**word pictures.**"

The Six Seal Allegory of the Entire tribulation Period

That's precisely what Revelation **6:1-17** is, one giant "**allegorical**" depiction of the entire seven-year tribulation period. It begins by metaphorically depicting the emergence of the dictator who will rule the world in the wake of the global resurrection and rapture of the saints,[102] and it ends with the Lord showing John the universally destructive *"Second Coming of Christ,"* which will dramatically conclude that seven-year period. Then,

[102] 1Th. 4:13-18, 1Cor. 15:51-54

starting in the very next chapter of John's vision (*Rev. 7:1*) and continuing throughout the remainder of John's book, the Lord reveals the actual significance of everything John was "**allegorically**" shown in **Rev. 6:1-17.** Therefore, by prophetically revealing these latter-day events to John in this manner, the Lord insured that John's book of Revelation would follow the same divinely established format as have all other prophetic scriptures.[103] Hence, understanding this simple truth enables us to properly interpret virtually all end-time prophecy, including John's exciting Revelation vision.

So, if we're willing to humbly study what John recorded experiencing, passing everything *"we think we know"* about end-time prophecy through the refining fire of pure Scripture, not allowing ourselves any assumptions or preconceived ideas, and not taking anything for granted — just because it's been taught that way for years — then and only then will the hope of attaining eschatological accuracy lie within our grasp. If we can muster the humility, the Holy Spirit and divine Word of God will provide the answers. So let's get to it. This is going to be a fun and exciting adventure!

The Mean Man on the White Horse

Rev. 6:1-2

Jesus — *"the Lamb of God"* — having been found worthy to take the book from the right hand of God the Father, who sits on the throne, began this sixth chapter of John's vision by opening the first of the book's seven seals. As He did this, John heard the thunderous voice of one of the four beasts say: ***'Come and see.'*** Thus, John looked and saw ***'a white horse: and he that sat on him had a bow; and a crown was given unto him: and he went forth conquering and to conquer.'*** This begins the allegorical portion of John's end-time vision.

While the allegorical nature of this chapter is already becoming obvious, it's commonly taught that during the tribulation period there will first be seven *"seal-judgments,"* followed by seven *"trumpet-judgments,"* and, finally, seven *"bowl"* or *"vial-judgments."* However, as we continue moving through the remainder of John's vision it will become clear that the opening of the first six seals in **Rev. 6:1-17** was not intended to indicate an actual commencing of tribulation events. Instead, the allegorical visions John saw as the first six seals were being opened were intended to give John a general understanding and "**preview**" of the effects of those future tribulation period events. That statement is not based on personal opinion. In fact, it's quite provable, and the purely allegorical significance of the

---

[103] Gen. 37, 41, Jdg. 7:12-15, Dan. 2 thru 7, Acts 10:9-28 and many others.

opening of the first six seals in John's vision will become unmistakably evident before we finish assessing the opening of those seals.

And the First Seal is Opened

Rev. 6:1-2 ~ *continued*

As we just read, after Jesus opened the first seal on the book from God's right hand, John looked and saw:

> ***'. . . a white horse: and he that sat upon him had a bow; and a crown was given unto him: and he went forth conquering and to conquer.'***

This rider on the white horse makes it immediately obvious that what John recorded seeing in **Rev. 6:1-2** is allegorical, because nobody is really going to be riding around on a white horse with a bow in their hand and a crown on their head during the tribulation period.

Although some teach that the man on the white horse is Jesus, nothing about that option fits. In the first place, the white horse and rider are intended to represent what will be happening on earth after the seven-year tribulation period begins, which explains why the verse states that a crown (*a symbol of authority and power*) was ***'given'*** to the rider of this white horse. There is no scriptural reason for Jesus to receive either a crown or a bow at the beginning of the tribulation period. At that time, Jesus will not be going forth ***'conquering and to conquer'*** anything. Moreover, when Jesus does return to conquer the earth, He will do so with a mighty sword (*the Word of God*), not a bow, and, according to Scripture, He'll be wearing many crowns, not just one! [104]

The son of perdition,[105] however, the man who will begin going about the earth deceiving the world into submitting to his newly acquired demonic power and authority, will be going forth ***'conquering and to conquer.'*** Therefore, this man on the white horse in John's vision can only represent one thoroughly evil figure — *the son of perdition*. Later, we'll see that this interpretation perfectly aligns with Daniel's parallel vision of this thoroughly wicked world leader and his actions during this period.[106]

---

[104] Rev. 19:11-15

[105] Paul wrote to the Thessalonians and explained about the coming of this wicked *son of perdition (2Th. 2:3-12),* and the *false-prophet (to whom Jesus referred in Mt. 24:15-24 and Mk. 13:22)* is the same *son of perdition* of whom Paul prophesied. Many incorrectly refer to this wicked individual, labeling him *"the anti-Christ,"* but the Bible never does. We'll cover this thoroughly as we make our way through John's vision.

[106] In Daniel's vision of this world leader, he saw him as a formidably stout little-horn, with a mouth speaking great blasphemous things against God—Dan. 7:7-8.

~ *But why is the rider on the white horse wearing a white garment?* ~

White is a symbol of purity, holiness, and most of all righteousness. Therefore, since the son of perdition's mission will be to deceive the whole world into believing him to be both holy and good, this white horse and rider is a perfect allegorical image of the deception with which he (*through Satan and his powers of darkness*) will cloak himself, in order to mislead those on earth into submitting to his (*what will appear to be divine*) authority. Thus, the crown John saw this figure wearing symbolizes that authority. Paul explained this in his second letter to the Thessalonians, stating that the son of perdition, through the act of extreme deceit, will:

> *'. . . opposeth and exalteth himself above all that is called God, or that is worshipped;* ***so that he as God sitteth in the temple***[107] ***of God, shewing himself that he is God****.*

2Th. 2:4

We all know that Satan frequently disguises himself as an angel of light in order to draw souls into darkness. So, because this is true, Paul warned the church at Corinth with the following words:

> *'For such are false apostles, deceitful workers, transforming themselves into the apostles of Christ. And no marvel;* ***for Satan himself is transformed into an angel of light****.'*

2Cor. 11:13-14

The preceding passage is important to remember, because, as we will see later, the son of perdition will cause the world to believe that he is God in the flesh. He will be demonically empowered by Satan (*not possessed*),[108]

---

[107] Some maintain that Paul's reference to "*the Temple*" in this passage indicates that the anti-Christ will emerge from within the body of Christ (*the Church*), but Paul's words clearly refer to the actual Jewish Temple, not the Christian Church. The *Greek* word "*naos*" *(which means "to dwell")* was used by Paul in reference to the literal, *"inner"* Temple, not the Church. This is because the Spirit of God dwelt within the *"inner"* sanctuary of the Temple; thus, when referring specifically to the Holy of Holies and the Holy place – *naos* - rather than - *hieron (the word used in reference to the entire Temple and surrounding structures)* - is respectfully used. To more thoroughly grasp this, it might also be helpful to read Mt. 24:11-24.

[108] This will be proven as we continue.

and, with that demonic power, he will deceive the world into following him, instead of obeying the preaching of God's two end-time witnesses.[109]

What we'll learn as we continue . . . .

As we move into the interpretive portion of John's vision, which begins with **Rev. 7:1** and continues throughout the remainder of John's book, we are going to learn that during the first 3½ years of the seven-year tribulation period God will use two unprecedentedly powerful witnesses to call the world to repentance. And to affirm the divine nature and origin of those witnesses and their preaching, God will enable them to perform great, extremely destructive and persuasive plagues throughout the 3½ years of their ministry. Hence, because the global plagues of these two witnesses will cause such unrelenting destruction, agony, and death, it will be easy for the son of perdition to deceive the world into believing that God's two tribulation period witnesses are actually evil rather than good.

We must remember, however, that the plagues during the first 3½ years will be plagues of mercy, "tough-love" from God the Father and our Savior, Jesus Christ. That's right! In reality, those plagues will neither be punishment nor wrath, though they'll certainly feel as though they are. They'll be God's final effort to save the stubborn left-behind world (*our unrepentant loved ones and friends*), which, without God's severe prodding, just won't repent. I realize this is hard for some believers to accept, but we'll see later that this is most definitely true. God never allows the faithful to suffer His wrath.

When it's time for wrath, we'll definitely know it!

As we continue through John's vision we'll identify every pertinent verse that indicates wrath. Thus, it will quickly become clear that the plagues of God's two witnesses (*during the first 3½ years*) will not be plagues of wrath.[110] This makes sense, because some of the people on earth during the first half of the tribulation period will later accept Christ and prove their faith by choosing to be beheaded instead of taking the damnable *"mark of the beast."* John will refer to that special group as being "**the remnant**." God will not allow that remnant of temporarily disobedient children (*who'll have been left-behind after the Rapture*) to suffer His vengeance and wrath. However, God will, through the plagues of His two witnesses, give them a little taste of "HELL ON EARTH" in order to cause them to repent. If God were to actually subject "**the remnant**" to His

---

[109] We'll learn about God's two witnesses very soon. Presently, we should note that it's also possible that the son of perdition (*the anti-Christ or false-prophet*) could be of Islamic origin and claim to be the *"Twelfth Imam."*

[110] 2Kgs. 10:23, John 3:36, Ro. 1:18 and 5:9, Eph. 5:6-7, 1Th. 1:10 and 5:9

wrath, which will be much more severe than the witnesses plagues, His doing so would be contradictory to His divinely inspired Word.[111]

"PLAGUES" don't always = "WRATH"

The plagues during the first 3½ years will be absolutely horrific, but they're not going to be God's wrath. When God's wrath is poured out there will be no question it has begun. The difference will be terrifyingly clear, because, unlike the restrained plagues of God's two witnesses, when God's actual wrath begins to be poured out on the perpetually rebellious inhabitants of the earth, it will be poured out virtually without measure!

The first 3½ years of the tribulation period (*which the opening of these first four seals from the book in God's right hand represent*) will be filled with unimaginably powerful deception, confusion, and globally-impactive wars and plagues. This will be due to a combination of the unrelenting plagues of God's two prophets and the wicked conquests of the son of perdition and his growing army of followers. Speaking in reference to this future wicked time of great deception, Jesus said the following:

> *'And then if any man shall say to you, Lo here is Christ; or, lo, he is there; believe him not: For false Christs and false prophets shall rise, and shall shew signs and wonders, **to seduce**, **if it were possible**, **even the elect**.'*
>
> ☙ **Mark 13:21-22** ❧

Given that we who believe in and follow Christ are the "**elect**" to whom Jesus was referring in the preceding verse, I'd say that the son of perdition will be capable of creating some extremely powerful deception!

Some things don't need to be interpreted . . . .

There are times when the Bible makes a crystal clear statement that's not open to interpretation. The 3½ year ministry of the two witnesses (*during the first half of the tribulation period—Rev. 11:3-12*) is an excellent example of Scripture telling us something straight-out, without our having to interpret its meaning. Unfortunately, for many, interpreting what John saw when Jesus opened the first five seals in **Rev. 6:1-11** is not as straight forward. Therefore, to properly interpret John's vision, we must use all the scriptures and, through the process of elimination, decide which interpretation most accurately aligns with "THE WHOLE OF SCRIPTURE."

---

[111] Ro. 1:18 and 5:9, Eph. 5:6-7, 1Th. 1:10 and 5:9

SOMETHING TO KEEP IN MIND:

We don't want to spend a lot of time trying to establish the significance of the 2nd thru 5th seals in this allegorical portion of John's vision (*Rev. 6:1-11*), because they will be thoroughly explained as we continue moving through the remainder of John's book. So, as Jesus opens these seals, one-by-one, we'll simply state each seal's symbolic relevance, without stopping to scripturally prove it. Then, after finishing Rev. Chapter 6, we'll move right into Rev. Chapter 7 and the ensuing chapters, which will clearly reveal the full significance of each of these seven seals.

So much for - "3½ years of Peace"

Rev. 6:3-4

> ***'As Jesus opened the second seal John heard the second beast say; Come and see.***
>
> ***And there went out another horse that was red: and power was given to him that sat thereon to take peace from the earth, and that they should kill one another: and there was given unto him a great sword.'***

The rider of this red[112] horse doesn't represent an actual person. Instead, as is indicated by his having the power to take peace from the earth, he represents the global destruction and calamity that will unexpectedly overtake the world as the tribulation period begins (*after the rapture of the Church suddenly causes the disappearance of hundreds of millions of saints*). Sadly, though the Rapture[113] will be unbelievably devastating, it will only partially account for what we just read in the preceding verses, which foretell of "PEACE" being stricken from the earth.

'Behold, I shew you a mystery; We shall not all sleep, but we shall all be changed, ***In a moment, in the twinkling of an eye****, at the last trump: for the trumpet shall sound, and the dead shall be raised incorruptible, and we shall be changed . . .'*

☙ 1Cor. 15:51-52 ❧

'For the Lord himself shall descend from heaven with a shout, with the voice of the archangel, and with the trump of God: ***and the dead***

[112] According to the original *Greek*, this color red would likely resemble fire.
[113] 1Th. 4:13-18

in Christ shall rise first: Then we which are alive and remain shall be caught up together with them in the clouds*, to meet the Lord in the air: and so shall we ever be with the Lord.'*

ꕥ 1Th. 4:16-17 ꕥ

We should easily be able to understand why this rider on the red horse represents a complete lack of peace on earth. When the Rapture (*which the preceding two scriptures describe*) unexpectedly takes place, peace on earth will instantly become a thing of the past — at least for the next few years. That brings the following thought to mind: *'I wonder how many eager seekers of knowledge on this end-time journey have been taught that the first 3½ years of the tribulation period will be relatively peaceful?'* With the opening of these first two seals, we can already see that peace will definitely not be attainable for those left on earth. Instead, once the seven years of great tribulation have begun, peace will be nearly nonexistent.

Surprisingly, some still teach Peace

Sadly, though it's hard to believe, there are many very distinguished and successful authors, film makers, and pastors still teaching that the first half of the tribulation period will be relatively peaceful. In fact, when I was a younger, enthusiastic student of Scripture, that's what I was taught. It seemed that every book I read and every movie or video I saw regarding the tribulation period made it seem as though the global plagues of God's two witnesses (*which will dominate the first 3½ years of the tribulation period*) are going to be barely noteworthy — "practically insignificant!" According to what I currently hear being taught on the radio and what I've read, both on-line and in books, much of what is being taught did not "**self-emerge**" from the text — any text! I wouldn't say this without being able to support it, and we're going to see this truth clearly established as we eagerly make our way through the rest of John's end-time vision.

With Anarchy and Chaos comes Famine

Rev. 6:5-6

After seeing Jesus open the third seal, John wrote:

> ***'. . . I heard the third beast say, Come and see. And I beheld, and lo a black horse; and he that sat on him had a pair of balances in his hand.***
>
> ***And I heard a voice in the midst of the four beasts say, A measure of wheat for a penny*** *(i.e., a day's wage)*, ***and three***

> ***measures of barley for a penny; and <u>see thou hurt not the oil and the wine</u>.'***

The opening of the first two seals represented peace being taken from the earth due to the aftermath of the Rapture and the brutal triumphs of the son of perdition, who will immediately go forth ***'conquering and to conquer.'*** Now, let's think: *'who is it that's always following war and destruction around, like a couple of snotty-nose, winey little sisters?'* That's right, "FAMINE" and "DISEASE." And, when those miserably pesky little brats barge their way in for an unwelcomed visit, the people of the world better brace themselves, because two far worse kin-folk are somewhere nearby! Prowling around in the rubble of humanity's despair and destroying any hope for future economic stability, will, of course, be the hopelessly reckless, blasphemously irreverent, big, fat, and ugly older brothers of Famine and Disease — "**ANARCHY**" and "**CHAOS**!" And guess what, once these guys show up, they're not leaving for at least three and a half years!

The global economy will collapse!

Since the **white**, **red** and **black** horses collectively represent the first 3½ years of the seven-year tribulation period, which will begin after the promised resurrection and rapture of the saints, it's logical to conclude that the opening of this third seal (*the black horse and rider*) signifies the subsequent, instantaneous, total collapse of the world's economic structure. After the Rapture, those who are suddenly left-behind will be forced to try and somehow survive the resulting chaos and global mayhem. Being non-believers, they won't understand why they've been instantly left-behind, in a terrifying world, where they can no longer trust even their closest friends and neighbors. That formerly friendly neighbor, with whom they enjoyed a chat and a cool drink at the family BBQ last summer, will sadly become the terrified survivor they'll catch sneaking over their back fence in the middle of the night, desperately attempting to steal the last little bit of water that's left in their swimming pool!

If you're wondering if I'm just being overly dramatic — "I'M NOT!" In fact, because I know that many who are on this journey with us don't realize just how bad even the first 3½ years of the tribulation period are going to be, I've toned this down a great deal, hoping to gently prepare us for the impending shock of the ensuing chapters. Jesus didn't refer to this final seven-year period as a time of "GREAT TRIBULATION" for nothing.[114]

Before moving on we need to lightly assess the metaphoric significance of the words John heard the voice in the midst of the four beasts say following the opening of the third seal:

---

[114] Mt. 24:21

'. . . A measure of wheat for a penny, and three measures of barley for a penny; <u>and see thou hurt not the oil and the wine</u>.'

The combination of this *"black horse and rider,"* the *"pair of balances,"* and the *"wheat and barley"* clearly suggests a state of physical misery and economic distress.

~ Okay, but what does the oil and the wine represent? ~

We can't perfectly prove the scriptural significance of the *"oil"* and the *"wine,"* but let's give it a shot. The answer might be found in one of Christianity's most beloved parables, *"The Good Samaritan."*[115] With this parable, Jesus taught the true meaning of loving thy neighbor as thyself. In so doing He spoke of using *oil* and *wine* medicinally. Stopping to clean and bind the brutalized man's wounds, the Good Samaritan used both *oil* and *wine.*

After the Rapture there will be hundreds of millions who'll desperately need medical attention, yet they'll have little to no hope of getting it from a hospital. Plainly stated, the *oil* and *wine* will likely be used to clean and bind wounds during the tribulation period, just as they've been used during centuries past. If not, we can at least deduce that the *oil* and *wine* probably indicate *"universal suffering"* and *"great injury."* Either way, a lot of people, all over the world, will have to endure prolonged agony and/or slow death without the comfort of professional medical assistance.

Summing up the Third Seal - *(Rev. 6:5-6)*

A world without "PEACE" implies constant violence, injuries, and death, which is suggested by the **red** and **black** horses and the need for *oil* and *wine*. Electricity will instantly become a thing of the past for most, if not all, of the world. Hence, after the Rapture, hospitals will almost immediately cease to be staffed and will, therefore, be looted and over-run. And yet, as we will soon see, all of this will account for just a fraction of the certain global anarchy that will erupt. Thus, it's logical to conclude that John's having witnessed the rider on the black horse carrying ***'a pair of balances'*** (*a common symbol of commerce or trade*) and his having heard a reference to ***'a measure of wheat for a penny, and three measures of barley for a penny'*** (*clearly suggesting a severe scarcity of food and basic, daily sustenance*) are intended to indicate a complete collapse of the world's economic structure and monetary systems. This will open the door for the universal administering of the *"mark of the beast"* (*at the beginning of the final 3½ years of the tribulation period*) as a means of achieving total civil

[115] Luke 10:25-34-37

compliance to a new, thoroughly wicked, globally autocratic economic system.

IT MIGHT HELP TO CONSIDER THE FOLLOWING:

Have you ever had someone try to briefly describe a movie without ruining it by telling you all the exciting details? Well, *"Hi friend,"* that's me. So much will be happening during the first 3½ years of the actual tribulation period that in order to prevent confusion I'm waiting until just the right time on our journey to address specific details of those events. We need to keep this in mind, because **Rev. 6:1-17** is only an allegorical *"table of contents"* of sorts for the rest of John's exciting vision. As I've stated, God used the first six seals in John's vision, which is all of Rev. Chapter 6, to metaphorically summarize the global degradation and suffering of the entire tribulation period, thereby enabling John to see a very helpful "**preview**" of the entire seven-year period before he was shown the detailed explanation of that same seven-year period in the ensuing chapters. If, for some reason, you're struggling with this, don't worry; you won't be after we've finished examining the rest of these six seals.

Chapter 13

The Middle of John's Allegorical Preview

Rev. 6:7-8

> ***'And when he had opened the fourth seal, I heard the voice of the fourth beast say, Come and see. And I looked, and behold a pale horse: and his name that sat on him was <u>Death</u>, and <u>Hell followed with him</u>...'***

The Son of Perdition will be allowed to rule the Earth

The opening of this fourth seal brings us to the middle of our allegorical preview of the seven-year tribulation period. Thus, the emergence of this symbolic pale horse and rider indicates an almost volcanic eruption of purely evil events, events so horrific that they'll literally emerge from the deep recesses of a place called, "THE BOTTOMLESS PIT!" During this period the son of perdition will intensify his murderous rampage by killing God's two witnesses and the 144,000 Jewish servants (*which we'll discuss shortly*) and by desecrating the newly constructed Third Temple in Jerusalem. Once that's accomplished, he'll begin to force every Left-behinder on earth to submit to his authority by receiving the eternally damnable *"mark of the beast."* All who choose to resist will die!

Wielding the thoroughly wicked son of perdition and his emerging one-world empire like a mighty sword, Satan will kill every saint and eternally captivate the soul of every faithless Left-behinder on the planet. We don't actually know how many millions or hundreds of millions the son of perdition will have already killed during the first half of the tribulation period, while amassing his army of followers, but before his damnable reign of terror is over the 144,000 Jewish servants and "**the remnant**" of newly repentant saints will all have been slaughtered.

The remnant (*those who'll be the very last to repent and be saved*) will have to choose to be beheaded instead of taking the damnable *"mark of the beast."*[116] And yet, the killing of "**the remnant**," though certainly ruthless

---

[116] Rev. 20:4. We'll cover this in detail at the appropriate time.

and extreme, won't be anywhere near as horrific as the killing of the faithless (*those who'll choose to eternally reject Christ*) with "**death**!" Some of you are probably scratching your heads and asking:

"What in the world does that mean?"

When Satan (*through the son of perdition*) kills the last of the saints he'll actually be doing them a huge favor. That's right! Saints are filled (*eternally sealed*)[117] with the Holy Spirit; that's what makes them saints. For that reason they're not going to want to stick around, trying to survive, in a wicked one-world kingdom, fueled by unfiltered demonic trickery and pure unharnessed evil. No way! Without a doubt, though they may be a little fearful, those new saints will consider themselves blessed once they've been martyred and quickly resurrected.[118] Their deaths will be the beginning of life-eternal, not death. Heaven isn't a last resort for saints; it's our long awaited reward!

~ But what about being killed with death? ~

In the second half of **Rev. 6:8**, John explained that when he saw the opening of the fourth seal, the rider on the pale horse emerged and was given power:

> ***'. . . over the fourth part of the earth, to kill with <u>sword</u>, and with <u>hunger</u>, and with <u>death</u>.'***

To be killed with "**death**" is to die without having faith in the true God. Man has always been justified by faith. Thus, whether under the Old Testament or the New, our path toward a right standing before God has always been that of *"grace"* on God's part and childlike *"faith"* on ours.[119] Before we understood God's plan to redeem the world through the atonement of one (*i.e., Christ*), man was simply justified by his obedient, childlike faith in God. Thus, it was said of Abraham: ***'And he believed the Lord; and He** (God) **counted it to him for righteousness.'*** Abraham, like all those prior to Christ's coming, didn't know just exactly how God would fulfill His promises or make atonement for his sins; therefore, complete trust in God, in the form of faith inspired obedience to His will, was his only way of salvation.[120] This was, of course, true for all mankind.

---

[117] Eph. 1:13, 1Jn. 3:15

[118] We will see these saints resurrected, all at once, as a "group," just before God's wrath is poured out.

[119] Rom. 1:16-17

[120] Gen. 15:6, Hab. 2:4, Rom. 1:17

When someone died under the Old Testament, without having had that *"faith-in-God,"* they were essentially being killed with "**death**," just as those today who choose to reject Christ. Thus, having no hope of redemption, faithless souls are doomed to an eternity of indescribable suffering, fear, and, worst of all, the loneliness that will come of knowing they've been eternally separated from God.[121] That's what it means to have been killed with "**death**."

In this world Satan may pummel us, hinder and confuse us, or cause us all manner of humiliation and anxiety. He may even attack our faith in God or kill our bodies (*if God lets him*), but, once we've been born into the eternal kingdom of God, Satan can never kill us with "**death**." Truly born-again believers have forever become part of God's eternal family of saints, and absolutely nothing can change that. Therefore, from a purely spiritual perspective, once we've been born into God's family of saints, we've become eternally indestructible, and God is currently extending that gracious invitation to all who choose to humbly receive it.

The Powers of Hell will be at his Disposal

Rev. 6:8 ~ *continued*

This fourth seal is an analogy of the overwhelming power Satan will exercise through his little *"puppet-leader"* (*the son of perdition*) and through the global kingdom he'll establish. Thus, this reference to the **pale** horse and rider's being given the power to kill a fourth part of the earth with ***'sword, hunger and death'*** is likely an allusion to the complete power and authority Satan will exercise while forcing the Left-behinders to submit to his total, global supremacy.

In order to bring what's left of the devastated, post-plagued[122] world's economy back to life, the son of perdition will demand complete, uncompromising submission from every citizen of his new one-world government. That will necessitate insisting that each citizen take a mark of compliance and worshipful submission to that new, global empire. Those who refuse (*and instead choose to receive Christ*) will be beheaded but will become children of God. Those who acquiesce will be sealed with a mark of eternal doom (*the mark of the beast, which we'll cover later*). Therefore, by choosing to take that mark, they will essentially be "**being killed with death**," because they can never be forgiven once they've received that damnable mark. Thus, they'll eventually die without hope of forgiveness.

---

[121] Mk. 9:42-50

[122] The plagues of God's two witnesses (*the trumpet-plagues*) will end when the witnesses are killed by the son of perdition and his followers at the end of the first 3½ years. We'll cover this in detail as we continue.

I'm sure most of us have heard it said that, as Christians, we are born twice (*once in the flesh and once in the spirit*), but we only die once (*or we get raptured*). That's definitely true. Unfortunately, those who choose to reject Christ's atonement are born only once (*in the flesh*), but they die twice (*once in the flesh and once in the spirit, when they're judged*).[123] This is what we will later see referred to as the "**second death**," which is the ultimate reality of being condemned to eternal spiritual damnation.

The Opening of the Mysterious, Fifth Seal

Rev. 6:9-11

I get really excited reading the following verses, because, once God showed me how to properly study Jesus' end-time revelation, these verses finally became clear and easy to understand. The final sixth seal in this Chapter six allegorical preview of tribulation events is going to prove a great deal, so I'll just state, straight-out, who these souls being depicted as Jesus opens this fifth seal are and move on to that final sixth seal. When this fifth seal was opened John saw:

> ***'. . . under the altar the souls of them that were slain for the word of God, and for the testimony which they held:***
>
> ***And they cried with a loud voice, saying, How long, O Lord, holy and true, dost thou not judge and avenge our blood on them that dwell on the earth?'***

I stated earlier that I would make it clear when what we are studying can't actually be proven; therefore, I wish to state that (*by my standards*) it's not possible to actually prove the identity of these souls John saw *"crying out"* from under the altar in Heaven. However, there is an extremely logical answer, which we will see self-emerge from the text in the chapters ahead. In reality, much of what we consider to be scripturally accurate could not actually be proven by any other standard than logic. "Logic," however, can sometimes be a pretty supportive step-brother for "Fact," which is why I'm comfortable writing that the following interpretation is scripturally the purest, most logical response to the following question:

"Who are the souls John saw crying out to be avenged when Jesus opened this fifth seal?"

The souls under the altar in the preceding verses are the 144,000 Jewish servants loudly *"crying out"* for God to avenge the shedding of their

---

123 We'll discuss this in more detail when we reach the later chapters of John's vision.

righteous blood. Thus, **Rev. 6:9-10** is an allegorical indication that we've reached the middle of this tribulation period preview, and the 144,000 Jewish servants[124] have been slaughtered. As we continue evidence will arise from the text and reveal the absolute logic of this interpretation and the absolute absence of any other explanation for what John witnessed.

~ *Hey, how'd you reach that conclusion?* ~

When the first 3½ years of the tribulation period are over God's two witnesses will no longer have the power to defend themselves or the 144,000 Jewish servants against the satanic power of the son of perdition. Thus, the 144,000 will be completely defenseless. Knowing this, the son of perdition (*most likely as part of his plan to deceive the world into believing him to be God on earth—2Th. 2:3-4*) will slaughter God's two prophets. Furthermore, since God's two witnesses will no longer be able to protect the 144,000 Jewish servants, there's a good chance that the son of perdition will also (*at or about the same time*) slaughter the 144,000 as proof that he, alone, is all-powerful. We'll study this in depth as we venture through Chapters 7 thru 14 of John's vision.

~ *How do we know this?* ~

The 144,000 Jewish servants of God are the only saints who fill all the requirements for being these souls John heard crying out to God for retribution.

Here's a condensed picture of what we're going to find later, when we get into the actual tribulation period:

As I've stated, the 144,000 Jewish servants will be sealed (*with the name of God on their foreheads*),[125] just moments before the Rapture, to prevent them from being hurt when the Rapture occurs and to protect them from the events of the first 3½ years of the tribulation period. Hence, they'll survive the world-wide calamity that will result from the global rapture of the saints totally unscathed. Then, soon after the Rapture, the 144,000 will repent. This will most logically happen after they've heard the preaching of God's two witnesses (*God's tribulation period prophets*). When we get a little deeper into John's vision the scriptures will clearly indicate that the 144,000 Jewish servants will be protected by these two witnesses for exactly 3½ years.

---

[124] We'll learn precisely who these 144,000 servants of God will be in Rev. 7:1-8.
[125] Rev. 7:1-8, 14:1-5

During the first half of the seven-year tribulation period, those two powerful prophets (*God's two witnesses*) will make one final effort — using all manner of plagues — to persuade "**the remnant**" (*the last of the saints*) to repent. Thus, when we put all the scriptures together, it will seem most logical that the 144,000 servants are going to build the new Third Temple and worship God on the Temple Mount, while, at the same time, God's two prophets continually witness to the rebellious Left-behinders. Of course, by that time, the 144,000 will be Messianic Jews (*Jewish Christians, like the founders of our faith*) and will, thus, worship accordingly.

Commonly Taught does not mean - "Proven"

Although it's taught by virtually everyone that the 144,000 Jewish servants will be global evangelists, there's not a single scripture that, when properly interpreted, truly suggests that as being a possibility. Not only is there no biblical evidence for that unsupportable theory, as we will clearly see, it just doesn't fit within the framework of all the other teaching we're going to study. The truth is, even with God's two prophets (*possibly Moses and Elijah*)[126] witnessing to the whole world and backing up their preaching with dreadfully powerful, globally devastating plagues, the Left-behinders will not heed the witnesses' preaching and repent until after the first 3½ years of the tribulation period are over. That's right! This is an absolute "**fact**," which is clearly stated in scripture, and we will see this fact powerfully self-emerge from the chapters ahead.

If, therefore, initially no one will heed the warnings of God's two powerful witnesses, who (*with the power of Heaven*) will be unleashing globally devastating plagues in their attempt to get people to listen and repent, why would God send the 144,000 Jewish servants out witnessing when the Church has already been faithfully committed to that effort for the past 2,000 years? The answer is: He won't! And the Scriptures don't teach that He will. The Church has just assumed this to be scripturally supported.

We are going to see absolute proof that not a single soul (*other than the 144,000*) will repent and be saved until after the two witnesses have been killed, resurrected, and called back into Heaven. This may be hard to accept, but this is not an opinion. The scriptures ahead will clearly bear this out.

The 144,000 will worship God in the new Temple

The 144,000 will be preserved. Thus, while all the rest of the world will be defiantly sinning and mocking God and His two prophets, the 144,000 new Jewish Christians will be worshipping God on the Temple Mount.

[126] I'll explain this when we reach that portion of John's vision.

However, as I stated earlier, when the son of perdition kills God's two witnesses, at the end of their 3½ year ministry, the 144,000 Jewish servants will no longer have anyone to protect them. Therefore, they'll also be killed (*just before, at the same time, or soon after the prophets die*). Hence, Jesus gave us the following general warning regarding that violent time:[127]

'And when you shall see Jerusalem compassed with armies, then know that the desolation thereof is nigh.[128] *Then let them which are in Judea flee to the mountains; and let them which are in the midst of it depart out . . . '*

Luke 21:20-21

With these words, Jesus warned the world about the abomination of desolation,[129] which will occur in the middle of the seven-year tribulation period. Later, when we're looking back at this Chapter 6:1-17 allegorical preview of the whole seven-year tribulation period, it will be quite clear to us that the anguished souls John saw *"crying out to be avenged from under the altar"* are intended to symbolize that the 144,000 Jewish servants of God will be martyred during the middle of the tribulation period, soon after the son of perdition assumes full control.

As **Rev. 6:9** states, the 144,000 will be brutally killed for holding the testimony of Christ, but after they're killed they'll be quickly resurrected. This is indicated in this allegorical portion of John's vision by the words: ***'And white robes were given to every one of them'*** (*Rev. 6:10, 14:1-5*). Thus, after being resurrected and taken to Heaven, the 144,000 are told to ***'rest yet for a little season, until their fellow servants also and their brethren'*** *("the remnant" - the last to repent)* are also killed. Hence, John is symbolically seeing God tell the 144,000 martyred Jewish souls that He will not avenge their deaths until the last of the saints have repented and been resurrected. The remnant (*those whom we will see finally repent after seeing the resurrection of God's two witnesses*) will have been warned that, after repenting, they (*like the 144,000*) will have to die for their testimony. Thus, after they are also martyred, God will avenge not only the deaths of the 144,000 Jewish servants and the two witnesses but also every saint who has ever been slain.

---

[127] Luke 21:20-21, Mt. 24:15-24

[128] Jesus is warning all future Left-behinders that immediately prior to the *abomination of desolation*, nearing the end of the first 3½ years of the tribulation period, Jerusalem will be surrounded by the armies of the son of perdition and overrun. Zechariah's prophesy gives greater detail about this dreadful event — Zec. 14:1-2.

[129] Mt. 24:15-24, Dan. 9:27

The Son of Perdition will Rule the World

Once God's two witnesses have ascended into Heaven and "**the remnant**" has repented, the son of perdition will be given power over the entire population of the earth, including this "**remnant**" of new believers. When this happens, the son of perdition's army of followers will hunt every non-compliant Left-behinder down, if need be, and kill them. According to John's vision, not a single believer in Christ will survive! His power will be such that he'll even be able to use animals as instruments of death to accomplish this.[130] Thus, when he's finished, a world population consisting entirely of citizens of his beastly empire will exist. Consequently, every person alive will have worshipped Satan and his demonic empire by taking his damnable mark, *"the mark of the beast."* For the first time in human history there will not be a solitary God fearing man, woman or child on earth. Not one! Hence, once the world is completely free of saints, then and only then will God begin to pour out His wrath!

~ Why is this so important? ~

This is important because as we move ahead we're going to see clear, scriptural evidence, which will prove that God will not pour out His wrath while even one saint is left on earth.

God will withhold His wrath until . . .

Rev. 6:11 ~ *continued*

John's having heard the Lord tell the 144,000 to wait ***'until their fellow servants also and their brethren'*** (*"the remnant"*) have also been killed before He avenges their deaths strongly supports our earlier assertion that the globally impactive plagues of God's two prophets (*during the first 3½ years*) will not be plagues of wrath. As has been stated, when it's time for God's wrath to be poured out, it will be far more severe and final than the plagues of the two prophets. And so, as we continue it will become clear that God has no intention of subjecting even the least of His temporarily unrepentant children (*the remnant*) to any of it.

One last note about the 144,000 Jewish servants of God

Many have assumed that the 144,000 Jewish converts will be evangelists simply because they can see no other way through which the message of God's two witnesses could be spread around the world. Nonetheless, the message of God's two witnesses will most likely be miraculously heard universally and by every living soul, through the power of God, not man.

---

[130] Rev. 6:7-8

Once we've moved into the corresponding chapters of John's vision we will thoroughly cover this topic, so we would do well not to hastily form any firm opinions until we've properly examined the remainder of the text.

A QUICK WORD OF ENCOURAGEMENT:

If you're having a difficult time, because what we've learned thus far is different from much of what you've been taught in the past, please do yourself a favor and stick with the rest of us until we reach the end of John's vision. You'll be extremely excited as you begin seeing everything in the book of Revelation begin to perfectly fall right into place! When that happens, every other end-time scripture in the Bible will also fall into place. Thus, having witnessed this for yourself, you'll never go back. Instead, you'll continue moving forward, growing in end-time knowledge, as everything in the Bible continues to reinforce what you've learned.

These verses are what I mean when I say – FACT!

Rev. 6:12-17

This sixth seal Jesus is about to open represents the end of the seven-year tribulation period. Thus, these verses will absolutely prove that the opening of the first six seals (*on the book from God's right hand*) are intended to allegorically characterize the "**effects**" of the events that will occur during the seven-year tribulation period, which will climax with the triumphant return of Christ. Hence, with the opening of this sixth seal, John actually witnessed Jesus' glorious return to earth, known in Scripture as the Second Coming of Christ.

For many on our journey this is already clearly understood; unfortunately, however, some of our loved ones have been convinced (*by others*) that the events depicted by these six seals in **Rev. 6:1-17** will actually occur at the start of the seven-year tribulation period. Hey, that's how I first learned it. As a matter of fact, that's how I first taught it, and I would have respectfully argued with anyone who tried to tell me differently. Fortunately, God granted me the necessary humility to broaden my perspective and take in the complete "BIGGER–PICTURE." In order to do that I had to honestly challenge what I rigidly believed to be correct, which, incidentally, is precisely what I believed I was already doing. But I was wrong, and these next few verses of John's vision clearly prove it.

A truly - "one of a kind" - Earthquake

Rev. 6:12-17 ~ *continued*

When the sixth seal was opened, John saw a clear vision of the Second Coming of Christ, which was preceded by a mighty earthquake. That is an absolute fact. This sixth seal is like a puzzle all by itself, and when we properly examine and connect all the scriptural pieces of that puzzle they unmistakably portray the Lord's triumphant return to earth at the end of the seven-year tribulation period.

~ *How can we be sure of this interpretation?* ~

This would actually be very easy to prove in court and here's why. John wrote that, when this sixth seal was opened, he beheld, *'. . . and, lo, there was a great earthquake . . . .'* John's description of that earthquake is exactly like the one he later recorded witnessing towards the end of his book, in the interpretive portion of his vision (*during Christ's triumphant return to judge the inhabitants of the earth—Rev. 16:17-21*). So, how do we know that John saw the same earthquake in both the early and later portions of his vision (*Rev. 6:12-17 and 16:17-21*)? In **Rev. 6:14** John wrote that the earthquake he saw when the 6th seal was opened was so strong that every mountain and island was moved out of its place! Those few words confirm this to be the same earthquake that John saw precede the Second Coming of Christ, and here's how we know. Look ahead with me at the 7th and final plague of "**wrath**," which will be poured out as Jesus returns to judge the earth:

> *'And the seventh angel poured out his vial into the air; and there came a great voice out of the temple of heaven, from the throne, saying, **It is done**. And there were voices, and thunders, and lightnings; and **there was a great earthquake, such as was not since men were upon the earth**, so mighty an earthquake, and so great. And the great city was divided into three parts, and the cities of the nations fell: and great Babylon came in remembrance before God, to give unto her the cup of the wine of the fierceness of his wrath. **And every island fled away**, **and the mountains were not found**.'*[131]

℘ Rev. 16:17-20 ℘

---

[131] Ezekiel describes this precise Second Coming earthquake—Ez. 38:18-23.

The absolute proof that the massive earthquake John described seeing in **Rev. 6:12-17** (*the allegorical portion of his vision*) is a description of the same earthquake he later saw in the preceding interpretive portion of his vision, just before witnessing the Lord's triumphant return to earth, is evidenced by John's following specific choice of words:

'. . . and there was a great earthquake, <u>such as was not since men were upon the earth</u>.'

This verse states that when the earthquake described in the preceding verses (*which will coincide with the Second Coming of Christ*) actually occurs there will <u>never</u> have been a previous earthquake of that same magnitude. Therefore, since the earthquake described in **Rev. 6:12-17** is described as being the same magnitude as the earthquake described in **Rev. 16:17-20**, we must acknowledge that both passages are describing the same event. What's more, while prophesying about the Lord's final judgment of the nation of Israel (*the Second Coming of Christ*), Ezekiel clearly describes this *"one of a kind"* earthquake and the effects of God's wrath being poured out on the nations of the earth (*Ez. 38:18-23*).

It doesn't get any simpler than that! Thus, **Rev. 6:1-17** can only be one thing, an allegory of the entire seven-year tribulation period, ending with John seeing Christ's vengeful return to earth.

This is going to be one massive earthquake!

Take a second to go outside and look around. Try to imagine every mountain on the planet being reduced to rubble and every island disappearing or fleeing away. That's what John witnessed, and an earthquake of that global magnitude will certainly not happen at both the beginning and the end of the tribulation period. If it did, it would doubtlessly kill most of the earth's population. That's why the Scriptures clearly state that this earthquake will occur only once, when Christ returns to judge the earth.

~ It's vital that we understand this! ~

If we don't understand this there's simply no point in going on. Understanding this is the key to understanding John's whole tribulation vision. If we fail to recognize that, with the opening of these six seals in **Rev. 6:1-17**, Jesus was showing John an allegorical "**preview**" of the entire tribulation period, we will also fail to understand the interpretive significance of the rest of John's end-time vision. There are so many other equally revealing clues that prove the allegorical nature of these six seals that I hardly need to go over them one at time. Nonetheless, for any of you who need a little more scriptural proof before moving on, the following list should help.

Here are some obvious Second Coming indicators from John's tribulation period preview in Revelation 6:12-17

- ❖ The **sun** became **black** as sackcloth of hair (*this will only happen once, just prior to Christ's return to earth—Joel 2:10, Mt. 24:29, Rev. 16:10*).
- ❖ The **moon** became as **blood** (*both Joel and Jesus prophesied that this will be part of Christ's Second Coming—Joel 2:30-31, Luke 21:25.*)
- ❖ The **stars** of heaven fell unto the earth (*Jesus said this will happen at the end of the tribulation period—Mt. 24:29, Mk. 13:25, Luke 21:25, Isa. 13:6-13.*)
- ❖ The **heaven** (*sky and space*) **departed as a scroll when it is rolled together**. This event will reveal God's throne and the Lamb of God's (*Christ's*) triumphant return to earth (*Isaiah prophesied of this same event in roughly 713 BC—Isa. 34:1-4, Rev. 19:11.*)
- ❖ **Rev. 6:15-16** states that John saw "*every man on earth*" as they hid themselves in the dens and in the rocks of the mountains, ***'And said to the mountains and rocks, Fall on us, and hide us from the face of him that sitteth on the throne, and from the wrath of the Lamb: For the great day of his wrath is come; and who shall be able to stand?'*** Since John's description clearly includes "*every man on earth,*" it should be obvious that there won't be a single Christian on earth during this event.

Every word in the following list of scriptures refers to the same end-time event, which is *"the wrath of God and the Lamb"* (*Christ's triumphant return to judge the earth*):

Isa. 2:10-21, **Joel** 2:11, **Luke** 23:30, **Rev.** 19:11-18.

The end of the Chapter six Allegory of Tribulation Events

Rev. 6:12-17 ~ *continued*

It should now be abundantly clear that what John recorded seeing after Jesus opened the 6th seal is a clear depiction of Christ's triumphant return to earth, which will be the final event of the seven-year tribulation period. Thus, this 6th seal (*at the end of Chapter 6*) combines everything the Bible teaches about the Second Coming of Christ into just a few powerful verses. In doing so, this seal unmistakably concludes the "**allegorical**" portion of John's tribulation period vision.

First the allegorical vision, then the interpretation

Having first shown this allegorical "**preview**" to John in Chapter 6, next, starting with Chapter 7, the Lord will begin to reveal the actual physical fulfillment and interpretation of what John saw during the opening of these first six seals. Thus, as we study the rest of John's Revelation vision, we will see that God revealed this end-time vision to John in perfect order. So, when we continue to study John's vision in that same order, it will continue to miraculously unfold right before our eyes!

Chapter 14

The Allegory Begins To Be Revealed

Here, in this Chapter 7:1-8 portion of John's vision, we're about to see irrefutable proof that the earth has not yet been "**hurt**" in any way, because the Rapture has not yet occurred. And the tribulation period hasn't, as of yet, begun. Thus, the horrific effects and destructive events John saw being symbolically depicted in **Rev. 6:1-17** (*the allegorical portion of his vision*) have not actually come to pass — but they're about to.

Just minutes away from the Rapture

Rev. 7:1

When Jesus finished opening the first six of the seven seals from the book in God's right hand, He immediately made sure that John understood that he had only been shown an "**allegory**" of the actual tribulation events, by showing John that no destruction of any kind had, thus far, taken place on the earth. John recorded this as follows:

> ***'And <u>after</u> these things** (after the opening of the first six seals) **I saw four angels standing on the four corners of the earth, holding the four winds of the earth, that the wind should not blow on the earth, nor on the sea, nor on any tree.'***

Jesus Waited before Opening the Final Seal

Rev. 7:2-3

As John continued watching he saw:

> ***'. . . another angel ascending from the east, having the seal of the living God: and he cried with a loud voice to the four angels, to whom it was given to hurt the earth and the sea,***
>
> ***Saying, <u>Hurt not the earth</u>, <u>neither the sea</u>, <u>nor the trees</u>, till we have sealed the servants of God in their foreheads.'***

That's pretty clear, isn't it? John saw the angels who have the power to hurt the earth still holding back. This means that the earth has not, as of yet, been hurt. If any of the calamities described in **Rev. 6:1-17** had already occurred, the preceding verses would make absolutely no sense. That means that at this point in John's vision the tribulation period hasn't actually begun. If we choose not to believe this, we're forced to believe that God should have revealed this Chapter 7 portion of John's vision to John before allowing him to witness what he recorded seeing in Chapter 6. God, however, doesn't make mistakes, and He didn't make one here.

The Four Corners of the Earth

John wrote that he saw ***'four angels standing on the four corners of the earth.'*** Given that the earth is round, those words are a little hard to understand, but ***'the four corners of the earth'*** is simply a reference to the earth's extremities. As John watched, he saw another angel ascending from the east with the *seal* of the living God.[132] That angel cried with a loud voice, telling the other four angels not to hurt the **earth**, the **sea** or any **trees** until the servants of God have been *sealed* in their foreheads. That angel is, of course, referring to the future 144,000 Jewish servants of God, whom he will *seal* so as to protect them from the global destruction that will result from the ensuing Rapture and plagues of God's two prophets.

John was told that the 144,000 servants of God, to whom the angel was referring, will be virgin male[133] descendants from twelve of the fourteen tribes of Israel. Thus, one by one, starting with the tribe of Judah, John heard each of the twelve tribes listed, until 144,000 Jewish servants were *sealed*. However, as most of you know, while we can be confident that John didn't make a mistake, there appears to be a problem with John's patriarchal list of tribes.

~ *What happened to the tribes of Ephraim and Dan?* ~

If you're an eschatologist you're probably hoping I have some brilliant answer to that question. Unfortunately, I don't. I've heard endless theories and possible explanations as to why the mysterious tribe of **Dan** is not listed here, but I don't personally believe any theory can be scripturally and historically verified beyond doubt. Furthermore, speculating will not help us understand this passage. I will, however, briefly refer to **Nu. 1:20-**

---

[132] Later, at the end of the first 3½ years of tribulation, when the 144,000 are killed and resurrected, they will immediately be seen standing before the Throne of God with His name written in their foreheads. Therefore, it's possible (*but perhaps not provable*) that the *seal* John is witnessing them receive before the Church is raptured is the name of God being written on their foreheads.

[133] Rev. 14:4

53, where we'll find a list of the tribes of Israel (*the descendants of Jacob*), who sojourned for forty years in the wilderness after being freed from slavery in Egypt. On that list, God told Moses not to number the tribe of Levi among the tribes that would go to war. Moses' list does include the tribe of **Dan** and lists[134] **Manasseh** as a whole tribe. The tribe of **Ephraim** is included as part of the tribe of Joseph, just as it is on John's list. Therefore, John's list (*Rev. 7:5-8*) is basically the same as Moses' list, with the exception of the tribe of **Levi** taking the place of the tribe of **Dan**.

There is no explanation given as to why Dan is not listed. Perhaps, by the time the 144,000 are sealed, there will no longer be 12,000 descendants from the tribe of Dan to take their place among the other tribes of Israel. We simply don't know.

How'd we ever miss this?

If I could, I would ask everyone on our expedition to join me in closing their book and getting out a piece of paper. Next, I would suggest we all write a 120 word description of what we imagine it would be like to be standing directly in front of God's throne at that very moment when, ***'in the twinkling of an eye,'*** the Lord will instantly resurrect and assemble before His throne all Old and New Testament saints, who, from one generation to the next, have believed in and trusted God to be their redeemer.

~ *Why would I suggest our doing that?* ~

If we were standing near the throne at that exact moment — before we could even blink an eye — an innumerably vast multitude of resurrected and raptured saints, ***'out of every kindred, and tongue, and people, and nation,'*** would instantly manifest right before us! We wouldn't even see Jesus leave the throne! All the resurrected saints would just appear, right before our eyes, clothed in brilliant, radiantly white robes, with palms in their hands and tears of unspeakable joy and elation running down their newly radiant faces.[135] We would witness, firsthand, their cheering and worshipful thanksgiving to God for His having so graciously bestowed upon them such unmerited mercy, grace, and eternal salvation!

Therefore, the answer to the question: "*Why would I ask everyone to write a description of the Rapture?*" is that I'd like to see if any of us could write a better, more complete description of that event than did John in the following verses.

---

[134] Manasseh and Ephraim were originally half-tribes until Jacob adopted them—Gen. 48:3-6

[135] There will apparently be tears in some of the eyes of the raptured saints. We'll examine why that might be significant when we reach the corresponding portion of John's vision. Don't worry; we're almost there.

An enormous multitude materializes before John!

Rev. 7:9-10

Immediately after seeing the *sealing* of the last member of twelve of the tribes of Israel, before any destruction or calamity of any kind had occurred on earth, John wrote the following:

> ***'After this*** *(after seeing the 144,000 sealed)*, ***I beheld, and, lo, a great multitude, which no man could number, of all nations, and kindreds, and people, and tongues, stood before the throne, and before the Lamb, clothed with white robes, and palms in their hands;***
>
> ***And cried with a loud voice, saying, Salvation to our God which sitteth upon the throne, and unto the Lamb.'***

This is only the beginning of John's description of the Rapture, and yet, a very important clue can be found in the simplicity of John's words. If we stop and take a careful look at that clue it may help us to properly interpret what John wrote.

John certainly beheld a shockingly awesome sight! He conveyed this by writing: ***'After this I beheld'*** *(i.e., after this, I saw or looked)*. That's simple, right? Okay, let's add the next two words: ***'After this I beheld, and, lo . . . .'*** Putting these words together, as John did in this verse, would most accurately be translated today by saying something like: *"After this I looked, and wow!"* or *"I looked, and oh my word!"* When John added, ***'and, lo,'*** he revealed his great surprise, which resulted from having just witnessed the instantaneous Rapture of the saints![136]

This is why the 144,000 were Sealed First

Having ***'the seal of the living God'*** on their foreheads is what will protect the 144,000 Jewish servants from being injured both during and after the Rapture. Hence, only after the last Jewish servant was sealed did John witness an innumerable multitude of saints, ***'of all nations, and kindreds, and people, and tongues,'*** suddenly appear before God's throne. Thus, when that glorious event actually occurs, it will mean that the dreaded seven-year tribulation period will have unexpectedly begun!

---

[136] We should acknowledge that as many as several billion saints will instantly appear in Heaven, before the throne, when the Rapture occurs, so John shockingly witnessed the instantaneous manifestation of many billions of people in glistening white robes. We'll cover this in more detail as we continue through the remainder of John's book—1Cor. 15:51-58, 1Th. 4:13-17, Mt. 24:34-44, Jam. 5:7.

So why didn't John see Jesus leave Heaven?

The resurrection and catching-away (*rapture*) of the saints will happen suddenly, ***'in the twinkling of an eye,'*** which is much faster than a blink and much too fast for the eye to consciously perceive.[137] In fact, it's so fast that some scientists estimate it to be between an 1,100th and a 1,700th of a second. And, while the saints are being caught up to the throne, God's two witnesses will be descending from Heaven (*either at the same time or shortly thereafter*) to begin their 3½ year earthly ministry.[138]

Speaking in reference to how instantaneously the rapture of the Church will occur, it was Paul who used the term: ***'. . . In a moment, in a twinkling of an eye . . . .'***[139] Hence, based on what Paul said, if we were standing in front of God's throne, right next to John, staring straight at Jesus when the Rapture occurred, we wouldn't even notice Jesus leave Heaven to meet the saints in the air and return. Instead, we would experience precisely what John recorded. All of a sudden an innumerable number of saints would instantly appear before our eyes! If John would have recorded actually seeing Jesus descend to meet the saints in the clouds and return to the throne, John's vision would not have agreed with Paul's description of that event. This is one reason why most of the Church has neglected to recognize what John wrote in **Rev. 7:9-17** as being his record of having witnessed the Rapture. Unfortunately, for centuries we've failed to take into account the obvious scriptural clues that reveal this truth.

All Power and Might be unto our God

Rev. 7:11-12

Let's go ahead and read some more of John's narrative and imagine that we too are in Heaven experiencing (*with John*) exactly what he wrote:

> ***'And <u>all the angels</u> stood round about the throne, and about the <u>elders</u> and the <u>four beasts</u>, and <u>fell before the throne on their faces</u>, and worshipped God,***

---

[137] (1Cor. 15:50-58, 1Th. 4:13-18, Rev. 7:8-17) Don't be thrown by the words, *'at the last trump (trumpet)'* when reading Paul's reference to the Rapture in 1Cor. 15:50-58. Though many have allowed Tunnel-vision to constrain their understanding of these verses, 1Cor. 15:50-58 is not a reference to the actual *last trumpet* of the tribulation period. It's a reference to the powerful voice of Michael, the Archangel (*1Th. 4:16*). Everything we've learned thus far and will learn as we continue will make this perfectly clear. What's more, God's realm of existence is beyond time; therefore, the speed of the Rapture would be immeasurable by any scientific means.

[138] Rev. 11:3-6

[139] 1Cor. 15:51-54

Saying, A'-men: Blessing, and glory, and wisdom, and thanksgiving, and honour, and power, and might, be unto our God for ever and ever. A'-men.'

These words, all by themselves, are pretty compelling; moreover, they make perfect sense. The resurrection and rapture of the saints will quite possibly be the most exciting event of all time.[140] Thus, it's no surprise that all the angels will gather around the throne, with the *elders* and the *four beasts*, and fall on their faces, while worshipping and praising God.

Why ask me?

Rev. 7:13

While John was still amazed at the innumerable congregation of saints who had instantaneously appeared before God's throne, one of the twenty-four elders asked him: *"**What are these which are arrayed in white robes? and whence came they?**"* In other words, the elder asked: *"Who are these people, and from where did they come?"* After all these years I still chuckle a little every time I read this verse. The elder couldn't have expected John to know the answer; could he? It's kind of like a father asking his young admiring son a question just so he, in all his great wisdom and experience, can proudly tell him the answer. Was the elder playing the role of the father here? That's possible, but maybe God just wanted the elder to ask John this question in order to further emphasize the fact that this innumerably large mass of people wasn't in Heaven prior to John witnessing its sudden and mysterious appearance. If we had to guess, that option seems most logical.

> I'm sure some of our more seasoned eschatological adventurers are probably just itching to present their debate about what John wrote in the preceding verses. We'll definitely deal with that, but first we need to finish examining the remainder of John's narrative of this event. We wouldn't want to begin trying this case before at least reading the remainder of John's testimonial, so let's continue.

---

140 Mt. 24:34-44, Luke 17:23-37, 21:28-36, 1Cor. 15:51-58, 1Th. 4:13-17, Js. 5:7, 2Pt. 2:9

~ Hey, I've noticed that the words in my Bible are sometimes different from these quotes from the text. Isn't that a problem? ~

As we touched on earlier, most translations of the Bible will enable us to lay hold of a general end-time understanding. However, after having studied all the different, major translations, I've personally found the King James Version (*KJV*) of the Scriptures to consistently be the most accurate version with respect to facilitating eschatological study. And while many highly esteemed pastors and instructors will agree with my assessment, there are just as many (*if not many more*), whom I love and greatly admire, who hold varying and, often times, contrary points of view. Their opinions demand our most sincere consideration, recognition and respect.

We all have particular translations of the Bible with which we're more comfortable, but Heaven help us if we allow ourselves to get caught-up in that whole—"My translation is best!"—argument. That immature squabble is a pointless pride-fest on a dead-end street! Even if the person making that claim happened to be right, proving it would almost certainly cause division, with a capital **D**! As Christians, we should be lovingly helping each other get down this path of understanding together, as a family of believers. So let's just stay focused on what's before us, get back on the trail, and learn some more fun and exciting end-time stuff. *"Stuff?" – now that doesn't sound very scholarly, does it?*

Who are these, and from where did they come?

Rev. 7:14-15 ~ *continued*

Before we digressed, the elder had asked John this question: ***'What are these which are arrayed in white robes? and whence came they?'*** That elder was, of course, referring to the vast multitude who had surprisingly and instantaneously appeared before the throne. John answered the elder, saying: ***'Sir, thou knowest.'*** To this, the elder responded:

> ***'These are they which came out of great tribulation, and have washed their robes, and made them white in the blood of the Lamb.***
>
> ***Therefore are they before the throne of God, and serve Him day and night in His temple: and He that sitteth on the throne shall dwell among them.'***

Hold that thought!

Let's get the rest of the passage out and on the table before we begin thoroughly dissecting it; then we'll be able to see it as God intended. As a matter of fact, it's a good practice to always prayerfully read the entire passage before stopping and extracting information that may or may not support an interpretation.

Rev. 7:16-17

The elder continued explaining to John about this massive sudden appearance of saints before the throne:

> ***'They shall hunger no more, neither thirst any more; neither shall the sun light on them, nor any heat.***
>
> ***For the Lamb which is in the midst of the throne shall feed them, and shall lead them unto living fountains of waters: and God shall wipe away all tears from their eyes.'***

Now that we can see this passage as a whole, I know from experience that some of our expedition buddies are wondering why the word "**the**" is missing from the middle of **Rev. 7:14** in this quote from the King James Version (*KJV*) of the Bible.

~ Wait a minute; you lost me! What are you saying? ~

Well, if you're reading from just about any version other than the King James, in the middle of **Rev. 7:14**, the word "**the**" is inserted before the words "great tribulation." Thus, the text has been changed to read: ***'the great tribulation'***, instead of simply, ***'great tribulation'***, as John originally intended. Although it shouldn't, the insertion of this word has caused many Christians to mistakenly believe that **Rev. 7:14** indicates that the Church will be raptured sometime during (*rather than before*) the start of the seven-year tribulation period. And, given that so many new Bible translations contain this added word (*the*), many Christians are confident that their translation, which happens to be more current than the *King James Version*, must, therefore, be correct. However, while that groundless notion has progressively hindered the Church's understanding of this passage, whether or not it's actually true makes no difference with regard to our interpretation of this verse. As Christians, we should know better than to just follow the masses. The truth, as always, lies within the text.

The fact that many modern translations have decided to add "**the**" to this verse doesn't irrefutably indicate that the older manuscripts, which wisely chose to refrain from doing so, were wrong! As a matter of fact, the words of the elder speaking with John prove that the earlier translators had good reason not to make that mistake. As we move through the remaining chapters of John's vision, we're going to learn that if this vast multitude of saints in **Rev. 7:9-17** is not John's record of having witnessed the instantaneous occurrence of the Rapture, then John never recorded having witnessed the Rapture's occurrence at all. That's right! Nothing we read prior to these verses (*Rev. 7:9-17*) and none of the remaining scriptures in John's Revelation vision are a reference to the occurrence of the Rapture. Therefore, if these verses in **Rev. 7:9-17** are not John's description of that event, then John never recorded having witnessed the resurrection and catching-away of the saints! This will become evident as we continue moving forward, and this interpretation will prove to be clear and incontestable.

The key to understanding John's vision is to **not** assume nor change the order of John's record of events. God didn't haphazardly reveal this tribulation period vision. Every event John recorded was purposefully laid out by the Lord, in perfect order, with the intent of enabling us to fully understand this future end-time period.

~ Then how come so many Christians continually fail to recognize this passage as being the Rapture? ~

Now that's a good question. If we read **Rev. 7:9-17** from any modern translation and focus only on the words "**the**" and "**tribulation**" in verse 14, we might also fail to recognize that John was actually recording his having witnessed the pre-tribulation rapture of the Church. The stumbling block lying in the Church's path of understanding has always been John's use of the words: "**great tribulation.**"[141]

A Lost and Forgotten Word

Today, people just don't use the word "**tribulation**" in everyday conversation. Thus, when we read that the elder told John that this innumerable number of saints (*who suddenly appeared before John and the throne*) had come — ***'out of great tribulation,'*** — we just can't accept that the elder was referring to the instantaneously resurrected and raptured saints. And, if we can't accept that, then we're forced to come to the conclusion that the Church must be intended to endure at least part of the tribulation period. Well, the truth is the elder "**was**" talking about the instantly resurrected and raptured saints, and they "**will not**" go through any of the final seven years of "**great tribulation**!"

John Understood This

As we earlier noted while reading John's declaration in **Rev. 1:9**, John declared himself to be our ***'brother, and companion in tribulation, and in the kingdom and patience of Jesus Christ.'*** Therefore, from John's statement we can begin to see what the words "**tribulation**" and "**patience**" actually meant to the early Church.

---

[141] Reviewing our discussion of Rev. 1:9 may be helpful before continuing.

In the original text, *tribulation* means: *affliction, anguish, trouble, oppression, distress, pressure and (of course) tribulation*. These are all powerful words, and each of these words could be used to describe the everyday persecution that we should all, at one time or another, experience as we openly declare and share our faith in Christ. Paul wrote to Timothy, telling him that all who will live Godly in Christ Jesus shall suffer persecution (*2Tim. 3:12*). These words are as true and relative today in many parts of the world as they were when Paul first encouraged Timothy with them during the early formation of the Church. As believers, in every generation, we are commissioned — commanded actually[142] — to endure daily persecution and ridicule as part of our open declaration of faith. For some, this persecution is an immediate and severe reality. For others, it's slow coming and scarce, but eventually we all experience some degree of persecution if we're truly saved. Here are several excellent supporting scriptures, which, if you take the time to prayerfully study, will make this truth abundantly clear:

Rev. 2:9, Mt. 13:21, Jn. 16:33 Act. 14:22, Ro. 5:3, 8:35 & 12:12, 2Cor. 1:4 & 7:4, 2Th. 1:4

A Powerful Word from the Past

While it's true that in today's world we would scarcely use the word tribulation while referring to our daily persecution, in the fifteenth, sixteenth and seventeenth centuries, when the King James Version of the Scriptures was being formed, the use of the word tribulation was not at all uncommon. In fact, there are only a handful of times when the word tribulation was used in Scripture to refer to something other than the daily *suffering, persecution* and *trials* of those who followed the teachings of Christ.

Currently, in most of the western world, Christianity is legal and, for the most part, tolerated, but that's not the case for many of our brothers and sisters in other parts of the world where just preaching the Gospel or simply possessing a Bible has gotten many of them tortured and/or killed. It's happening every year to thousands of faithful saints in the East. Many of whom, having been imprisoned for openly confessing their faith, are, at this moment, praying for deliverance from the severe "**tribulation**" and anguish that has become a consequential part of their everyday Christian lives. If, in order to worship and learn about Christ, we too had to secretly attend a forbidden underground church (*e.g., somewhere in China, Saudi Arabia, North Korea or Iran*), it would be easy for us to relate to the elder's use of the words "**great tribulation**" in reference to our daily confession

[142] Luke 22:35-36

of faith. However, having had the freedom to worship and openly preach the Gospel, as many Christians in the western hemisphere do, truly understanding this can be difficult.

In today's modern Church we tend to only link the word "**tribulation**" with a specific seven-year end-time period. That's one of the biggest reasons why the Church has failed to recognize John's words in **Rev. 7:14** as being an obvious prophetic reference to the raptured Church. This is a mistake, and when we make that mistake it reveals our failure (*as the body of Christ*) to daily sympathize with and address the needs of our brothers and sisters who, at this moment, are suffering great "**trials**" and "**tribulations**," while bannering the Gospel of Christ in other parts of the world.

The Proof is in the Elder's Message

Fortunately, as is usually the case, God didn't leave us without proof of this within the text. Let's take a closer look at **Rev. 7:15**. This vast multitude, which John suddenly saw appear before God's throne, is said to: ***'serve God day and night.'*** No matter which major translation of the Bible we use, the word *serve* seems to indicate either *present* or *past present* tense, as if these saints have already been *serving* God ***'day and night in His temple.'*** However, according to what John was shown prior to the appearance of these saints, the seven years of tribulation hadn't even started. Therefore, these saints couldn't have been in Heaven for very long. In fact, John made it perfectly clear that He had just witnessed their sudden arrival.

Nonetheless, for the sake of argument, we need to at least consider the possibility that these saints were somehow already in Heaven before John got there. In **Rev. 4** and **5** John was taken up to Heaven and immediately shown, *the elders, the four beasts, hundreds of millions of angels around the throne* but **not** an innumerable assembly of saints anywhere. Therefore, if these saints were somehow already in Heaven, where were they?

~ But couldn't the saints have been there without John seeing them? ~

Of course that is possible! Heaven must be at least potentially an eternally large place. But, as to whether or not God would keep John from seeing billions of saints and then suddenly and inexplicably spring them on him, in a flash, as John's testimony reveals — well, that seems highly unlikely! As we all know, God is not the author of confusion.[143] Therefore, if in **Rev. 7:13** the answer to the elder's question: ***"What are these which are arrayed in white robes? and whence came they?"*** is not that John

[143] 1Cor. 14:33

had instantly — ***'in a moment, in the twinkling of an eye'*** [144] — witnessed the resurrection and rapture of the saints, then we're forced to believe that hundreds of millions of saints were already in Heaven when John first got there, and yet, John was totally clueless as to their existence. From my perspective that seems well beyond the boundaries of what could be considered a rational interpretation of what John wrote.

Moreover, if all these saints were already in Heaven when John arrived, why didn't John mention them in **Rev. 5:8-10**? When we examined that passage, we posed the question: *"If hundreds of millions of saints were already in Heaven, shouldn't they have been the individuals John witnessed singing, instead of the four beasts and the twenty-four elders?"* I strongly suggest rereading that passage to see if you agree.

Finally, if these saints were somehow already in Heaven, mysteriously hidden, for whatever reason, from John's view, then in order to surprise John (*as he clearly testified they did when they suddenly appeared before the throne*), they would have had to be instantly translated to God's throne, all at the same time, from wherever they were in Heaven. There again, one would have to admit that such an occurrence doesn't seem likely and would not mesh with the rest of John's vision.

~ So, where does that leave us? ~

It leaves us admitting that, since there is absolutely no scriptural proof to support the possibility of these saints having already been in Heaven when John was initially caught-up to the throne, there is no reason not to believe that **Rev. 7:9-12** is John's record of having witnessed the long awaited resurrection and rapture of both Old and New testament saints. And why not?! As we'll soon see, this interpretation fits perfectly within the boundaries of "THE ENTIRETY OF SCRIPTURE." The only reason we didn't recognize this before is because the words "**great tribulation**" or, for some of you with modern translations, "**<u>the</u> great tribulation**," caused us to stumble. We (*the Church*) had a bad case of "tunnel-vision!"

The Church figured that, since the Rapture is going to take place before the start of the tribulation period, if the saints John saw before the throne in **Rev. 7:9-17** are to have come out of "**<u>the</u> great tribulation**," then those saints couldn't represent the raptured saints. That's true, but the saints John saw instantly appear before the throne didn't come out of "**the**" great-tribulation; they simply came out "**of** " great-tribulation. There's a big difference. Thus, the wiser translators of the *King James Version* of the text got it right and chose not to mistakenly add the word "**the**" before the words "**great tribulation**" in their translation of the earlier text.

---

[144] 1Cor. 15:51-55, 1Th. 4:13-18, Luke 21:36

I realize that this may still be a little confusing for some, but once we've finished examining the rest of the elder's message, this will not only be proven but will also fall neatly into place.

Thankfully, we don't have to guess . . . .

When we read what John experienced in **Rev. 7:9-17** as one complete message, starting with verse 9, it's obvious that John wasn't the only one excited and surprised by the sudden arrival of an innumerable sea of saints before the throne. According to verse 11, *the twenty-four elders, the four beasts, and all the angels* were also excited and began worshipping and praising God when these saints suddenly arrived. I doubt this would have been the case if this multitude of saints had not instantly appeared. If the saints were already there, why the sudden excitement?!

As we read this passage, we read that the elder who was speaking with John began to explain just who this innumerable multitude of saints will be. It is then that the passage seems, at least on the surface, to indicate that these saints had already been in Heaven for at least a little while. That's where, if we're not careful, "**tunnel-vision**" can kick-in. But if we pay close attention and just keep reading, the last three verses of the elder's message make it clear that everything God promised to do for that vast group of saints, He had not already done. Since that's true, they must have just arrived. If they were already somewhere in Heaven, do you suppose they would still be *hungry, thirsty* or *crying*? I seriously doubt it.

Let's examine the latter part of the Elder's Message

In **Rev. 7:16-17** the elder says:

> ***'They shall hunger no more, neither thirst any more; neither shall the sun light on them, nor any heat.***
>
> ***For the Lamb which is in the midst of the throne shall feed them, and shall lead them unto living fountains of waters: and God shall wipe away all tears from their eyes.'***

It's pretty clear from these scriptures that at least some of those saints, just moments before having been caught-up to Heaven, must have been *hungry, thirsty* or *weeping,* because if they weren't, God wouldn't be assuring them that He and the Lamb ***'shall'*** (*future tense*) feed them and lead them to fountains of living waters. Moreover, if none of those saints were crying, God wouldn't be promising to wipe the tears from their eyes.[145] Therefore, the only logical conclusion is that this vast multitude of saints must have just arrived. I doubt any of us are expecting to continue to

145 Isa. 25:8

suffer *hunger, thirst, sorrow,* or *exposure to the heat of the sun* after we've been caught-up to Heaven. What's more, these scriptures couldn't reveal the identity of these saints more clearly than they do. Looking at it any other way would simply defy logic. Besides, we'll soon see (*as I stated earlier*) that if these verses are not John's record of having witnessed the rapture of the saints, then John never recorded having witnessed that monumentally important event. Additionally, and of equal importance, this interpretation perfectly fits into John's complete vision of the entire seven-year tribulation period.

If, for whatever reason, you're still struggling with this, that's okay. As you begin to see the whole, "COMPLETE PICTURE" of the tribulation period, which all the Old and New Testament scriptures (*together*) so perfectly create, this portion of John's vision will also clearly come into focus.

~ *Why are the raptured saints holding palm branches?* ~

Some 500 years before the coming of Christ, Zechariah prophesied the following words:

'Rejoice greatly, O daughter of Zion;
shout O daughter of Jerusalem:
behold, thy King cometh unto thee: He is just,
and having salvation; lowly, and riding upon
an ass, and upon a colt the foal of an ass.'

Zec. 9:9

God inspired Zechariah to speak these words in anticipation of the glorious prophetic day that we now look back on as Palm Sunday.[146] On that extraordinary day our precious Savior meekly rode into Jerusalem on a donkey, just as Zechariah had prophesied. As Jesus did this, many of those who gathered to celebrate the coming Passover worshipfully waved and spread palm branches on the ground before Him. They had no idea how providential their actions would be. With that in mind, I don't think the resurrected and raptured saints in **Rev. 7:9-17** worshipfully waving palm branches, while singing and praising God, on the day of their ascension into Heaven will be coincidental.

---

[146] Zech. 9:9, Jn. 12:13, Rev. 7:9

HERE'S AN UPDATED OUTLINE OF TRIBULATION EVENTS:

- **Before** the start of the 7 year tribulation period, the 144,000 Jewish servants will be marked with **'the seal of the living God,'** to protect them from the, soon to occur, resurrection and rapture of the saints and the following plagues of God's two witnesses.

- **After** the 144,000 are "**sealed**," the long-awaited resurrection and rapture of both Old and New Testament saints will instantly occur. Thus, the saints will be resurrected and instantaneously "caught-up" to Heaven, and God's two witnesses, at the same time or shortly thereafter, will be sent down to begin their earthly ministry. This will kick-off the seven year tribulation period. Hence, during the next 3½ years, God's two prophets will powerfully pronounce God's final call to repent, while unleashing powerfully persuasive plagues to affirm the divine nature of their ministry.[147]

- **Next**, now that the resurrected saints and the Church are safe in Heaven, in Revelation Chapter 8, the formal launch of the seven-year great tribulation period will take place, and the "trumpet-plagues" of God's two witnesses (*which are not wrath*) will begin. "Simple!"

It really will be simple to follow and understand John's vision if we just keep moving ahead, leaving everything in the same order as God revealed it to John.

[147] The powerful plagues of God's two tribulation period witnesses will be analogous to the persuasive plagues God formerly unleashed through Moses and Aaron on the Pharaoh and all Egypt, prior to the great exodus—Ex. Chap. 7-12.

Chapter 15

The Loudest Silence Eternity Will Ever Hear

Rev. 8:1

> ***'And when he*** *(Jesus)* ***had opened the <u>seventh seal</u>, there was <u>silence in heaven</u> about the space of half an hour.'***

It's easy to rush right by this first verse without recognizing its significance. The fact, however, that a half hour of silence will immediately follow the opening of this final, seventh seal should be, to us, like a trumpet blast, loudly warning that whatever is about to follow must be tremendously important. But, if we wish to fully grasp the significance of this half-hour of silence, we must first acknowledge the significance of what we learned in the previous two chapters of John's vision. After showing John an allegorical preview of the entire seven-year tribulation period in **Rev. 6:1-17** (*which ended with a powerful depiction of the Second Coming of Christ*), Jesus just stopped, having only opened the first six of the seven seals on the book from God's right hand,[148] and waited, before opening this final, seventh seal.

~ Why didn't Jesus just open the seventh seal back in Chapter Six? ~

From our perspective, Jesus waited an entire chapter (*Rev. Ch. 7*) before opening this final important seal so we wouldn't make the mistake of confusing the allegorical portion of John's vision (*Rev. Ch. 6*) with its interpretation, which began in **Rev. 7:1** and continues throughout the remainder of John's book. This is where it gets really exciting. As we continue exploring the remainder of John's vision, we will see both the *"heavenly"* and the *"earthly"* fulfillment (*the actual interpretation*) of everything John witnessed allegorically in Rev. Chapter 6. Hence, once we've finished, the brilliant, perfectly sequential manner through which the Lord revealed this vision to John will have become abundantly clear.

---

[148] Rev. 5:1

All of Heaven will stand in Silent Recognition

The resurrection and rapture of the saints will kick-off the seven-year tribulation period, causing global pandemonium and chaos. Millions of unsuspecting individuals will die, be killed, or be seriously injured in the wake of this event, yet few will receive professional medical attention. This, of course, explains why John witnessed the sealing of the 144,000 Jewish servants before he witnessed the rapture of the Church.

Unexpectedly, ***'like a thief in the night,'*** [149] the whole world will be terrifyingly plunged into anarchy when the Church is suddenly caught-up to Heaven! Only God's two witnesses (*the prophets*) will be able to explain the empty graves and the sudden, universal disappearance of hundreds of millions of people. And, though it's hard for us to imagine the world not believing God's two prophets' explanation of what will have happened, we will soon find out that, during the first half of the tribulation period, only the 144,000 Jewish servants of God will believe the witnesses' explanation and, thus, repent. The rest of the world will continue in disbelief throughout the remainder of the first half of the seven-year tribulation period.[150]

The Scene in Heaven will be much different from that on Earth

While **CHAOS** and **ANARCHY** (*in the wake of the Rapture*) are initiating their dreadful reign of terror around the world, the scene in Heaven will be wonderfully different and spectacular! Having just been resurrected, gloriously transformed, and, at long last, caught-up into God's presence, the faithful in Christ will be rejoicing and praising God before His throne, just as John described in the preceding passage (*Rev. 7:9-17*). Thus, an innumerable sea of white robed saints, spanning as far as the eye can see in every direction, will surround the throne, waving palm branches in joyful worship of God the Father and the Lamb. In Heaven, the long awaited event now commonly referred to as "THE RAPTURE" will have finally brought us face to face with our blessed Savior and Lord. Unfortunately, however, at the same time, all those who'll have been left-behind down on earth will be horrifically plummeted into sudden, global mayhem and despair. Thus, the saints will finally be safe at home in Heaven, and the dreaded seven years of "GREAT TRIBULATION" will have just begun.

~ So, who will be Left Behind? ~

I don't know how much time you've spent thinking about "**the remnant**" (*our future brothers and sisters who'll have to endure great suffering,*

---

[149] 1Thes. 5:2, 2Pet 3:10, Mt. 24:36-44

[150] This is scripturally provable, and the truth of it will "self-emerge" from the text as we continue. It's by no means an opinion.

during the tribulation period, before eventually repenting), but those who know me best know that I've spent endless hours contemplating the global effects that the Rapture will have on all those who'll be tragically left-behind. Severely heavy hearted at the thought of it, I've imagined those woeful individuals being forced to fight for their survival in a degenerate world, spiraling downward on its way toward finally becoming a total spiritual "**wilderness**." It's a soul wrenching assessment, yet, sadly, as we're about to learn, before the tribulation period is over that is precisely what the world will be — a total spiritual "**wilderness**!"[151]

We're going to see that those who'll be left-behind (*we'll refer to them as "the Left-behinders"*) will fall into two stubbornly defiant groups. The larger of the two groups will be the perpetually rebellious "**majority**." They, despite God's efforts, will never repent; thus, full of hatred for God, they'll eventually perish. The second group (*which we'll see referred to as, "the remnant"*) will be the last group of souls throughout all eternity to eventually repent. Hence, after enduring God's tough-love, via the persuasive ministry and plagues of His two witnesses (*the prophets*), this "**remnant**" will finally prove their contrition by choosing to be beheaded, rather than denouncing their new faith in Christ and receiving the damnable *"mark of the beast."*

Only the extremely hard of heart will be Left-behind

Because the first 3½ years of the tribulation period will be so horrific, I'm confident that before Jesus catches away the Church, leaving our future brothers and sisters (*"the remnant"*) behind to suffer the consequences, He will have first used every means of earthly persuasion available to bring them to repentance. And yet, despite all of Jesus' and the Church's efforts, they will have remained defiant right up to the day of the Rapture and beyond. Because we love our family and friends so much, it's sometimes easy to forget that God's love for them greatly surpasses our own. But, in reality, while we will be excitedly rejoicing and celebrating our instantaneous arrival in Heaven (*having just been raptured*) Jesus will still be mindful of our wayward — *"not-yet-repentant"* — eternal brothers and sisters, who'll be fighting for survival down here on earth.

After the Rapture, those who've been left-behind will be in desperate need of God's extreme redemptive intervention; they just won't know it. Without that intervention, however, they'll have no hope of ever being saved. These people, who will make up "**the remnant**" portion of Left-behinders, aren't going to be left-behind by accident. They'll be the ones

---

[151] Later, as we move through John's vision, it will become essential for us to understand God's use of the word *"wilderness."* The world will actually become a spiritual *"wilderness."* In time we'll see just exactly what that means—Isa. 14:17.

who'll eventually repent but not until the start of the second half of the tribulation period and, then, only after they've witnessed the resurrection and ascension of God's two prophets.[152]

Preaching alone isn't going to get it done!

These Left-behinders will be genuine hard-cases, not people who could have simply been talked into accepting Christ — not even if witnessed to by one of the 144,000 Jewish converts. In fact, not even God's two prophets will be able to talk the Left-behinders into repenting, at least not without the use of extremely powerful and persuasive plagues. That's why we haven't found and will not find any truly solid scriptural evidence in support of the errant teaching that suggests that the 144,000 Jewish servants will be evangelists. Since it's going to take the death, resurrection, and ascension of God's two witnesses to finally convince "**the remnant**" to repent, I don't see how mere words from any mortal evangelist could get the job done. Let's face it, not even the thousands of miracles Jesus performed[153] were enough to convince the majority of those in Judea that He was and is the Messiah. Hence, it stands to reason that if "**the remnant**" had soft enough hearts to simply be talked into repenting, God would mercifully see to it that those individuals had a chance to accept Christ before Jesus returns to catch-away the Church. That's just one opinion, but perhaps it could be argued to be a logical conclusion when viewed in light of the Lord's love for His kids. And let's not forget, we're talking about the last lingering sheep to be gathered into God's eternal fold.

What's more, I can't imagine God allowing even one of His future children to be left-behind to endure such unimaginably agonizing plagues and spiritual depravity if that individual actually had enough humility to repent but, sadly, just didn't know how. The plagues of God's two witnesses have not been designed to bring the average little lambs into the fold. They've been designed to powerfully persuade all those who are severely self-willed and rebellious to fall to their knees in repentance. And yet, as severe as those plagues will be, they'll still be nothing more than God's merciful parental arm reaching out to the last of His temporarily rebellious and confused future saints.

Life on Earth for those who'll have been Left-Behind

We haven't really talked about the global panic and devastation that will follow in the wake of the Rapture. Think of all the accidents that will result from the millions of cars, buses, trains, subways, and airplanes that

[152] That's also not an opinion. The proof of this is just around the corner in John's vision.
[153] Jn. 21:24-25

will instantly be unmanned once all the believers in Christ are instantaneously taken out of the world. Even in cities where the Rapture will happen in the middle of the night, the sparse accidents that will occur will prevent the public from being able to use the main streets and highways for several weeks, months or even years.[154]

How many times have we all sat, "stuck in traffic," because of a minor fender-bender somewhere ahead on the road? Eager to get to work or back home, most of us have helplessly waited for what seemed like hours until we finally got to the scene of an accident and were outraged to find that the accident wasn't even on our side of the freeway! If just one incident can shut down an entire freeway for hours, what do you suppose thousands of accidents,[155] on both sides of the freeways and side streets, all at the same time and in every city around the world will do? Picture perhaps as many as one car out of thirty or forty being instantly abandoned and left to crash! In an instant, immobile vehicles with injured passengers in desperate need of emergency medical attention will cover the roadways.

Those who'll be left-behind in cities during business hours will really be up a creek! From the new "auto-graveyard" that was once their freeway home, Left-behinders (*in many cities around the world*) will scan the horizon, panic-stricken and completely bewildered, as they gaze in amazement at the hundreds or even thousands of burning cars, houses, buildings, and fields surrounding them. Terrified by the prospect of one of those houses or apartments being their own, the smart Left-behinders will quickly abandon their cars and make a desperate attempt to get home any way they can. Many Christian homes with a burning candle, stove, or fireplace, will eventually catch fire and burn to the ground — taking other homes, apartment complexes, trailer parks, and even whole neighborhoods with them!

Neighboring cities won't be able to help

City and state emergency plans currently rely on help from unaffected neighboring cities and counties, and those plans anticipate additional state and federal support for more severe emergencies. But, sadly, in many cases there will be no unaffected neighboring cities. Virtually every city on the planet will be overwhelmed (*of course some cities much more than others*) as they're instantly plunged into varying states of disarray, confu-

---

[154] Let's not forget that the powerfully devastating *"trumpet-plagues"* haven't even begun! We'll discuss the future effect of those plagues just ahead.

[155] Keep in mind, many of those accidents will have caused serious or fatal injuries to those involved, but there will be no way for emergency personnel to respond. Thus, initially, it won't be possible to just bulldoze those vehicles out of the way.

sion, and uncontrollable panic; thus, there will be nowhere for individual cities to turn for help.

Chaos and Anarchy will Rule *(the red horse – Rev. 6:4)*

The inability of government authorities to respond to such formerly unthinkable, universal calamity will cause the public to panic and become dangerously fearful and territorial. Without Christians and authority figures helping to keep the peace, minor quarrels will quickly turn violent, even deadly.

Picture civilians trying to clean up after just one massive, multiple car, train, or subway accident — good-luck! What will they use to clean up the mess or help the injured? The fire department sure won't be able to assist. Even the military is nowhere near adequately staffed or supplied to deal with universal calamity on such a global scale.

Moreover, not only will most of the roads and freeways be blocked but, once the meager amount of water on their trucks runs out, firemen will have no water and no way of responding to the tens of thousands of traffic accidents and countless fires. Within a few hours, virtually all water, gas, and electricity will (*of necessity*) be permanently shut-off. The inability to control and contain the thousands of residential and commercial fires, which will blanket both cities and rural areas alike, will allow field and forest fires in many areas to grow to monstrously devouring proportions. Unable to meet the sudden massive demand, water pressure will nearly instantly drop-off, leaving any remaining firefighters (*few as they may be*) completely powerless. Thus, having nothing with which to fight these fires and fearing for the safety of their own relatives, even the "faithful-few" will eventually abandon their posts and head toward home in hopes of protecting their own homes and families.

Past books and movies don't even come close!

The real aftermath of the Rapture will be nothing like the books we've read or movies we've watched. Not having a plan capable of dealing with such truly universal chaos and mayhem, in many cases, there will be little more than a minimally coordinated effort made by government officials to control the pandemonium. The chaos and lack of resources will simply be far too overwhelming to manage! Thus, having no other option and powerless to suppress the panicked rioting public or to bring the massive fires and looting under control, eventually most civilian and government authorities will have no choice but to either "lock-down" and protect themselves from the terror-stricken mobs or to abandon their posts, head for home, and try and fend for themselves. This level of severity just isn't what's being illustrated by most end-time books and movies, is it? Nonetheless, in some cities around the world (*especially here in the United States*) the aftermath of the Rapture will be every bit this devastating.

The Situation isn't going to Improve any time Soon

Uncontained, some fires will continue burning for several days or even weeks, devouring thousands of homes and businesses before they finally burn out. With fires damaging and irreparably destroying the main telephone lines, gas pipes, water pipes, and power lines to millions of structures and substations (*not to mention the countless thousands of electrical transformers that will catch fire and/or explode*) it will be unsafe, negligible even, for authorities to **ever** turn these services back on once they've been shut-off. That's assuming, of course, that government and civilian authorities will choose to dutifully stick around and do their jobs, despite the monumental lack of supplies and nagging fear for the welfare of their families and homes.

Being old or sick will almost certainly equal death!

The personnel in hospitals, nursing homes, board and care facilities, and retirement homes (*without receiving any relief or support from the government*) will quickly become exhausted and overwrought. Fear for their own family's well-being and the overall continually hopeless conditions will quickly outweigh their loyalty to their patients; thus, caregivers will eventually be forced to head for home — leaving the sick and helpless to survive or die on their own, without power, water, or food. Each patient's hope for survival will depend on their loved ones' ability to rush to their aid, but a slim hope that will be.

Seriously, can it get any worse?

Unfortunately, the answer is, *"Yes; – absolutely!"* If you haven't accepted Christ and you're stuck in prison when the Rapture occurs, you'd better get comfortable, because, with their homes and families in jeopardy, I strongly doubt prison guards are going to report to work.

Endeavoring to deal with these issues and hoping to control the rioting masses, some countries may attempt to implement martial law but will quickly find it impossible to initiate and even harder to sustain.

There are other severe repercussions we haven't even mentioned, which will result from this global pandemonium. To name just one, the United States alone has over a hundred nuclear reactor sites, and at least fifty of those sites contain large spent-fuel pools. The water levels and circulation in those pools are maintained around the clock to prevent the radioactive spent fuel rods from overheating and releasing deadly radiation (*i.e., cesium-137*) into the air. This slow cooling process must continue around the clock for a minimum of 3 to 5 years before the spent fuel can be moved to the next phase of slow cooling, which includes a special dry-storage system.

If the water level in just one of these pools were to fail to be properly maintained and circulated, the spent fuel would soon overheat, causing a radioactive fire to ensue, which would violently release deadly toxins into the atmosphere. Hundreds of square miles would eventually (*like Chernobyl*) become uninhabitable, not to mention the sickness and lingering deaths that would follow. If just one of these spent fuel pools can cause that kind of catastrophe, what do you suppose will happen when many of the more than 400 active nuclear power plants around the world can't maintain their status quo?

What's even more alarming is the knowledge that most of these spent fuel storage pools are not presently required to back-up their "off-site" power with "on-site" emergency generators. Therefore, when "off-site" power is lost, they'll have no way of keeping the spent fuel rods cool and safe. Consequently, I have a hard time believing that the employees of those power plants are going to leave their families and homes unprotected (*if they haven't burned to the ground*) and, in the midst of all the global chaos and uncertainty, head off to work. What's more, how will they get to work? Most likely, they'll just warn their friends and loved ones to join them in getting as far away from those nuclear facilities as is humanly possible!

And, while imagining being caught in the middle of all of this is definitely terrifying, we're still only scratching the surface. At this point, God's only earthly intervention will have been the catching-away of the Church (*the Rapture*), and all this calamity will just be part of the aftermath of that event. God's two witnesses will not have even begun to call the world to repentance; therefore, none of the powerful "**trumpet-plagues**" — which will mightily dominate the first 3½ years of the tribulation period — will have been unleashed.

Silence in Heaven

Rev. 8:1 ~ *continued*

Therefore, in light of the globally horrific aftermath that will result from the resurrection and rapture of the saints and given that soon after the saints are caught-up to Heaven God's two witnesses will begin unleashing one globally powerful plague after another, it's easy to see why John witnessed the Heavenly observance of a half hour of silence immediately following Jesus' opening of the seventh and final seal on the book from God's right hand. That seal represents the beginning of the seven-year tribulation period, during which God will deal more severely with His creation than at any time since He flooded the earth, some 4,300 years prior.

Thus, in loving acknowledgment of the severity of the Left-behinders suffering, immediately after John saw Jesus open that final seventh seal, in his vision, John witnessed all of Heaven, including those who had just been raptured, observe a half hour of silence. When that silence is over it will be time for God (*through His two powerful witnesses*) to wreak even greater havoc and terror on the earth as part of His final effort to call the defiantly impenitent world to repentance. Jesus will do whatever it takes to bring the last of His children to their knees, and these powerful "**trumpet-plagues**," which will begin soon after the Rapture, have been designed to do just that!

John didn't just say: "*And I saw seven angels . . .*"

Rev. 8:2

John said:

> ***'And I saw <u>the</u> seven angels which stood before God; and to <u>them</u> were given seven trumpets.'***

John could have simply written: ***And I saw seven angels*** *. . . .* Instead, however, he specifically wrote that he saw – "**the**" - seven angels. Adding the word "**the**" before angels may (*though we can't be sure*) indicate that John had seen these seven specific angels before. Could it be that John recognized these angels as being the same seven angels Jesus had earlier declared to be the ***'seven stars'*** of the ***'seven churches'*** in **Rev. 1:12-20**? It certainly seems to be a logical possibility. In fact, that does make a great deal of sense.

If we remember back to the beginning of John's Revelation experience, we'll recall that John was visited by the angel of the Lord while he was still on earth and in prayer on the island of Patmos. And, although John almost immediately began seeing a glorious vision of Jesus, he wasn't actually taken up into Heaven until **Rev. 4:2**, after he had finished recording all of Jesus' messages for the seven churches in Asia.

~ *Why wasn't John immediately taken up into Heaven?* ~

I believe the answer to be quite simple. John probably (*though we're not told*) received the letters to the seven churches while he was still on earth because, at that time, the seven churches and their angels were also still on earth. The letters to the seven churches are Jesus' direct instruction not only for those particular churches that were recognized as actually existing in Asia during John's lifetime but also for the Church of today as a whole. Thus, when we study and interpret John's vision, leaving it in the same order as John recorded it (*just as God intended*) we find that, once John was taken up into Heaven in **Rev. 4:2**, although he recorded seeing many other angels and incredible heavenly beings around the throne, he never recorded seeing these seven "specific" angels until here, in **Rev. 8:2**, after he had witnessed the rapture of the Church (*Rev. 7:9-17*). Therefore, if, as Jesus seemed to indicate in the earthly portion of John's vision,[156] there are actually seven angels, whom Jesus has commissioned to oversee the true Church on earth (*the body of Christ*), John would not be expected to see them appear in Heaven until after they, with the Church, are caught-up to Heaven. This likely explains why immediately after having witnessed the half hour of silence in Heaven (*which John was shown will launch the seven-year tribulation period*) John recorded that he saw ***'the seven angels'*** (*i.e., seven specific angels*) standing before the throne. I don't see how this could be coincidental, though the intrinsic significance of it may presently be impossible to prove.

For centuries Christians have been reading and gleaning wisdom and instruction from all seven of Jesus' letters to the early churches in Asia, and we will continue to do so until that final day when Christ returns to redeem us to Himself. Thus, there's no reason not to believe that these seven specific angels are still connected to the Church and are somehow working in unison (*here on earth*) with the Holy Spirit and the *Seven Spirits of God* on the Church's behalf. Whatever the case may be, it certainly remains a mystery to me. And, no, I did not intend for that to rhyme. But I like it!

---

[156] John experienced the first three chapters of his vision before he was taken up into Heaven.

Chapter 16

Hopefully Scared Straight

Based on what we're about to read, the ministry of God's two tribulation period prophets will be a divinely designed *"Scared Straight Program"* on a global scale! Through these two unprecedentedly powerful prophets, God will preach the Gospel message throughout the earth one final time. But motivating these skeptically defiant Left-behinders to repent won't be an easy mission by any means. Once the tribulation period begins and the Left-behinders are directly exposed to the demonically empowered lies and trickery of the son of perdition (*the false-prophet, the anti-Christ*),[157] it will be more difficult than ever for the Left-behinders to distinguish between truth and deception. And, making things even more difficult will be the reality that the Church, God's current beacon of light in the world,[158] will no longer be here to help expose that deception. What's more, the Holy Spirit will already have been ***'taken out of the way'*** (*pulled back*),[159] in order to allow the son of perdition to be revealed.

We touched on this earlier. Although both Christian and secular writers have profited millions through their creation of suspense movies and novels that attempt to depict the terrifying events of the tribulation period, even truly sincere writers have made one common mistake. They've consistently created characters in their stories that have repented and become believers in Christ before the end of the first half of the tribulation period. Sadly, however, as we're about to see, John's vision clearly reveals that nobody, not a single soul (*with the exception of God's 144,000 Jewish servants*), will repent during that initial 3½ year period.[160] This is why we

---

[157] We're going to see conclusive proof that the *"son of perdition," "the false prophet"* and *"the anti-Christ"* are all <u>one</u> person. I realize this is not commonly taught; nonetheless, by the time we finish our journey, the Scriptures will have proven it to be accurate.

[158] John 12:36, Phil. 2:15, Rev. 18:23

[159] 2Th. 2:3-12

[160] As have many of you, I've been teaching about the end-times for quite a while. Therefore, I know that, for those of you who've spent years reading and studying eschatological books and sermons, some or much of this is hard to process. And

won't find any scriptures explaining how God will miraculously provide for and/or protect new-believers during any of the tribulation period. The Left-behinders who will eventually repent won't do so until the first 3½ years have expired, and will, subsequently, have to choose to be martyred in order to maintain their hope of salvation through Christ.[161] Thus, according to John's vision, the only saints God will be protecting from the terrors of the tribulation period will be His specially chosen and *"sealed"* 144,000 Jewish servants, and even they will eventually have to suffer martyrdom to maintain their testimony of faith in Christ.[162]

~ *Why is this so important?* ~

We intentionally digressed, here, to make one important point clear. Every disbelieving individual who (*in an instant*) shockingly finds that they've been left-behind after the Rapture will have to endure 3½ years of what will seem like "HELL ON EARTH" — with both God and Satan contending for their soul.

As we earlier noted while warning about the powerful deception that will surface during the tribulation period, Jesus said: ***"If it were possible, they shall deceive the very elect."***[163] With those words Jesus warned the Church that the deception of the tribulation period false prophets will be so strong that, if exposed to it, even true Christians (*the elect*) would be deceived. Therefore, if, as believers, we would be deceived, it's easy to see why none of the Left-behinders will believe the testimony and preaching of God's two witnesses until after they see irrefutable proof that those witnesses have been divinely sent. That proof will come as God spectacularly raises them from the dead at the end of their 3½ year ministry and calls them back up Heaven. Thus, those two witnesses will be God's final effort to reach the lost before it's eventually too late for them to repent and be saved.

The Plagues will be Horrific, but they won't be Wrath!

We're about to learn about the "**trumpet-plagues**" of God's two witnesses, and, because those plagues will be so severe, it has been assumed that God will use them to punish the Left-behinders. However, no scriptural evidence to support that theory exists. The prophets are <u>not</u> being sent back to Earth to punish non-believers. If they were, during this first

---

that's to be expected, but when we get to the proof in the next few chapters, this will all become clear and irrefutable. I love it when that happens, and so will you!

[161] Rev. 13:15, 14:9-13, 20:4

[162] Rev. 6:9-11, 7:1-8, 14:1-5

[163] Mt. 24:24

3½ year portion of John's vision of the tribulation period we would eventually find the word "**wrath**" attached to the unleashing of the prophets' plagues. That, however, won't be the case, because God's two prophets will be sent back to do what most past prophets have done. They'll warn the people to either *"repent"* or *"expect to perish."* This first 3½ year period is all about one thing – "MERCY." Amazingly, God intends to give all those who will have been left-behind one final chance to repent before He eternally shuts the allegorical "Door of Salvation"[164] and begins dishing out His vengeance and wrath on what will be left of this obstinately wicked and defiantly rebellious world.

~ *But this just isn't how I learned it!* ~

If that's how you feel, I understand, and I'm not at all surprised. Most people, including many of my favorite pastors and teachers, don't teach that John's "allegorical" vision (*the opening of the first six seals—Rev. 6:1-17*) is simply a chronological "preview" of the entire seven-year tribulation period. Thus, when they read in **Rev. 6:12-17** about the Second Coming of Christ and ***'the wrath of the Lamb,'*** they misinterpret the text and teach that God will begin pouring out His wrath at the beginning of the tribulation period. The truth is (*as we learned earlier and will continue to see proven*) John wasn't actually shown the start of the tribulation period until he witnessed the rapture of the saints in **Rev. 7:9-17**. That's why immediately afterward (*in Rev. 8:1*) we read about the ***'half hour of silence'*** that will follow the Rapture and precede the unleashing of the seven "**trumpet-plagues**." Six of those plagues will be unleashed as part of the two witnesses' ministry, during the first half of the tribulation period.

The Rapture and its inevitable aftermath (*as we've discussed*) will be unimaginably devastating and will likely cause the injuries or deaths of many tens of thousands or even hundreds of thousands of Left-behinders. And the global calamity that will ensue will be absolutely horrific! That's no little thing to God, which explains the half-hour of silence at the beginning of the tribulation period.

Sadly, mistaking what John saw when the six seals in **Rev. 6:1-17** were opened as being the actual beginning of the seven-year tribulation period is a common mistake. And, unfortunately, because so many have made this mistake, when readers get to this "**trumpet-plague**" portion of John's vision, they just can't see how these plagues can be anything other than God's wrath. To most people the words *"plague"* and *"wrath"* are synonymous; however, that's not scripturally accurate. Plagues don't necessarily equal wrath.

---

[164] Luke 13:24-28, Mt. 25:10

For example, the ten plagues God unleashed through Moses and Aaron on Pharaoh's kingdom were not plagues of wrath. They were simply God's means of displaying His omnipotence and global sovereignty to the reigning Pharaoh and the future children of Israel. There's not a single scripture that can truly support a claim that those plagues somehow represented the wrath of God. However, once God had delivered His people safely out of the land of Egypt and the Pharaoh and his army decided to race after them in a rage, God did exercise His wrath, eventually overthrowing the Pharaoh's army by closing the waters of the Red Sea upon them.[165]

When the perfect divinely ordained time for the pouring out of God's wrath actually arrives (*at the end of the tribulation period*) there will be absolutely no way of failing to recognize it. In fact, it will be just about the most identifiable event in the history of the world! Not even Noah's flood will be comparable to it.

Are we that particular, fateful Generation?

I don't know for certain if we will be that final end-time generation that will actually see the start of the tribulation period, but, if we are that generation, then some of our closest friends and loved ones (*for whom we've diligently prayed and to whom we've continually witnessed*) will unfortunately make up part of that rebellious "**remnant**" who'll be left-behind when the saints are instantly caught-up to Heaven. Thus, having been unsuccessful in our attempt to reach them for Christ, in a fraction of a second, they'll shockingly find themselves part of a global panic-stricken group of confused and terrified Left-behinders. Looking at it from that personal perspective and imagining that it's our own son, daughter, brother, sister, husband, or wife, who'll horrifyingly find themself feeling abandoned and exposed to the powerful, dark deception of the emerging earthly kingdom of Satan certainly can give us some frightful insight into why God will need to forcefully intervene on our loved ones' behalves.

John's view from the Altar

Rev. 8:3

In every direction, as far as John could see and far beyond, a sea of glistening white robes and radiant smiling faces covered the landscape. And, if you're a faithful follower of Christ, one of those youthful, radiant faces was yours! Hence, after witnessing the raptured saints praise God for their redemption (*Rev. 7:9-12*) and, after having observed a fittingly solemn half-hour of silence in Heaven, John watched, as:

[165] Ex. 15:7

'. . . another angel came and stood at the altar, having a golden censer; and there was given unto him much incense, that he should offer it with the prayers of the saints upon the golden altar which was before the throne.'

I'm not sure if this had ever been done before, but John actually witnessed this angel mix our prayers with the holy incense upon the golden altar — "WOW!" Thanks to what John recorded in **Rev. 5:8**, we've already learned that God is currently saving our prayers, preserving them, year after year, in vials of pure gold. *Seriously, how sweet is that?!*

Rev. 8:4

'And the smoke of the incense, which came with the prayers the saints, ascended up before God out of the angel's hand.'

We will all be standing right there, before God's throne, watching as our own past fretful pleas for the redemption of our unrepentant loved ones ascend to God from the golden censer in the angel's hand. God will not have forgotten a single prayer; thus, the dreadful seven trumpet-plagues, which God's two witnesses will be ready to unleash, will, in reality, be God's righteous, loving response to our own persistent pleas for Him to intervene on behalf of our lost family and friends who'll have been left-behind.

The Tribulation Period will have Officially Begun

Rev. 8:5

'And the angel took the censer, and filled it with fire of the altar, and cast it into the earth: and there were voices, and thunderings, and lightnings, and an earthquake.'

The preceding verse is an example of how we must distinguish between what John saw occur in the spiritual realm of Heaven and what he actually saw occur down on earth. The thunder, the lightning, and the earthquake John witnessed as the angel cast the censer into the earth will most likely only be perceptible to those in Heaven. Having been taken into Heaven, as John was when he saw this vision, he had the unique ability of simultaneously seeing both the spiritual (*the heavenly*) and the physical (*the earthly*) perspectives of these tribulation events. In the same way, we know from Scripture that angels are currently intervening, both physically and spiritually, in our lives, accomplishing God's will for us on earth.[166] Yet, while we know this to be true, we're often unable to determine precisely how or

[166] Heb. 1:14, Mt.1:20-24, 2:13-19, 4:11, 13:41, 26:53, 28:5, Mk. 1:13, Luke 1:11-38, 2:10-15, 2:21, 4:10, 22:43, 24:23, John 5:4, 20:12

when angels intercede. John's having witnessed the angel cast the golden censer down to earth is a great example of how some of what John saw from his heavenly perspective was purely symbolic or was only perceptible to those in Heaven. To put it simply, I seriously doubt that those who'll be left-behind on earth will need to wear hardhats in order to protect themselves against angels throwing golden censers and burning incense! If we simply remember that some of what John was shown in his vision only has symbolic relativity to the actual events that will occur on earth, we'll find these symbolic portions of John's vision easier to discern.

The Seven Angels prepare themselves to Sound

Once the half hour of silence ends the earthly ministry of God's two powerful witnesses will begin. During that same 3½ year period, however, the *"son of perdition"* and the *"powers of darkness"* (*Satan and his army of fallen angels*)[167] will be forcefully taking the world by storm, while going forth building Satan's blasphemous one-world empire. Sadly, as we're about to read, since John gave no indication of having witnessed anyone other than the 144,000 Jewish servants immediately respond to the two witnesses' warnings, as the following verses reveal, God's two prophets will have no choice but to exercise their heavenly powers of persuasion in the form of powerful plagues — the "**trumpet-plagues**!"

'And I will give power unto my two witnesses . . . .'
*'These have power to shut heaven, that it rain not in the days of their prophecy: **and have power over waters to turn them to blood**, **and to smite the earth with all plagues**, **as often as they will**.'*

Rev. 11:3 & **6**

Rev. 8:6

'And the seven angels which had the seven trumpets prepared themselves to sound.'

John watched while these seven mighty angels were given the most severe implements of heavenly persuasion the Lord has ever devised — the seven trumpet-plagues. With those plagues God will give new meaning to the term, "tough-love." Thus, just as the Lord proved Moses' words to be divinely ordained — unleashing plague after plague upon Pharaoh's kingdom and filling it with blood, pestilence, darkness, and death, until the Pharaoh and his magicians finally relented, God will also powerfully confirm the divine origin of His two final witnesses and their message.

[167] Eph. 6:12-16, 2Pt. 2:4, Jude 6, Rev. 12:7-9

Chapter 17

And You Thought Your Tough-love Was Tough

The first Trumpet-plague

Rev. 8:7

> ***'The first angel sounded, and there followed hail and fire mingled with blood, and they were cast upon the earth: and the third part of the trees was burned up, and all green grass was burned up.'***

Hail mingled with blood? For years I've heard teachers try to explain away these trumpet-plagues by claiming that some sort of humanly generated catastrophe or nuclear explosion is responsible for their effects on the earth, but that just doesn't wash. The truth is there's absolutely no reason for us to interpret these trumpet-plagues as being anything other than exactly what John recorded them to be — "Heaven-sent plagues!"

~ But John doesn't actually call them plagues, does he? ~

If the preceding question was on your mind, the answer is, "No!" In this chapter John does not refer to these events as plagues. However, he will make that clarification later in Chapter 11. Much of our ability to correctly interpret Scripture depends on our being able to recognize **2** + **2** (*scripturally*) and get **4**. When we (*in the following chapters*) add up everything John recorded about the tribulation period, the sum will prove that these seven angels and their powerful trumpet-plagues will be God's supportive response to the earthly preaching ministry of His two witnesses — the two tribulation period prophets.

~ But I thought war would cause this destruction!? ~

It's possible, even likely, that the sudden resurrection and rapture of the saints will spawn panic-driven wars and skirmishes, especially in the Middle East. But that doesn't negate the fact that the devastation John recorded witnessing in **Rev. 8:1** thru **9:20** will be produced by angelic intervention in support of the preaching of God's two end-time prophets.

Furthermore, it seems obvious that God designed these plagues in such a way as to make it impossible for us to mistake them as being anything other than His divine intervention on earth. This will definitely become obvious as we continue.

What's amazing is the thought of anyone even hinting at a human or natural cause for effects like ***'hail and fire mingled with blood,'*** and all the ***'green grass'*** and ***'the third part of** [the]* ***trees'*** being burnt up. Moreover, without getting into an extensive *Greek* word study, the word *hail* (*in this verse*) is only used in the book of Revelation and always refers to only one thing — "God's judgment." By itself that fact would seem to suggest God's wrath. However, judgment doesn't always indicate wrath, which is a truth that will be confirmed by the text as we continue.

Nothing mankind has created could cause **hail** and **fire** to fall on and *"burn-up"* only *"green-grass"* and only *"one-third of the trees,"* leaving all the dry grass unharmed! Furthermore, what logical earthly explanation could there be for burning hail to be mingled with blood? Before we attempt to answer that we must first be ready to prove our answer with Scripture alone. Obviously this plague is precisely what John indicated it to be, an act of God, carried out by angels, intended to force "**the remnant**" to repent before it's eventually too-late for them to do so.

When will the first trumpet sound?

Rev. 8:7 ~ *continued*

Nothing John wrote gives us any real clarity as to how much time will pass between the rapture of the Church and the sounding of the first angel's trumpet. Fortunately, thanks to **Rev. 11:1-7**, we know that God's two witnesses will minister for 3½ years before being killed in the middle of the tribulation period. Thus, we can logically conclude that they'll begin preaching as soon as the tribulation period begins. Just exactly what they'll say and by what miraculous means everyone on earth will hear their global "CALL TO REPENTANCE" is a mystery, but we're safe in presuming that the worldwide-web will not be their method of global communication.

~ *Wait! — Why do you say that?* ~

Let's look at this logically. During the tribulation period God will be loudly proclaiming His final offer of salvation (*the Gospel*) to every inhabitant on the planet through His two witnesses. Today, even under perfect conditions, the internet is not setup to reach every remote area around the world, especially during a massive global power failure. And, since God would never impose plagues that He has carefully designed to turn the rebellious inhabitants of the earth towards repentance on those who have not even heard His call to repent, it's likely that every person on the planet will hear the witnesses' global message. What's more, the prophets' message will continue to be heard throughout their 3½ year ministry, which means it will be heard right through the first six trumpet-plagues. Thus, after learning of the unprecedentedly destructive nature and global effects of those plagues, we would have to be irrationally open-minded to even consider the possibility of power-grids being continually operational throughout the full, earth-shaking ministry of God's two witnesses. If that's not already obvious, John will make this abundantly clear in the next few verses.

Let's not assume . . . .

Just because our current ability to communicate on a nearly global scale (*via the internet*) seems to be a fulfillment of prophecy doesn't mean that God actually needs our help in doing so on behalf of His two witnesses. If God can simply will an angel to blow a trumpet and, thereby, cause all the *green grass* and *a third of all the trees on earth* to be burnt-up, without lifting a finger or speaking a word, we would certainly be foolish to imagine that God will have any difficulty causing the salvation message of His two powerful prophets to be heard all around the world, by every living inhabitant of the earth, including those in the most remote of remote locations. Therefore, I think we can safely conclude, based on what we've learned from Scripture about the righteous ways of God, that every person on earth — even those who choose to hide in caves[168] — will clearly hear the voices of God's two witnesses when they begin calling the world to repentance. And, just as on the day of Pentecost,[169] they'll hear those words in a language they can understand. What's more, as we continue surveying the next few exciting chapters of John's vision, we're going to learn that projecting their voices so as to be heard around the world won't even come close to being the witnesses' most remarkable accomplishment.

These have power to shut the heavens . . . .

Rev. 8:7 ~ *please read Rev. 11:2-12 before continuing.*

As the sun begins setting (*all around the world*) at the end of that fateful day when Jesus will have come to *"catch-away"* the Church, thousands of fires and dark, towering columns of smoke will dominate the horizon, in every direction, as far as the eye can see. Varying in size and ferocity, these frightening pillars of smoke will loom heavily over the earth, reaching high into the stratosphere, where they'll spread out to form thick, intimidating, chemically-toxic canopies over both cities and rural areas alike. If just a

---

[168] 1Kg. 19:9
[169] Acts 2:4-12

single wildfire, under normal circumstances, can turn the evening sky over an entire city eerily red and dark, what do you suppose thousands of fires of varying size and origin will do?

Some of those clouds will contain deadly fallout from out of control fires in chemical factories, refineries, nuclear-power plants, and countless other types of manufacturing plants. The chronically sick, the elderly, all those with breathing disorders (*like, e.g., asthma, emphysema and chronic-bronchitis*), and those who need special oxygen mixtures will find it painful and nearly impossible just to take a breath. And yet, rather than simply obeying the constant pleading of God's two witnesses to repent, the Left-behinders will stubbornly continue to refuse.

Now, on top of everything else, let's also try to imagine that *"all of the green grass and a third of all the trees"* have been burnt to a cinder! What should we expect will happen to the remaining barely breathable air? The global scene in the wake of the Rapture alone will be nearly indescribable! Just the effects of hundreds of millions of people instantly disappearing from the face of the earth, without a single plague having been released, will have thrust the world's inhabitants back to their primitive tent and cave dwelling existence. This time, however, along with tents, abandoned-houses, hospitals, military bases, concrete bunkers and the like, the Left-behinders will fiercely occupy and defend any dwelling they can find. And yet, sadly, the tribulation period will have only just begun!

Once God's two witnesses commence unleashing one catastrophic trumpet-plague after another (*over roughly 4 to 6 month intervals*), they're certain to shake the surviving population of the earth right out of its perpetually defiant, spiritual slumber. Every person on the planet will be forced to fight for their lives just to maintain a meager existence. In many ways it will be even worse than the panic-stricken day when the torrential rains began to fall and the Lord miraculously reached down and shut the door on Noah and his family in the Ark.[170]

Hail mingled with blood?

Rev. 8:7 ~ *continued*

We haven't even mentioned the inescapable stench that will permeate the barely breathable, air after only a few days, once the ***'hail mingled with blood'*** begins to putrefy, thus, creating an ideal environment for flies and other insects to abundantly multiply. I would imagine it will smell something like a well-trodden battlefield, strewn with millions of bloated and decaying bodies, of which, incidentally, there will be plenty! Anyone who's ever worked in a butcher's shop, grocery store, or a restaurant will

---

[170] Gen. 7:15-16

attest to the foul, pungent — *"stop you in your tracks"* — odor that arises from putrefying blood, when a meat box or tray has accidently been overlooked and allowed to spoil — YUCK! The fly population will think it has died and gone to insect heaven.

Even still, no one will listen . . .

There's little doubt that God's two witnesses will begin their 3½ year ministry by explaining to all the Left-behinders precisely why such universal calamity has befallen them, but it just won't matter. All but the 144,000 Jewish converts will initially remain defiant. With the son of perdition going forth ***'conquering and to conquer,'*** [171] supernaturally deceiving the whole world into believing that he alone is God,[172] the Left-behinders will hold on to their foolish hope of being able to resume their self-willed, Godless lifestyles without ever having to repent. And they'll be looking to the miraculous (*though covertly demonic*) powers of the son of perdition to make that happen.

Can we at least get a weather report?

We're not told for certain if God's prophets will allow it to rain during this first half of the tribulation period, but, since they'll have been given the power to keep it from raining during the entire 3½ years of their ministry,[173] rain isn't likely to be in the forecast. With all that smoke and bloody hail stinking-up the atmosphere and no fresh rain water to cleanse the earth or sky, the inhabitants of the earth, like haughty, defiant teenagers who've been locked in their rooms on the night of the big party, will seethe with hatred and resentment towards God for having intentionally subjected them to such miserably unrelenting conditions.

And all the green grass was burnt up . . . .

Rev. 8:7 ~ *continued*

The consequences of all the *"green grass"* being burnt up in the raw aftermath of the hundreds of thousands of fires, which will have been triggered by the Rapture, would be unimaginably devastating all by itself. But, when we add to that the burning of *"one-third of all the trees"* around the world, life on earth will be nearly unbearable! God has designed both grass and trees to produce and filter the very air we breathe. In fact, those trees are so perfectly designed that just one mature tree can produce enough oxygen to sustain eight to ten adult humans, so it's not hard to imagine the

---

[171] This is what the rider on the white horse signifies—Rev. 6:1-2.
[172] 2Th. 2:3-12, Mt. 24:21-35
[173] Rev. 11:6

diminishing effect that a sudden loss of all green-grass and one-third of the trees will have on the rapidly dwindling, breathable air. What's more, the elaborate root systems of the billions of trees on the planet not only stabilize the earth's surface *(working to prevent landslides and the like)*, they're also a major part of God's global air purification system. Those glorious trees and grasses are largely responsible for the daily absorption of toxic airborne pollutants and hazardous particles, not to mention the ingenious way in which their root systems also filter ground water, efficiently absorbing and diluting dangerous pollutants and chemicals that have entered the soil through sewage and/or animal waste.

To begin to grasp the wide reaching impact that one out of three trees and all the green-grass catching fire and completely burning to the ground will have on the earth, take a look outside. Scan the landscape all around you. Imagine that the Rapture has already occurred and, now, on top of all that devastation, you're seeing new, aggressive fires breaking out everywhere ***'green grass'*** exists. And, while this is happening, one out of every three trees (*all over the horizon*) are also bursting into flames, even those growing near factories, commercial buildings, school, hospitals, apartment complexes, and houses — until one-third of all the trees on the planet (*that have not already been destroyed in the wake of the Rapture*) and all green grass has been incinerated.

Consider all the great forests around the world (*like the Boreal Forest of Taiga, the Giant Sequoia and Redwood Forests of California or the mighty Amazon Forest of South America*). When the first trumpet-plague finally comes to an end and the fires cease (*whenever that will be*), there will be no more *"green grass"* and *"one-third fewer trees"* in the world to help purify the air and make it breathable for the miserably suffering, yet still rebellious, inhabitants of the earth.

The Second Trumpet-plague

Rev. 8:8-9

> ***'And the second angel sounded, and as it were a great mountain burning with fire was cast into the sea: and the third part of the sea became blood;***
>
> ***And the third part of the creatures which were in the sea, and had life, died; and the third part of the ships were destroyed.'***

Every time we read "third-part" or "one-third" after the sounding of a trumpet, we should be thinking "ACT OF GOD." I stated earlier that when it's time for God's wrath to be poured out there will be no mistaking it. That's because when that time comes the Lord will not hold back as He is here with these trumpet-plagues. With the first four trumpet-plagues God will give the inhabitants of the earth a bitter taste and smell of "HELL ON EARTH," measured out in thirds! *"Why thirds?"* you ask. We're not told, but perhaps that's all the Left-behinders will be able to physically endure.

As I stated earlier, God won't be unleashing these plagues to be cruel. On the contrary, He'll be doing it to give the Left-behinders an advanced taste of the eternal damnation that will inevitably overtake them should they allow their wayward rebellion to eventually lead them beyond His loving, redemptive grasp. And, while these plagues will be horrific, they won't even come close to accurately representing the unbearable despair and perpetual loneliness that all lost souls will ultimately experience when their sad day of judgment inevitably comes and they spiritually awaken to find themselves being cast, *"live, into the lake of fire"* (*in outer-darkness*),[174] where they'll forever be separated from God, Heaven, and all that's good!

It's got to be a comet, or a meteor, or something - right?

Rev. 8:8-9 ~ *continued*

Even allowing my imagination to wildly explore beyond the realm of rational thought, I can't comprehend how an asteroid, a comet, a meteor, or any other manner of galactic debris could cause one-third of the seas to be turned into blood. It's obvious, without even looking ahead at the clarifying verses in the coming chapters that this plague will be a perfectly calculated "ACT OF GOD" directed from Heaven in support of God's two witnesses and their preaching. And, while this should already be apparent, we would be remiss if we failed to acknowledge that turning water into blood is listed in **Rev. 11:3-6** as being one of the specific powers to be possessed by God's two witnesses. God didn't take the time to give us that little bit of essential information for nothing. Those powerful prophets will most definitely be turning water into blood on a truly global scale as part of their persuasive, final call to repentance.

In **Rev. 8:8-9**, the ***'great mountain burning with fire'*** (*which John witnessed being cast into the sea*) will most likely originate and be violently cast directly down from Heaven, by the power of God, at the appropriate time. It is possible, however, though not necessary, that God created this astronomical mountain of fire and set it on an earthbound course during the week of creation, when He created everything else. However, given the enigmatically bloody effect it will have when it violently crashes into the oceans and seas around the world, there's really no reason for our assuming that to be the case.

---

[174] Mt. 8:12, 22:13, 25:30

According to what John wrote, when this heavenly object hits the earth it will have been miraculously designed to turn precisely one-third of all the ***'seas'*** *(i.e., seas and oceans)* into ***'blood'*** *and* ***'kill'*** one-third of all the creatures in them. In order for this prophecy to be fulfilled, this burning mountain doesn't need to break into smaller pieces and be evenly dispersed around the globe, though it probably will do just that. It could simply make impact in one location (*like the Atlantic Ocean, for instance*) and be divinely limited to affecting just one-third of the earth's oceans.

I guess those must be some seriously bloody fish - huh?

Because many writers have failed to give God full credit for the origin and initiation of these globally devastating tribulation events, they've been forced to use naturally impossible happenstance to explain inexplicable occurrences, like this one-third of the seas being turned to blood. That, however, is an impossible task! Nothing other than an "ACT OF GOD" could turn precisely one-third of the water in all the oceans and seas on the planet (*according to some estimates, roughly one fourth of the total surface of the earth*) into blood. I've heard more than just a few teachers attempt to explain away this future event by claiming that a giant meteor (*possibly radioactive or something*) or a comet, on a path towards earth, will make impact in an ocean, thus killing one-third of the creatures in the oceans and seas and turning one-third of them to blood.

Let's consider that perspective one step at a time. The scripture says that only one-third of the creatures in the sea will die. The word ***'sea'*** in these verses is a scriptural reference to both "**oceans**" and "**seas**." The seas of the world are so enormous that even if every mammal on earth and every fish in the seas were to be killed and all the blood were to be drained into the oceans, it still wouldn't be sufficient to turn even one one-thousandth of the sea into blood, let alone one-third! The geometrical logic of that fact should be obvious. Furthermore, a precise interpretation of the scripture suggests that it will be the water being turned into blood that will be responsible for the creatures in the sea dying — not the other way around. What's more, the text clearly states that the effected waters will be turned into blood; they won't just become bloody.

But what does the word - "Sea" - actually mean?

There are a few who would have us believe that, when John wrote ***'sea'*** in these verses, he was referring specifically to the *Mediterranean Sea* and nothing more. However, if we accept that teaching, we'll soon run into serious obstacles while interpreting what John wrote about the next two trumpet-plagues. So, rather than jumping ahead into that unfamiliar territory to see why that's true, let's first see if we can find a precedent from within the previous text, where John used the same *Greek* word (*thalassa*) to indicate both "**oceans**" and "**seas**." Fortunately, this exact *Greek* word can be found in five previous verses.

- ❖ In Rev. 4:6 it is used to refer to the "**sea of glass**" before God's throne.
- ❖ In Rev. 5:13 it is used while referring to "**all the bodies of water on the planet**" — Hello!
- ❖ And in Rev. 7:1, 2 and 3 we find the words "**earth**" and "**sea**" being used three times to refer to "**all the land and water on earth.**"

That's enough precedent for me. But if you're still not convinced, not to worry; there are even stronger, more exciting scriptural clues around the corner.

A flaming mountain hits the Atlantic?

Rev. 8:9 ~ *continued*

We could only guess where this great mountain — ***'burning with fire'*** — will hit the earth (*assuming it hits all in one piece*), so let's not. Sufficient for our understanding of these end-time events is the knowledge that one-third of the waters on the planet will be affected by the impact, causing one-third of the creatures and ships in the oceans and seas to be destroyed, as one-third of the water is miraculously turned into blood. It certainly won't be the bloody water that will destroy one-third of the ships, but when that mountain-size meteor (*or whatever it is*) hits the seas, even if it first breaks into smaller pieces, it's likely to cause monstrously huge title waves, which will destroy sea fairing vessels and devastate coastal areas and harbors all around the globe. Heaven help those tragically defiant sailors who, despite the persistent warnings of God's two witnesses, will foolishly allow themselves to be trapped at sea when this burning mountain size meteor hits the earth. Jesus spoke generally about this event in one of His end-time addresses:

> *'And there shall be signs in the sun, and in the moon, and in the stars; and upon the earth distress of nations: with perplexity;* ***the sea and the waves roaring****; Men's hearts failing them for fear, and for looking after those things which are coming on the earth:* ***for the powers of heaven shall be shaken****.'*

Luke 21:25-26

Before we move on, it's important to understand . . . .

When reading Jesus' end-time discourses, we must remember not to extract chronological timelines or chains of events. Jesus' sermons were not necessarily given with the intent of enabling us to do so. Jesus often spoke of the "Day of the Lord" in general terms. Sometimes He prophesied of the future persecution of the early Church, the resurrection and rapture of the saints, and of His triumphant Second Coming all in the same address (*Mt. 24:1-30, 31-51*). Therefore, while studying Jesus' end-time teachings, it's important that we take into account the following fact:

> Although frequently misunderstood, according to Scripture, the "Day of the Lord" is actually a reference to a future period consisting of more than a thousand years.

As we make our way through the remainder of John's vision we will learn that the Day of the Lord will begin with the "catching-away" of the Church,[175] continue through the seven-year tribulation period and the millennial[176] period, and end with the "Great White Throne Judgment," which will occur immediately following the last physical day on earth. We'll discuss this in detail later.

Uh-oh, — I have a feeling some of our expedition buddies are starting to get a little riled, saying:

"Hey, the Day of the Lord is the return of Christ!"

That is, of course, correct, but the Day of the Lord is also a great deal more. If we had time to further digress and thoroughly study everything the Scriptures reveal about the Day of the Lord, we would find that particular day to be a very long day. Giving us a little insight into the length of that day, Peter wrote the following:

> *'But the day of the Lord will come* ***as a thief in the night****; in the which the heavens shall pass away with a great noise, and the elements shall melt with fervent heat,* ***the earth also and the works that are therein shall be burned up****.'*

2Pet. 3:10

[175] 1Th. 4:13-18, 5:1-3
[176] Rev. 19:1 thru 20:15

Peters preceding explanation of the Day of the Lord begins with a reference to the unpredictable day of the Rapture. Then, it continues right through the seven-year great tribulation period and the Millennial Period and concludes with a description of the total dissolution of the earth. Thus, Peter declared the Day of the Lord to be at least 1,007 years long. Therefore, according to Peter, the Day of the Lord includes much more than just Christ's triumphant return to earth.

~ *Will you please explain that?* ~

First of all, the fact that Jesus will return to earth at the end of the seven-year tribulation period has been clearly established throughout Scripture; therefore, the *"Second Coming of Christ"* will not occur unexpectedly, ***'as a thief in the night.'*** The spontaneous *"catching-away of the saints"* (*the Rapture—1Th. 4:13-18*), however, will definitely occur like a thief in the night. Consequently, since Peter clearly stated that the Day of the Lord must begin as unexpectedly as ***'as a thief in the night,'*** we can logically conclude that the Day of the Lord must begin with the Rapture, not the Second Coming of Christ. Secondly, during that particular "**day**" or "**period**" (*the Day of the Lord*), Peter also stated that the earth will completely melt away — dissolve! Thus, the Day of the Lord must be more than just a reference to Christ's Second Coming, because the earth won't be completely dissolved until the end of Christ's millennial reign on earth (*which will end 1,000 years after Jesus' Second Coming)*. This will all emerge from the text as we continue.

The Third Trumpet-plague

Rev. 8:10-11

> ***'And the third angel sounded, and there fell a great star from heaven, burning as it were a lamp, and it fell upon the <u>third</u> part of the <u>rivers</u>, and upon the <u>fountains of waters</u>;***
>
> ***And the name of the star is called <u>Wormwood</u>: and the <u>third</u> part of the waters became wormwood; and many men died of the waters, because they were made <u>bitter</u>.'***

At this point we still don't have any clear knowledge of how much time will pass between the unleashing of each of these trumpet-plagues. All we really know is that the first six trumpets will sound sometime during the first 3½ years. If, therefore, we were to spread these plagues out evenly, over the first 3½ years, the trumpets would continue to sound successively, about every five to six months, until the sounding of the final seventh trumpet, which John was told will sound immediately after God resurrects and calls His two witnesses back up to Heaven, at the start of the second half of the tribulation period. This means that God and His two witnesses will keep giving the rebellious inhabitants of the earth plenty of time after the sounding of each trumpet to repent before unleashing the next trumpet's dreadful calamity. Sadly, however, at least initially, it won't seem to matter. As we will soon see clearly stated, the Left-behinders will not repent until they've witnessed the divinely validating resurrection and ascension of God's two witnesses.

A great and bright Star hits the Earth

Rev. 8:10-11 ~ *continued*

When this third angel sounded his trumpet John saw what he described as a ***'great star'*** falling from heaven (*the sky, space*). What's most remarkable about this object is that it will burn ***'like a lamp.'*** When John witnessed the effects of the first two trumpets he saw ***'hail and fire mingled with blood'*** and ***'a great mountain burning with fire.'*** Each of which were markedly similar to this third meteor (*or whatever it will be*), yet John describes this particular falling object as having been something like a great lamp.

Whatever it was, it appeared to John to be luminous, possibly radioactive or at least capable of radiating its own internal heat. Either way, when it hits the earth's atmosphere it will apparently break-up and spread around the globe. Miraculously, God will divinely direct those fragments to land in preordained ***'rivers'*** and ***'fountains of waters,'*** which will render precisely one-third of the fresh water on earth undrinkable — "**bitter**." Therefore, while this third trumpet-plague's purpose will be to bring "**the remnant**" (*the last of the saints*) humbly to their knees, it will cause tens of millions, possibly even hundreds of millions to die, as desperate survivors all over the world reluctantly drink the bitter, contaminated water.

What's most horrific is the reality that, since those who'll die from these plagues will not have first accepted Christ, they'll have been (*as John was told in Rev. 6:8*) killed with "**death**." That means that they'll have no hope of ever being forgiven and, therefore, no hope of ever attaining eternal life. That's absolutely terrifying! And, regrettably, this will be true for every casualty during the first 3½ years of the tribulation period.

This brings up another point. I'm curious how many on our expedition have come to the conclusion, as have I, that there will not be 3½ years of "PEACE ON EARTH" during the first half of the seven-year tribulation period, contrary to the teaching of many scholars?

~ *Why do I ask this?* ~

For many years, Christians have mistakenly taught that the son of perdition (*most commonly referred to as "the anti-Christ"*) will sign a seven-year "peace-treaty" with Israel, which will indicate the start of the seven-year tribulation period. It has also been taught that, after 3½ years, this son of perdition will break this treaty, thus ending that peaceful era. While it is true that a seven-year *"covenant"* will be *"confirmed"* at the start of the tribulation period, there is no actual promise of "PEACE ON EARTH" as part of that covenant (*Dan. 9:27*). As we've already learned while trekking through the first eight chapters of John's Revelation vision, there will be absolutely no peace during the first half of the tribulation period, and very little, if any, real peace during the second half.

The kind of reasoning from which the 3½ years of peace teaching evolved could have only emerged amidst a radically severe attack of "**tunnel-vision**." It's definitely true that a seven-year treaty of sorts will be signed with Israel (*and many others—Dan. 9:27*) at or near the beginning of the tribulation period — perhaps necessitated by the global unrest and chaos that will ensue following the Rapture. However, as we've discovered, that treaty in no way indicates a subsequent 3½ year period of universal peace. As a matter of fact, it doesn't even indicate that there will be peace in Israel. Peace will exist, but only among the 144,000 newly born-again Jewish converts, who (*during the first 3½ years of the tribulation period*) will be serving God in a "Goshen-like"[177] existence on and, most logically, around the Temple Mount in Jerusalem.[178]

The Fourth Trumpet-plague

Rev. 8:12

> ***'And the fourth angel sounded, and the <u>third part</u> of the sun was smitten, and the <u>third part</u> of the moon, and the <u>third part</u> of the stars; so as the <u>third part</u> of them was darkened, and the day shone not for a <u>third part</u> of it, and the night likewise.'***

It's pretty easy, while reading about these trumpet-plagues, not to fully appreciate the compounding global impact that they'll have on the earth and its inhabitants. In addition to the universal chaos and worldwide environmental destruction that will have been caused by the Rapture, by the time this fourth angel finishes releasing his powerful plague, the world will be an absolute mess! All the green grass and a third of the trees will have been completely incinerated, and much of the air will be filled with

---

[177] (Ex. 8:22 thru 9:26) This will be revealed as we continue.

[178] We'll cover this in detail as we journey through the next few chapters of John's vision—Revelation Chapters 11 and 12.

chemically toxic smoke.[179] One-third of the oceans and seas will have been turned into blood, killing one-third of the creatures in the seas and destroying one-third of the ships. The insect populations (*e.g., flies and mosquitoes*), thanks to all that blood and putrefying flesh, will also have greatly multiplied. This will make the already noxious, barely breathable air absolutely reek with the smell of dead, rotting fish and sea mammals; not to mention the constant annoyance and spreading of diseases that all those bacteria breeding flies, mosquitoes, and other insects will facilitate.

In addition, one-third of the remaining drinkable water in the rivers, lakes, streams, and reservoirs will have become ***'bitter'*** (*i.e., it will have been rendered undrinkable by the sounding of the third trumpet*), killing hundreds of millions more and contaminating both fields and crops. And let's not forget that rain won't likely be in the forecast. So, after this fourth angel sounds his trumpet the already dismal state of the earth will get even worse, as one-third of the *sun*, *moon* and *stars* are smitten, causing them to emit and/or reflect one-third less heat and light.

The Lucky Ones

Rev. 8:12 ~ *continued*

For the slightly more fortunate survivors who'll be fighting for their lives on or near the equator, the sounding of the fourth trumpet-plague may not be immediately harmful. But, for those who will be trapped at higher latitudes or altitudes, the loss of heat and sunlight might prove to be instantly fatal. Less sunlight will rapidly cause the polar icecaps to become drastically enlarged, distressing global tidal activity, reshaping coastal regions and increasing glacier formation around the world. Snow storms and blizzards will occur in new locations and at lower altitudes everywhere, even in places where it had never before been possible. Many newly planted crops will immediately freeze in the fields, as will many animals and frail or newborn human survivors.

With no modern rapid-transportation still operational, millions who'll have been stranded in the extreme northern and southern regions will quickly die, due to their inability to migrate to lower, warmer climates. Thus, the surviving population of the world will forcibly become "compressed," as those in extremely exposed locations are forced to migrate to less affected areas. This will radically intensify the already volatile social

---

[179] Given that by this time more than a year will have passed since the first angel will have sounded his trumpet, when this fourth angel is ready to sound, at least some of the green grass will probably have regrown. But, we must acknowledge that, since God's two witnesses will have power to keep it from raining during their entire ministry, regrowth of any kind will likely be slow and gradual at best.

climate, especially in highly populated regions. If, currently (*under pre-tribulation period conditions*), both men and women can, with slight provocation, be moved to selfishly exhibit their more primal instincts to the point of "going-to-blows" over something as petty as a parking space, what do you suppose they'll be willing to do during the tribulation period, when their only chance to survive the night may hinge on their ability to acquire a warmer blanket, a cup of untainted water, or simply a dry piece of cardboard on which to lie?

~What will the full geological impact of this plague be? ~

Not being a geologist or an oceanographer, I couldn't even begin to assess the total, global affect that this plague will have on the earth, on animals and marine life, on the global tidal flow, or on humans in general. One thing I do know, however, having no electricity with which to generate either heat or light, it's not only going to get very "**cold**" and "**dark**," it's also going to be really scary as well! From the moment the fourth trumpet begins to sound until the end of the tribulation period (*when the Lord will begin to unleash His vengeful plagues of wrath upon the earth*), both day and night will be at least one-third colder and darker, and the surface of the earth will never be the same.

Chapter 18

Three Truly Terrifying Words

By the time the fourth trumpet-plague will have finished sounding, the formerly beautiful earth will look scarred and ravaged, like some sort of distant, bloodied, battle-ground planet in the throes of having barely survived hundreds of years of constant, full-scale, interplanetary war. And, with the Left-behinders still defying God's patient, persistent call to repentance, the Lord will have no choice but to give the world an even more severe taste of the inescapable suffering that will ultimately become the eternal fate of all who continue choosing to rebel against His will.

Rev. 8:13

John watched as an angel, flying through the midst of Heaven, loudly proclaimed:

> ***'Woe, woe, woe, to the inhabiters of the earth by reason of the other voices of the trumpet of the three angels, which are yet to sound!'***

It's doubtful that anybody on earth will actually be able to see or hear this angel's warning, but it won't really matter. God's two witnesses will have clearly warned the Left-behinders about the severe increase in the intensity of the coming plagues.

The Fifth Trumpet-plague

Rev 9:1

> ***'And the fifth angel sounded, and I saw a star*** *(an angel)* ***fall from heaven unto the earth: and to him was given the key to the bottomless pit.'***

I find this verse uniquely interesting, because in the same verse the words *angel* and *star* are both used in reference to angels. When we get to the end of the tribulation period (*Rev. 20:1-3*), before Jesus begins His one thousand year reign on earth, an angel will appear again, also having a key, and he'll use that key to bind Satan in that bottomless pit for a thousand years. That angel may actually be the same angel John saw falling as a star from heaven in the preceding verse, but we have no sure way of proving that to be the case. What's important for us to grasp at this point in John's vision is that angels are powerful spiritual beings; therefore, like God, they're simply not bound by mortal, earthly constraints. In fact, it's entirely possible (*likely even, though not provable*) that, in Rev. 8:10-11, after the sounding of the third trumpet, when John saw the great "**star**" falling from heaven and burning as it were a lamp, he may have actually been witnessing another angelic being, just like the angel John recorded seeing here.

The Bottomless Pit

Rev. 9:2-6

'And he opened the bottomless pit; and there arose a smoke out of the pit, as the smoke of a great furnace; and the sun and the air were darkened by reason of the smoke of the pit.

And there came out of the smoke locust upon the earth: and unto them was given power, as the scorpions of the earth have power.

And it was commanded them that they should not hurt the grass of the earth, neither any green thing, neither any tree; but only those men which have not the seal of God in their foreheads.'

'And to them it was given that they should not kill them, but that they should be tormented five months: and their torment was as the torment of a scorpion, when he striketh a man.

And in those days shall men seek death, and shall not find it; and shall desire to die, and death shall flee from them.'

If you weren't sure why I used terms like *"severe"* and *"inescapably agonizing"* when I alluded to the aftermath of this fifth trumpet-plague, it should be quite clear now. When this ***'star'*** (*angel*) actually descends from Heaven and spiritually unlocks that massive earthly cauldron of evil in the heart of the earth, known in Scripture as the *"bottomless pit,"*[180] he will quite literally be unleashing "HELL" upon the face of the earth! As those devilish, locust-like creatures eagerly surge up and out with the smoke from the pit, they'll be focused on fulfilling their only command. That command will be to brutally torment every stiff-necked, self-willed inhabitant of the earth who doesn't have the seal of God on their foreheads. That

[180] That which is spiritual (*for example, demons*) can occasionally manifest physically, as do angels. Therefore, the spiritual beings in the bottomless pit may not always be visible to humans, but God can allow that to change in an instant.

means that everybody but the 144,000 Jewish servants will be excruciatingly tormented for five full months!

~ *Are you actually saying that Hell is in the heart of the earth?* ~

Surprisingly, though it has been estimated that as many as eight out of ten North Americans believe in a physically real Heaven, many don't firmly believe in a spiritually/physically real Hell. And, while many true Christians do believe (*as they should*) in a future lake of fire and brimstone, which will be somewhere in outer-darkness,[181] many don't believe that Hell (*spiritually or physically*) is currently within the heart of the earth. That's not hard to understand. The idea of several billions of lost souls actually being tormented somewhere within the earth's core is barely fathomable, yet verses like those we've just read (*Rev. 9:1-2*) are hard to ignore.

ꟷ Illuminating scriptures about the bottomless pit: ꟷ

Isa. 5:14, 14:9-19, **Ez.** 28:8-19, **Rev.** 20:1-3, **Num**.16:30-33, **Job** 17:16, 33:24-, **Psa**. 9:15, 28:1, 30:33, 55:23

When God, through His two witnesses, gives the command and this fifth angel sounds his trumpet, that dreadfully dark, locust-filled smoke will most definitely surge up and out — *"as if from a great furnace"* — and begin ominously towering high over the earth, exactly as John witnessed. Bursting out from the deep recesses of their bottomless prison, those demonic locusts will swiftly ascend, in a flurry, and aggressively begin encircling the globe. Hence, from that massive bottomless hole somewhere in the earth's crust, these wicked beings will eagerly hunt down and violently attack only humans wherever they'll be futilely attempting to hide. Once that happens, any questions the Left-behinders may have had regarding the actual existence of a physical Hell in the heart of the earth or as to the reality of a demonically inhabited "bottomless pit" will instantly vanish!

~ *Will anyone be immune to this plague?* ~

According to John's record of events, only the 144,000 Jewish servants will have God's protective "**seal**" in their foreheads, and there's simply no scriptural indication that anyone else will have been sealed before the sounding of this fifth trumpet. Though we (*from our mortally limited perspective*) may wish to believe otherwise, the Scriptures just don't support the assertion that anyone other than the 144,000 Jewish servants and the two prophets will be immune to the locusts' relentless attack.

---

[181] Mt. 8:12, 22:13, 25:30, Rev. 19:20, 20:10-15

Moreover, while it's been commonly assumed, nowhere in Scripture are we told that during the tribulation period *"new-believers in Christ"* will be instantly sealed in order to protect them from any of these plagues (*as will have been the 144,000 Jewish converts—Rev. 7:1-4*). I realize that various renowned authors, teachers, and pastors, whom we all love and admire, have taught this as though it were provable, and have, therefore, incorrectly anticipated the immediate repentance of thousands of Left-behinders, but, as hard as it may be to accept, no truly substantive scriptural support can be found for that teaching.

Instead, John's vision will clearly reveal that, while the son of perdition powerfully goes about deceiving and subjugating the world to his demonic authority, the Left-behinders will continue in their obstinance, being either too stubborn and/or confused to repent, which explains why they'll have been left-behind in the first place. Let's face it, as I stated earlier, if these Left-behinders couldn't be convinced to repent prior to the Rapture, with both the Church and the Holy Spirit vigorously working in a unified effort to reach them, how hard do you suppose it will be for God's two tribulation witnesses to persuade them to repent after the Church has been taken up to Heaven and the Holy Spirit has been pulled back (*2Th. 2:7)?* It's certainly not going to be easy, not even for God's two witnesses!

Once Satan is allowed to empower the iniquitous son of perdition to perform astounding acts of deception in direct opposition to the divinely inspired plagues of God's two witnesses, people on earth are going to quickly become confused.[182] Jesus plainly warned that even those who will fear God enough to listen to the prophets' salvation message will be uncertain as to who they should believe. Throughout the entire ministry of God's two witnesses, the son of perdition will be working against them, feeding the Left-behinders whatever lies and half-truths are necessary to get them to believe and follow him instead of God's two prophets.

Since, today, most of the world's population is already eager to believe just about anything other than the truth, most of the son of perdition's tribulation period work is already being accomplished. This is precisely why it's so important that we neither faint nor become weary[183] in our effort to fulfill Jesus' mandate[184] of globally sharing the Gospel message. While we (*the Church*) are still here, we are powerfully emboldened by the Holy Spirit to fulfill Christ's command. Let's not forget what we learned earlier. Speaking generally about the Church and also specifically about this future period of "great deception," which will immediately precede the tribulation period and continue through it, Jesus said the following:

---

182 2Th. 2:3-11, Mt. 24:15-24

183 Gal. 6:6-9, 2Th. 3:13-15, 1Pet. 2:15

184 Mt.28:18-20, Mk. 16:15-18

*'For there shall arise false Christs, and **false prophets**,*[185] *and shall shew great signs and wonders; insomuch that, **if it were possible, they shall deceive the very elect**.'*[186]

Mat. 24:24

Imagine that you had never read the book of Revelation, heard anything about the son of perdition or God's two tribulation period prophets, or been taught anything regarding the end-times. What if you knew nothing about the resurrection and rapture of the saints, and yet, instantly and without any warning you were to horrifyingly find yourself "left-behind" after hundreds of millions of people, from all over the world, inexplicably disappeared? How baffling would it be to suddenly be faced with the realization that you've become helplessly trapped in the middle of a chaotic world, where discerning the difference between "GOOD" and "EVIL" has become nearly impossible — with Satan and his little *"puppet-dictator"* (*the son of perdition*) performing devilishly deceptive miracles on one side and God's two globally prominent prophets preaching the truth and unleashing powerfully persuasive plagues on the other? It's not hard to understand why it will be so difficult for "**the remnant**" to eventually make the right decision and repent. And we should keep in mind that the few who will make up that final remnant of saints will likely be a very small minority among billions of lost and bewildered souls.[187]

These will be no ordinary locusts!

Rev. 9:7-8

'And the shapes of the locusts were like unto horses prepared unto battle; and on their heads were as it were crowns like gold, and their faces were as the faces of men.

And they had hair as the hair of women, and their teeth were as the teeth of lions.

---

[185] Thousands of false teachers and false prophets already exist, but in this verse Jesus is referring to a specific seven year period of extreme demonic activity that will be so powerfully deceptive that it would even fool Christians.

[186] Based on Jesus' words, the only way the elect (*i.e., the saints*) will not be deceived is if they are not exposed to the deception; therefore, it's possible that Jesus proved the pre-tribulation rapture interpretation with just these few words.

[187] While the word *"remnant"* may seem to refer to a small group of future believers, we actually have no way of knowing how many Left-behinders will end up repenting after they witness the two prophets' deaths, resurrection, and glorious ascension into Heaven—Rev. 11:9-19. It could be a vast multitude or just a few thousand weary souls—Rev. 15:1-4.

'And they had breastplates, as it were breastplates of iron; and the sound of their wings was as the sound of chariots of many horses running to battle.

And they had tails like unto scorpions, and there were stings in their tails: and their power was to hurt men five months.'

Not only will the sky grow hauntingly dark and ominous as these locusts emerge but the terrifying sound of this demonic army of horse-shaped, scorpion-tailed, lion-toothed, human-faced, long-haired locusts from Hell will be nearly deafening! Witnesses who've endured just an ordinary plague of locusts have testified that the darkening sky and low, progressive roar of an approaching swarm can be absolutely terrifying. Try to imagine the escalating, thunderous roar that will precede the arrival of this seemingly infinite, demonically charged swarm of locusts — a swarm so perniciously ravenous and aggressive that it will eagerly continue rushing up and out of that colossal bottomless-pit until its numbers are sufficiently vast to torturously assault the entire population of the world all at once!

Not even Death will be a means of Escaping

The very old and the weak and sickly will probably not have survived even the first few months of the tribulation period, but if they've made it to this point, they're going to be around for at least 150 more of the longest, most miserably excruciating days in history.[188] We have no way of comparing the suffering of this first "**woe**" plague to the unbelievable agony that our righteous big brother Job endured, but unlike Job's suffering, this plague will be absolutely inescapable. Not even suicide will be a means of escape! In fact, even if one of these Left-behinders were to take the advice of Job's wife (*Job 2:9*) and irreverently curse God, hoping to provoke Him into slaying them, it just won't work. Once this excruciating, five month, 24 hour a day plague begins, there will be no way of avoiding the misery.

When those scorpion-tailed embodiments of pure evil arrive and begin their ferocious attack, sleep will in all probability become a matter of having luckily passed out! That's the whole point of this plague. God will be forcing the Left-behinders to sample just a little taste of the eternal suffering and interminable exhaustion for which they're certainly destined should they continue abusing their right of "free-will" by foolishly rejecting His plan for their eternal redemption. Therefore, in order for this fifth trumpet-plague to be a realistic taste of eternal damnation, those who experience the suffering must have no-way of escaping the extreme agony

---

[188] If He wills, God can enable even the weakest Left-behinder to survive long enough to repent and be saved.

it will cause. Consequently, when people try to kill themselves or just waste away and die, according to what we just read from John's vision, God won't let them.

What's even more horrifying is the reality that by preventing the Left-behinders from dying God will actually be doing them a favor. Think about it. If God were to allow them to die, prior to having repented, their agony would instantly increase, as their souls would begin swiftly slipping irrevocably into Hell. Thus, for those individuals, there would no longer be any hope of ever repenting and escaping perpetual damnation.

Is God truly long-suffering?

Difficult as it is for us to respect our unrepentant loved ones' right to wander foolishly through their spiritually blind lives, failing daily to recognize the thin, eternally dangerous path of destruction on which they're treading, how upsetting do you suppose it will be for our Father in Heaven when He eventually has no choice but to force-feed this five month long sample of "HELL ON EARTH" to our future brothers and sisters in Christ and the rest of the rebellious, left-behind world? And yet, as much as God will detest doing it, without this severe reality check, none of the Left-behinders would have the slightest hope of ever wising-up and accepting Christ.

~ But this seems flat-out cruel, and I wouldn't call five full months of inescapable, unrelenting, hellish torment just a reality check! ~

If you agree with the preceding statement, you'll get no argument from me. But, just to put everything into its proper perspective, five months of tormenting locusts will be no comparison to what being eternally separated from God and cast into the eternal lake of fire, where the soul never dies and the agony never ceases, would be! Take a look at the following eternal timeline and see if you agree:

THE FIRST DOT MARKS THE BEGINNING OF ETERNITY ....

.... *By the way, each dot represents 1,000 years in the eternal lake of fire, and, horrifically, these dots will never end...................*

.... ⟹

"WHAT'S FIVE MONTHS OF ANYTHING WHEN COMPARED TO THAT?!"

These Locusts will have a Destructive Leader

Rev. 9:11

> ***'And they** (the locusts) **had a king over them, which is the angel of the bottom less pit, whose name in the He'-brew tongue is A-bad'-don** (destruction), **but in the Greek tongue hath his name A-pol'-ly-on** (destroyer).'*

There is no reason to conclude that this demonic *"angel of the bottom-less-pit"* (*Apollyon*) is actually Satan. Being *"the prince of the power of the air"* here on earth,[189] Satan currently rules over many powerful fallen-angels and apparently allows some of them to assume positions of authority beneath him. Thus, this *"angel of the bottomless-pit"* is likely just one of many such demonic spirits.

Unrelenting - now that's the word!

What if you were a terrified survivor of the first four trumpet-plagues and now, after having endured two horrific years of fighting and foraging for your food, water, and basic existence, you were to suddenly hear the bone chilling trumpet-blast that you've been warned will signify the beginning of the first of three radically more devastating plagues?[190] Having only barely survived the first couple of years, what if you were a bewildered and still unrepentant Left-behinder when the first of these three "woe-plagues" (*Rev. 8:13*) was about to begin?

> ❧ Let's try for just a moment to imagine the icy-terror that will seize the heart of every wearied and bewildered Left-behinder once that fifth angel's trumpet has sounded and the first of these three horrific "woe-plagues" has begun. ❧

A few minutes as a terrified Left-behinder . . .

Hiding in a building or a cave won't stop them. Even if you're one of the few who'll consider themselves lucky to have found a missile-silo or a bank vault in which to hide, you'll still need fresh air, food and water. More importantly, you better believe that if God (*because of His great love for you*) intends to use these next two radically more severe "woe-plagues" to

---

[189] Eph. 2:2-3, Rev. 12:3-13, 2Pt. 2:4

[190] We have no way of knowing if the trumpets will be audible on earth, but, if they are, hearing them will most assuredly be a terrifying experience!

spiritually wake you up before it's ultimately too-late to repent, you're not going to be able to escape any of the agonizing torment of these plagues, no matter how well you hide! God loves you far too much to allow that.

As I said earlier, the Lord has designed these powerful "woe-plagues" to give you and all the other terrified, but still unrepentant, Left-behinders a tiny sample of eternity in Hell. If that's where you ultimately choose to end up (*and presently the choice is yours*), the never-ending sorrow, the soul-wrenching hopelessness, and the eternal loneliness you'll feel will be the result of having realized too-late that Satan's plan of drawing your attention away from what was truly important (*during your short time on earth*) worked! Using your own selfish desire and prideful nature against you, Satan will have successfully kept you from recognizing that there is no more significant goal in life than that of attaining your prepaid ticket to Heaven through Christ!

Terrified and Waiting For the Coming Plague

Chilled to the core by the sound of it, you suddenly hear the powerful blast of the fifth angel's trumpet as it reverberates through the sky above and the terror of it leaves you shaking so violently that you're helpless to control the painful muscle spasms now sending tremors throughout your body.[191] Having fearfully buried yourself under whatever debris you could scavenge, you futilely death-grip the smelly old piece of tarp you've been using as a covering and desperately rack your brain, trying to recall the exact words of the prophets' warning:

"The locusts will have the appearance of horses dressed for battle and powerful, stinging, scorpion-like tails. On their chests they'll appear to have breastplates of iron and on their heads crowns like gold."

Oddly enough, their horse-like bodies and scorpion-like tails aren't the physical characteristics you find most distressing. What's most troubling, the thought you just can't shake from your mind's eye is the knowledge that those locusts will have hair like women, teeth-like lions, and faces like little-men! Envisioning little evil creatures with human-like features actually being released from some deep, dark place within the heart of the earth absolutely terrifies you! Imagining just one freakish little lion-toothed, human-faced locust actually landing on your chest and arrogantly

---

[191] We should reiterate that John doesn't indicate whether or not those on earth will actually be able to hear the sounding of the angel's trumpets before each of the seven trumpet-plagues are released. It's possible that those trumpets will only be heard by those in Heaven.

glaring, hatefully, with piercing human-like eyes straight up at you turns your already frayed nerves to mush. Practically insane with fear, you scream out:

"This just can't be happening!"

But it is happening! And, while that terrifyingly surreal image is still fresh in your mind, an even greater reality suddenly grips you. Like ice water being forced through your veins, you chillingly realize that, when that hellishly vicious little bundle of demonic torment inevitably arrives with his scorpion-like tail poised threateningly up to strike, he won't be alone! No, not by a long shot! He'll only be the first of hundreds of billions of wicked little demonic creatures of misery. And, in a few minutes, when that haunting image in your mind actually becomes a reality, the five month long fifth trumpet-plague will have only just begun. Thus, totally helpless and nearly out of your mind with fear, you wonder:

'How can I possibly survive for five full months?'

The whole disturbing thought is way more than you can handle. Desperate in your attempt to push the image from your mind, you hastily decide to use the precious little time you have left to try and find a thicker, yet still pliable, covering with which to protect yourself from the painful stings of the coming locusts. Unsuccessful (*as you expected*) and the sky growing even darker, you again wrap yourself up from head to toe and wait! Quivering so fiercely that you find it impossible to calm the rippling spasms in your stomach, you're now learning how truly painful spiritual fear can be, and the plague hasn't even reached you. Before today you'd have said nothing could make you forget your gnawing hunger pains, but how wrong you were. Nerves shot and stomach knotted, you'd gladly give your last morsel of bread to only have hunger about which to worry now.

Risking a peek at the horizon, you carefully peel back just a small opening around your eyes and see that the sky is growing eerily dark from mostly one direction. Curiously petrified, you watch as, in just a matter of seconds, the thickest, blackest smoke you've ever seen envelopes more than half of the visible atmosphere. Strangely, it appears to be overshadowing only areas of human habitation. Now, a low, guttural reverberation has begun to grow stronger and stronger beneath you.

'What's that sound?'

Another chill runs up your spine as you horrifyingly remember having foolishly scoffed at something the two prophets said during their most recent call to repentance. They warned that the fifth trumpet-plague would originate from a place deep within the heart of the earth, a place they referred to as "THE BOTTOMLESS-PIT."

The memory of that warning quickly paralyzes you, as the menacing dark cloud you were watching rapidly approaches and continues to totally devour the sky. It's becoming perfectly clear that that cloud is directly related to the powerful, subterranean vibration you feel growing stronger and stronger beneath you. That monstrous sound is nothing less than the powerful reverberation of countless billions of locusts ferociously escaping their evil, bottomless prison. Like thousands of mighty, high-speed trains rushing up towards the earth's crust from deep within its core, the locusts are headed up and out in a hurry! Beyond panicked, again, you cry out:

"They're coming, and their coming fast!"

The unmistakable sound of Left-behinders being torturously attacked can now be faintly heard in the distance, and their tormented screams are growing louder and louder with every passing second. That can mean only one thing. The locusts must be getting much closer! Easily penetrating your tattered, hole-riddled canvas, the thick, death-like stench of sulfuric smoke from the bottomless-pit has now engulfed the air around you. You thought the stench of the bloody waters and dead fish from the 2nd and 3rd plagues was nauseating, but this is ten times worse! This disgusting odor is so powerfully pungent that you immediately begin to uncontrollably gag and dry-heave. Like being buried alive, you're now feeling the weight of spiritually oppressive darkness pushing so stiflingly down on you that if you were weaponless, stripped bare, and abandoned in a den of ravenous lions you couldn't feel more vulnerable than you do at this moment! And, on top of it all, a thunderous, painfully piercing metallic roar is mysteriously preceding the approaching cloud of locusts.

'What's that horrible, piercing sound?'

Then it hits you. The prophets said:

"The locusts will have breastplates like iron."

That's something you certainly hadn't expected. Hiding in the cellar of a scrap metal yard while a massive tornado ripped through overhead couldn't be more deafening! Again, you vainly struggle trying to block out the awful noise, while, at the same time, wrestling to be certain that every inch of your body is covered. Completely out of control, you scream:

"They're here!"

The agonizing, unrelenting screams of tens of thousands of tormented Left-behinders can be heard all around you. And now that you can actually feel what must be hundreds of those little, evil, demonic beasts landing on your tarp, a sobering reality grips you; there's just no way to stay covered for five full months! Pure, undiluted wickedness has physically overtaken you and every other Left-behinder on the planet, and the first of 150 days of literal "HELL-ON-EARTH" has only just begun!

The preceding scenario is merely a fabrication, not an interpretation. Its sole purpose is to aid us in our attempt to imagine what life on earth will be like for the Left-behinders after the first of three "woe-plagues" has begun. That having been said, I don't believe this scenario to be an over-dramatization of the sheer agony and terror that those on earth will experience once the fifth angel has sounded his trumpet and the fifth trumpet-plague has begun.

Chapter 19

An Hour, a Day, a Month, and a Year

Rev. 9:12

> ***'One <u>woe</u> is past; and, behold, there come <u>two woes</u> more hereafter.'***

If the first five trumpet-plagues are to be unleashed over reasonably equal intervals (*and we have no way of knowing if that will be the case*), then roughly two and a half years will pass before the first "woe-plague" ends and the demonic, scorpion-tailed locusts from the bottomless pit finish their five month long attack on the inhabitants of the earth. Once they do, it will be time for the second "woe-plague" to begin.

Rev. 9:13-15

> ***'And the sixth angel sounded, and I heard a voice from the four horns of the golden altar which is before God, Saying to the sixth angel which had the trumpet, <u>Loose the four angels which are bound in the great river Euphrates</u>.***
>
> ***And the four angels were loosed, which were prepared for <u>an hour</u>, and <u>a day</u>, and <u>a month</u>, and <u>a year</u>, for to slay the third part of men.'***

By using the information found in the preceding verses and counting backwards from the end of this second "**woe**" (*Rev. 11:14*), we can reasonably conclude that when this sixth angel's trumpet begins to sound the Left-behinders will be somewhere in the middle of their 29th or 30th month of unspeakable suffering and carnage.

~ Wait; how did you come to that conclusion? ~

First of all, it's important to recognize that we are not attempting to create a daily timeline of tribulation events. We could never confidently accomplish that task without first knowing the exact day when the tribulation period will begin and the precise hour when the abomination of desolation[192] will take place. Our goal is simply to use the information within the text to achieve a basic understanding and approximate timeline of the most impactive tribulation events. Claiming to be able to achieve anything more would be a mistake. That having been said, we do know that the son of perdition will make a seven-year covenant with Israel (*and many others*)[193] at the beginning of the seven-year tribulation period. Then, after only 3½ years, he'll break that covenant by invading Jerusalem, killing God's two witnesses, and desecrating the new Third Temple.

In **Rev. 11:3-14**, we'll soon see that John was told that God's two witnesses will prophesy 1,260 days.[194] Afterward, they'll be killed and, 3½ days later, ascend into Heaven, followed by an earthquake in Jerusalem and the repentance of "**the remnant**." This will bring an end to the sixth trumpet-plague — the second of the three "**woes**."

The Sixth Trumpet

Rev. 9:13-15 ~ *continued*

Interpreting the first five trumpet-plagues was fairly easy and straightforward. This sixth trumpet-plague, however, is a different story entirely. Thus far we've been careful not to allow ourselves the irreverent use of supposition while endeavoring to understand John's vision. The simple truth is even those who will be here to experience this deadly sixth plague will not likely fully understand what's happening when it happens!

~ *So where does that leave us?* ~

---

[192] The abomination of desolation is the day that will mark the middle of the tribulation period, when the son of perdition will break his covenant with Israel, kill God's two witnesses (*and most likely the 144,000*), enter the Temple, desecrate it, and proclaim himself to be God — Dan. 9:27, Zec. 14:1-2, Mt. 24:15-21,22-30, Mk. 13:14-25, Luke 21:20-26, 2Th. 2:3-4-12.

[193] Dan. 9:27

[194] Here's a little clarification for nerds like me: Biblically speaking, we're talking about a 360 day year, not 365. Therefore, one year equals 360 days, and one month equals 30 days. Thus, we know that 3½ years equals 1,260 days. Hence, our rough time-line is calculated as follows: 1,260 days (*the length of the two witnesses' ministry before being killed*) plus 3½ days (*the time between the death of the two witnesses and the end of the sixth trumpet-plague*) equals 1,263½ days. Therefore, if we count backwards, subtracting the 391 days (*the length of the sixth plague {an hour, and a day, and a month, and a year}*) from the 1,263½ days (*leaving off the extra hour*), we get approximately 872½ days. Now, if we divide the 872½ days into 30 day months, we find that the sixth plague (*the second "woe"*) will begin sometime between the 28th and 30th months of the tribulation period. Hopefully that helps, but it's neither important nor precise.

The wisest thing to do after praying for the Holy Spirit's help when we're faced with the task of determining which part of a prophecy *"is being," "has been"* or *"is yet to be"* revealed is to extract from the text only that which is clearly evident and filter the remainder with logic. So let's begin with **Rev. 9:13-15**. After the sixth angel sounded his trumpet, John heard a voice from the golden altar before God's throne give the sixth angel the following command:

> ***'. . . Loose** (unbind) **the <u>four angels</u> which are <u>bound</u> in the great river Euphrates.'***

I could be mistaken, but I can't recall any heavenly hosts (*angels*) ever having been bound. Only the insane, the rebellious, or the disobedient need to be bound; therefore, I doubt anyone would consider us presumptuous for inferring that these four angels must be four *"fallen-angels"* who've been bound and are presently being reserved solely for the purpose of accomplishing this future lethal and destructive plague.[195]

Will God give total control to the son of perdition?

If John had heard the command to — ***'loose the four angels'*** — come from Satan (*down on earth*), rather than from Heaven, our view of the resulting deaths of one-third of the earth's population would, of necessity, be altered. However, as John witnessed, the command will come directly from the altar before God's throne. Therefore, given the fact that during the first 3½ years of the tribulation period God will be unleashing one trumpet-plague after another (*through His two witnesses*), it's certainly logical for us to consider the probability of God using these deaths as a powerful, final warning — intended solely for the purpose of persuading the surviving Left-behinders to repent. Let's face it, even when God does choose to pull back His earthly authority and allow the son of perdition to rule the world, He will still (*as He always has*) maintain complete control of earthly events. The very fact that we're reading about these future tribulation events prior to their occurrence is proof of this.

Not a hair from our heads or a sparrow from a tree falls to the ground without God's foreknowledge.[196] Therefore, since God's two prophets will

---

[195] FOOD FOR THOUGHT: Since the original location of the Euphrates River was most likely changed between the years 1,656 and 1,658 (*when the flood waters were upon the earth*), we don't actually know how long these four *"fallen-angels"* have been bound (*Gen. 2:14 and Gen. 6, 7 and 8*). NOTE: Year zero would begin with the week of creation and count forward towards the year of the flood. Researching this opens a truly amazing and accurate study, which can be calculated using the information recorded in Genesis 5:1 thru 9:29.

[196] Mt. 10:29-30

still be in control when this sixth plague is unleashed, it's also logical for us to consider the likelihood that, with the sounding of this sixth trumpet, God's two witnesses may be unleashing their final plague, in hopes of persuading the stubborn, still unrepentant "**remnant**" to repent.[197] That prospect would fit the pattern of the first five plagues perfectly!

An army of "200,000,000" Killer-horsemen

Rev. 9:16-19

> ***'And the number of the army of horsemen were two hundred thousand thousand: and I heard the number of them.***
>
> ***And thus I saw the horses in the vision, and them that sat on them, having breastplates of fire, and of jacinth, and of brimstone*** *(deep-red, almost black)****: and the heads of the horses were as the heads of lions; and out of their mouths issued fire and smoke and brimstone.***
>
> ***By these three was the third part of men killed, by the fire and by the smoke and by the brimstone, which issued out of their mouths.***
>
> ***For their power is in their mouth, and in their tails: for their tails were like unto serpents, and had heads, and with them they do hurt.***

The obvious question is: *"Just what is this demonically commanded army of 200,000,000 killer-horsemen, and from where will they come?"* This sixth plague will kill one out of every three survivors on earth, and before this second "**woe**" is over, even God's two witnesses will have been killed and resurrected (*though not by this plague*).

So - who are these evil horsemen?

Just because God knows when each hair on our head will fall to the ground doesn't mean that He actually plucks them from our head! That is to say, God sometimes allows calamity to come about through natural causes or through the existence of evil in order to accomplish His divine plan, and He will certainly be doing just that during this seven-year tribulation period. These destructive demonically led horsemen could actually be supernatural embodiments of the powers of darkness. Thus, God may release them Himself,[198] intending to force "**the remnant**" to either repent

[197] Absolute proof that no one has repented will soon emerge.
[198] We must remember that it is Christ Jesus who controls the keys to the "bottomless-pit," not Satan!

or die. Let's not forget that these 200,000,000 killer horsemen will be released by one of God's Heavenly hosts (*an angel—Rev. 9:14-16*).

And — "NO" — I haven't been watching too much Sci-Fi!

During this period the demonic powers of darkness[199] will be violently unleashed upon the earth, and these end-time events will be like nothing the earth has ever experienced. Hence, these four fallen-angels will have been prepared to slay a third of the earth's surviving inhabitants (*Rev. 9:15*), and they'll do this by empowering 200 million horsemen to kill, using – *fire, smoke and brimstone (sulfur)*. Therefore, that being the case, the unleashing of these four fallen-angels from the great Euphrates River will be a prime example of God's using the powers of darkness to accomplish His will? We must remember that when this plague is unleashed it will be by the power of God, through His two witnesses. And, just moments before this plague ends, the very last of the saints will repent, and, shortly afterwards, the analogous "Door of Salvation" will immediately slam shut!

I don't wish to digress, but the story of our beloved brother Job[200] is another prime example of God having used Satan and his demonic cohorts to bring about His divine will. In fact, if we chose to do so, we could bring to light several other occasions during which God usurped His divine authority over the powers of darkness in order to accomplish His will. Is it possible that we've already forgotten the relentless demonic torment that followed the sounding of the fifth angel's trumpet as the first of these three "**woes**" began to take effect? From where did those terrifying demonic locusts come? That's right! They came from the bottomless pit!

~ How do these events align with the allegorical portion of John's vision (the preview) in Rev. 6:1-17? ~

It's times like these when the brilliant manner through which God revealed this vision to John really shines. By first giving John a condensed, chronological "**preview**" of the entire tribulation period in **Rev. 6:1-17**, God has wisely provided us with an accurate timeline of tribulation events. Thus, if we view the length of this sixth plague (*which, we've been told, will be a year, a month, a day and an hour*) in the light of our chronologically correct timeline from **Rev. 6:1-17**, we'll be able to get a clearer view of just how this vast, 200,000,000 strong army of killer-horsemen will fit into the whole seven-year tribulation period picture.

---

[199] Eph. 6:12-17

[200] Job 1:1-22

Let's not forget the man with the bow on the white horse

When God gave John the allegorical preview of the tribulation period in **Rev. 6:1-17**, it began with a man on a white horse going forth – ***'conquering, and to conquer'*** – immediately after the sudden rapture of the saints:

> ***'. . . and he that sat on him had a bow; and a crown was given unto him: and he went forth conquering, and to conquer.'***

We need to remember that as John's **Rev. 6:1-17** tribulation preview reveals, the man on the white horse (*the son of perdition*) will begin his surge toward world domination at the beginning of the tribulation period. And, although John also witnessed him being given a crown (*signifying a limited measure of authority*) and carrying a bow (*but apparently no arrows — possibly indicating that he will not initially be given full reign on the earth*), it will actually be God and His two witnesses who'll be controlling even the powers of darkness during the first half of the tribulation period.

Satan may very well be the leader of the rulers of darkness here on earth, but he is nothing more than a *"puppet-on-strings"* to God. What's more, Satan didn't sneak into the Garden of Eden without God's foreknowledge when he tempted Adam and Eve; it was all part of God's eternal plan. Likewise, when God allows these four fallen-angels to orchestrate the killing of one-third of the earth's population, in spite of how merciless that reality may sound, it will also still be part of God's perfect plan.

What about the son of perdition's army of Followers?

When the sixth trumpet sounds, the son of perdition will have already been ***'going forth conquering and to conquer'*** for about 2½ years. Therefore, it does seem at least possible that by the time this sixth trumpet-plague begins the son of perdition could have enlisted and organized hundreds of millions of followers as part of his demonically inspired army. And yet, while that may be true, it doesn't necessarily follow that the 200 million killer-horsemen in John's vision will be human. Before we, in our eagerness to claim to have properly interpreted this prophecy, choose to just *"lazily-embrace"* or *"wearily-cling-to"* the path with which we're most familiar, let's first dutifully consider a few essential facts.

200,000,000 - now that's a lot of horsemen!

Rev. 9:13-15 ~ *continued*

For more than thirty years I've heard it taught that China could easily mount an army large enough to fulfill this prophecy. Whether that's true or not, as of 2012, just the countries that make up the Asian continent comprise more than 4 billion people — roughly 60% of the earth's population. Therefore, if the scripture simply stated that, from the start of the tribulation period, the son of perdition will ***'go forth conquering and to conquer,'*** uniting the world, as he builds an army of 200,000,000 soldiers (*instead of horsemen*), which will kill one-third of the earth's population over a thirteen month period, I would most likely have little difficulty accepting that interpretation. The prospect of the son of perdition being able to mount such an army would, in that case, seem plausible. However, that's not what the prophecy indicates.

The prospect of an army of 200,000,000 "foot soldiers" is one thing. But 200,000,000 "horsemen," riding "killer-horses," with "lion-like" heads that violently spew deadly *fire, smoke,* and *brimstone* from their mouths, while violently injuring people with their "serpent-like" tails, well that's an entirely different proposition!

Let's Look at the Facts

Let's start with the 200,000,000 horses. John has no difficulty in describing the bodies of these horse-like beings, so there's no reason for us to assume that he actually saw some type of futuristic war machine and just likened it to a horse. If we were to make that assumption in this portion of John's vision, we would, likewise, have to make the same assumption about the stinging "horse-like" locusts John described in **Rev. 9:1-10**.

According to John's description of this sixth trumpet-plague, these 200 million killer beings (*whatever they'll be*) will only differ from actually being horses in their heads and in their tails. For years, I slackly figured that by using his satanically enhanced knowledge[201] the son of perdition will probably fulfill this prophecy through the devising of — *fire, smoke, and brimstone–spewing* — mechanical headdresses for these 200,000,000 horses. If that ends up being the case, then, in order to align with John's vision, the mechanical headdresses will have to resemble a lion's face. And, to complete the ensemble, the son of perdition will also have to create something similar and "serpent-like" for their tails. However, there are several serious problems with that interpretation.

~ So, what's the problem? ~

First of all, embracing that interpretation requires us to embrace pure supposition, without any logical scriptural support, and we detest supposition! Once we start wandering off the well established pathway of *Sola-Scriptura* (*Only Scripture*), to begin meandering down the countless overgrown paths of endless supposition, there are no clear scriptural markers to help get us back on the straight path of "TRUTH." Thus far, we've been

[201] This will be revealed in the coming chapters.

sticking as closely as possible to the path of pure-Scripture and logic on our quest for truth; now is not the time to allow ourselves to be lazily wooed off course.

Looking at this from a purely logical perspective, these 200,000,000 sets of head and tail mounted killing machines would have to be fabricated totally by hand, from raw materials. Furthermore, all the work would have to be done by Left-behinders, who, at the same time, will be enduring such unrelentingly severe torment that they'll be futilely trying to kill themselves (*Rev. 9:6*) in hope of escaping their agonizing existence.

Leaving aside for just a second the frightfully dismal condition of the earth during this period, the Left-behinders will have already endured the aftermath of not only the rapture of the Church but also the first five globally destructive trumpet-plagues. Taking all of this into account, we must ask the following question:

> Is it still logical for us to consider it possible that the barely surviving Left-behinders will be capable of fabricating anything at all, despite the incessant agony of their painfully swollen feet, fingers, eyelids, lips, and other body parts?

By no means an easy task . . . .

These mechanical head and tail dresses would have to be incredibly intricate apparatuses. What's more, they would have to be manufactured from raw materials in a world where one-third of the oceans and seas will have been turned into *"blood,"* one-third of the drinkable water on the planet will have been made *"bitter"* (*killing hundreds of millions*) and one-third of the heat and light from the *sun*, *moon* and *stars* will have been blotted out? Can we honestly say that we believe it logical to expect the nearly dead inhabitants of the earth, who'll be wearily malnourished, severely dehydrated, dangerously sleep deprived, almost certainly and perpetually dysenteric, and barely able to exist from one day to the next, to be able to accomplish such an enormous undertaking?

If we can imagine that humans could actually work under those horrific, inhuman conditions, then remember this: While the Left-behinders will be slaving away, struggling to miraculously create these 400 million sophisticated head and tail mounted killing machines for the son of perdition,[202] little demonic, scorpion-like *"locusts from Hell"* will be ceaselessly

[202] A machine would need to be manufactured for both the head and tail of each horse, totaling 400 million machines, not including spares, fuel or munitions.

stinging every inch of their bodies, including their eyes, lips, hands, and feet!

Once again, the books we've read don't even come close . . .

Most (*if not all*) of the movies and books that attempt to depict the fifth trumpet-plague (*the plague of scorpion-tailed locusts*) make it seem more like an attacking swarm of wasps than demonic locusts.[203] If you've ever seen an actual plague of locusts, you already know that locusts cover the affected area so completely that nothing but locusts can be seen. Close your eyes and try to imagine them. They not only cover every inch of everything in sight, but the swarm is usually a few inches thick. Now imagine that all those locusts have scorpion-like stingers and that they're not interested in eating plant life. No, they'll be interested in only one thing, continually stinging and tormenting humans for five long months!

There is no way I can logically imagine people working while being subjected to those underworld-like conditions, and there's no reason to assume that the son of perdition will be able to thwart God's plagues and do anything to stop or even inhibit any of their agonizing effects.

Therefore, as I earlier stated, we should keep in mind that if these 200,000,000 killer-horses are actually going to be fitted with physically real mechanical weapons, then in order for those weapons to bear the resemblance of a lion and the tail dresses to resemble serpents, those weapons will have to be intricately and artistically designed. What's more, they'll need to be incredibly well-made in order to continue to function without failing for more than a year. Furthermore, they'll require billions of precisely designed and complex moving parts and hundreds of millions of tons of ammunition and fuel, if they're to successfully continue spewing fire, killer-smoke, and brimstone — ***for an hour, and a day, and a month and a year.***

Actually manufacturing all these sophisticated weapons, fuel-packs and brimstone-type munitions, in such a short period, would be an unbelievably remarkable accomplishment, even if it were to be accomplished today, before the start of the tribulation period, under the most ideal of conditions. But that, however, won't be the case. Instead, in order for this to be accomplished, it will have to be achieved without having electricity, essential food and clothing, functioning factories and machinery, or even a healthy, skilled workforce. And, to make things even worse, there will be very little (*if any*) readily available tools or materials with which to do the intricate work and almost no running water.

---

[203] Incidentally, if we were to assume that the fifth plague (*the plague of scorpion-tailed locusts*) will be no more severe than would be an attack of wasps; would it be logical to suggest that the Left-behinders could work under those conditions?

And yet, as utterly impossible as it would be for the Left-behinders to accomplish this task, if we are to believe that these killer-horses will be real horses, fitted with both head and tail mounted killing apparatuses, then, despite all their suffering, that is exactly what the barely surviving Left-behinders will have to accomplish. But that's not all. They'll also have to manufacture the 200,000,000 fiery breastplates John saw the horsemen wearing.[204]

Now let's talk logically about the Horses

Presently, the United States has the largest horse population in the world, and yet, even the United States can only boast a total horse population of somewhere around ten million. According to a study completed in 2012, there are only somewhere between 60 to 70 million horses on the planet. This includes all breeds, ages and conditions, whether healthy, unhealthy, young or old. And, while it is true that race horses are frequently ridden while they're still relatively young, most experts agree that it's not wise to ride a horse, even lightly, before they're two to three years old, because their skeletal structures take at least four years to fully develop. I would imagine it's already pretty easy to figure out where I'm going with these facts and line of thought. If the son of perdition were to attempt to assemble an army of 200,000,000 killer-horsemen right now, prior to the occurrence of the Rapture (*the beginning of the tribulation period*) and prior to the unleashing of the first five trumpet-plagues (*which will essentially turn the earth into a wilderness within 2½ years*), it would be absolutely impossible for him to do so. Even if all the horses in the world were healthy, 3 to 7 year old war-horses, which very few are, there simply aren't anywhere near enough horses on the planet to accomplish that task.

Moreover, attempting to create such an army of horses, to be readied for service by the 29th or 30th month of the tribulation period, would require the son of perdition to radically begin breeding millions upon millions of horses several years before the start of the tribulation period and without anyone noticing. And, as if that wouldn't be hard enough, after the Rapture, in the midst of all the global chaos and anarchy, the son of perdition would also need to somehow continually protect, water, and feed all 200,000,000 horses and their offspring, plus tens of millions of additional spare mounts.

~ Hey, — good-luck with that! ~

---

[204] A closer look at the actual *Greek* translation suggests that these breastplates will have a *"shiny, fiery"* appearance — like that of a deep red and yellow burning stone. Thus, they'll certainly be frightening to behold!

What's more, soon after the tribulation period begins, according to John's tribulation preview in **Rev. 6:4-8**, starving people all over the world will fight and kill each other while foraging for food and safe drinking water. If I were a horse, with all those desperate, hungry people around, I'd quickly jump my stall and head for the hills before I became the stable boy's dinner!

So - what's the Verdict?

Once we carefully consider all that an army of this magnitude would entail, the prospect of these 200,000,000 killer-horsemen actually being something other than spiritual beings, who'll be used by the four fallen-angels from the great river Euphrates to kill one-third of the remaining Left-behinders, becomes absolutely unthinkable!

Okay - but why will it take four Fallen-angels?

God does nothing without purpose; thus, there may be a specific reason why four angels are presently bound in the great river Euphrates.[205] As we've learned, when these 200 million horsemen are released, they'll kill one-third of the earth's inhabitants. From a heavenly perspective, the earth is divided into four sections, which are sometimes referred to as the four *"winds"* or *"corners"* of the earth.

Before being shown the actual start of the seven-year tribulation period, John witnessed four angels (*heavenly hosts—Rev. 7:1-3*) standing on the ***'four corners of the earth,'*** holding back the ***'four winds of the earth'*** until the 144,000 Jewish servants of God were sealed. John understood those four heavenly hosts to have the power to hurt the earth and the sea, yet, unlike the four angels in the great river Euphrates (*Rev. 9:13-14*), those heavenly hosts were not bound. The following scriptures may help to shed a little more light on the subject:

Isa. 11:12, Jer. 49:36, Dan. 7:2, 8:8, Zec. 2:6, Mt. 24:31, Mk. 13:12, Rev. 20:8

And yet, they repented not . . . .

Rev. 9:20-21

Finally, the undeniable proof for which we've been waiting:

'And <u>the rest of the men which were not killed by these plagues yet repented not</u> of the works of their hands, that they should not

[205] The Scriptures aren't clear as to whether or not these four fallen angels are presently bound in the great river Euphrates, but it does seem a likely possibility.

worship devils, and idols of gold, and silver, and brass, and stone, and wood: which neither can see, nor hear, nor walk: *(notice it doesn't say talk; we'll see why later—Rev. 13:15.)* ***Neither repented they of their murders, nor of their sorceries, nor of their fornication, nor of their thefts.'***

There is no mistaking the meaning of the preceding two verses and absolutely no reason not to interpret them precisely as John wrote them. John plainly states: ***'And the rest of the men which were not killed by these plagues yet repented not . . . ,'*** which means that the Left-behinders "still" refused to repent. From John's words, we can logically infer nothing other than that the Left-behinders have not, thus far, been repenting. Furthermore, up to this point in John's vision, regardless of what we may wish to believe and teach, there hasn't been a single verse that could, in any way, be twisted or manipulated into suggesting that even one person, during the first 3½ years of the tribulation period, will have repented before dying. The evidence just isn't found anywhere in the text, and irreverently manipulating what John actually recorded to suit our emotional needs just won't change that fact!

In **Rev. 9:20**, when John wrote: ***'And the rest of the men which were not killed by these plagues yet repented not . . . ,'*** he was referring to every survivor of the first six trumpet-plagues. Those six plagues will all occur during the first 3½ years of the tribulation period, with the sixth plague ending immediately following the resurrection and ascension of God's two prophets (*Rev. 11:7-14*). Being careful to infer only that which John and Scripture have made abundantly clear, we can conclude with complete confidence that not a single soul, during that first 3½ year period, will have repented before the prophets are killed.[206] Therefore, everyone up to that point, whom God will have allowed or enabled to survive, will "still" or ***'yet'*** be unrepentant. Thus, they'll all be wearily struggling to decide who to believe and with whom they should align. Should they trust God's two witnesses or the son of perdition, who'll have declared himself to be God in the flesh?

How do we know this? We know this by looking at the complete picture of John's entire vision, while reverently refraining from inadvertently reading anything into the text that hasn't clearly been stated by John. While some may suggest that there's no reason not to expect that some of the Left-behinders may repent before dying during the first 3½ years of the tribulation period, according to what John wrote, the possibility of people repenting before God's two witnesses rise from the dead is scrip-

---

[206] There is no scriptural record of anyone, other than the 144,000, having repented during the first 3½ years—Rev. 9:20-21.

turally unsupportable. If that's not true, then why did John go to the trouble of recording that the people who were not killed by these first six trumpet-plagues "still" did not repent?

The sad truth . . . .

Based on what we just read (*Rev. 9:20-21*), it would be wrong to assume that even one of the hundreds of millions of Left-behinders, whom God will have allowed to die during the first 3½ years of the tribulation period, will have first repented before dying. And, though that reality is very distressing, as we continue moving through John's vision, we're going to find that the only accounting for the resurrection of those who do die during that first 3½ year period will be at the Great White Throne Judgment.[207] That means that those who die during this first half of the tribulation period will not have been saved; therefore, they will not return to earth with Christ at the end of the tribulation period.

Conversely, those who choose to repent at the end of the first 3½ years, after seeing the two witnesses rise from the dead, will be martyred for having done so but will soon after be resurrected and caught-up to Heaven before God begins to pour out His wrath. I realize that at this point on our journey this may sound a little complicated, but we're getting very close to the scriptures that will enable everything we're learning to fall neatly into place.

These are all little pieces of one "BIG PICTURE"

What's important to acknowledge is that the complete, bigger picture, which John's vision and *"the whole of Scripture"* exhibit, does not indicate that any individual who will die before the end of the first 3½ years of the tribulation period will ever be seen resurrected and counted among the redeemed. We'll discover why this is so powerfully significant as we move a little deeper into John's vision. Sadly, though we may wish to believe that millions will repent before dying, the truth is, other than the 144,000 Jewish servants of God (*who will have been sealed prior to the rapture of the Church*), the Scriptures don't even hint at the possibility of anybody repenting before the death and resurrection of God's two witnesses. In fact, John's statement at the end of **Rev. 9:20-21** makes it abundantly clear that even after 3½ years of unbelievable pain and suffering the Left-behinders will still be obstinately refusing to obey God and repent!

~ *Why is this so important?* ~

---

[207] That resurrection will occur at the end of the Millennial Period and will be a resurrection unto damnation, not eternal life. We'll cover this later.

If we were to irreverently state that those who die before God's two prophets are resurrected might have first repented before dying, without having a single verse of Scripture with which to back up that interpretation, we would be in serious danger of willfully disregarding a direct warning from the Lord. I'm not being dramatic. John ended his book with the following clear, direct warning:

> *'For I testify unto every man that heareth the words of the prophecy of this book, If any man shall add unto these things, God shall add unto him the plagues that are written in this book: And **if any man shall take away from the words of the book of this prophecy**, **God shall take away his part out of the book of life**, and out of the holy city, and from the things which are written in this book.'*
>
> **Rev. 22:18-19**

The Holy Scriptures Account for every Soul

There's actually another important and excitingly logical reason not to assume that some of the people who will die during the first 3½ years will have first repented. As we continue venturing through the fascinating chapters ahead, we're going to find that John's vision gives an extraordinarily accurate account of the resurrection and redemption of every repentant soul in God's eternal kingdom. That's how amazingly detailed and inspiring John's Revelation vision of God's eternal plan is.

~ *So why won't people be repenting?* ~

Due to the powerful, relentless plagues of God's two witnesses during the first 3½ years, most of the confused Left-behinders will passionately hate God. Even the hopeful "**remnant**" (*those who'll eventually repent*) will find it hard to understand and trust that God's two witnesses will have been sent as ambassadors of God's love for the sole purpose of inspiring the world to change direction and repent.[208] What's more, adding to the confusion will be the son of perdition, who will be feverously working on a global scale (*throughout the entire tribulation period*) promoting his false, pagan religion and causing all manner of confusion.[209] And, unfortunately,

---

[208] After 3½ years of experiencing the plagues and preaching of God's two witnesses "the remnant" will begin to hope the witnesses' preaching is true, but they'll wait to see if the witnesses actually rise from the dead before they finally repent. That's not an opinion; we'll see this clearly emerge from the text.

[209] Eventually the son of perdition will come right out and declare himself to be God on earth—2Th. 2:3-12

as if the global scene isn't already going to be confusing enough, when the son of perdition is strategically allowed[210] to kill God's two seemingly indestructible witnesses, those who hate God will easily be convinced that he (*the son of perdition, also referred to as the false prophet or the anti-Christ*) is the one and only true God; thus, they'll rejoice when God's witnesses are killed. The hopeful "**remnant**," however, will wisely wait, eagerly hoping to see God's two witnesses rise from the dead, just as they will have forewarned. And when God's witnesses do rise, their resurrections will finally confirm, beyond any doubt, that their witnessing and plagues were truly inspired by God, as a final, merciful call to repentance. Thus, after seeing the prophets arise and ascend into Heaven, the remnant will finally repent, and their repentance will conclude God's more than 6,000 year long harvest of souls. That's precisely what we will see self-emerge from the remainder of John's amazing vision.

[210] Just as God the Father allowed Satan to provoke the world into crucifying Christ and then, three days later, confirm Jesus' authority over "hell" and "death" by raising Him from the dead, so also will God allow His two witnesses to be killed and, 3½ days later, raise them from the dead—Rev. 11:3-12.

Chapter 20

The Mystery of God

An angel like no other

Rev. 10:1

> ***'And I saw another <u>mighty</u> angel come down from heaven, clothed with a cloud: and a rainbow was upon his head, and his face was as it were the sun, and his feet as pillars of fire . . .'***

When John said he saw a mighty angel he certainly wasn't exaggerating! According to his description this angel was clearly impressive, but if we neglect to compare the words John used here with the same *Greek* words and their usage in other parts of the New Testament we might be left with the impression that John has seen angels as mighty as this before. Not surprisingly, however, after thoroughly searching the Scriptures, I can't find a description anywhere that even comes close to equaling John's description of this unprecedentedly impressive heavenly host. The Scriptures do record several other impressive angelic beings, but, as remarkable as their descriptions are, none of them can measure up to this particular extraordinary messenger from Heaven. Translating what John wrote in **Rev. 10:1** into English, by writing: ***'And I saw <u>another</u> mighty angel . . . ,'*** would be analogous to our suggesting that King David would have described seeing Goliath by saying something like:

"Hey, I met another imposing Philistine today."

I realize that we would be talking about *Hebrew*, rather than *Greek*, in this case, but the comparative significance of the words in their proper context would be the same. The point is the use of the word "**another**" (*in this case*) would not imply that all or other Philistines are giants, as was Goliath. Likewise, if we examine the common usage of the actual *Greek* word for *mighty* as it was originally used in **Rev. 10:1**, we'll find it most commonly interpreted to mean, "**Mightier**." Therefore, John was most likely intending to relay something more along the lines of: ***"And I saw***

***another even mightier angel . . . .*"** This becomes apparent when we carefully reread John's impressive description of this magnificent angel, so let's try to imagine actually seeing what John saw.

From the way John described this glorious heavenly-host he must have been observing this vision from either somewhere between Heaven and earth or from the earth's surface, because John wrote that he saw the angel come down from heaven. This colossally large being was so massive that John describes him as having been clothed with a cloud (*possibly representing the heavens*),[211] with a rainbow upon his head (*perhaps signifying God's throne and authority*),[212] as having feet (*and lower legs*) like pillars of fire, and a face as radiant or as bright as the sun (*this is usually an indication of the refiningly unapproachable Holiness of God*).

Since this mighty angel's appearance was apparently intended to powerfully represent all of God's creation we can logically conclude that his message must have been as monumentally significant as was his appearance. So, after assessing the following few verses, we'll see just what this monumentally significant angel's message was.

The Seven Thunders mysteriously speak?

Rev. 10:2-4

> ***'And he*** *(the mighty angel)* ***had in his hand a little book open: and he set his right foot upon the sea, and his left foot upon the earth,***
>
> ***And cried with a loud voice, as when a lion roareth: and when he had cried, seven thunders uttered their voices.***
>
> ***And when the seven thunders had uttered their voices, I was about to write: and I heard a voice from heaven saying unto me, Seal up those things which the seven thunders uttered, and write them not.'***

When John watched this powerful angel, spanning both earth and sea, cry out, he heard the Seven Thunders utter their voices, but when he started to write what they said he was told to ***'seal-up'*** the words and write them not. We lightly covered this at the beginning of our journey, when we made our way through John's salutation to the seven churches in Asia. There, we found that the apostle Paul also recorded having known a

---

[211] John doesn't explain the significance of the angel's characteristics; therefore, we don't want to draw any hard and fast conclusions as to their meaning. However, we can get a feel for the relative significance of the angel's characteristics by comparing them to their significance in other similar scriptural settings.

[212] Rev. 4:3

man (*which was most likely Paul's humble way of referring to himself in the third person*), who, like John, had also been taken up to the third heaven (*the dwelling place of God*) where he, too, heard ***'unspeakable words, which it is not lawful for a man to utter.'*** Is it possible that Paul also heard the voices of these Seven Thunders? Perhaps he did, but the Scriptures don't tell us. The truth is we don't know just who or what the Seven Thunders are. I can't help wondering, however, if they have something to do with the fact that there are also Seven Spirits of God who are symbolized in numerous ways throughout Scripture, especially here in John's vision. Having sufficiently covered this ground earlier,[213] we'll avoid supposition and just move on.

Many theories but not a shred of proof!

Over the years I've been exposed to many theories regarding the explanation of these Seven Thunders. Some of those theories go as far as to claim that the Seven Thunders actually represent seven plagues or major events of some sort, but none of those theories have any real scriptural foundation. That's because there simply isn't any. Without employing supposition in hopes of stumbling upon the truth (*which has not been revealed*), no scripturally logical conclusion can be reached. The simple fact is John was told not to record the words he heard the Seven Thunders speak for a reason, and we don't know what that reason is. I'm okay with that. Remember this:

Supposition without foundation = "**CONFUSION**!"

John clearly recorded having heard seven ***'voices.'*** Nowhere did John record having witnessed seven actual events; therefore, we shouldn't jump to that completely irresponsible conclusion. Furthermore, the original *Greek* word for ***'voices'*** in this verse is the same *Greek* word as was used in **Matthew 3:17** to record the words spoken by God, while Jesus was being baptized — there again, an indication that the Seven Thunders were voices, not events. Moreover, asserting the possibility that these Seven Thunders are actually events, rather than voices, just doesn't fit within John's complete vision of the entire tribulation period. If these voices were an indication of actual events we would read evidence to that affect in the ensuing verses, but, instead, John immediately obeys the heavenly command to ***'seal-up'*** the words the Seven Thunders ***'uttered'*** (*spoke*) and moves on. Having done so, John set a good example for us to follow.

[213] It may be helpful to review our earlier discussion of Rev. 1:4, regarding the Seven Spirits of God—Rev. 1:4, 3:1, 4:5, 5:6, Zec. 4:1-6, John 1:1-4-9-12.

The Revelation of the Mystery of God!

As I suggested earlier, the unprecedentedly glorious appearance of this mighty heavenly-host is likely intended to signify the eternal importance of his message, so let's see what that message is.

Rev. 10:5-7

> ***'And the angel which I saw stand upon the sea and upon the earth lifted up his hand to heaven,***
>
> ***And sware by him that liveth forever and ever, who created heaven, and the things that therein are, and the earth, and the things that therein are, and the sea, and the thing which are therein, that there should be time no longer:***
>
> ***But in the days of the voice of the seventh angel, when he shall begin to sound, the mystery of God should be finished, as he hath declared to his servants the prophets.'***

There it is, a whopper of a declaration! Although most of us have mistakenly trampled right over these verses without recognizing their eternal significance, this mighty angel's declaration is a clear heavenly warning to every individual who has not yet committed their heart and life to Christ.

~ *What are you talking about?* ~

The angel's statement reveals a specific point in time when the temporarily open "Door of Salvation" will be forever "SHUT!" [214]

~ *How do you figure that?*

During Jesus' earthly ministry He explained that there will come a day when He — ***'the master of the house'*** — will rise up and forever "SHUT" the temporarily open "Door of Salvation." The absolute finality of that day will be every bit as severe for those who continue to choose to reject Christ's offer of salvation (*through faith in His name*) as was the day when God shut the massive door on the Ark and sent rain to kill every wicked individual who refused to believe the preaching of Noah.[215] Thus, once Jesus decides it's time to eternally shut that symbolic door, not another soul, no matter how much they beg or plead, will ever be able to be counted among those who'll have wisely chosen to receive God's gracious invitation and become members of His eternal family of saints.

---

[214] Luke 13:24-28, Mt. 25:10

[215] Gen. 7:16, 2Pt. 2:5

'Strive to enter in at the strait gate: for many, I say unto you, ***will seek to enter in****,* ***and shall not be able****.* ***When once the master of the house has risen up****,* ***and hath shut the door****, and you begin to stand without, and to knock at the door, saying, Lord, Lord, open unto us; and he shall answer and say unto you,* ***I know ye not whence ye are****: Then shall ye begin to say, we have eaten and drunk in thy presence, and thou hast taught in our streets. But he shall say, I tell you, I know you not whence ye are; depart from me, all ye workers of iniquity.* ***There shall be weeping and gnashing of teeth****. . .'*

Luke 13:24-28

Most people live in willful ignorance, having little or no regard for the fact that their soul is eternal. Being eternal, however, every soul will spend eternity somewhere, if not in Heaven (*with God*), then in *"outer darkness,"* away from God and His merciful loving-kindness. The average individual believes themselves to be basically good. Thus, most believe God's merciful "Door of Salvation" will always be open to them. However, the truth is so called *"good-people"* don't go to Heaven; repentant, forgiven people do.[216] And today (*right now*) is the day of salvation. Tomorrow isn't promised to any of us. Consequently, once that temporary door of mercy and grace has been shut, it will never again be open, not to anyone — "EVER!" This is in no way a reach or a supposition.[217] If anything has ever been a scriptural fact, this is it, and the key to our comprehending this truth lies in our ability to understand the "MYSTERY OF GOD."

So what is the Mystery of God?

The answer to this question is revealed throughout the New Testament and is both fun and inspiring to explore. The *Greek* word ***mystērion*** *(i.e., mystery or mysteries)* is used 27 times in Scripture. Of which, there are only four places where it is not being used either directly or indirectly in reference to God's eternal kingdom and plan of salvation. Whether we're reading Jesus' parables about the hidden mysteries of the kingdom of God or are simply being inspired by one of Paul's letters to the early Church, the "Mystery of God" has always been a reference to just one thing — God's

[216] Mt 19:16-17, Mk 10:17-18
[217] 2Cor. 6:2

plan for the establishment of His eternal, heavenly kingdom and family of angels and saints.

Initially, God's mysterious plan for the salvation of the world, though foretold through His prophets, was not fully revealed even to them.[218] Jesus began teaching the mystery of God's redemptive plan in parables, which even His disciples only began to understand after the day of Pentecost had come. Had Jesus' disciples understood the "Mystery of God" prior to Pentecost they would, no doubt, have continued preaching during that forty day period between Christ's resurrection and His final ascension.[219] But, instead, Jesus' disciples proved they didn't understand by going[220] fishing after Jesus' rose from the dead. They simply couldn't understand why their long awaited Messianic leader had been killed; thus, they were left down-trodden and confused. But Jesus' sacrificial life created the only gateway (*or doorway*)[221] to salvation, and it's only through that door that any of us can gain hope of an eternal Heavenly existence and right standing with God. There's simply no other way. But, as the preceding scripture from Luke's Gospel (*Luke 13:24-28*) clearly reveals, that allegorical door will not remain open forever.

> *'. . . But we speak the wisdom of God* ***in a mystery****,* ***even the hidden wisdom****,* ***which God ordained before the world unto our glory****: Which none of the princes of this world knew: for had they known it, they would not have crucified the Lord of glory. But as it is written, Eye hath not seen, nor ear heard, neither hath entered into the heart of man, the things which God hath prepared for them that love Him.'*

∞ 1Cor. 2:7-9 ∞

> *'. . . Whereof I am made a minister, according to the dispensation of God which is given to me for you, to fulfill the word of God;* ***Even the mystery which has been hid from ages and from generations****, but now is made manifest to His saints: To whom God would make known what is the riches of* ***the glory of this mystery*** *among the Gentiles;* ***which is Christ in you****,* ***the hope of glory*** *. . .'*

∞ Col. 1:25-27 ∞

---

[218] 1Pt. 1:9-10-12, Ro. 1:1-2, 3:21, Mt. 13:17, Acts 3:18-24, 10:43, Eph. 3:3-5
[219] 1Cor. 15:3-7
[220] Jn. 21:1-19
[221] Mt. 7:13-14, Jn. 14:16

'Now to him that is of power to stablish {establish} you according to my gospel, and the preaching of Jesus Christ, ***according to the revelation of the mystery****,* ***which was kept secret since the world began****,* ***But now is made manifest****, and by the scriptures of the prophets, according to the commandment of the everlasting God,* ***made known to all nations for the obedience of faith*** *. . . .'*

Rom. 16:25-26

We could spend hours exploring the wonderful mystery of God's plan of salvation, but instead I'll just leave you with some insightful scriptures to explore on your own:

1Pt. 1:9-12, **Mt.** 13:11, **Ro.** 11:25, 16:25-27, **1Cor.** 15:51-57,
Eph. 1:3-9-14, 3:1-3, 4-12, 5:25-32, 6:19-20, **Col.** 2:1-3, 4:3, **1Tim.** 3:9-16

Let's not forget the "BIGGER–PICTURE"

Rev. 10:5-7 ~ *continued*

Although we may consider this mighty angel's warning about the mystery of God ending to be a harsh reality, the angel's message definitely fits perfectly within the framework of the complete, bigger–picture of the entire tribulation period that God gave John. The sad reality, which we will soon discover, is that the majority of Left-behinders will remain disobedient even after having witnessed the resurrection of God's two prophets and will not care in the least that the symbolic "Door of Salvation" has been shut. The remnant (*the minority, who will repent after witnessing the prophets' resurrection and ascension into Heaven*), however, will care, and they'll prove it by eventually allowing themselves to be martyred in order to hold on to their newly acquired hope of salvation.

Let's take a quick peek at the trail ahead.

In most cases it's better to refrain from looking ahead on the trail, but in this case it may be helpful for us to take a quick glance at a pertinent supportive clue from **Rev. 11:7-19**. When we get to that portion of John's vision, we're going to find that, immediately after God's final two witnesses are killed, resurrected, and called back into Heaven, "**the remnant**" (*the very last souls to be saved*) will repent, and the seventh angel will immediately sound his trumpet. Then, just as this mighty angel told John would happen, the "MYSTERY OF GOD" will end. The Gospel call to repent will never again be heard! Thus, precisely as one would expect, as soon as that seventh trumpet finishes sounding, John will hear great voices in Heaven making the following joyful proclamation:

"The Kingdoms of this world are become the kingdoms of our Lord, and of His Christ; and He shall reign for ever and ever . . . ."

The preceding words are only the beginning of the whole magnificently exciting celebratory discourse John recorded hearing after witnessing the seventh angel sound his trumpet. And that grand discourse is precisely the type of exuberant declaration we would expect to follow something as eternally significant as the end of God's more than 6,000 year long harvest of souls![222]

Hence, as we move ahead in John's vision, we're going to read that, immediately after witnessing "**the remnant**" repent and give glory to God,[223] John recorded hearing the seventh angel sound his trumpet. In that very instant, the "Door of Salvation" will permanently shut! Thus, when these events actually occur, that remnant of newly born-again saints will immediately become the final members of God's eternal family. And so, just as we would expect, when that last group of souls are ultimately saved, all of Heaven will rejoice, as never before, because every lost sheep in God's eternal family of saints will have been brought into the fold. This is precisely what John witnessed in his vision and, thus, a perfect fulfillment of everything Jesus taught.[224]

Jesus explained to His disciples that every time a soul is saved Heaven rejoices. The angels don't wait for our resurrection before celebrating. When someone truly repents and surrenders their life to Christ that soul instantly becomes a member of God's eternal kingdom of saints, just as surely as if he or she were already standing before the throne. But, for those who've defiantly chosen not to repent, when that seventh-trumpet sounds it will be too-late. Christ will have already risen up and eternally "SHUT" the allegorical "Door of Salvation!" After that day, the purifying hope for forgiveness — about which John wrote (*1Jn. 3:1-3*) — will have become a thing of the past. Not a single soul will ever again be saved!

~ But what about the Old Testament saints? ~

Christ's death and resurrection also paved the way for our faithful brothers and sisters who lived in hope of redemption under the original Old Testament. Thus, those saints will have already been resurrected and

---

[222] Mt. 9:36-37, 13:36-43

[223] This will be clearly understood when we get to the related scriptures in Rev. Chapters 11 thru 15.

[224] Luke 13:24-28, 15:1-10, John 10:9-18, Mt. 25:1-10-13, Rev. 11:15-19, Gen. 7:16

raptured with the Church at the start of the seven-year tribulation period. The 144,000 (*who will be sealed immediately before the tribulation period begins—Rev. 7:3-8*) will repent[225] in the wake of the Rapture (*most likely as soon as God's two witnesses begin to preach*). That only leaves "**the remnant**." They'll be the very last saints to repent, which is precisely why they are referred to (*by John*) as "**the remnant**." Every bit of this will be clearly evident in the scriptures ahead.

After God's two witnesses (*the prophets*) ascend into Heaven and the "**the remnant**" finally repents, God will begin resurrecting and *"catching-away"* (*taking up to Heaven*) all those who will have repented during the tribulation period. The first group to be martyred, resurrected, and taken up to Heaven will be the 144,000 Jewish servants. And, while John doesn't tell us precisely when the 144,000 will be killed, they will most likely die and be resurrected at or near the same time as will God's two prophets, because the prophets will no longer be here to protect them. Thus, the newly born-again "**remnant**" will be the last Christians left on earth, and (*as I've stated*) they'll have to prove their new faith in Christ by choosing to be beheaded rather than submitting to receiving the mark of the beast.[226]

John's vision doesn't reveal how long it will take the son of perdition to kill the remnant after they've repented; however, we do know that every born-again believer will have been killed, resurrected, and seen standing before God's throne before any of God's wrath is poured out. That's how precious we are to God; not even a fragment of bone from the least of God's martyred children will be left behind to suffer the shame and agony of God's righteously indignant wrath. That's right! Even "**the remnant**" (*who will have needed to be powerfully persuaded to repent before doing so*) are God's kids; thus, God will not allow a single hair on their heads to be punished with the wicked.

And so, only after God has safely united His entire eternal family before His throne, as one massive body of sanctified saints (*the body of Christ*),[227] will He then fiercely deal with those obstinately defiant Left-behinders, who'll have brutally martyred and blatantly blasphemed His faithful prophets, His Church, and (*worst of all*) His Son and Holy Name.

~ But aren't people going to be born during the Millennial Period? ~

---

[225] The Scriptures don't reveal any "rock–solid" evidence with regard to how and when the 144,000 will repent. They do, however, clearly indicate, as we will soon see, that the 144,000 will be protected by God's two witnesses for 3½ years. Then, shortly thereafter, they'll be seen standing before God's throne.

[226] Rev. 20:4

[227] Rev. 7:9-17, 14:1-5, 15:2-4. You may also wish to read Eph. 1:9, 10-14, regarding the body of Christ.

For those of you who are wondering about all those who'll repopulate the earth during the Millennial Period (*Christ's 1,000 year reign on earth*), the "Door of Salvation" will definitely have already shut! However unfair or merciless that may presently seem to be, when we get to the scriptures that directly address this issue, we will clearly discern how unambiguously the Bible reveals and resolves that understandably disquieting concern.

As we continue and each piece of this puzzle falls neatly into place, the entire seven-year tribulation period, the following Millennial Period, and even the glorious revealing of God's eternal City will become clearly visible, until we're finally able to see the complete, "BIGGER—PICTURE" that all these little pieces of John's vision create.

The bitter-sweet little Book

Rev. 10:8-9

> ***'And the voice which I heard from heaven spake unto me again, and said, Go and take the little book which is open in the hand of the angel which standeth upon the sea and upon the earth.***
>
> ***And I went unto the angel, and said unto him, Give me the little book. And he said unto me, Take it, and eat it up; and it shall make thy belly bitter, but it shall be in thy mouth sweet as honey.'***

Is it just me, or does this angel sound a little perturbed about John's telling him to give him the little book? The angel's response — ***'take it, and eat it up'*** — sounds a little like the response one might get from a selfish little boy after mom has forced him to share the last piece of cake with his little sister. Of course I'm just kidding, but this does seem to be worded a little funny.

The Gospel - Sweet on the Tongue but Bitter to Deliver

Rev. 10:10-11

> ***'And I took the little book out of the angel's hand, and ate it up; and it was in my mouth sweet as honey: and as soon as I had eaten it, my belly was bitter.***
>
> ***And he said unto me, Thou must prophesy again before many peoples, and nations and tongues, and kings.'***

Roughly 600 years before Christ came the prophet Ezekiel had a similar experience.[228] He too was given a scroll containing the Words of God, and,

---

[228] Ez. 2:6 thru 3:7

likewise, was told to eat it. After having done so, Ezekiel also wrote that the book tasted as sweet as honey. I don't think we would be correct in drawing any direct correlation between what John recorded experiencing in **Rev. 10:10-11** and Ezekiel's earlier experience, but Ezekiel's words might help us gain a little perspective. In both cases it seems that the Word of God, when eaten, was sweet as honey, but delivering it (*in both Ezekiel's and John's cases*) proved to be a bitter task.

If the symbolism of what John wrote wasn't so straightforward, I would hesitate to comment about its meaning. But, stepping back and taking it all in, we'll remember that John took the little book from the hand of a mighty angel. That mighty angel appeared to be both adorned and postured in such a way as to represent all of heaven and earth. Given that that angel made a mighty proclamation (*essentially declaring precisely when Jesus, the Master of the house, would rise up and eternally shut the Door of Salvation*), it does seem fairly obvious that the little book the angel was holding, while making his announcement, served to represent the Gospel of Christ — "THE MYSTERY OF GOD."

Anyone who's done any serious witnessing can relate to the sweet, yet bitter reality that comes of sharing their faith while preaching the Gospel in a faithless world. Before dying, Jesus warned His disciples to anticipate this *"bitter"* reality, which they soon faced after His ascension.

> *'And Jesus answered and said unto them, Take heed that no man deceive you. For many shall come in my name, saying, I am Christ, and shall deceive many. And ye shall hear of wars and rumours of wars: see that ye be not troubled: for all these things must come to pass,* ***but the end is not yet****. For nation shall rise against nation, and kingdom against kingdom: And there shall be famines, and pestilences, and earthquakes, in divers places.* ***All these are the beginning***[229] ***of sorrows****. Then shall they deliver you up to be afflicted, and shall kill you: and ye shall be hated of all nations for my name's sake. And then shall many be offended, and shall betray one another, and shall hate one another.* ***And***

[229] Jesus is making it clear that, from the first century (*AD*) onward, wars, famines, pestilences, and earthquakes will just be the beginning of the many sorrows to befall the inhabitants of the earth until He returns. And, yet, many continue to teach that an increased number of earthquakes are an indication that the tribulation period and the Rapture are soon to occur. The truth is (*which most seismologists will confirm*) the actual number of earthquakes is not necessarily increasing, but, rather, we're just getting better at detecting them.

***many false prophets shall rise*, *and shall deceive many*. *And because iniquity shall abound*, *the love of many shall wax cold*.** *But he that shall endure unto the end, the same shall be saved. And this gospel of the kingdom shall be preached in all the world for a witness unto all nations; and then shall the end come.'*

ꟹ Matthew. 24:4-14 ꟹ

We're going to see that God's two tribulation witnesses will be the very last individuals to preach the Gospel before this figurative "Door of Salvation" is eternally shut. Thus, when that door shuts the preaching of the "MYSTERY OF GOD" will forever be finished, precisely as the mighty angel loudly proclaimed:

'. . . But in the days of the voice of the seventh angel, ***when he shall begin to sound*, *the mystery of God should be finished*,** *as he hath declared to his servants the prophets.'*

ꟹ Revelation 10:7 ꟹ

Chapter 21

A Covenant and a New Third Temple

Rev. 11:1

> ***'And there was given me a reed like unto a rod:*** [230] ***and the angel stood, saying, Rise, and measure <u>the temple of God</u>, and <u>the altar</u>, and <u>them that worship therein</u>.'***

The obvious question is: *"Which Temple is John being told to measure?"* Herod's Temple was destroyed in 70 AD and has never been rebuilt. In order for a new Third Temple to be erected, *"the Dome of the Rock"* and the less popular *"Dome of the Spirits"* (*also known as the Dome of Tablets*) would have to be removed. Or would they? That's debatable. The exact location of the original Holy of Holies (*the heart of the original Temple*) is such a controversial subject that I don't frankly see how anyone could defend, with complete confidence, any claim to know the precise location or footprint of the original Temple. And, with so many brilliant historians and archaeologists widely differing in their opinions, even if we were experts on the subject (*which I'm not*), I doubt we would feel led to boldly argue our points of view. Thankfully, we don't have to figure this out in order to understand John's vision.

If building the new Third Temple in a specific location is important (*and we should acknowledge that most scholars agree that the Scriptures demand that the new Temple be built on a divinely preordained site*), then, presumably, God's two witnesses will tell the 144,000 Jewish servants exactly where to build it. That's assuming, of course, which we're loathsome to do, that (1) the new Temple will not have already been built prior to the start of the tribulation period and (2) that the 144,000 will definitely be the ones to build the new Temple. That's too much assuming for me.

So, what do the experts say?

Some experts seem to believe that the little structurally unobtrusive *Dome of the Spirits* was actually built directly over the original location of

---

[230] John was simply given a measuring stick.

the Holy of Holies, which everyone agrees was the heart and most holy portion of former Jewish Temples. In fact, the alternate name for the *"Holy of Holies"* is *"The Most Holy Place."* Presently, the little *Dome of the Spirits* is standing roughly 300 feet to the north of the easily visible and very massive *Dome of the Rock* [231] and is positioned west of the beloved eastern *Golden Gate,*[232] near (*but not on the crest of*) the Temple Mount.

Due to the little *Dome of the Spirits'* current frail condition, if a large camel, wishing to relieve an itch, were to aggressively rub himself against one of the Dome's eight feeble posts, the ancient, gazebo-sized structure would likely collapse.

Many experts, however, have several serious problems with any theory that includes the little *Dome of the Spirits* being the actual site of the original Holy of Holies. Without going into a lot of confusing detail, the main issue is its elevation. Many feel that the actual site on which the *"Mercy Seat"* (*"the Ark of the Covenant"*) originally sat, inside the former Holy of Holies, was positioned at the highest elevation on the Temple Mount. If that's true, then the famous *"Shtiah"* stone, which is positioned directly under the massive Islamic *Dome of the Rock,* is roughly 4.5 meters (*15 ft.*) higher (*in elevation*) than the much smaller *Dome of the Spirits*. That could mean that the current *Dome of the Rock* is positioned directly over the true site of the original Holy of Holies. If (*and it's possible that God only knows*) this is indeed the case, the *Dome of the Rock* will have to come down before the new Third Temple can be built.

A new Third Temple must be built

The only way these scriptures[233] can be fulfilled (*and they will be fulfilled*) is if a new Third Temple is built, in Jerusalem, on the Temple Mount. The rebuilding of that Temple will enable God's two tribulation period witnesses and the specially chosen 144,000 Jewish servants to restore true worship (*divinely inspired worship of God the Father, God the Son and God the Holy Spirit*) to Israel.[234] And, without question, one way or another, a new Altar and Temple will be built precisely where God wants it, either before or during the tribulation period. Any religious group or belief system having a problem with that statement should direct their conten-

[231] The Dome of the Rock is considered by many to be the third holiest Islamic site. Jews and Christians, however, consider the temple Mount, on which that structure sits, to be the holiest site on earth!

[232] Some believe Ezekiel prophesied of this gate being shut until Christ returns and enters the city by way of that porch or gate—Ez. 44:1-3. However, as we continue moving into the Millennial Period scriptures, we may see it differently.

[233] Dan. 9:25-27, Mt. 24:15-24, Rev. 11

[234] Mt. 17:1-11

tions or hostilities heavenward. I'm simply restating the obvious, in complete accord with the angel of the Lord's statement:

> ***'. . . measure the temple of God, and the altar, and them that worship therein.'***

It's estimated that John experienced his Revelation vision sometime between AD 70 and AD 95, presumably after Herod's Temple (*the Second Temple*) had already been destroyed. It may be that only God knows if that's truly accurate. Fortunately for us, it doesn't matter. Whatever the case may be our inability to determine the precise future Temple location in no way hinders our understanding of end-time scripture as a whole. From a purely logical point of view, it would have made no sense for Christ's angel to have told John to measure a Temple, which either no longer existed or was about to be destroyed! Therefore, the angel must have been telling John to measure the future Third Temple, which, as I formerly stated, will likely be built by the 144,000 Jewish servants, under the protection of God's angels and His two globally dominant prophets.

~ How do we know if the 144,000 are going to build the temple? ~

We don't know if the 144,000 servants will actually build the new Temple by themselves,[235] but we do have good reason to believe that they will at least be "involved-in" or "in-charge-of" the work. How do we know this? Consider the following question: *"Would we expect a thief to knock before breaking in?"*

~ That's a dumb question! What does that have to do with it? ~

Well, this is where the second part of Daniel's dual-nature prophecy comes into play. Later, when we look closely at **Dan. 9:25-27**, we'll find that it speaks of the coming Messiah (*Christ Jesus*) and of the destruction of the Second Temple (*Herod's Temple*).[236] Here, in **Rev. 11:1-6**, John is being told of the impending defilement (*the abomination of desolation*) of the, future Third Temple. That Temple, as I just stated, will most logically be built quickly and by God's chosen 144,000 Jewish servants or *(possibly)* under their direct supervision, with God's two witnesses overseeing and miraculously protecting those who do the work.

---

[235] Based on what we've learned about the effects of the trumpet-plagues, it's not likely that any mortals will be healthy enough to help construct the new Temple.

[236] In AD 70, just as Jesus prophesied (*Mt. 24:2*), Titus' army destroyed the Second Temple (*Herod's Temple*) – not leaving one stone upon another.

~ So, why couldn't the Third Temple be built before the start of the tribulation period? ~

It is possible that "**a**" Temple but not "**the**" Temple could be built prior to the start of the tribulation period, but I seriously doubt that the true Third Temple will be built before the Church has been raptured. I say this mainly because in order for the true Third Temple to be built, as has been stated, a seven-year *"covenant"* will first need to be initiated, allowing only non-Gentiles access to the immediate Temple areas. And the initiating of that *"covenant"* would be, to the Church, like a thief knocking before breaking in! Jesus, Peter and Paul all taught that the *"catching-away"* of the Church (*the Rapture*) will come as a surprise — ***'like a thief in the night!'***

'But the day of the Lord will come ***as a thief in the night*** *. . .'*

ᢒ 2Pet. 3:10 ᢓ

'For yourselves know perfectly that ***the day of the Lord so cometh as a thief in the night****.'*[237]

ᢒ 1Th. 5:2 ᢓ

'Verily I say unto you, that this generation shall not pass, till all these things be done {fulfilled}. Heaven and earth shall pass away: ***but my words shall not pass away****.*[238] ***But of that day and that hour knoweth no man****, no, not the angels which are in heaven, neither the* ***Son****,*[239] *but the Father. Take ye heed, watch and pray:* ***for ye know not when the time is****.'*

ᢒ Mark 13:30-33 ᢓ

Therefore, if the Church were to actually witness the initiation of a seven-year *"covenant"* with Israel — prohibiting Gentiles from accessing the Temple area and allowing the new Third Temple to be built — it would be, to the Church, like a thief knocking on the door before breaking in. Only a new-born, scripturally unaware Christian would fail to recognize that the

---

[237] As has been stated, the Day of the Lord will begin with the Rapture.

[238] This prophecy — stating that Christ's words shall not pass away — is one of the most powerful confirmations that Jesus is truly the Messiah, aside, of course, from His having risen from the dead. Hello!

[239] When Jesus refers to Himself as the *"Son of man"* He's speaking only of His mortal existence on earth. After His resurrection, Jesus returned to His original glorious status as "God the Son," the Creator of all things—John 17:5, Col. 1:12-20.

seven-year tribulation period was about to or had already begun. That would make Jesus, Peter and Paul false prophets.

It is possible, though (*from a logical perspective*) extremely improbable, that Israel could unwittingly compromise and build a Temple in the wrong location, over the site of the *Dome of the Spirits*, right next to the existing *Dome of the Rock*. However, if that were to happen, that new Temple would eventually have to be removed or disassembled and reassembled exactly where God wants it. Let's make no mistake about it, God's Temple will be built precisely when, where, how, and by whom God chooses.

Forty and two months, an obvious clue!

Rev. 11:2

> ***'But the court which is without the temple leave out, and measure it not; for it is given unto the Gentiles: and the holy city shall they tread under foot forty and two months** (3½ yrs.).'*

When I stated that this verse is an obvious clue, I meant a clue so blatantly recognizable that you'd have to be totally blind to trip over it! As we lightly covered while making our way through **Rev. 8:10-11** and **9:13-15**, Daniel's prophecy (*Dan. 9:25-27*) about *"the prince that shall come"* (*the son of perdition, the anti-Christ*) doesn't clearly indicate, at least not to my satisfaction, precisely with whom this future *"prince"* will confirm his seven-year covenant. Nonetheless, a covenant or (*to more closely align with the Hebrew text*) an *"alliance"* will be enforced with a future *"prince"* (*a leader or ruler*). Paul referred to this particular future purely wicked *"prince"* and global dictator in the same way as did Jesus when He referred to His former betrayer (*Judas Iscariot*), calling him *the son of perdition.*[240] This is a suitable name for both men, considering that this future prince of darkness will also, like Judas, be foolishly wicked enough to resist God's obvious divine authority, even after having witnessed the world-shaking, awe-inspiring power and plagues of God's two Heaven-sent prophets.

Daniel, like John, also prophesied of a 3½ year Period

The first portion of Daniel's dual-nature prophecy[241] has already been fulfilled. It foretold the coming of the Messiah and of Titus' 70 AD destruc-

---

[240] 2Th. 2:3, Jn. 17:12

[241] In Dan. 9:25-27, Daniel prophesied that after 70 weeks of years God's plan for our salvation and the fulfillment of prophecy will be completed. Most experts agree that 7 + 62 weeks *{of years}* equals 69 weeks or 483 years, which, as was prophesied, is precisely when Jesus came and made atonement for all sin. That leaves the 7 year tribulation period to account for the final 7 years of Daniel's prophecy *{one week of years}*. It was necessary for God to leave this roughly 2,000

tion of the Second Temple (*the Temple Herod rebuilt*). We'll thoroughly examine that prophecy in just a moment. The obvious clue to which I was referring lies within the second portion of Daniel's prophecy (*Dan. 9:27*). That portion deals with the future Third Temple and a seven-year *"covenant"* (*alliance*), which will be enforced with *"many."* The 3½ year period, of which the angel spoke while speaking with John in the preceding verse (*Rev. 11:2*), perfectly aligns with Daniel's prophecy of a future seven-year *"covenant,"* because Daniel's prophecy indicates that the *"covenant"* will be broken after only 3½ years. During the first 3½ years of the tribulation period, that *"covenant"* will prohibit Gentiles from entering the holy courtyards where the new Third Temple will be built. So let's take a look at Daniel's prophecy:

> *'And **he** {the son of perdition} **shall confirm the covenant with many** {We don't know precisely with whom or with how many.} for one **week** { 7 yrs.}: and in the midst of the week {after 3½ years} he shall cause the **sacrifice** and the **oblation** {worship} to cease, and for the overspreading {the entirety, the completion} of **abominations he shall make it desolate**,[242] even until the consummation {until the end}, and that determined shall be poured upon the desolate. '[243]*

Daniel 9:27

Will the covenant be of a political or spiritual nature?

Daniel's prophecy (*Dan. 9:25-27*) makes it quite clear that the son of perdition (*'the prince that shall come'*) will be the most significant of the ***'many'*** parties who'll be involved in the confirmation of a seven-year

---

year gap {*the Church age*} between the first 483 years and the final 7 years of Daniel's prophecy, so as to prevent us from being able to calculate the exact date of the Rapture. So, all together, Daniel's prophecy covers a total of 70 weeks of years plus *"the Church age"* {*the period between the establishment of the Church and the beginning of the 7 year tribulation period*}. At the beginning of the last week of Daniel's prophecy {*which speaks of the tribulation period*} the *"false-prophet"* {*the 'prince that shall come'*} will agree to a 7 year *"covenant;"* however, after only 3½ years he'll break his agreement (*covenant*) and invade Israel.

242 This is a reference to the *abomination of desolation*.

243 God's wrath shall be poured out on the desolate (*The desolate are those who will follow the son of perdition.*).

covenant, but Daniel's prophecy doesn't reveal whether or not the son of perdition will actually be the initiator and/or enforcer of that covenant. If that covenant is spiritually (*rather than politically*) inspired, there could be another very logical alternative to consider, and we'll discuss that alternative in just a minute.

Only after this covenant or *"treaty"* (*however you wish to label it*) has been enforced will the world actually know the precise identity of its ***'many'*** participants. Whoever the many participants will be, as we just read in Daniel's prophecy, the covenant will be confirmed for seven years. However, Daniel also revealed that this ***'prince that shall come'*** will break the covenant in the midst of that seven-year period by desecrating the new Third Temple.[244] Thus, he'll cause the Temple sacrifice and oblation (*worship*) to cease, just as Daniel, Jesus and Paul formerly prophesied.[245]

In the past I leaned toward the belief (*as have many others*) that the son of perdition (*also called the anti-Christ*), through feigning a desire for peace, will be the initiator of this covenant. I firmly believed that he would be the one to agree to its confirmation as a means of preventing or ending a war with the nation of Israel. However, while that, at least to some degree, may be the case, scripturally speaking, it seems just as plausible to conclude that God's two powerful prophets may be the ones to both initiate and enforce this restrictive covenant, thereby, forbidding all Gentile access to the inner courtyards of the new Third Temple.

These two divinely powerful witnesses (*God's two prophets*) will be ministering (*'prophesying' — as Jesus' angel put it*) from the holy city Jerusalem[246] and will be the most powerful men on the planet, so it's entirely possible that God might enforce this restrictive covenant to ensure the safety of the 144,000 Jewish servants and to preserve the sanctity of the new Third Temple. We'll get back to the likelihood of this just ahead.

Heaven will back-up the earthly ministry of God's witnesses

All the powers of Heaven will enforce the 3½ year ministry and authority of God's two witnesses for the entire first half (*'forty and two months'*) of the tribulation period. This is why I'm personally finding it easy to allow for the possibility that God's two witnesses may actually be the initiators of this future covenant (*treaty*).

As we just read in **Rev. 11:2**, the angel told John that the outer court of the Temple would be given to the Gentiles until *"the times of the Gentiles"*[247] is fulfilled. That's exactly how it was with the last Temple, which is

---

[244] This wicked event is referred to as *"the abomination of desolation"*.

[245] Dan. 9:26-27, Mt 24:15-28, 2Th. 2:3-12

[246] We will cover this when we get to Rev. 11:7-8.

[247] Luke 21:24, Rom. 11:25, Rev. 11:1-3

why that particular courtyard was referred to as *the Court of the Gentiles.* The angel also told John that the Gentiles would tread the holy city under foot for ***'forty and two months'*** *(3½ years).* Therefore, it's very possible that the angel may have been foretelling of a sacred restriction that will be initiated and enforced by God, through His two witnesses, upon all Gentile Left-behinders. If so, this restriction — the *"covenant"* or *"treaty"* — would prevent the Gentiles from desecrating and/or interfering with the construction of the new Third Temple and/or any future worshipping therein. Thus, the *"covenant"* would establish spiritually inspired physical boundaries, which would serve to preserve the sanctity of the Temple Mount and new Temple.

Given the fact that God's two witnesses will be His instruments of authority and power on earth when this future covenant is enforced, this would make a great deal of sense. However, at this point, with several very insightful chapters ahead of us, it would be irresponsible to firmly embrace any opinion. This future covenant could just as logically (*and at the same time*) be both a *"politically"* and *"spiritually"* inspired agreement. Fortunately, once we get into the next few exciting chapters of John's vision, a lot of divinely inspired light will be shed on the future global dominance of the *"son of perdition,"* the definition of *"the beast,"* and the reason for the preservation of God's 144,000 Jewish servants.

Won't the Son of Perdition be powerful?

The son of perdition will certainly be powerful, but he will not have the spiritual authority to kill God's two witnesses until the end of the first ***'forty and two months'*** *(3½ years).* This is why Jesus' angel spoke specifically of a 3½ year period of restriction with regard to the Gentiles and the Temple Mount,[248] rather than the full seven-year period, which will be the initial length of the covenant (*treaty*). God knows full well that the son of perdition will break his agreement in the midst of the seven years. And, though it may be difficult for us to understand, that too is part of God's perfect plan.

~ I'll bet that really ticks Satan off! ~

It's possible (*though not provable*) that the son of perdition will agree to the terms of this covenant and stay out of Jerusalem during the first 3½ years, simply because during that period he will not have the power to kill God's two prophets. No doubt his subjects will be miserably suffering under the plagues of God's two witnesses, so it's logical to expect that the Left-behinders will wonder why their new powerful leader (*the son of perdition*) doesn't just kill their afflicters (*the prophets*) and put an end to

[248] Rev. 11:2

the miserable plagues and suffering. Thus, it does seem likely that the son of perdition could easily claim to be righteously withholding his vengeance and wrath while honoring his *"covenant"* with Israel and the prophets. This would allow him to appear to be morally superior to the prophets, while also enabling him to save-face among his millions of followers.

Off-Limits to all Gentiles

Rev. 11:2 ~ *continued*

> ***'But the court which is without the temple leave out, and measure it not; for it is given unto the Gentiles . . .'***

A quick on-line study of either Solomon's or Herod's Temples will give you a relatively clear picture of this larger, outer *Court of the Gentiles.* The inner courts, which in the past have always been off-limits to Gentiles, were referred to as: *the Court of the Priests, the Court of Israel, and the Court of Women.* These three courts were reserved for those who observed God's Laws and had either become a Jew ceremonially or were considered to be a Jew by birth. Once the Third Temple is built and the future covenant has been enforced, Gentiles will once again be completely restricted from entering those specific holy areas. We can be certain that this restriction will inspire the son of perdition and his hordes of wicked subjects to absolutely love Israel and the two witnesses, I'm sure!

~ *But hasn't Daniel's prophecy about the destruction of the Temple already been fulfilled?* ~

While it is true that "**Antiochus IV Epiphanes**," during his psychotic reign over the *Seleucid Empire* (*roughly 175-164 BC.*), did indeed horrifically desecrate and defile the rebuilt Second Temple, ***'causing the sacrifice and oblation*** *(i.e., offerings and tributes)* ***to cease,'*** there is no record of his having first agreed to a seven-year covenant. Therefore, Antiochus could neither scripturally nor historically be said to have met all the specifications of Daniel's prophecy. Hence, only a weak, unsupportable argument at best could be made, claiming that "**Antiochus IV**" fulfilled any part of Daniel's, Jesus' or Paul's interrelated prophecies regarding this future covenant.[249] Furthermore, we'll soon see that, as usual, there's good reason not to just lazily follow the masses and assume that Antiochus IV was the specifically wicked individual who was described in Daniel's prophecy. So, before we embrace any particular view, let's first be sure we've prayerfully taken-in the entire "BIGGER–PICTURE."

---

[249] We're getting ready to thoroughly dig into this subject — Dan. 9:26-27, Mt 24:15-28, 2Th. 2:3-12.

What about Titus in - AD 70?

"**Titus**" — son of Vespasian — eventually succeeded his father as the emperor of Rome (*AD 79-81*) and did, without a doubt, destroy the Second Temple, causing the sacrifice and oblation to cease, but he did not claim to be God. There is also no record of Titus having signed any seven-year treaty or covenant, which, if he had, could have fulfilled Daniel's prophecy regarding the ***'prince that shall come.'*** This is vitally important, because both Jesus and Paul clearly prophesied that this future false-prophet (*the son of perdition*) will stand in the Holy Place professing himself to be God. It's because this world dictator will do this that Jesus spoke in clear affirmation of the dual-nature of Daniel's prophecy, thus referring to this future false-prophet as *"the abomination of desolation."*[250] We'll discuss that portion of Daniel's dual-nature prophecy very soon. What's important to understand, at this point, is that most agree that, by destroying the Second Temple (*Herod's Temple*), Titus only fulfilled the following first part of Daniel's dual-natured prophecy:

> *'. . . from the going forth of the commandment to restore and to build Jerusalem unto the* ***Messiah the Prince*** *shall be* ***seven weeks****,* ***and threescore and two weeks*** *{of years}:*[251] *the street shall be built again, and the wall, even in troublous times. And after threescore and two weeks {of years}* ***shall Messiah be cut off*** *{killed},*[252] *but not for himself {meaning, for us};* ***and the people of the prince that shall come shall destroy the city and the sanctuary****;*[253] *and the end thereof shall be with a flood, and unto the end of the war desolations are determined.'*

℘ Daniel 9:25-26 ℘

---

[250] Mt. 24:15

[251] Most believe this to be a reference to Artaxerxes' 445 BC decree {*Neh. 2:1-8*}, which allowed Nehemiah to return to Jerusalem and rebuild both the city and its walls. Amazingly, exactly 483 years later, just as was prophesied, Jesus triumphantly entered Jerusalem, perfectly fulfilling this prophecy—Mt. 21:1-11.

[252] Starting in 9:25-27, Daniel explains that after 70 weeks of years all prophecy concerning God's entire plan for salvation and the establishment of His millennial and eternal kingdoms will be completed. This will fulfill all prophecy, thus, completing the full 70 week period. God left the final week of years *(the tribulation period)* to be fulfilled at a later date, because He didn't want to reveal precisely when the rapture of the Church would occur.

[253] This is a reference to Titus and his army. In our discussion of Rev. 11:2 we looked at Dan. 9:27, which is the second-part of this dual prophecy.

Titus' destruction of the Second Temple was a fulfillment of an important prophecy from the Savior. Jesus' teachings about the ensuing persecution of the Jews, the early Church, and the end of the world were documented by Matthew, Mark and Luke.[254] Each recorded Jesus' words, giving us slightly different bits of information — all of which are critically relevant with regard to our ability to understand this complete end-time picture of events. And the fact that they each recorded Jesus' words a little differently actually adds to the authenticity of their work, while, at the same time, giving us a clearer picture of both past and future events. The following scripture is a reference from Christ, which foretold of the formerly impending destruction of the Second Temple. As I stated, Titus fulfilled this shortly after Christ's glorious resurrection:

'And Jesus said unto them, See ye not all these things
{Jesus was referring to Herod's Temple}? verily I say unto you,
There shall not be left here one stone upon another,
that shall not be thrown down.' [255]

Matthew 24:2

As we've learned, ***'the prince that shall come'*** *(i.e., the son of perdition, the man who'll fulfill the second part of Daniel's dual-prophecy—Dan. 9:27)* will make a seven-year covenant and break it in the midst of the seven years. This is something neither "**Antiochus IV**" nor "**Titus**" ever did; therefore, neither Antiochus nor Titus could have fulfilled the second part of Daniel's prophecy. While it's true that Antiochus did desecrate the Second Temple, Jesus' prophecies[256] refer to a future, rather than past, fulfillment of Daniel's prophecy about the abomination of desolation. Thus, just as the apostle Paul prophesied (*2Th. 2:3-12*), at that future time the son of perdition will desecrate the new Third Temple by standing in the Most Holy Place and claiming to be the one true God.

There's no question about it; the second half of Daniel's prophecy, like the second part of Malachi's prophecy,[257] is still to come. Both prophecies will be fulfilled sometime in the near future. We don't know exactly when, but Jesus left us with the following warning about that future, supremely evil period:

---

[254] Mt. 24:15-24, Mk. 13:14-31, Luke 21:20-36

[255] Presently, just as was prophesied, only the Temple Mount remains.

[256] Study <u>all</u> of these (*Mt. 24, Mk. 13, and Luke 21*), but remember, Jesus' teachings cover more than 2,000 years. They we're never intended to be chronologically interpreted verse-by-verse. We will cover this further in the chapters ahead.

[257] Malachi 4

*'And **when ye shall see Jerusalem compassed with armies,**[258] then know that the desolation thereof is nigh. Then let them which are in Judaea flee to the mountains; and let them which are in the midst of it depart out; and let not them that are in the countries enter thereinto. **For these be the days of vengeance, that all things which are written may be fulfilled.**'*

Luke 21:20-22

*'. . . **Behold the fig tree, and all the trees;**[259] When they now shoot forth, ye see and know of your own selves that summer is now nigh at hand. So likewise ye, **when ye see these things come to pass,** know ye that the kingdom of God is nigh at hand. Verily I say unto you, **This generation shall not pass away, till all be fulfilled.** Heaven and earth shall pass away: but my words shall not pass away.'*

Luke 21:29-33

---

[258] This is a warning that the Left-behinders will witness the armies of the son of perdition surround Jerusalem prior to the *abomination of desolation*. Thus, with these words, Jesus is warning the Left-behinders to *'flee to the mountains.'* We'll see why later.

[259] It's been assumed that Jesus' reference to a *"fig tree"* was His way of specifically referring to the reestablishment of Israel as a nation, which occurred in 1948. Jesus, knowing that some would hastily rush to that assumption, clarified His prophecy by including the words, *and all the trees*. With those words Jesus included every other nation, which should have prevented us from making that assumption. Sadly, however, some still hastily drew the wrong conclusion and began teaching that that 1948 generation will be the generation to see the Second Coming of Christ. That particular generation may very well end up seeing the Lord's return, but Jesus' words are in no way an indication of that possibility.

Chapter 22

The Two Olive Trees Who Stand Before God

Rev. 11:3-4

> ***'And I will give power unto my two witnesses, and they shall prophesy a thousand two hundred and three score days*** *(3½ years)*, ***clothed in sackcloth.***
>
> ***These are the two olive trees, and the two candlesticks standing before the God*** *(capital "G")* ***of the earth.'***

Through His angel, Jesus relayed to John the significance of these two witnesses as though they are currently permanent fixtures before God. That might very well be the case, yet, since there are so few scriptural references capable of helping us to zero in on just who these two prophets are, we must again be careful not to get carried away while attempting to ascertain the true meaning of this passage.

Since Jesus' angel referred to these prophets as being both *"candlesticks"* and *"olive trees,"* his words may be linked to an earlier prophecy of Zechariah's, dating back to when the Second Temple was first rebuilt, which was roughly around 525-518 BC. In Zechariah's prophecies, he saw a prominent *"golden candlestick."* Apparently, the candlestick was similar in some ways to those John saw Jesus standing ***'in the midst of'*** in **Rev. 1:12-20** (*at the beginning of his vision*). Zechariah's candlestick had seven lamps (*bowls of burning oil*) with an additional lamp (*or stem*) elevated above the others.[260] We don't want to wander back into the subject of the mysterious Seven Spirits of God, so we'll just note (*for those who wish to look into this later*) that Zechariah's prophecies include many Messianic references.[261] The two references we are about to read may shed a bright light on our two tribulation period witnesses and also on the *"seven eyes"* John saw in his **Rev. 5:6** vision of the *"Lamb of God,"* who was seen standing in the midst of the throne.

---

260 The elevated stem represented Christ.

261 Zec. 2:6 thru 6:13

*'. . . for, behold, I will bring forth my servant **the BRANCH**.*[262]
For behold the stone that I have laid before Joshua;[263] *upon*
***one stone** shall be **seven eyes** . . . .'*[264]

Zec. 3:8-9

Zechariah's book contains so many historical references to both past and future events that, although it would be exciting to venture through them, we'd better just note what's immediately pertinent to our end-time journey and move on. Zechariah recorded[265] having seen two prominent figures, which he (*like the angel in John's vision*) referred to as ***'olive trees.'*** He also noted that he saw these two anointed figures standing before the Lord — one on the left side and one on the right side of the prominent ***'golden candlestick'*** *(which represented Christ).* Zechariah was told the following about the two olive trees in his vision:

*'These are the **two anointed ones**,*
*that stand by **the Lord of the whole earth**.'*

Zec. 4:14

Likewise, in his vision, John was told:

*'These are the **two olive trees**, and the **two candlesticks***
*standing before **the God of all the earth**.'*

Rev. 11:4

The remarkable similarity of the preceding scriptures could be an indication of their shared prophetic significance. Certainly, no one could deny that Zechariah and John seem to have seen the same heavenly beings, and it's not likely that their having done so was a coincidence.

~ So why didn't John see these anointed beings
when he first saw God's throne? ~

---

[262] The BRANCH is an obvious reference to Christ—Zec. 6:12-13, Ex. 25:33, 37:17-19, Isa. 11:1, Jer. 23:5, 33:15.

[263] In roughly 521-515 BC, Joshua, son of Jehozadak, was to be the high-priest of the rebuilt Second Temple.

[264] John saw Jesus as a Lamb – having *seven horns* and *seven eyes*, which, John was told, are the *Seven Spirits of God* sent forth into all the earth—Rev. 5:6, 1:4-9, 3:1, 4:5, Zec. 4:10.

[265] Zec. 4:3

Zechariah and John were both shown visions. Visions can be a God's-eye revelation of an actual past or future event or they can be powerful visual analogies, consisting of actual or merely symbolic objects. In the same way that Jesus isn't really a ***'Golden Candlestick'*** *(as Zechariah's vision symbolized)* or a ***'Lamb, having seven horns and seven eyes'*** *(as John saw in Rev. 5:1-10)*, the two prophets are not really ***'olive-trees'*** or ***'candlesticks.'*** John was simply shown this symbolic representation of the prophets standing together, ***'before the God of the whole earth,'*** so we would understand that God has placed them in a position of respect and authority as supportively submissive servants of Christ (*'the BRANCH'*).[266]

So who are the two witnesses?

Moses and Elijah are the only prophets whom we have good scriptural reason to believe will actually be these two ***'olive trees'*** in John's vision.

~ *Wait a minute! How in the world did you come up with that?!* ~

The preceding two passages (*Zec. 4:14, Rev. 11:4*) are the only directly relevant places in Scripture where two ***'olive trees'*** are seen standing ***'before the God of the whole earth,'*** and these scriptures are, as I've stated, nearly identical. Thus, it certainly wouldn't be illogical for us to allow for the possibility that Zechariah's two olive trees may very well be the same two olive trees and candlesticks John saw in his Revelation vision. Therefore, the obvious question is: *"Who are the two olive trees standing before God's throne?"*

To grasp this, we need to look at the "BIGGER–PICTURE"

I don't think Jesus allowed Peter, James, and John to witness His glorious, yet mysterious, mountaintop transfiguration[267] — in the presence of both Moses and Elijah — for nothing. When that event was over, Jesus told His three core disciples the following:

'Tell the vision to no man, until the Son of man {speaking of Himself} be risen again from the dead.'

Mt. 17:9

Jesus, of course, knew that if His many followers heard that Elijah had appeared they would also mistakenly jump to the same conclusion as did Peter, James, and John, who (*because of seeing Elijah*) had apparently

---

[266] Zec. 3:8-9, 6:12-13

[267] It is commonly believed that this event occurred on Mt. Tabor, west of the *Sea of Galilee*—Mt. 17:1-9.

assumed that *"the Day of the Lord"* had begun. My question is: *"Did Jesus allow Moses and Elijah to be seen with Him during His transformation for the purpose of revealing the identity of the two tribulation period witnesses?"* That doesn't seem likely. The Lord's mountaintop experience, by itself, proves nothing. That having been said, however, when we look at all the scriptures, "AS A WHOLE," a very logical reason for considering Moses to be the most likely second prophet in John's vision begins to emerge.

~ But I've read that Enoch will be the second prophet! ~

If you're one of those who've read or been taught that Enoch is the only possible person who could be the second tribulation period prophet, you certainly didn't read it in the Scriptures. But, before we start rolling through the exciting scriptures ahead, I know many have been exposed to this clearly unscriptural assumption about our big brother Enoch, so let's quickly get that errant teaching out of the way.

Apparently Enoch was such a great guy that God just took him into Heaven while he was still alive.[268] That, however, doesn't mean that Enoch is presently in a new body (*although he could be*) any more than is Elijah.[269] Nevertheless, since God just took Enoch, he must be a pretty special child of God. One day we'll all meet him and find out for ourselves. The fact that he never died, however, does not necessitate or prove, in any way, that he will be the second tribulation period prophet. The main reason for the surfacing of that unsubstantiated belief is directly tied to **Heb. 9:27**, in which the author states: ***'. . . it is appointed unto men once to die, but after this the judgment . . . .'***

Some have errantly interpreted the preceding verse to state that man can only die once before facing judgment. So, since neither Enoch nor Elijah have died, some believe them to be the only individuals who are qualified (*according to the preceding verse*) to be the two tribulation witnesses. We don't want to take the time to cover the total tonnage of scripture that, when properly interpreted, actually presents a much stronger case for Moses being that second prophet than it does for Enoch, so we won't even start down that lengthy trail. I'm confident a prayerful study of the complete book of Hebrews, in its proper context, will give clarity to the author's purpose for having written the preceding verse (*Heb. 9:27*).

Simply stated, the author of Hebrews was just making a general statement with regard to the natural fact that we all must die and, afterwards,

---

[268] We don't actually know why God took Enoch. It's possible that God just really liked him or wanted to spare him from a painful death or illness. The Scriptures just don't reveal this mystery.

[269] Since the son of perdition will be able to kill God's two witnesses at the end of the first 3½ years of the tribulation period, Elijah must presently be a mortal.

face judgment. Therefore, Christ Jesus, in like manner, died once, making atonement for all sin. That doesn't mean a person can't be resurrected in their mortal body (*as was Lazarus and several others*)[270] and die again. And, while digressing more deeply into the wonderfully illuminating book of Hebrews would be an exciting study, we need to stay the course and continue on our current end-time path.

If, however, we were to try and make a case for Enoch, we could refer to His end-time prophecy, which is recorded in the book of Jude (*verse 14*). There, Enoch (*father of Methuselah and great grandfather of Noah*) gave a very revealing end-time prophecy, which will greatly enlighten us when we get to the end of the first seven years of John's end-time vision. Enoch's prophecy reveals vitally important information about the triumphant return of Christ. And, while that is interesting, it is not a solid foundation for declaring Enoch to be the second tribulation period prophet.

If some of you (*for whatever reason*) still believe the *"Enoch Theory"* to be reasonably supported by Scripture, ask yourselves this question: What about Lazarus, whom Christ raised from the dead? He died twice. For that matter, what about all the people who were raised from the dead by Jesus, His disciples, and various other prophets? They've all already died twice. So, let's move ahead and see what pure Scripture reveals.

How could we fail to recognize their divine power?

Rev. 11:5

> ***'And if any man will hurt them** (God's two witnesses), **fire proceedeth out of their mouth, and devoureth their enemies: and if any man will hurt them, he must in this manner be killed.'***

Can you imagine even entertaining the thought of tangling with these two Heaven-sent prophets? Only a completely irreverent fool could be spiritually anesthetized enough to aggressively approach these two powerful witnesses! But, should a defiantly arrogant Left-behinder arise who'll be brazen enough to willfully attack these divine extensions of God's authority on earth, all I can say is: "I HOPE THEY CAN TAKE THE HEAT!"

Will God's two powerful witnesses be sociable?

The fact that God's two witnesses will have the power to instantly incinerate any foolishly aggressive attackers doesn't necessarily indicate that they'll be unapproachable, though that notion has been frequently put forth in many books and movies. The truth is the two prophets will be

---

[270] John. 11:1-44

mortals,[271] despite their great power, and they'll have descended with a commission to share the Gospel of Christ and compel the world to repent. They won't be coming to exact revenge. Therefore, there is no reason to assume that a humble Left-behinder will not be able to safely approach the witnesses, so long as he or she does so with good intent. Whatever ends up being the case, whether they're approachable or not, we can be sure that if strict boundaries will be enforced, those boundaries will be clearly defined by the two witnesses.

War will only play a Small Part

Rev. 11:6

> ***'These** (the two witnesses) **have power to shut the heaven, <u>that it rain not in the days of their prophecy</u>: <u>and have power over waters to turn them to blood</u>, <u>and to smite the earth with all plagues</u>, <u>as often as they will</u>.'***

It's pretty obvious that these two witnesses will be representing God's awesome power on earth, so I can't understand why these incredibly powerful prophets, who'll literally be indestructible and will have virtually unlimited power (*until they've completed their witnessing*), never seem to be recognized as being the instruments of God who'll be responsible for all the horrific plagues that will sequentially (*not randomly*) occur during the first half of the tribulation period! *(I know; that sentence was a mouthful!)* But how can we just mildly acknowledge the mind-boggling, "hand-of-God-incredible" authority of these two witnesses?! Their divinely, preordained ministry will be so miraculous in its enormity that they'll even be able to ***'shut heaven, that it rain not in the days of their prophecy.'*** This means that these two prophets will have the power to prevent it from raining, globally, for the entire 3½ years of their earthly ministry.

Can we actually imagine a 3½ year global drought? And, as if that were not enough, by their command, one-third of the world's oceans and seas will be turned into blood, and one-third of the drinkable water will be turned into poison! As the angel put it, these two prophets will have the divine authority ***'. . . to smite the earth with all plagues, as often as they will.'*** In fact, every terrifying plague John witnessed during the first half of the tribulation period can be directly attributed to the divinely persuasive powers that these two Heaven-sent witnesses will be employing as a final act of mercy from God the Father. This may sound incredible, but it's

---

[271] If the prophets were not mortals they wouldn't be able to be killed, as we know they will be, at the end of their 3½ year ministry.

precisely what the Scriptures reveal. Each of the trumpet-plagues we examined in Revelation Chapters 8 and 9 can clearly be attributed to God's severely "tough-love" and final attempt to "gather-in" the still stubborn "**remnant**" (*the last of the saints*) before the allegorical "Door of Salvation" is irrevocably shut. As we earlier established, when the two witnesses finish preaching the Gospel (*for the very last time*) and that door closes, not another soul will be saved;[272] the "MYSTERY OF GOD" will be finished, just as the mighty angel in John's vision loudly declared.[273]

Most of the Global Calamity will have a Spiritual Origin

If you've been erroneously taught that all the catastrophe during the first 3½ years of the tribulation period will be due to something other than God's plan for the redemption of His final group of rebellious kids (*the last of the saints*), I'd suggest that you stop and prayerfully reread Revelation Chapters 8 and 9 along with the corresponding notes from this book. As was earlier stated, God has designed these first 3½ years of plagues so as to prevent us from making the mistake of believing them to be anything other than His divine handiwork. Certainly the son of perdition will be employing every means of deception possible during his desperate attempt to redirect the focus away from God's two witnesses and on to himself, but the powerfully persuasive plagues of God's two prophets will still dominate world events during the first half of the tribulation period. The suffering that will be caused by their plagues will not be mere random happenstance or the result of global war. If we've learned anything from what we've read thus far, we should have learned that. War will certainly contribute to the global anguish and suffering, but its effect will pale when compared to the aftermath of the Rapture and the globally devastating effects of the trumpet-plagues of God's two witnesses.

As we surveyed the last few chapters of John's vision, we noted several obvious indicators that prove beyond any reasonable doubt that the trumpet-plagues will be "ACTS OF GOD," not for revenge, but for the purpose of giving the surviving Left-behinders a small taste of "HELL ON EARTH." There's simply no other rational explanation for unnatural, global effects like:

- "bloody hail" and all the green grass and **one-third** of the trees being burnt-up
- exactly **one-third** of the *seas* and *oceans* being turned into "blood"

---

[272] We'll see absolutely irrefutable proof of this as we move through Revelation chapters 11 thru 15.
[273] Rev. 10:1-7

- exactly **one-third** of the fresh water being "poisoned" (*made bitter*)
- exactly **one-third** of the *sun, moon* and *stars* being "darkened"
- demonic, scorpion-tailed locusts being released from within the bottomless pit in the heart of the earth.

Nothing man can produce could cause such unimaginable effects and neither could meteors, comets or asteroids. What's more, we haven't even included the 200,000,000 demonic killer-horsemen who will slay another **one-third** of the earth's population.

One final important thought:

As we've learned while examining the first six trumpet-plagues, God designed clear indicators into each plague, so as to prevent us from mistaking them to be something other than His powerful handiwork. We need to keep this in mind, since we've now reached the middle of the seven-year tribulation period and haven't discovered a single verse that could correctly be interpreted to indicate the repentance of even one Left-behinder. At this point in John's vision (*which depicts the middle of the seven-year tribulation period*) we still have no reason to assume that anyone (*other than the 144,000 Jewish servants*) has repented. That's about to change, but, for now, we must not forget that John was clearly told the following:

> *'And the rest of the men which were not killed by these plagues* ***yet repented not*** {still did not repent} *of the works of their hands, that they should not worship devils, and idols of gold, and silver, and brass, and stone, and of wood: which neither can see, nor hear, nor walk:* ***Neither repented they of their murders****,* ***nor of their sorceries****,* ***nor of their fornication****,* ***nor of their thefts****.'*

Rev. 9:20-21

I realize that we've digressed from identifying the two witnesses. But, not to worry; we'll do so in the next chapter.

Chapter 23

God's Tribulation Period Prophets

One of the two prophets will definitely be Elijah

In roughly 400 B.C., Malachi recorded the following two-part prophecy, through which the Lord foretold of a forerunner to the Messiah and also of a "latter-day" return of Elijah.

> *'Behold, I will send you Elijah the prophet before the coming of* ***the great and dreadful day of the LORD****:*[274] *And he shall turn the heart of the fathers to the children, and the heart of the children to their fathers, lest I come and smite the earth with a curse.'*
>
> **Malachi 4:5-6**

Fortunately, because Matthew recorded Jesus' explanation of Malachi's prophecy, we can understand its "earlier" and "latter-day" significance:

> *'. . .* ***Elias truly shall first come, and restore all things*** *{with these words, Jesus was confirming a latter-day return of Elijah}. But I say unto you, That Elias is come already and they knew him not {Jesus was referring to John the Baptist}, but have done unto him whatsoever they listed {whatever they willed}, Likewise shall also the Son of man suffer of them {Jesus was, of course, referring to His own death.}.'*
>
> **Mt. 17:11-12**

---

[274] Malachi's reference to *"the dreadful day of the Lord"* is a reference to the *Second Coming of Christ* (*Joel 2:31-32*), not a reference to Jesus' initial coming as the Messiah. Therefore, since the angel Gabriel explained to Zacharias (*the priest, Luke 1:11-17*) that his son (*John the Baptist*) would fulfill the first part of Malachi's prophecy (*by acting as a forerunner for Christ*) and, since Jesus clearly affirmed that Elijah will return to earth sometime in the future and fulfill the second part of this prophecy by *"restoring all things"* (*which he has not, as of yet, done*), we can conclude that the second part of Malachi's prophecy is yet to be fulfilled.

Through Jesus' words in the preceding verse, His disciples understood that He was referring to His forerunner, John the Baptist.[275] They didn't, however, initially understand that He was also revealing the dual-nature of Malachi's prophecy by affirming the future latter-day return of Elijah during the seven-year tribulation period.[276]

Remember their Mountaintop Experience

The fact that Jesus clearly told Peter, James, and John that Elijah's return will happen sometime in the future is solid proof that Daniel's prophecy[277] about the confirmation of a future seven-year covenant (*or treaty*), which will be signed at the beginning of the tribulation period, has not yet been fulfilled. Therefore, it's important that we understand the circumstances surrounding Jesus' statement.

Prior to Christ's death, His disciples fully expected that He would eventually lead them and the rest of the Jews in a revolt against the oppressive Roman Empire. Doing so, they believed, would prove Him to be the Messianic leader who, possibly with Elijah's help,[278] would ***'restore all things.'*** Therefore, having recently witnessed Elijah's glorious appearance with Moses and Jesus on the mountaintop (*where Jesus was miraculously transfigured—Mt. 17:1*), the disciples certainly couldn't have understood that, when Jesus told them: *"Elias (Elijah) truly shall first come, and restore all things,"* He wasn't speaking of the present but, rather, of a time in the distant future. In fact, Jesus was actually revealing that the second parts of both Daniel's and Malachi's prophecies (*which foretell of the same end-time period*)[279] were yet to be fulfilled.

When we read the whole Mount Transfiguration passage, we must keep in mind that, as I just stated, Peter, James and John believed Jesus would eventually show Himself to be the conquering Messianic King of Israel. Therefore, witnessing the appearance of Moses and Elijah (*the two most prominent and powerful prophets in history*) during Jesus' transformation must have seemed to be a confirmation of that expectation. How then could Jesus, after having been magnificently transformed right before their eyes, now be talking about dying? Instead of telling Peter, James, and John not to tell anyone what they had seen on the mountaintop until after His resurrection, from their perspective, Jesus should have been telling them how to prepare for war. Certainly they couldn't be expected to understand

---

275 Mt. 17:13

276 Mal. 4:1-6, Mt. 17:11, Mark 9:12

277 We covered this in Chapter 21 of this book—Dan. 9:27.

278 Please read the following insightful scriptures: Acts 1: 1-6 thru 8.

279 Mal. 4:1-6, Dan. 9:25-27

that! They thought that they had just witnessed the beginning of the fulfillment of Malachi's prophecy:

> *'Behold I will send you* ***Elijah*** *the prophet* ***before the coming of the great and dreadful day of the Lord*** *. . .'*
>
> **Malachi 4:5**

Peter, James, and John believed that ***'the great and dreadful day of the Lord'*** would begin with the coming of Elijah, which they believed they had just witnessed. That's why they asked Jesus about the future coming of Elijah as they descended from the mountaintop; they were confused. But Elijah's appearance on the mountaintop with Jesus and Moses was not the precursor to ***'the great and dreadful day of the Lord.'*** It is possible that Jesus, Moses, and Elijah talked about that future day (*period*), but we have no way of knowing if that was the case. We do, however, know that the dreadful day of the Lord is still to come.[280] And when it comes, Elijah and his partner (*most likely Moses*) will be instrumental in fulfilling Jesus' prophecy by restoring true worship to Israel.[281] What's more, they'll do it while heralding God's final call to repent to this lost and rebellious world. Once they've accomplished that task, they too will be martyred, resurrected, and called back to Heaven.

During Jesus' earthly ministry, He certainly didn't expect His disciples to understand these things, but He knew that later, after His resurrection and the descent of the Holy Spirit (*the Comforter*),[282] His words would begin to open doors of understanding for all believers. Collectively, all these scriptures reveal God's perfect plan for the salvation of all truly repentant souls and His plan for the wondrous establishment of His eternal Kingdom. The next few chapters of John's book will beautifully tie this all together.

Is it possible that Jesus meant something else?

Let's look at it logically. When the disciples asked why the Scriptures spoke of Elijah's future coming,[283] if Jesus' response (*Mt. 17:11-12*) was not

---

280 The Day of the Lord is a complex subject, of which the vengeful return of Christ, known as the Second Coming, will only be a part. We'll cover this later.

281 They'll do this with the help of God's special 144,000 Jewish servants — the "first-fruits" of Israel. That's not to say, however, that all Israel will turn to the Lord and repent; in fact, far from it! We'll see this explained in Chapter 14 of John's vision.

282 John 14:26, Acts 2:1-4

283 Mal. 4:4-6, Mt. 17:11-12

intended to be an affirmation that Elijah is still to come, Jesus would have simply told the disciples that Elijah's appearance on the mountaintop, coupled with John the Baptist's ministry, was a complete fulfillment of Malachi's prophecy. But that's not what Jesus said, and no one can scripturally support an argument that claims Jesus' prophecy regarding Elijah's future coming *"to restore all things"* has already been fulfilled. Simply put, Elijah has not, in any capacity, fulfilled Jesus' words by returning and restoring all things. What's more, while referring to that particular end-time generation, Jesus also said the following:

> *'Verily I say unto you, This generation {Jesus was referring to the tribulation period generation} shall not pass,* ***till all these things be fulfilled****.'*

℘ Matthew 24:34 ℘

Therefore, while it's true that Jesus declared John the Baptist to be the greatest of prophets,[284] John certainly did not fulfill Jesus' prophecy about the future coming of Elijah by having restored all things.[285] John did just as was prophesied in the first half of Malachi's two-part prophecy; he prepared the way for the Lord. Likewise, when God's two witnesses descend during the first half of the tribulation period they'll turn the hearts of the 144,000 Jewish converts and "**the remnant**" (*the last of those who will be saved*) to the Lord, and they'll restore true worship to Israel. But their preaching will be far more powerful than was John's and will be divinely established through the unleashing of unspeakably powerful plagues!

One final note about the 144,000 before moving on:

While making our way through the first half of John's end-time vision, we have found absolutely no scriptural evidence to support the assumption that the 144,000 Jewish servants will be reserved for the purpose of evangelizing the already heavily evangelized world. Therefore, since that supposition has absolutely no scriptural foundation, it shouldn't be taught. What we have learned is that (*as was just stated*) God intends to powerfully endorse the two witnesses preaching by unleashing powerful trumpet-plagues at their command throughout their entire 3½ year ministry. Thus, these two prophets will be more than capable of delivering God's message without additional help. What's more, in the next chapter of John's vision we will find solid scriptural evidence that will reveal why God intends to preserve a specially selected group of 144,000 Jewish servants. Hence,

---

[284] Luke 7:28
[285] Mt. 17:11-12

once we've learned what God's plan for those special 144,000 Jewish servants is, our understanding of this formerly enigmatic end-time period will be greatly enhanced.

~ But every book I've read says that the 144,000 will be evangelists!? ~

I realize that there may be a few who are still having trouble acknowledging that the Scriptures simply do not teach, anywhere, that the 144,000 will be evangelists, and that's okay for now. But when we get into Chapters 12 thru 14 of John's vision we'll see definite proof that God's two witnesses will be used, by God, to protect the 144,000 Jewish servants in one, specific, preordained location. The 144,000 simply will not be roaming the earth!

Chapter 24

Is It Presently Possible to Identify the Second Prophet?

The correct answer to the preceding question is, "No." It's not scripturally possible to know, with complete certainty, who Elijah's partner will be. That was easy. Disheartening as that may be, it is true. But does that mean that the Scriptures don't give us any clues? *Scriptural clues?*, now that's a different matter. The Scriptures may, in fact, give us some very exciting clues, so let's take a quick look at a few very interesting passages that may shed a powerful spotlight on just who this second tribulation period prophet will be.

Now that I've clearly stated that it's impossible to scripturally prove who the second prophet will be, I'll tell you that, personally, I have no doubt that Moses will be Elijah's partner. And, while, as I stated, I don't believe that this can be proven, I do believe we need to be mindful of all the scriptures — from Genesis to the book of Revelation — if we want to gain a proper perspective. Taking the time, however, to give this subject the attention it deserves would delay our end-time journey, so we'll just cut right to the heart of the subject.

In a Nutshell:

The Scriptures reveal that God made a covenant with Abraham[286] that the Law, which was initiated some 430 years later,[287] could in no way annul or make void. Though, originally the Hebrew exiles unanimously agreed to uphold God's righteous laws, they, like the rest of us, have miserably failed to do so. Fortunately, God never expected us to succeed. God is pure-holiness, perfect, and thoroughly righteous; whereas, we are sinful, selfish, self-willed, unholy, and unrighteous in the extreme. There's just no way even the best, most generous person could be seen as a reflection of perfect innocence when standing before the mirror of truth, which is God's Law and Holy Word. We all know the story. That's why the whole world,

---

[286] Gen. 12:1-3-7, 13:14-17, 15:4-6 and 15:12-21, 17:1-16, 22:16-18 — God extended His promise to Isaac and his descendants: Gen. 26:2-5, 26:24, 27:28-29, 28:3-4 and 13-15, 32:27-28, 35:10-12, 46:2-4, and also to David — Gen. 49:8-10

[287] Gen. 15:12-21, Gal. 3:17

not just Israel, needs a Savior. This was no surprise to God. The Law was designed to reflect our sin and, thereby, enable us to clearly see our desperate need for God's divine mercy and grace.[288] When Jesus came on the scene He began to reveal this truth, saying:

'But go ye and learn what that meaneth,
***I will have mercy, and not sacrifice**: for I am not come to*
call the righteous, but sinners to repentance.'[289]

ꕤ Matthew 9:13 ꕤ

Jesus didn't expect the world to offer Him a sacrifice. His eternal purpose has always been to be that holy, sacrificial Lamb.[290] The Law was merely imposed to serve as our teacher. It was intended to help us recognize the inescapable reality of our sinful nature. The Law never replaced or annulled God's original Abrahamic Covenant, a covenant which promised that mercy and grace would be extended to the world through faith in God's ability to provide the necessary atonement for sin. Thus, after having given the Law to the children of Israel (*as a schoolmaster—Gal. 3:22-25*), before dying, Moses prophetically explained that a special prophet would come and do that which neither he nor the Law could do.[291]

Not even Moses fully understood how significant the ministry of that future Prophet, the Messiah, would be.[292] Thus, nearly 1,500 years later, the Jews were still waiting for that Prophet of whom Moses had foretold. So, when John the Baptist came on the scene, the Jews sent priests and Levites to ask John if he was that prophet:

> *'And this is the record of John, when the Jews sent priests and Levites from Jerusalem to ask him, Who art thou? And he {John} confessed, and denied not; but confessed, **I am not the Christ**. And they asked him, What then? **Art thou Elias** {Elijah}? And he saith, I am not. **Art thou that prophet** {i.e., the prophet of whom Moses had prophesied} And he answered, No.'*

ꕤ John 1:19-21 ꕤ

---

[288] Gal. 3:21-26
[289] None of us, without Christ, are righteous before God; thus, righteousness can only be attained through faith in Christ's atonement, not through good works or religion.
[290] 25:34, Eph. 1:4, 1Pt. 1:20, Rev. 13:8
[291] Deut. 18:15-19
[292] 1Pt. 1:9-12

Since John already told them that he wasn't the Christ, their asking him if he was *"that prophet"* proves that they didn't understand that *"the Christ"* and *"that prophet"* would be one and the same person. Our heavenly Father provided Jesus — *the Son of Man, the Christ, that Prophet of whom Moses spoke* — for our redemption. This was always His plan. With Jesus' perfectly sinless life, death, and resurrection, God successfully atoned for the sin of all mankind.

~ Okay, but what about Moses? ~

Moses was and is no ordinary Prophet

Referring to Moses, Joshua wrote the following:

> *'And there arose not a prophet since in Israel like unto* ***Moses, whom the LORD knew face to face****, In all the signs and the wonders, which the LORD sent him to do in the land of Egypt to Pharaoh, and to all his servants, and to all his land, And in all that mighty hand,* ***and in all the great terror which Moses shewed in the sight of all Israel****.'*

Deut. 34:10-12

Sadly, the Jews rejected Jesus (*that prophet of whom Moses spoke*), saying:

> *'. . . we are Moses' disciples.* ***We know that God spake unto Moses****: as for this fellow {*irreverently referring to Jesus*}, we know not from whence he is.'*

John 9:28-29

This pridefully irreverent rebellion is why many Jews still refuse to recognize Jesus as their Messiah, even though Jesus fulfilled every Messianic prophecy (*with the exception of those that will be fulfilled during or after His return*). As is always true of religion,[293] it's much easier to conform to a strict set of traditions and worthless religious rituals than it is to humbly and completely surrender one's life to the true, living God, who knows our deepest, darkest thoughts and our every sinful desire.[294] Sadly, since Moses clearly warned the nation of Israel to anticipate the coming of

---

[293] The only true religion is that of which James spoke — Js. 1:27.
[294] Jer. 17:9-10

the Messiah (*that prophet*), their continual rejection of Jesus' divine authority leaves them without excuse.

~ *Why is this pertinent to our end-time study?* ~

Because the descendants of Jacob (*the Jews*) continue to deny the obvious Messianic status of Jesus, many Christians believe that God will send Moses back to Israel with Elijah. The Jews boast to be disciples of no one but Moses and, therefore, will not accept the teachings of Jesus. Thus, it makes a great deal of sense for God to send Moses back to Israel so Moses can openly declare that Jesus is the Messiah, the true High Priest and Son of God. What excuse will the Jews or anyone else have for rejecting Christ Jesus then, especially while seeing God bear witness to Moses' and Elijah's preaching by dispensing plague after plague in accordance to their words?

More support for Moses as one of the Witnesses

We all know that God met with Moses on top of Mount Nebo and kindly showed him all of the land that the Hebrews would eventually conquer and claim once they crossed over the Jordan River. Thus, while revealing this to Moses:

> '. . . *the LORD said unto him {Moses}, This is the land which I sware unto* ***Abraham****, unto* ***Isaac****, and unto* ***Jacob****, saying, I will give it unto thy seed: I have caused thee to see it with thine eyes, but thou shalt not go over thither.*'

Deut. 34:4

The Lord's words give us a little more perspective as to just how eternally significant God's covenant with Abraham and his descendants is. The Law had already been in force for forty years by the time Moses died on that mountaintop, yet God's preexistent covenant with Abraham — a covenant of grace and mercy rather than works — had not diminished one bit! This is probably why God chose Joshua (*whose name means "Jehovah is salvation"*), rather than Moses (*who represents "the Law" and "works"*), to lead the Hebrew children through the Jordan River and into the land God had promised to Abraham's descendants with an everlasting covenant, a covenant of grace, not works. Joshua is a symbol of God's merciful plan of salvation and justification through faith alone; whereas, Moses represents justification through the works of the Law, works that never could sanctify to the cleansing of the conscience (*the inner man, the soul*).[295]

---

[295] Heb. 9:6-9 thru 28, 10:1-5 thru 31, Gen. 12:1-3, 15:4-21, 17:1-22, 22:18, 26:2-4-5, 28:13-14-15, 35:10-12, 49:8-10

We made this little historical detour because, in the next few chapters of John's vision, we're going to see how monumentally important God's relationship with Abraham's descendants is. Presently, however, we just need to understand that, as far as God is concerned, from the day of Moses' death until now, absolutely nothing has happened to invalidate God's 3,900 year old covenant with Abraham. In fact, the Law, which was and still is a stumbling block to the people of Israel, was completely satisfied (*fulfilled*) when Jesus willfully offered His sinless life to atone for the sins of the world.[296] Jesus affirmed this with His final words on the cross:

*'. . . **It is finished**: and he bowed his head, and gave up the ghost.'*

℘ John 19:30 ℘

Moses' interesting Death, Burial and Resurrection

When Moses died on the mountaintop, God buried him that very day in a valley near *Beth-pe'-or* — somewhere in Moab. That, in itself, is an interesting mystery to me. If God didn't have some special plan for Moses' future, why didn't he send Joshua with some Levites up to retrieve Moses' body so it could be placed in a fittingly prominent location as was the usual custom? The Scriptures clearly reveal that Moses was a close and cherished friend to God, whom God wanted the people to continually remember and respect. Therefore, God's having buried Moses in this seemingly insignificant manner just doesn't fit! Moreover, it doesn't align with past patriarchal interment methods.

Though Moses had passed his authority on to Joshua in the sight of all the children of Israel — demanding that they harken to and respect Joshua as they had him[297] — it still seems that, if ever a special burial was in order, one would have been in order in the case of Moses' death. So what was God's reason for dealing with Moses' death as He did?

I have an unprovable, though very logical, reason for bringing this subject up. An incredibly insightful, possibly relevant (*we don't know for sure*), even more enigmatic scripture can be found in the tiny, though powerfully illuminative book of **Jude**. Later, we'll see why I declare this little letter from Jude to be so wonderfully prophetic and insightful, but, for now, let's just see how Jude's mysterious words — which could only have been revealed by the Holy Spirit — directly relate to Moses' burial. In the following passage, Jude wrote that, after burying Moses, God sent Michael (*the archangel*)[298] to retrieve his body:

---

[296] Col. 2:6-23

[297] Deut. 34:9

[298] Michael's name means: *"Who is like God?"* How cool is that?!

'Yet Michael the archangel, when contending with the devil ***he disputed about the body of Moses****, durst not bring against him a railing accusation, but said, The Lord rebuke thee.'*

℘ Jude 9 ℘

Don't you just love that? Michael didn't even waste time listening to Satan's accusatory words. Instead, Michael simply said: *"The Lord rebuke thee,"* and proceeded to take Moses' resurrected body to Heaven.[299]

The question is: *"Did God send Michael to resurrect Moses in his original mortal body, as He had Lazarus and various others, or did God resurrect Moses in a new, spiritually perfect body, like that of Christ's?"* There's certainly no scriptural reason to assume that Moses has already been resurrected to immortality before the appointed time.[300] That theory just doesn't fit within the overall framework of God's complete redemptive plan. I doubt that God sent Michael (*long before the coming of Christ*) to resurrect Moses for the purpose of making him the first mortal to receive a new, spiritual body. The Scriptures clearly regard Jesus as being: *the first begotten from the dead.*[301] That means that neither Moses, nor Enoch, nor anybody else could have been resurrected to immortality before Christ.

When God took Elijah (*alive*) into Heaven[302] He didn't give him a new spiritual body either. How do I know that? It's simple logic. If God had changed Elijah or Moses into new spiritually eternal beings, it would be impossible for either of them to come back as one of the two tribulation prophets, because God's two prophets (*the witnesses*) will be killed at the end of their earthly ministry. Of course, we don't know, with complete certainty, that Moses will be one of the two tribulation period prophets, but we have clearly proven that Jesus said Elijah will return. Therefore, we can state, with complete confidence, that Elijah is still a mortal being. Thus, Enoch and Moses may be as well.

During the abomination of desolation (*when the two witnesses will be killed*), their ministry will end. Only then will the Left-behinders see, to their great surprise and terror, the immortal resurrection of God's two faithful prophets. Thus, since Moses, like Elijah, could not have been the *"first begotten from the dead,"* he must also still be in his original mortal body. That means we have another very good reason to suggest that Moses

---

[299] We know Moses' body was, at some point in time, resurrected (*in the flesh, not to immortality*) and taken up to Heaven, because he later appeared with Elijah and Jesus on Mount transfiguration—Mt. 17:2-3.

[300] 1Th. 4:13-18

[301] Rev. 1:5

[302] 2Kgs. 2

is logically the most likely candidate to be Elijah's tribulation period partner. Let's face it, who could do a better job of convincing the Nation of Israel that Jesus is the fulfillment of God's covenant with Abraham and also a fulfillment of the Law (*and, therefore, the only way of salvation*) than Moses? What's more, why else would God send Michael to resurrect Moses and take him up to Heaven, instead of just waiting and resurrecting him with the rest of the saints?

Let's sum up:

Finally, since Jesus taught that Elijah will definitely be one of the two tribulation period witnesses and John recorded in **Rev. 11:3-4** that the angel referred to those two witnesses as, ***'the two olive trees' 'standing before the God of the whole earth,'*** we can logically conclude that Elijah is one of the two "olive trees" in Zechariah's earlier prophecy.[303] As for Moses, let's consider the following sound reasons for his candidacy:

- Moses has an unparalleled relationship with God
- Moses, more than anyone else, is uniquely important to the people of Israel and the Law
- Moses' body was mysteriously reclaimed and taken to Heaven
- Moses miraculously appeared on the mountaintop with both Jesus and Elijah
- The Jews declare themselves to be disciples of "**only**" Moses
- According to Rev. 11:8, Jerusalem (*where the Lord was crucified*), the spiritual hub of all Jews, is where God's two witnesses will preach the Gospel message for the very last time.

It's pretty clear that Moses is, by far, the most logical second olive tree in both John's and Zechariah's end-time visions. Therefore, after having considered all the evidence, Moses seems to be the most probable candidate for being the second tribulation period witness. Of course, we still can't actually prove our case for Moses, but, thus far, I haven't heard a better, scripturally pure argument put forth for another candidate.

---

[303] Rev. 11:1-6, Zec. 4:1-14

Chapter 25

The Abomination of Desolation

Rev. 11:7-9

> ***'And when they*** *(God's two witnesses)* ***shall have finished their testimony, the beast that ascendeth out of the bottomless pit*** *(keep in mind, a man could not ascend out of the bottomless pit)*[304] ***shall make war against them, and shall overcome them, and kill them.***
>
> ***And their dead bodies shall lie in the street of the great city, which spiritually is called Sodom and Egypt*** *(Jerusalem),* ***where also our Lord was crucified.***
>
> ***And they of the people and kindreds and tongues and nations*** *(apparently everybody on earth)* ***shall see their dead bodies three days and an half, and shall not suffer their dead bodies to be put in graves.'***

Although a seven-year covenant will have been initiated between Israel, the son of perdition, and many others,[305] 3½ years into the tribulation period God will allow the son of perdition to break his covenant, kill the two witnesses, and desecrate the new Third Temple — an event referred to in Scripture as *"the abomination of desolation."* Therefore, since the son of perdition will kill God's two witnesses,[306] it would not be illogical for us to allow for the possibility that, when this occurs, he may also choose to

[304] The beast is not a man, though many have mistakenly taught this. A mere mortal could not ascend out of the bottomless pit. Satan will use the *"son of perdition,"* the *"anti-Christ"* (*who will be nothing more than a "puppet-leader"*) to kill the prophets. John's vision will reveal that this *"beast"* is nothing more than an allegorical representation of Satan's entire demonic kingdom, and that that demonic kingdom (*the powers of darkness—Eph. 6:12-16*) has been fighting against God's eternal plan for the salvation of man since the creation of Adam and will continue to do so until Christ returns, at the end of the tribulation period. This is scripturally provable, and we will clearly see this emerge from the text as we continue.

[305] Daniel 9:27

[306] The Scriptures do not reveal precisely how the 144,000 will be killed.

behead or slaughter the subsequently defenseless 144,000 Jewish servants, who will likely still be worshipping God in that Temple.

As most of you know, by entering God's Temple, erecting an image of the beast (*which will likely symbolize Satan's demonic kingdom*), and claiming to be God, the son of perdition will have fulfilled both Daniel's and Paul's prophecies[307] regarding the occurrence of the abomination of desolation. There are additional scriptures, from both the Old and New Testaments, that foretell of this supremely evil event, like the following prophecy from our Savior:

> *'And this gospel of the kingdom {"the Mystery of God" — Rev. 10:7} shall be preached in all the world for a witness unto all nations; and then shall the end come.* [308] *When ye therefore shall see* ***the abomination of desolation****, spoken of by Daniel the prophet,* ***stand in the holy place*** *{The word "stand" actually means: to "set-up," to "erect." Thus, the image of "the beast" will be "erected" in the midst of the new Third Temple.}, whoso readeth, let him understand:* ***Then let them which be in Judaea flee into the mountains*** *. . .'*

℘ Mt. 24:14, 15-28 ℘

By the time we've finished surveying this chapter of John's vision, we'll have seen why Christ Jesus gave the preceding warning to those who'll be left-behind. For now, I'll just say that Jesus was not likely warning the 144,000 Jewish servants to flee from Judea, because they, like the prophets, won't be afraid to die. Instead, they're goal, as Christians, will most likely be to set a good example for those who will eventually repent.[309]

---

[307] Dan. 9:27, 12:11 and 2Th. 2:3-12

[308] According to Paul's letters, the gospel message has already been preached throughout the world—Ro. 10:18, Col. 1:2. See also John 1:9.

[309] Those *'who will eventually repent' (the remnant)* are the Left-behinders who will hope the testimony of God's two witnesses is actually true and will, therefore, *'flee'* Judea, as we just read Jesus warned them to do. The two prophets will have warned the Left-behinders to—*flee into the mountains*—or to stay away from Jerusalem and await their resurrection. Once "the remnant" has witnessed the resurrection of the prophets and the prophesied earthquake that will follow, killing exactly 7,000 people in Jerusalem, they'll know that the two witnesses' plagues and preaching will have been divinely inspired. Thus, "the remnant" will finally—*'give glory to the God in Heaven' (i.e., they'll repent).* Hence, they'll become the last saints to be redeemed. We'll thoroughly cover this as we continue.

Christians will not survive this Period

We're about to learn that, after God resurrects His two witnesses and the undecided Left-behinders finally repent, they'll all eventually be killed for refusing to worship the beast. Therefore, since, once the son of perdition begins killing those who refuse to receive his mark of compliance (*the mark of the beast*) nothing will prevent him from succeeding, it isn't logical to assume that, in the previous passage (*Mt. 24:14-28*), Jesus was suggesting that by fleeing from Judea the Left-behinders will be able to survive the remainder of the tribulation period. John's vision makes it perfectly clear that survival, for new believers, just won't be possible.

Therefore, it's far more logical to conclude that Jesus is warning the Left-behinders not to enter Judea but to, instead, *"flee"* — before Jerusalem is surrounded and seized by the approaching armies of the son of perdition.[310] If they remain in Judea they may not survive the mayhem or the earthquake that will follow the witnesses' resurrection and ascension into Heaven. Hence, by fleeing into the mountains, the Left-behinders will at least have a chance to survive long enough to repent after seeing the witnesses' testimony validated by their glorious resurrection and ascension into Heaven.

Don't be a fool

If you haven't yet accepted Christ and you have visions of somehow hiding and actually surviving these seven years of great tribulation, forget it! And forget every book you've read or sermon you've heard about newly repentant Christians surviving this period. The Scriptures are very clear. Not a single soul who refuses to worship the beast will survive the tribulation period. That is an absolute fact, and we will plainly see it proven before we finish our end-time journey. Our opinions about the interpretation of Scripture (*mine included*) are worthless, so I don't share my opinions without clearly stating that I'm doing so. Our goal is simply to allow pure, scripturally supportable truth to surface and nothing more.

Paul's message will help us understand these Final days

The Thessalonian Christians were being taught that the vengeful *"Day of the Lord"*[311] was upon them. So, with the following divinely inspired words, Paul set things right and greatly advanced our understanding of the

---

310 Luke 21:20, Mt. 24:15-20, Mk. 13:14-15

311 As has been stated, *"the Day of the Lord"* includes much more than just the Second Coming of Christ. We'll study that glorious day thoroughly, at the appropriate time. Here are just a few insightful Scriptures—2Th. 1:7-10, Mal. 4:1-3, Isa. 2:12, 3:6-9.

end-times. In the following passage, each reference to the son of perdition (*the anti-Christ*) will be preceded with an asterisk (*) and will be explained by a footnote.

Please read each corresponding footnote while surveying the following prophecy from Paul:

'Let no man deceive you by any means: for ***that day***[312] *shall not come, except there come a* ***falling away first,***[313] *and that **<u>***man of sin***</u> *be revealed,*[314] *the **<u>***son of perdition***</u>*; Who opposeth and exalteth *himself above all that is called God, or that is worshipped;* <u>***so that he as God sitteth in the temple of God shewing himself that he is God.***</u>[315] *Remember ye not, that, when I was yet with you, I told you these things? And now* <u>***ye know what withholdeth***</u>[316] *that **<u>*he*</u> *might be revealed in his time. For the* <u>***mystery of iniquity***</u>[317] *doth already work: only he who now letteth {*the Holy Spirit*} will let, until he be taken out of the way. And then shall **<u>***that wicked***</u> *be revealed, whom the Lord shall consume with the spirit of His mouth, and destroy with the brightness of His coming; Even **<u>***him***</u>*, whose coming is* <u>***after the***</u>

[312] When Paul wrote *'that day,'* he was referring to the Second Coming of Christ, not the rapture (*the catching-away*) of the Church.

[313] There will be a general apostasy (*a rebellion against the Gospel of Christ*), which is already happening all around the world and will only continue to intensify.

[314] This is simply an acknowledgment that, before the Second Coming of Christ, which will occur at the end of the tribulation period, the son of perdition (*"the anti-Christ," also referred to as "the false-prophet"*) will have been revealed.

[315] Jesus and Daniel refer to this as *"the abomination of desolation."*

[316] This refers to the Holy Spirit's control over what happens spiritually here on earth. When it's time, the Holy Spirit will *"pull back"* (*though not totally*) His control and allow Satan to empower the son of perdition (*the false-prophet*) to rule over every inhabitant of the earth. This will happen as the Church is raptured but <u>not</u> before.

[317] Just as there's a "Mystery of God" (*God's formerly mysterious plan of salvation—see the discussion in Rev. 10:5-7*), there is also a "mystery of iniquity" (*Satan's foolish plan of rebellion against God and His <u>true</u> servants*). This may even predate Adam and will continue until the end of the final 24-hour day (*which will be the last day of the Millennial Period*). On that day Satan will be cast into the *"eternal lake of fire"*—Rev. 20:10.

working of Satan [318] ***with all power and signs and lying wonders, And with all deceivableness of unrighteousness in them that perish***; *because they received not the love of the truth {the message of the two witnesses}, that they might be saved.* [319] *And* ***for this cause God shall send them strong delusion,*** [320] ***that they should believe a lie***: *That they all might be damned who believed not the truth, but had pleasure in unrighteousness.'*

2Th. 2:3-12

Paul's preceding Thessalonian message makes it clear why Jesus made the following statement:

'For there shall arise false Christs, and false prophets, ***and shall shew great signs and wonders***; *insomuch that,* ***if it were possible,*** [321] ***they shall deceive the very elect****.'*

Mt. 24:24

But just who exactly are "the elect?"

When Jesus used the term, ***'the very elect,'*** He meant us. Scripturally, *"the elect"* refers to the saints (*God's faithful servants, from both before and after the coming of Christ*). This, as we briefly covered, is one way we can be sure, with complete confidence, that we won't be here, on earth, to be exposed to the son of perdition's powerful deception. If we were here

---

[318] The word—*'after'*—in this verse simply means—*in accordance with*. This implies that the son of perdition will be empowered to do the work of the devil. That doesn't mean he'll be possessed by Satan. Satan, unlike God, is not omnipresent and could not, therefore, effectively run his demonic kingdom if he were confined to just one body.

[319] Paul is referring to those future, still unrepentant Left-behinders, who, even after having witnessed the miraculous plagues of God's two prophets for 3½ years, will still not repent — not even after having clearly seen God raise His two witnesses from the dead.

[320] These last two verses of Paul's powerful prophecy mean exactly what the interpreters of the King James Bible wrote. They need no clarification; however, we will thoroughly discuss them as we continue our exhilarating journey through the rest of John's vision.

[321] Remember, Jesus said, *'if it were possible,'* because deceiving *'the elect'* won't be possible, since we won't be here when the tribulation period begins—John 3:36, Ro. 1:18, 5:9, Eph. 5:6, 1Th. 1:10 and 4:13 thru 5:9.

during the tribulation period, Jesus said that even we — ***'the elect'*** – would be deceived. That's how unbelievably powerful the deception of the son of perdition will be.[322] And it's why John's vision, as we will continue to see, doesn't indicate the repentance of a single individual (*other than the 144,000*) before the resurrection and ascension of God's two witnesses. In affirmation of this truth, Jesus stated the following:

> *'Watch ye therefore, and pray always, **that ye may be accounted worthy to escape all these things** that shall come to pass, and to **stand before the Son of man**.'{If we go through any of the tribulation period, we will not have escaped all these things!}*[323]

Luke 21:36

> *'The Lord knoweth how to deliver the godly **out of temptations**, and to reserve the unjust unto the day of judgment to be punished . . .' {As we've already learned, there will be no real peace during the first half of the tribulation period. Therefore, it's simply not scriptural to suggest that God would subject His faithful, already repentant children (the saints) to the plague infused ministry of His two witnesses, a ministry intended to call the blatantly rebellious inhabitants of the earth to repentance.}*

2Pet. 2:9

When we put everything we've studied together, we have good reason to be very encouraged. We don't have to go through any of these awful events. Jesus clearly assures us that we have a choice. We can "**escape**" this entire end-time period by simply repenting and fully surrendering our lives to Christ before the tribulation period begins. The 144,000 Jewish servants will apparently not have done this. Thus, though they'll be protected (*at least to some degree*) from the effects of the witnesses' plagues, they will have to endure the first half of the seven-year tribulation period.

---

[322] 2Th. 2:7-12

[323] To be counted worthy of escaping all the events of the tribulation period, we must put all of our faith in Christ and, thus, be (*as Jesus termed it*) "born-again," into the Kingdom of God, before the tribulation period begins. Please read John 3:1-21.

The world will rejoice and party, but not for long!

Rev. 11:10

> ***'And they that dwell upon the earth shall rejoice over them, and make merry*** *(when the two witnesses are killed)*, ***and shall send gifts one to another; because these two prophets tormented them that dwelt on the earth.'***

According to everything Jesus' angel told John, the witnesses bodies will be irreverently left *"dead in the streets"* for three and a half days, like trophies! Killing these two formerly indestructible prophets will prove to the son of perdition's foolish followers that he is more powerful than the God of the two witnesses. At least it will seem that way. Since no one else will have been able to kill the two prophets, their deaths, at the hand of the son of perdition will appear to validate his claim to be the one true God. Sadly, his massive foolish group of followers will not recognize the obvious truth, which will be that the son of perdition will be nothing more than a *"puppet-on-strings"* to Satan. Most of the Left-behinders will be so wicked-hearted and foolish that they won't even wait for 3½ days to see if God's two powerful witnesses will actually rise from the dead, as the prophets will likely have forewarned.

We've seen time and time again how disrespectfully the bodies of murdered ambassadors, reporters, contractors, fallen Israeli or American soldiers, or even just ordinary Christians have been treated in the middle-east and elsewhere, often after having been brutally tortured to death. It's not a pretty sight! So, how should we expect the hundreds of millions of hatefully motivated, defiantly rebellious Left-behinders to treat the martyred bodies of God's two prophets after having suffered through 3½ years of the prophets' tormenting plagues? Once God's two witnesses are dead and the son of perdition has taken over and defiled the Temple (*by erecting the image of the beast in the Holy of Holies and boldly declaring himself God*), the defiant Left-behinders will believe there's no longer any reason to hold back or restrain their hostility.

As we've established, John doesn't give us any real details about how God's two witnesses will be killed, so we really don't know just how far God will allow the torturing and killing of the two witnesses to go. In fact, we don't even know if they will be tortured. But, if we consider the former conduct of the children of Israel at the base of Mount Sinai, when Moses stayed a little too long on the mountaintop,[324] or the current murderous persecution of Christians in Islamic countries, I'd guess that these future

[324] God immediately had 3,000 people executed because of that particular idolatrous outburst - Ex. 32:1-35.

worshippers of the son of perdition are probably going to eagerly break all records of malicious ill-restraint and unbridled debauchery during the celebratory killing of God's two witnesses and the 144,000.

What will happen to the 144,000 Jewish servants?

If the 144,000 are not killed on the same day as are God's two witnesses, they'll probably be the first to be symbolically beheaded when the damnable mark of the beast begins to be imposed. As I stated earlier, we don't know the specifics regarding the deaths of the prophets or the 144,000, so, since the Scriptures don't tell us, let's not guess! The good news is as we survey the next three chapters of John's vision we'll see irrefutable proof that, after John saw the eternally damnable mark of the beast being forced upon the surviving Left-behinders (*which won't begin until after God's two witnesses have been resurrected and "the remnant" has repented*), God's special 144,000 Jewish servants will immediately be seen resurrected, clothed in white, and jubilantly singing before God's throne!

Even a Mule flees from Danger

The foolishly wicked "majority" of Left-behinders will not have *"fled to the hills"* as Jesus warned, nor will they have stayed away from Judea with the much wiser "**remnant**." Instead, many of them will have remained in Jerusalem (*or wherever they'll be around the world*) celebrating, rejoicing, and sending each other gifts, just as the scripture reveals. They'll defiantly mock God and His two witnesses just as they mock God and Christians today. In fact, as followers of the false-prophet (*which is another name for the son of perdition*),[325] when they enter Jerusalem and the Temple to help *"set-up"* the wicked image of the beast (*whatever that will be*), they'll have become willful participants in *"the abomination of desolation"* — the ultimate desecration of God's Holy City and Temple.

Thus, just as was true of those who formerly mocked Jesus while He was willfully allowing Himself to be publicly humiliated and tortured for our atonement, I doubt it would be presumptuous of us to expect that the future hate inspired Left-behinders will also irreverently mock God's two witnesses and make sport of His special 144,000 Jewish servants. It won't matter in the least that those two witnesses will have been God's final attempt to save the last of the lost and rebellious world from what will surely be an eternally dark and agonizing fate if they don't repent!

---

325 The "false-prophet"(*in Mt. 24:15-24, Mk. 13:22 and Rev. 16:13, 19:20*) is the son of perdition of whom Paul wrote—2Th. 2:3, 4-12. This is, as the Scriptures will clearly reveal before we're through, <u>not</u> an opinion.

Party-on folks, but you're in for the shock of your lives!

I'm sure the deaths of God's two witnesses and His 144,000 servants will be violently gruesome, something about which we'd rather not read, so we'll just embrace the knowledge that neither the prophets nor the 144,000 Jewish servants will stay dead for long and move on into the exciting second half of Revelation Chapter 11. As we do, we'll see how God intends to respond to the killing of His two faithful witnesses.

Chapter 26

The Power Shift

As we made our way through the previous chapters, we learned that during the first half of the seven-year tribulation period a symbolic beast of sorts will ascend from the depths of a spiritual place called *"the bottomless pit"* and make war with God's two witnesses. Then we read, in **Rev. 11:7-10**, that that beast will eventually kill God's two prophets and desecrate the new Third Temple in Jerusalem. That being the case, we've obviously reached the middle of the seven-year tribulation period. So, since we're about to enter the second half of this extremely wicked period, it's important that we understand just what this analogous "**beast**" John saw rise up out of the bottomless pit actually represents.

Could all this be said of a mortal being?

I realize that it's difficult for some to accept that the beast John saw rise up and out of the bottomless pit will not be a mere mortal, and I understand why. But we will clearly see that John's having been told that this beast will – ***ascend out of the bottomless pit and make war with God's two witnesses*** – was not an indication that the false-prophet (*the son of perdition, the anti-Christ*) will be possessed by Satan. In fact, there's no scriptural indication that he'll be possessed at all, and yet, even without any proof, many have embraced that assumption. The false-prophet will, however, be completely manipulated by Satan and his wicked subordinates (*fallen-angels—Rev. 12:7-9*) — "**the beast**." Therefore, though Satan (*through the use of "demonic principalities and powers of darkness"—"the beast"*) will certainly manipulate humans and nations in order to accomplish his will, as we continue we will see that this reference to "**the beast**"[326] will be irrefutably proven to be a reference to much more than just a demonically manipulated man.

~ So then, to what or to whom was the angel referring when he spoke of a beast rising up out of the bottomless pit? ~

---

[326] Rev. 11:7

When Jesus' angel referred to "**the beast**" in **Rev. 11:7**, he was simply giving John some spiritual insight — a port-hole view as it were — into the demonic principalities and powers of darkness that neither we nor John would be able to see or understand without God's help. Most of the time (*though not always*) the powers of darkness that make up this "**beast**" are visually imperceptible. However, if we were still here, on Earth, during the tribulation period, we would see this spiritual beast manifest in many forms, starting with the powerful *"signs and lying wonders"* [327] that will be demonstrated by the false-prophet (*the anti-Christ*) as he powerfully goes about the earth deceiving the nations into submitting to his authority.

God used Paul to teach us these things

We've been studying Paul's clarification of these spiritual principalities that make up "**the beast**" all along.[328] Paul taught that the powers of darkness under Satan's control exist in a spiritually real, though mostly invisible world — just as do God's heavenly hosts (*angels*). We don't want to further digress into this subject, so we'll just leave the study of angels and principalities to our individual exploration. For now, let's focus on the future power and authority that this spiritual, beastly kingdom will have over the inhabitants of the earth. Through "**the beast**" (*the powers of darkness*) and the "**false-prophet**," Satan will powerfully dominate most of the final 3½ years of the tribulation period. In fact, Satan's demonic subjects are going to be allowed to kill every survivor who refuses to submit to the authority of the false-prophet's tyrannical, global kingdom (*Rev. 13:15*). This (*at least in part*) is why, in the following passage, Jesus warned those who survive the first 3½ years to expect and prepare for even greater tribulation during the second half of this seven-year period:

> *'When ye therefore shall see* ***the abomination of desolation****, spoken of by Daniel the prophet,* ***stand*** *{set-up, erected}* [329] *in the holy place, (whoso readeth, let him understand:) . . . .' '. . . For* ***then shall be great tribulation****, such as was not since the beginning of the world to this time,* ***no****,* ***nor ever shall be****.'*

Mt. 24:15 & 21

---

327 2Th. 2:2-12

328 Eph. 6:12-18, 2Th. 2:8-12

329 According to Dan. 12:11, the image of the beast will be *"set-up"* (*erected*) in the new Temple, so, since this world dictator will *"sit in that Temple, declaring himself to be God"* (*2Th. 2:3-4*), if *"the beast"* will represent a mere mortal, who will claim to be God, why wouldn't the citizens of this global empire simply worship that mortal, instead of erecting an image of him to worship in the same Temple?

Most still won't repent

The foolish Left-behinders (*who will disdainfully detest the idea of humbly submitting to God's authority*) will frantically flock to the false-prophet. They'll do so desperately hoping that his apparent divinity and supernatural powers will eventually be the means to their ultimate vindication for having chosen to rebel against God and the Church. Thus, when the false-prophet is eventually allowed to kill God's two witnesses, the proud majority of Left-behinders will rejoice in the power of their new, earthly god[330] — *"the son of perdition"* — *"the false-prophet."*

We've heard this Rhetoric for Years

The purposefully agonizing and persuasive trumpet-plagues of God's two witnesses will be perceived as being the exact opposite of tough-love and divine tolerance. Hence, it should be easy for the false-prophet to blame the pre-tribulation period's problems on Christians and the tribulation period's anarchy and suffering on the "INTOLERANCE" of God and His two witnesses. I can hear the lambasting now, because I've heard the same irreverently arrogant pomposity freely flow from the wicked hearts and mouths of countless lost and rebellious souls for years. The false-prophet and his subordinates will probably say something like:[331]

"These messengers couldn't have come from Heaven,
because no truly loving God would cause such merciless
suffering and universal calamity!"

Since we (*the true Church*) have heard this type of willfully ignorant rhetoric regarding God's allowing the existence of evil in the world, year after nauseating year, it should actually be relatively easy for the false-prophet to present himself as a savior of sorts — "God in the flesh."[332] Thus, his doing so will conversely make God's two witnesses appear to be merciless instruments of an intolerant and cruel god.

Everyone is primed and ready for this New-world Leader

For several years Satan has not so subtly been conditioning the world for the emergence of a new-world leader, especially during these last few generations. Through the almost cancerous influence of social progressiv-

---

330 Mt. 24:21-24, 2Th. 2:3-12, Rev. 16:13, 19:10, 20:10

331 Of course we have no way of knowing what the actual words or tactics of the false-prophet will be. Only God and those who'll be left-behind will know for sure, so let's not be here to find out!

332 It's also possible that he'll be seen as being the long awaited *"twelfth Imam."*

ism in most governments, secular schools, universities, and even (*in some cases*) through what the world loosely refers to as Christian religions, (*which, occasionally, are nothing more than social, religious gatherings or even cults*), Satan has succeeded in turning our perspective of what should obviously be "GOOD" or "BAD" and "RIGHT" or "WRONG" upside down.[333]

'Woe unto them that call evil good, and good evil; that put darkness for light, and light for darkness; that put bitter for sweet, and sweet for bitter!'

Isaiah 5:20

Not surprisingly, both Jesus and Paul also warned of this latter-day apostasy and falling-away from a reverent fear and love of God.[334]

'And because iniquity shall abound, the love of many shall wax cold.'

Matthew 24:12

Jesus' words flawlessly describe today's universally immoral, though *"politically correct,"* majority. And, sadly, we must acknowledge that the global majority, every day, is moving closer and closer to total alignment with Jesus' description of what will be that final, utterly depraved and profane end-time generation that will have to endure this horrific period of great global tribulation and unspeakable distress.

[333] Isa. 5:20, Rom. 1:18-32
[334] 2Th. 2:3

Chapter 27

What Jesus Taught About This Period

This is why I just love God's perfectly designed and inspired Word. As we lightly discussed earlier, there are three very similar accounts of Jesus' teaching about the end-time period John was shown in Revelation Chapter 11.[335] All three of those accounts contain important details regarding the *"abomination of desolation,"* which will occur in the middle of the tribulation period. If we want to clearly see the complete picture, as Jesus intended, we can do so by first gleaning the pertinent facts from all three, slightly different, yet perfectly accurate, accounts of Jesus' end-time message. But we must keep in mind that Jesus' entire prophetic sermon covers nearly 2,000 years, not just the end-times. And, while that's true, when we read Jesus' end time message in the light of Scripture as a whole, it becomes clear and easy to understand.

Jesus started His end-time sermon by explaining that the existing Temple (*the Second Temple—Herod's Temple*) would be completely destroyed: ***". . . there shall not be left one stone upon another . . . ."*** We earlier established that this was fulfilled by Titus in AD 70. Then, as Jesus continued, He warned His disciples and all future believers of the many trials and hardships that we, as believers, should expect to endure in the years preceding His eventual return. Finally, Jesus concluded His end-time sermon with a brief summary of the entire tribulation period, which included a prophetic description of His triumphant return to earth.

As I've stated, a close study of Jesus' end-time sermon will reveal that Jesus never intended us to interpret each event of His end-time message chronologically (*verse by verse*). Yet, sadly, many have mistakenly neglected to recognize this truth and have, consequently, caused many to unwittingly dart off of God's perfectly straight and level path of scripturally accurate interpretation and onto the treacherously steep and infinitely directional slopes of endless supposition.

The fact that there are many varying opinions and interpretations regarding the last days doesn't change the logical reality that there is always only one correct interpretation of every scripture. Paul taught that we all

---

[335] Mt. 24:14-30, Mk. 13:14-26, Luke 21:20-24

see through a glass darkly.[336] Hence, none of us — independently — have all the answers. That's why unified study, with the Holy Spirit (*the Comforter*)[337] as our teacher, is so critically important to the growth and understanding of the Church. God, through various prophets and apostles (*about 40*), has dispensed the pure, unadulterated TRUTH, and He did this over about a 1,500 year period so as to establish the Bible's obvious divine inspiration. Now, it's up to us, the body of Christ, to humbly submit one to another and, together, rightly divide God's Holy Word. What's more, if we will humbly allow it, these scriptures will miraculously interpret themselves! Thus, all we need to do is keep our *opinions, theories* and *presuppositions* from preventing the divine self-interpretation of God's Holy Word.

Pure-Scripture always Supports Pure-Scripture

Scripture supporting scripture is a simple logical reality. We've been referring to the following three accounts of Jesus' most prophetic end-time message over the entire course of our journey. Now it's time to look at how remarkably God's perfectly accurate Word uses all three separate accounts of Jesus' sermon to give us "**one**" clear picture of the *"abomination of desolation"* — the wicked event that will mark the middle of the tribulation period.

The following three Gospel accounts are kind of like an officer recording different testimonies from three separate individuals, each having witnessed the same accident but from different corners of the same intersection. Our three witnesses are **Mark** (*who told mostly Peter's account*), **Luke** (*who was an expert at collecting and recording historical information from everyone*) and **Matthew** (*one of Jesus' personally chosen disciples*). Their three testimonies will address the following important question:

> ☙ How do we know that "the remnant" will flee from the city of Jerusalem, head for the hills and escape the earthquake that will follow the ascension of God's two prophets? ❧

Nearly 2,000 years ago Christ warned that the severe suffering God will bring on the earth through His two witnesses, during the first half of the seven-year tribulation period, will be no comparison to the "**even greater**" suffering that will immediately follow, during the second half of that seven-year period. The following scripture is part of Matthew's account of that warning:

---

336 1Cor. 13:12

337 John 14:16-26, 15:26, 1Jn. 2:27

*'When ye therefore shall see **the abomination of desolation**, spoken of by Daniel the prophet, **stand** {i.e., set-up, erected} in the holy place, (whoso readeth, let him understand:) **Then let them which be in Judaea flee into the mountains** . . .' '. . . For then shall be **great tribulation**, **such as was not since the beginning of the world to this time**, **no**, **nor ever shall be**.'*

{Those last few words reveal a very important clue!}

Mt. 24:15 and 21

Jesus clearly warned that there has never been and never will be any tribulation that will compare to the *"even greater tribulation"* that will follow after the occurrence of the abomination of desolation. Not even the tribulation that will result from the plagues of God's two witnesses during the first 3½ years will compare to what will follow once this false prophet is allowed to totally take over and rule the world. I failed to fully grasp this fact for years, but the truth of this is as clear as scripture can get. Jesus is warning all the Left-behinders and especially "**the remnant**"[338] to brace for even more severe tribulation during the second half of the seven-year period than they will have already endured during the plague infused ministry of God's two witnesses![339] This will become unmistakably apparent as we explore the next few chapters of John's Revelation vision. By including the following words: ***'then shall be great tribulation, such as was not since the beginning of the world to this time, no, nor ever shall be,'*** Jesus proved He was referring specifically to the end-times.

There are still many who mean well but are continuing to teach that Jesus' words have already been fulfilled. Frankly, I can't see — considering Jesus' clear reference to the end-times — how anyone can continue holding to that belief. In order to do so we would have to believe that there will never be any future event or chain of events (*including the tribulation period*) that will be more devastating than those events that occurred shortly after Jesus' death. Furthermore, as if to emphasize the future severity of the last 3½ years of the tribulation period, which will be devastatingly concluded by the pouring out of God's seven plagues of wrath and the immeasurably destructive, triumphant return of Christ, Jesus continued by saying:

---

[338] This is a reference to the wiser Left-behinders, whom we will see repent 3½ days after the witnesses are killed.

[339] We should note that this period of *"even greater tribulation,"* to which Jesus is referring, includes the end of the second half of the tribulation period, when God's plagues of wrath will be poured out and the Second Coming of Christ will occur.

'And except those days should be shortened,
there should no flesh be saved: ***but for the elect's sake*** [340]
those days shall be shortened*.'*

࿐ Mat. 24:24 ࿐

Jesus warned that there will come a period of such utterly severe tribulation and universal carnage that, if God doesn't intervene, not a single soul will survive; however, for the elect's sake (*i.e., the saints*) God will prevent that from happening. There's a very exciting reason why Jesus gave the elect this assurance, and when we get closer to the end of John's vision that reason will emerge.

~So, what's special about Luke's account of Jesus' message? ~

Luke recorded the same message as did both Matthew and Mark, but before we look at Luke's account we should note that it was Jesus who originally warned the Left-behinders to flee into the mountains when they see the abomination of desolation about to occur. Hence, during their 3½ year ministry, God's two witnesses will most likely just repeat Jesus' earlier warning and tell the Left-behinders to *"flee from all of Judea"* before the false-prophet and his followers surround Jerusalem and takeover.

Luke reveals what will happen during this Chapter 11 portion of John's vision (*which depicts the middle of the tribulation period*), so we're going to examine those scriptures presently. But, before we do, we should also note that Mark's account of Jesus' end-time message is very similar to that of Matthew's[341] (*which we learned while surveying Rev. 6:1-2 and 11:1*), so we have no need of revisiting that passage.

Luke adds some insightful information about how the abomination of desolation and the killing of God's two witnesses will come about, information which neither Matthew nor Mark included. What's more, Luke's account reveals why Jesus warned everyone who will listen to flee from Judea:

> *'And* ***when ye shall see Jerusalem compassed with armies****, then know that the desolation thereof is nigh.* ***Then let them which are in Judaea flee to the mountains****;* ***and let them which are in the midst of it*** *{Jerusalem}* ***depart out****;* ***and let not them that are in the countries enter thereinto****. {With these words, Jesus is apparently warning everyone outside of Jerusalem*

[340] Mt. 24:24-31, Mk.13:22 and 27, Luke 18:7

[341] Mt. 24:15-30

and all over the world <u>*not*</u> *to follow the son of perdition into Judea.} For these be the days of vengeance, that all things which are written may be fulfilled . . . .'* [342]

'<u>**And they shall fall by the edge of the sword**</u>, <u>**and shall be led away captive into all nations**</u>: <u>**and Jerusalem shall be trodden down of the Gentiles until the times of the Gentiles be fulfilled**</u>.'*{In roughly 487 BC, Zechariah (14:1-11) prophesied in the same way, warning that, during the tribulation period, all the nations of the world will gather against Jerusalem. The city (Jerusalem) shall be taken, the houses rifled, the women ravished, and half of the city shall be taken into captivity. According to the end of Zachariah's prophecy, this period will end with the Lord's vengeful return to earth.}*

℘ Luke 21:20-22 and 24 ℘

Luke's account of Jesus' prophecy couldn't be any clearer. We can't simply ignore it, and why would we? Jesus clearly taught that these events will occur sometime in the future; therefore, neither "**Antiochus IV's**" attack and desecration of God's Temple (*170-167 BC*) nor "**Titus'**" attack and annihilation of Herod's Temple (*AD 70*) could have been a fulfillment of Daniel's and Jesus' parallel end-time prophecies.[343] But the time during which this prophecy will be fulfilled is certainly drawing near.

~ *How can we be sure of this?* ~

In the preceding scripture Jesus warned every Left-behinder that, after the abomination of desolation takes place, all that has been written (*i.e., prophecy*) will be fulfilled. This obviously has not, thus far, occurred. When Jesus said this, He was warning that, during *"the Day of the Lord"* (*which will begin with the Rapture and end with the White Throne Judgment*), <u>all</u> prophecy will be fulfilled. This would include <u>all</u> Old and New Testament prophecy and every prophecy concerning the Church, the latter days, the future pouring out of God's vengeance and wrath, and the Millennial Period Kingdom of Christ.

Because Jesus made this particular statement, His end-time message is one of the most revealing and conclusive end-time prophecies at our

[342] That's a huge statement from the Messiah, and we're about to read John's account of how he witnessed the future fulfillment of Jesus' words.

[343] Dan. 7 and 9:26-27

disposal. We certainly couldn't claim that either "**Antiochus IV**" or "**Titus**" ever accomplished the fulfillment of all prophecy. In fact, after reading Jesus' words, making the claim that any past event or combination of events has somehow already completely fulfilled all prophecy could in no way be considered to be a rational, logical, or scriptural premise. Thus, Jesus' warning can only be a reference to future events.

SOMETHING CHRISTIANS SHOULD NEVER FORGET

When Satan attacks our faith it will be our knowledge of God's perfectly prophetic, wholly inspired Word that will be the sword and shield of our defense. The Christian's foundation of faith is a proven foundation that's been mightily tempered, year after year, as prophecy after prophecy has been perfectly fulfilled. Upon that foundation, true Christianity has successfully refuted all manner of opposition, not because we have passionate or strong "feelings" about God or religion, but rather, because our foundation of faith is built upon a solid "ROCK," and that "ROCK" is Christ Jesus — "THE LIVING WORD OF GOD" — John 1:1-14.

"The Christian's faith rests on - FACT - not feeling!"

Unlike the thousands of false doctrines, cults, and religions that have evolved over the past thousands of years, the Christian Bible is filled with hundreds of detailed prophecies, most of which have already been 100% accurately fulfilled. No other belief system or religion on the planet can make that boast and truly support their claim. Our faith in Jesus as the Messiah (*the Son of God*) stands alone and is solidly grounded in the scientific, historically accurate, and logically conclusive **FACT** that God's prophetic Word has never failed nor, in any way, been proven to be false. Therefore, since not a single Bible prophecy or scientific statement has ever failed to be perfectly fulfilled or has been found to be even slightly inaccurate, we would be foolish not to expect the remaining prophecies, which foretell of these globally impactive future events, to also be perfectly fulfilled. Therein lies our foundation of faith; and it is, by far, the surest of foundations!

Chapter 28

Heaven Bound Party Crashers

(The Resurrection of the Two Witnesses)

Rev. 11:11

'And after three days and an half the Spirit of life from God entered into them** (God's two witnesses), **and they <u>stood upon their feet</u>; <u>and great fear fell upon them which saw them</u>.'

As God's two witnesses suddenly arise and mightily stand to their feet after lying dead in the streets for 3½ days, the Left-behinders in Jerusalem are probably going to need to go change their shorts, but they won't have time. Instead, they'll likely feel a sudden, intense chill rush up their spines as they begin to remember the resurrected prophets' earlier warnings regarding the powerfully fatal earthquake that will immediately strike the city of Jerusalem following their resurrection and glorious ascension into Heaven! And, though the Scriptures don't actually give us much in the way of specific details as to what is sure to be a naturally panicked reaction on the part of the Left-behinders when they see the prophets unexpectedly rise from the dead, simple logic would dictate that they'll immediately look to their self-proclaimed god — *"the son of perdition"* — for help. Regrettably for them, however, their new god (*small "g"*), whom some will likely have been following from before the start of the tribulation period, will also be totally helpless.

Once Jesus decides it's time to fulfill His divine Word, by miraculously raising His two witnesses from the dead, Satan won't be able to empower the son of perdition to hinder or prevent it from happening. In fact, Satan will be just as powerless to foil the two witnesses' resurrection as he was nearly 2,000 years earlier when the Holy Spirit raised Jesus, "the Messiah," from the dead. Thus, the son of perdition will be just like the rest of the foolish "**majority**" — absolutely powerless to resist God's will.

Hence, with the immortally resurrected prophets standing right in front of the blasphemously partying Left-behinders in Jerusalem and looking far more majestic than before, the foolish followers of the son of perdition will likely wonder in terror: *'What manner of horrific, deadly-plague will now be unleashed?'* Naturally, they'll expect that some sort of punishment will be in order, due to their blatant, sinful behavior in the wake of the prophets' deaths, and they'll be right! But, after 3½ days of debaucherous revelry, I wonder if they'll be lucid enough to remember that a massive earthquake is about to ruin what's left of their party. If not, God will sober them up with a powerful, ground shaking reminder to that effect.

The Resurrection of God's witnesses won't be quick!

The dissimilarity between the instantaneous rapture of the saints and the slow, dramatic resurrection and ascension of God's two witnesses is what will make the witnesses' resurrection such a monumentally unique and terrifying event for all those who'll be caught celebrating their deaths in the streets of Jerusalem when it occurs.

Conversely, "**the remnant**," the much wiser, now hopeful "**minority**" of Left-behinders, who will have obeyed the prophets' warnings and fled or stayed away from Judea, will be watching and waiting (*all around the world*) to see if the prophets actually rise from the dead.[344] Hence, when they witness, with their own eyes, the prophets' glorious resurrection, they'll collectively rejoice and watch to see if the prophets are also called up into Heaven as the prophets will have prophesied.

There can only be one - "First Begotten of the Dead"

Only one other time has something like this resurrection and ascension occurred, and, when it did, it took place in this same holy city and similarly unique manner. I'm of course referring to the glorious morning when Mary Magdalene and those with her found Jesus' tomb empty and ran back to share the good news with His sad and discouraged disciples. It's important to remember this, because the Scriptures clearly declare Jesus to be: *"the first begotten of the dead."*

'And from Jesus Christ, who is the faithful witness,
*and **the first begotten of the dead** . . .'* [345]

Rev. 1:5

The previous verse declares that, prior to Jesus' resurrection, no other individual had been raised to immortality. Others had been resurrected

[344] Taking into consideration the angel's clarification in Rev. 11:8, where he told John that the prophets will be killed in the same city as was Christ, it seems plausible, even likely, for many of "the remnant" to *"watch and wait"* from up in the hills just outside of Jerusalem.

[345] If any other individual had formerly been resurrected to immortality, these words would not be true. Therefore, Moses could not have been resurrected to immortality when Michael took him. Jesus was and is the first—Acts 26:23, Jude 9, Col. 1:18.

but not in immortal bodies.[346] When Jesus ascended to Heaven for the final time, having fulfilled His physical, earthly responsibilities as the one and only true High-Priest[347] and having appeared to His disciples and various other individuals over a forty day period, He was caught-up into Heaven in the same manner as will be God's two tribulation period witnesses. Thus, having made the ultimate sacrifice and having become *"the first begotten of the dead,"* Jesus returned to Heaven as the perpetual "HIGH PRIEST"[348] and reassumed His original, glorious status as the preeminent "SON OF GOD," the "KING OF KINGS AND LORD OF LORDS!"

Expectantly waiting . . . .

Alienated for having chosen not to align with the wick followers of the false-prophet and probably in hiding all around the world, the expectant "**minority**" (*"the remnant"*) will stand in desperate hope of seeing the now magnificently resurrected and glorified prophets ascend into Heaven, as they will have prophesied. An event as eternally pivotal and impactive as this will undoubtedly be visible to every eye, and why wouldn't it? The prophets' preaching and plagues certainly will have miraculously reached and affected every inhabitant on earth. So, enabling every Left-behinder to see the validating ascension of His two global witnesses certainly shouldn't be any more difficult for the Creator of the Universe than will have been His having turned a third of the oceans to blood or His having blotted out a third of the light from the sun, moon and stars![349]

---

[346] According to Mt. 27:52-53, after Jesus rose from the dead many saints were resurrected and were seen in Jerusalem. In order for them to have been recognized by their loved ones, which was likely the reason for their having been resurrected, they must have been recently deceased. Unfortunately, Matthew's Gospel doesn't record what happened to them afterwards. Thus, we don't know if they were given immortal bodies and taken up to Heaven (*which would be my guess*) or just allowed to live out the remainder of their mortal lives, as did Lazarus.

[347] Jesus is the only true High Priest, the Creator King. The Scriptures clearly reveal Jesus to be the same Melchizedek, King of Salem (*Jerusalem—Psa. 110:4*), who met and blessed Abraham after Abraham rescued Lot—Gen. 14:14-20, John 8:26-28. Thus, Jesus fulfilled His ministry as both the *Sacrificial Lamb of God (the Paschal Lamb)* and the eternal *High Priest* by offering Himself as the atonement for all sin. This is explained in the book of Hebrews 7 thru 10, which reveals the continual priestly ministry of Christ, "Melchizedek" — Acts 1:9.

[348] Heb. 5:10, 6:20

[349] (*Rev. 8:7-12*) Though the Scriptures don't directly reveal if all the inhabitants of the earth will actually be able to see the prophets' ascension, Rev. 11:12 does say that their enemies will behold (*see*) them when they ascend. That would likely include their enemies all around the world, but we can't be sure of this.

At least half of the Left-behinders will have Died

Although, by the middle of the tribulation period, at least half of the world's population will have died or been killed, there will still be hundreds of millions (*even billions*) who will have survived but will not be anywhere near Judea when the prophets are killed. We should also note that it's certainly conceivable that some Left-behinders, who will have wanted to flee but will not have been physically able to do so before Jerusalem is seized, could find themselves stranded in Judea when the abomination of desolation occurs. After 3½ years of plagues and famine, many of the Left-behinders will be far too weak, sick, or near death to travel.

The Apple truly doesn't fall far from the Tree

Even after having witnessed all the miraculous plagues of God's two witnesses, the foolish "**majority**" will put their faith in the false-prophet. Let's face it, if the false-prophet and his followers had believed there was any chance of God's two witnesses being resurrected, instead of leaving their carcasses in the streets to rot, John probably would have recorded seeing them burn the prophets' bodies and grind them to dust, so as to prevent that from happening. We know that wouldn't work, but they won't! So why didn't John see them do this? The answer is simple. They won't bother to totally destroy the prophets' bodies, because they, ***'being of their father the devil'*** *(unlike the wiser minority of Left-behinders who will eventually repent)*,[350] will be incapable of believing the truth. Therefore, if I had to guess, I'd guess that they won't believe that the broken and rapidly decomposing bodies of the two prophets could ever be brought back to life. And, should they be wrong, they'll likely expect their fearless leader (*the false-prophet*) to instantly respond by doing something incredible, like calling fire down from heaven to incinerate them.[351]

How will Satan explain this?

Rev. 11:11-12 ~ *continued*

> ***'And after three days and an half the Spirit of life from God entered into them*** *(the two witnesses)*, ***and they stood upon their feet; and great fear fell upon them which saw them.***
>
> ***And they heard a great voice from heaven saying unto them, <u>Come up hither</u>. <u>And they ascended up to heaven in a cloud</u>; <u>and their enemies beheld them</u>.'***

---

[350] John 8:44
[351] Rev. 13:13

Not being able to prevent God from raising His two prophets from the dead and calling them back up to Heaven, Satan will have to invent a plausible excuse for having allowed this to happen. And, though that may seem impossible, Satan is such a great liar that, even after seeing God's two witnesses ascend into Heaven, the thoroughly wicked followers of the false-prophet will just accept whatever outrageous lie Satan gives his little *"puppet-god"* (*the false-prophet*) to feed them. Since this thoroughly wicked majority of Left-behinders will have heartily chosen not to repent and receive Christ, they'll have no other option. Thus, they'll do this because, just as has always been the case, those who reject Christ are, as Jesus said, ***". . . of their father the Devil."***

Therefore, for most of the Left-behinders, the resurrection and ascension of God's two witnesses won't change a thing. And why should it? Even now, with the Holy Spirit powerfully at work all over the world, enabling the Church to reveal God's merciful plan of salvation to all mankind, the obstinate "**majority**" is still too proud and self-willed to humble themselves before God and be saved. For most, following an unprovable scientific theory or religion — "any theory or religion" — is much more intellectually satisfying and self-promoting than humbly serving the true Creator of all things. This explains the need for the following passage from Christ:

'Enter ye in at the strait gate: for wide is the gate, and broad is the way, that leadeth to destruction, and ***many*** *there be which go in thereat: Because strait is the gate, and narrow is the way, which leadeth unto life,* ***and few there be that find it****.'*

Matthew 7:13-14

After the Rapture, when the Holy Spirit is ***'taken out of the way,'***[352] we certainly shouldn't expect the followers of the new world leader to be more receptive to the truth then they are today. That would be both illogical and scripturally inconsistent. As we've learned, Jesus taught that even His *"elect"* (*the saints*) would be deceived by the ***'great signs and lying wonders'*** of the various false-prophets that will arise during the tribulation period. That means that, along with the son of perdition (*the false-prophet, the anti-Christ who will rule the world*), there will also be other subordinate false-prophets working to deceive the inhabitants of the earth (*Mt. 24:11-24*). That's probably because, unlike God, Satan and his puppet-leader won't be able to be everywhere at the same time, and the world's a big place!

---

[352] 2Th. 2:3-7-12

The Great Soul Harvest Comes To an End

Rev. 11:13

> ***'And the same hour** (as the prophets ascended to Heaven) **was there a great earthquake, and the tenth part of the city** (Jerusalem—11:8) **fell,**[353] **and in the earthquake were slain of men seven thousand: and the remnant** (the very last saints to repent) **were affrighted and gave glory to the God of heaven.'***

These are the only words in the entire book of Revelation that could correctly be interpreted as indicating a corporate act of contrition. Therefore, if the preceding verse isn't John's record of having witnessed the repentance of the last of the saints — "**the remnant**" — then there is no clear record of any Left-behinders repenting anywhere in John's Book.

After seeing, with their own eyes, the miraculous resurrection and ascension of God's two witnesses and the ensuing earthquake, which will kill exactly 7,000 rebellious Left-behinders in Jerusalem, "**the remnant**" will finally be fully persuaded that the two witnesses' message must have come from Heaven. Thus, having become ***'affrighted,'*** they'll immediately ***'give glory to the God of heaven'*** as John witnessed. That means that they'll repent! When this occurs, the very last of the saints will have finally repented, and the 6,000 year long (*give or take a few decades*) harvest of souls will be over. Hence, it will be time for Jesus, "THE MASTER OF THE HOUSE," to rise up and permanently "SHUT" the allegorical "DOOR OF SALVATION."[354]

~ But how do we know that that's what these verses reveal? ~

Recognizing John's words here and in the next few verses to be irrefutable evidence that the last of the saints (*"the remnant"*) will repent immediately following the earthquake in Jerusalem, may (*on the surface*) seem to be supposition, but I assure you this is not, in any way, an opinion. In fact, this is actually one of the easiest truths to substantiate in all of Scripture. I've never shared this with any rational student of Scripture, pastor or seasoned eschatologist and, afterward, had them fail to recognize the pure, scriptural logic and simplicity of what God is revealing through this portion of John's vision.

---

353 This is why Jesus warned the Left-behinders to *"flee from Judea."* Those who do will recognize the earthquake to be the final validation of God's two prophets' message and will, therefore, humbly repent — *giving glory to the God of heaven!*

354 (*Luke 13:24-28*) This will become obvious as we examine and discuss the next few verses of John's vision.

After the earthquake, John simply recorded what he witnessed by writing the following:

> ***'and the remnant were affrighted, and gave glory to the God of heaven.'***

We don't want to belabor the point, but, although John's words are fairly straight forward, there are still some on our journey who will need just a little more clarification before they can comfortably move on. If that's you, you've set a commendably proper standard for reverently and effectively studying Scripture. So let's look at this logically.

~ Couldn't the remnant just be the survivors of the Jerusalem earthquake? ~

Before we really dig into the obvious, straightforward interpretation of John's words, I've tried to answer the preceding question in the affirmative from every possible perspective, but it just isn't possible. Instead, everything in John's vision will confirm that what he recorded seeing in these verses was the last of saints – "**the remnant**" – finally repenting.

To start with, notice John's exact choice of words in **Rev. 11:13**. Rather than just recording that this remnant was *"scared"* and gave glory to God, John specified that this remnant was ***'affrighted!'*** In the *Greek* the word *"affrighted"* indicates that this particular remnant had a reverent fear; they weren't just afraid. Of course those who survive the earthquake will be fearful, but there's no logical justification for implying that they'll suddenly become reverent. We'll discuss this further just ahead, but before doing so we should also note that John witnessed this particular remnant ***"giving glory to the God of heaven"*** (*notice the capital "G"*). It would make absolutely no sense for the blasphemous followers of the false-prophet to suddenly give glory to a God they utterly hate, in fact, quite the contrary. What's more, John clearly recorded having seen the remnant, to whom he is referring in this passage, give ***'glory'*** *(worship, glory, honor and praise)* to the true God in Heaven, not the false god on earth.[355]

The Followers of the false-prophet will see this as Revenge

As I've stated, we should acknowledge that, for the hatefully motivated followers of the false-prophet, stopping to suddenly ***"give glory to the true God in Heaven"*** would be completely inconsistent with their previous conduct and disposition. Just moments before the resurrection of God's two witnesses — while their tattered and decaying bodies are still lying dead in the streets — this massive debaucherous group of rebellious

[355] 2Th. 2:3-12

Left-behinders will have been wholly devoted to worshipfully celebrating their new god, the false-prophet. For 3½ days they'll have been doing so by orchestrating what will probably amount to a drunken orgy and blasphemous pagan ceremony in God's holy Temple and in the streets of His holy city![356]

Seeing it as John saw it:

I'm confident that if we could actually see this future "**majority**" of vindictively motivated party-animals through the eyes of John — exactly as John saw them — not one of us would still consider the possibility that this evil group could actually be the same repentant souls John witnessed sincerely ***'giving glory to the God of heaven'*** after the deadly Jerusalem earthquake ended. Let's not forget that this particular group of defiantly wicked Left-behinders in the streets of Jerusalem will be the same hateful souls John earlier saw:

- Forcefully surround Judea and God's holy city (*Jerusalem*)[357]
- Violently storm God's Temple, while brutally slaying His prophets — most likely slaughtering the 144,000 Jewish servants in the process.
- Desecrate God's holy Temple, by erecting and worshipping the wickedly blasphemous "**image of the beast**" in the Holy of Holies[358]

Frankly, believing this spitefully motivated group of earthquake survivors to be the same people John saw meekly ***"giving glory to the true God in heaven"*** seems absolutely beyond the boundaries of what could be considered rational thought. What is rational to expect is that after God annihilates 7,000 of their family and friends with a powerful earthquake, literally crushing their victory celebration, those who survive will likely be even more vindictive and resentful than before! If we look a little deeper into John's vision we can see clear evidence of this hateful, rebellious attitude and response:

> *'And men were scorched with great heat, and blasphemed the name of God, which hath power over these plagues: **and they repented not to give him glory**.' ~*

---

[356] Rev. 11:7-11, Ex. 32:1-35

[357] Luke 21:20-21, 2Th. 2:3-12, Dan. 9:27, 12:7-12.

[358] Daniel 9:25-27, 12:10-11

'. . . And blasphemed the God of heaven because of their pains and their sores, ***and repented not of their deeds****.' ~ 'And there fell upon men a great hail out of heaven, every stone about the weight of a talent:* ***and men blasphemed God because of the plague of hail****; for the plague thereof was exceeding great.'*

༄ Rev. 16:9, 11 & 21 ༄

Once again, we're just not used to hearing these words.

In the preceding verses, John actually tied the words ***'repented not'*** to the words ***'to give him** (God)* ***glory,'*** thus, indicating that giving God glory would have been an act of contrition (*repentance*) on the part of the Left-behinders. Today, when we speak of soul changing contrition, we simply use the word *"repentance."* Unfortunately, though we know some of the Left-behinders will repent before the end of the tribulation period, the only references to repentance in the book of Revelation are found in Jesus' letters to the seven churches. Throughout the remainder of John's vision, the word *"repentance"* is nowhere to be found. Instead, John used words and phrases that were more commonly found in Old Testament passages. And, while John's choice of words may not be familiar to us today, well established scriptural precedent for their use in reference to an act of repentance does exist in both the Old and New Testaments:[359]

'And Joshua said unto Achan, My son, ***give****, I pray thee,* ***glory to the LORD God of Israel****,* ***and make confession unto him*** *. . .'*

༄ Josh. 7:19 ༄

'. . . There are not found that returned ***to give glory to God****, save this stranger. And he {Jesus} said unto him, Arise, go thy way:* ***thy faith hath made thee whole****.' {This man's returning to 'give glory to God' was recognized – by Jesus – to be a sincere act of contrition.}*

༄ Luke 17:18-19 ༄

---

[359] Here are just a few more examples: Jer. 13:16, Rev. 14:7, 16:9-11.

~ Will the prophets' ascension really be seen around the world? ~

Now that's a good question. While it's true that John recorded that the witnesses' enemies will behold them during their ascension into Heaven (*Rev. 11:12*), perhaps it could be argued that the Scriptures don't clearly reveal if their ascension will be visible to every living soul. However, since their preaching and plagues have been divinely designed to reach and affect every Left-behinder on the planet and since their ministry will be God's last attempt to call every living soul to repentance, it would be illogical for the one miraculous event that will unquestionably validate their ministry not to be witnessed by every survivor on earth. And, as has been stated, making that possible certainly wouldn't be a difficult task for the Creator of the Universe and the initiator of these global plagues!

It's important that we recognize that, just as did the resurrection and ascension of Christ, the prophets' resurrection will instantaneously affirm every word they'll have spoken and every plague they'll have unleashed. And, while it's true that we can't point to any particular scripture as absolute proof that their ascension will be seen around the world, since just seconds after the witnesses ascend into Heaven the seventh angel will sound his trumpet, declaring that the "MYSTERY OF GOD" has finished and the "Door of Salvation" has permanently "SHUT," it certainly seems reasonable for us to expect that God's last minute warning to repent (*which will be the ascension of His two witnesses*) will also be seen and heard all around the world! [360]

The prophets' Ministry will be unlike any prior Ministry

The ministry of God's two tribulation period witnesses will be the polar opposite of Christ's. A study of **Isaiah 42:1-2, 53:1-12** and **Matthew 8:4** will reveal that Jesus' earthly ministry, though far more significant, was never intended (*during His lifetime*) to be broadcast all over the world. That job falls to us, His disciples — the true Church.[361] Therefore, while Jesus' resurrection is the most important event in history, it was first a fulfillment of God's covenant with Abraham and his descendants.[362] Then, as was promised in that covenant, by extension, salvation was offered to the Gentile world.[363] This, of course, was always part of God's perfect plan for our redemption (*the Mystery of God—Rev. 10:1-7*).[364]

---

[360] Scripturally speaking, the "Mystery of God" is <u>always</u> a reference to God's plan of salvation, the Gospel—Rev. 10:3-7.

[361] Mt. 28:16-20, Mk. 16:15-20

[362] Acts 3:25-26, Mt. 10:5-6 and 15:22-28

[363] Acts 13:46, Isa. 53:6

[364] Gen. 12:1-3, 18:18, 22:18

The tribulation witnesses' ministry will also be radically different from that of Jesus' ministry, because their preaching and worldwide plagues will be intended to reach and affect every living soul on earth, right from the start. They'll only have 3½ years to persuade the last of the saints (*"the remnant"*) to repent, and their mission will be God's final attempt to redeem the lost. Therefore, when the witnesses are resurrected and called back to Heaven, their glorious ascension will be God's final, worldwide "CALL TO REPENT" before the "MYSTERY OF GOD" is finished. Thus, their ascension will happen just moments prior to the sounding of the seventh angel's trumpet. This is why I previously indicated that the sounding of the seventh trumpet will be the most soulfully sobering moment in history!

Remember, in **Rev. 10:1-7**, John recorded being told by a mighty angel that the sounding of the seventh and final trumpet will indicate to every unrepentant Left-behinder that the "MYSTERY OF GOD" is finished. God's merciful "Door of Salvation" will have forever shut. That means that the Gospel message (*the mystery of God*) will never be preached again. That's a big deal! And it explains why immediately after the Jerusalem earthquake, just moments before the sounding of the seventh trumpet, John observed "**the remnant**" (*the very last souls to be saved*) reverently ***"giving glory to the God of heaven."***

> *'Strive to enter in at the strait gate: for many, I say unto you, will seek to enter in, and shall not be able.* ***When once the master of the house*** *{Jesus}* ***is risen up***, ***and hath shut the door****, and ye begin to stand without, and to knock at the door, saying, Lord, Lord, open unto us; and he shall answer and say unto you, I know you not whence ye are . . .'*

Luke 13:24-25

~ But what about those who will be born during the Millennial Period? ~

As was earlier stated, when we venture through the corresponding portion of John's vision, the answer to the preceding question will beautifully self-emerge from the text. But it's an emotionally complicated topic, and there are many who hold varying points of view. Therefore, it's better for us to continue moving forward (*gathering a full perspective of this end-time period*) and wait until we reach those corresponding scriptures before addressing this question. Doing so will better enable us to see how clearly the answer fluently self-emerges from the text (*Scripture as a whole*).

Chapter 29

The Seventh Trumpet Is About To Sound

Rev. 11:14

> ***'The second woe is past; and, behold, the <u>third woe cometh quickly</u>.'***

Earlier, we learned that, with the sounding of the fifth angel's trumpet, John witnessed the unleashing of the first of three soberingly devastating woe plagues. The first woe subjected the Left-behinders to five full, excruciating months of torment from stinging locusts. Then, immediately following the sounding of the sixth angel's trumpet, the second woe plague began with the unleashing of four very powerful fallen-angels from ***'the great river Euphrates.'*** Consequently, when that second woe plague had ended, John had witnessed those four fallen angels lead a demonic army of 200,000,000 killer-horsemen, as they set out on a killing rampage — ***'for an hour, a day, a month and a year'*** — leaving one-third of the surviving inhabitants of the earth dead in their wake. And yet, as sobering as that thought is, just as sobering is the fact that we have no way of knowing how many hundreds of millions will have already died prior to the unleashing of those first two woe plagues.[365] Moreover, on top of the one-third slain by that second woe, God will have killed an additional 7,000 unrepentant Left-behinders during the Jerusalem earthquake. That earthquake, we just learned, will have finally led to the repentance of "**the remnant**" (*the very last soles to be saved*), thus, bringing us to the end of the second of three very powerful woes.

Rev. 11:15

> ***'And the seventh angel sounded; and there were great voices in heaven, saying, <u>The kingdoms of this world are become the</u>***

---

365 Many millions (*even billions*) will have died or been killed during the first half of the tribulation period, due to the effects of the Rapture, the first four trumpet-plagues, wars, skirmishes, territorial disputes and natural death and exposure.

kingdoms of our Lord, and of his Christ; and He shall reign for ever and ever.'

No more hope of Salvation for the Lost

Immediately after witnessing the repentance of "**the remnant**,"[366] the angel revealed to John that the second woe had ended (*Rev. 11:14*). Now, in verse 15, John is being told that the third and final woe will come *"quickly"* (*i.e., without delay*). As I stated, the sounding of a trumpet and the shutting of a door happen instantly, and when Jesus (*the Master of the house*) decides it's time to cease calling the wicked and rebellious inhabitants of the earth to repentance, the sounding of the seventh angel's trumpet (*precisely as the mighty angel declared—Rev. 10:5-7*) will indicate that the "MYSTERY OF GOD" is finished! The preaching of the Gospel message will have ended, and God's final two witnesses will have been called back to Heaven. Thus, the allegorical Door of Salvation will eternally slam shut!

A very Logical Perspective

In John's vision, after having seen "**the remnant**" repent, we are now being warned that the third and final woe will come *'**quickly**.'* Throughout the New Testament, when the original *Greek* word for *"quickly"* (*Rev. 11:14*) was used in the scriptures it was intended to indicate an immediate and instantaneous event, reaction, or response, and what John recorded witnessing after seeing the remnant repent and the seventh angel sound his trumpet (*which, in John's vision, initiated the third woe*) is no exception. This could explain why, throughout the remainder of John's vision, we won't find any declaration as to when the third woe will end. As a matter of fact, the third woe could both "**start**" and "**end**" with the sounding of that seventh and final trumpet. Therefore, the third woe may be an instantaneous event, like a trumpet blast or the slamming of a door.

*'. . . But in the days of the voice of the seventh angel, when he shall **begin** to sound, **the mystery of God should be finished**,*[367] *as he hath declared to his servants the prophets.'*

Rev. 10:7

[366] Rev. 11:13-15

[367] We thoroughly studied the significance of the "Mystery of God" and God's plan of salvation coming to an end during our survey of Rev. 10:5-7. If this isn't perfectly clear, it might be wise to "stop" and go over our earlier discussion of that passage. Remember, it's critically important that we don't allow our personal feelings to hinder us from properly interpreting what is actually written in God's Holy Word. By the time we've finished surveying John's vision all the answers will have self-emerged from the text.

But is that all that the seventh trumpet will represent?

Since John recorded witnessing that the sounding of the fifth and sixth angels' trumpets will unleash the first and second woes, it would not be illogical for us to allow for the possibility that the sounding of the seventh angel's trumpet may not only be a declaration that the Mystery of God is finished (*as John was told*) but also that the third and final woe is about to begin. Jesus did warn the inhabitants of the earth to anticipate even greater tribulation during the second half of the tribulation period than the first.[368] And the second half of the tribulation period will begin with the deaths of the two witnesses, just 3½ days before the seventh angel sounds his trumpet, and it will end with the unleashing of God's seven mighty plagues of wrath and the globally destructive return of Christ. Therefore, it is possible that the sounding of the seventh trumpet and the shutting of the Door of Salvation will only be the beginning of the third and most dreadful of the three very powerful "**woes**."

By far the most Terrifying Woe . . . .

These are truly frightening scriptures. The very thought that there will come a day when salvation and forgiveness of sin will never again be an option is beyond my calm comprehension, but Jesus clearly taught that that dreadful day would eventually come (*Luke 13:25*). More than all the plagues and wrath in John's vision combined, the irreversibility of that Door of Salvation closing is so terrifying that just thinking of it gives me a desperate, hollow feeling in the middle of my chest! What could be worse than absolutely no hope of ever being forgiven?

The Great Declaration of the Kingdom of God and Christ:

'And the seventh angel sounded; and there were great voices in heaven, saying, ***The kingdoms of this world are become the kingdoms of our Lord**, **and of his Christ***; *and he shall reign for ever and ever. And the four and twenty elders, which sat before God on their seats, fell upon their faces, and worshipped God, Saying, We give thee thanks, O Lord God Almighty, which art, and wast, and art to come; because thou hast taken to thee thy great power, and hast reigned. And the nations were angry,* ***and thy wrath is come**, **and the time of the dead**, **that they should be***

[368] Mt. 24:21

judged, and that thou shouldest give reward unto thy servants the prophets, and to the saints, and them that fear thy name, small and great; and shouldest destroy them which destroy the earth.'

Rev. 11:15-18

The preceding scriptures explain themselves. They are a clear proclamation that, when the seventh angel sounds his trumpet, God will have finished assembling His eternal family of saints, and His efforts to reach all lost and unrepentant souls will have come to an abrupt end. It will finally be time for the Lord to resurrect and catch-up to Heaven every individual (*still left on earth*) who will have been wise enough to repent, rather than follow the son of perdition. Thus, this will be accomplished in the following manner:

- First, God will resurrect and "**bring-in**" His faithful 144,000 Jewish servants
- Then, after the last of the newly repentant "**remnant**" has been martyred for rejecting *"the mark of the beast"* (*we're not told how long that will take*), they will also be resurrected and gathered into Heaven. This will end God's roughly 6,000 year long harvest of saints. For the first time, every saint will finally be in Heaven.

That means that only those who'll have taken the damnable mark of the beast will be left on earth when God begins to pour out His wrath.[369] What's more, every word you've just read will be irrefutably proven as we continue through the remainder of John's vision.

And the Tabernacle in Heaven was Open

Rev. 11:19

'And the temple of God was opened in heaven, and there was seen in his temple the ark of his testament: and there were lightnings, and voices, and thunderings, and an earthquake, and great hail.'

[369] The Mark of the beast is a mark that will be forcibly placed or branded on the right hand or forehead of every inhabitant of the earth. Those who receive it will be eternally damned. We'll cover this in the chapters ahead.

We should note that in the preceding verses John actually recorded having been allowed to see the original, heavenly Tabernacle and Ark of the Covenant. And, when I say that John saw the original Tabernacle and Ark of God, I'm not referring to the Tabernacle Moses instructed the descendants of Jacob (*the Hebrew exiles*) to build as they made their way through the wilderness. No! The Tabernacle John saw has always remained in Heaven and is the same Tabernacle of which God commanded Moses to build a replica. That replica was then used by the Hebrew exiles for hundreds of years until it was replaced by Solomon's permanent Temple. Eventually, the Ark of the Covenant was lost, taken to an undisclosed location and hidden, or taken as spoil (*which likely happened sometime either prior to, during, or after the Israelites were taken captive into Babylon by Nebuchadnezzar in roughly 610 BC*).

'According to all that I {God} shew thee {Moses},
after the pattern of the tabernacle *{the Tabernacle in Heaven}*[370]
and the pattern of all the instruments thereof,
even so shall ye make it {the replica Tabernacle}.'

Ex. 25:9

---

[370] For a better understanding of the significance of this heavenly Tabernacle you might enjoy reading Hebrews Chapter 8 before moving on.

Chapter 30

The Woman and the Dragon

(Revelation Chapter 12 begins...)

Having moved through the first eleven chapters of John's vision, we've now arrived at the beginning of the second half of the seven-year tribulation period. Hence, by this time, during that period, the last of the saints will have repented and the "Door of Salvation" will have been eternally shut. Now the Lord will use what we refer to as Rev. Chapters 12 and 13 to give us a clearer understanding of the tragically nefarious affect Satan and his wicked *"powers of darkness"* (*the fallen-angels*) have had on all the inhabitants of the earth, during every generation, starting with Adam.

These next three chapters of John's vision (*Rev. 12, 13 and 14*) are almost completely allegorical, so we must be careful not to allow supposition into our interpretation.

A Crown of Twelve Stars

Rev. 12:1

> ***'And there appeared a great wonder in heaven; a woman clothed with the sun, and the moon under her feet, and upon her head a crown of twelve stars . . .'***

In the preceding verse, John saw a woman clothed with the sun, with the moon under her feet, wearing a crown of twelve stars. If we start by focusing on the twelve stars it will become easy to identify just who this woman is and what she represents.

'Behold, I {Joseph, son of Jacob} have dreamed a dream more; and, behold, the ***sun*** *and the* ***moon*** *and the* ***eleven stars*** *made obeisance to me.'*

℘ **Gen. 37:9** ℘

Since the preceding verse speaks of only eleven stars and John saw twelve stars on the woman's crown, we appear to be missing a star. Genesis 37:9 chronicles one of Joseph's allegorical visions about the formation of the twelve tribes of Israel, and, incidentally, the tribe of Joseph represents that twelfth star. Hence, Joseph only spoke of seeing eleven stars (*his brothers*) in his dream. Every time I read about Joseph's two dreams in Genesis Chapter 37, I can't help laughing. It's a riot reading about Joseph telling his father and eleven brothers (*ten of whom were much older than he*) about his visions of them all bowing at his feet and paying him homage. At the start of our journey we discussed the significance of those visions. It's here, however, in John's end-time vision, that we see the relative significance between the stars in Joseph's vision and the twelve stars in this woman's crown.

The twelve tribes of Israel are the woman in John's vision

The Bible is filled with scriptures declaring Israel and the true Church to be one body and bride to God and Christ,[371] so we don't need to prove this woman's analogous significance. However, in this particular chapter, the woman wearing the crown is a specific reference to the original twelve tribes of Israel — not the Church — and to Christ being born through Jacob's posterity. This becomes obvious in the following verse.

Rev. 12:2

> ***'And she being with child cried, travailing in birth, and pained to be delivered.'***

'But thou, Bethlehem Ephratah,
though thou be little among the thousands of Judah,
***yet out of thee shall he come forth unto me that is to be ruler in Israel**;*
whose goings forth have been from of old, from everlasting.'
{This prophecy is a clear reference to Christ Jesus, the Creator.}

℘ **Micah 5:2** ℘

In **Rev. 12:2** John sees the woman in his vision travailing in pain to be delivered. For centuries prior to Christ's birth, the nations of the world, including Israel, abode immersed in sin and idol worship without truly understanding their need to be reconciled to God. Thus, more than ever, the world needed a savior, yet that savior could only come from one peo-

[371] Helpful Scriptures: Gen. 37, Isa. 54:1- 8, Jer. 31:32, 2Cor. 11:2, Eph. 5:24-27, Rev. 19:7-9

ple, the promised descendants of Abraham.[372] The Lord's original covenant began with Abraham and extended to Jacob's descendants (*"the Jews"*). Therefore, regardless of Jacob's descendants' unwillingness to truly honor that covenant, God would fulfill His holy prophetic Word by sending Jesus, the promised Messiah. This analogous prenatal woman in the beginning portion of **Rev. 12:1-5** is an obvious representation of that blessed event.

Behold, the Dragon is Revealed

Rev. 12:3-4

> ***'And there appeared another wonder in heaven; and behold a great red dragon*** *(Satan, the devil)*, ***having seven heads and ten horns, and seven crowns upon his heads.***[373]
>
> ***And his tail drew the third part of the stars of heaven, and did cast them to the earth: and the dragon stood before the woman which was ready to be delivered, for to devour her child as soon as it was born.'***

We don't want to spend time covering the significance of the dragon's seven heads and ten horns now, because this will be thoroughly explained as we venture through Chapter 13 of John's vision. At the moment we only need to embrace one significant fact. John's words reveal that the tail of this analogous dragon, at some point in time, drew one-third of the ***'stars'*** (*angels*) from Heaven and cast them down to earth.

> *'For if God spared not {past tense}* ***the angels that sinned, but cast them down to hell, and delivered them into chains of darkness****, to be reserved unto judgment . . .'*

2Pet. 2:4

> *'And* ***the angels which kept not their first estate****, but left their own habitation, he {God} hath* ***reserved in everlasting chains under darkness*** *unto the judgment of the great day.'*

Jude 6

---

[372] Gen. 12:1-3,7, 13:14-17, 15:4-6, 15:12-21, 17:1-21, 21:12-13, 22:16-18, 25:23, 26:2-5,24, 27:28-29, 28:3-4,13-15, 32:27-28, 35:10-12, 46:2-4,49:8-10, Ex. 6:6-8

[373] John's vision of a great red (*fiery-red*) dragon, wearing a crown on each of his seven heads, indicates that Satan and his *"powers of darkness"* have reigned, at least to some degree, during each major kingdom, from the emergence of the *Babylonian Empire* to Satan's end-time kingdom of the son of perdition.

While it's true that the preceding scriptures don't refer to angels as *"stars,"* the following scriptures do:

'And it waxed great, even to the host {angels} of heaven; ***and it cast down some of the host and of the stars to the ground*** *. . . '*[374]

Dan. 8:10

'The mystery of the ***seven stars*** *which thou sawest in my right hand, and the seven golden candlesticks. The* ***seven stars are the angels of the seven churches****: and the seven candlesticks which thou sawest are the seven churches.'*

{Given that the interpretation of the word – *angel* – in this verse is debatable, it may be helpful to review our conversation from Rev. 1:10-20.}

Rev. 1:20

'And the fifth angel sounded, and ***I saw a star*** *fall from heaven unto the earth: and to* ***him*** *{an angel} was given the key of the bottomless pit.'*

Rev. 9:1

Though the significance of the word *"star"* in **Dan. 8:10** and **Rev. 1:20** could open the door to debate, **Rev. 9:1** leaves no room for opinion as to its interpretation. John's words clearly indicate that he witnessed a heavenly host — ***'a star '*** — being given the key to the bottomless pit. There's just no other reasonable way to interpret that scripture. Thus, **Rev. 9:1** is a solid scriptural precedent. Given that Satan didn't actually draw one-third of the stars in the Universe down to earth, I feel confident that our interpretation regarding Satan having drawn one-third of the angels (*stars*) in Heaven down to earth (*where they're awaiting judgment—2Pet. 2:4*) is completely rational and accurate, so let's move on.

Nice try Satan

Rev. 12:4 states that the dragon (*Satan*) stood before the woman (*Israel, the descendants of Jacob*) who was about to give birth, intending to devour her child as soon as it was born. That's a pretty obvious reference to Herod's fearfully malevolent response, once he believed the wise men had mocked him by failing to do as he had instructed, which was to return

374 The word *stars* is poetically used to indicate the gloriously divine nature of God's heavenly host.

to Jerusalem so they could report the location of the newly born King of the Jews (*Jesus, the Christ*).

> *'Then Herod, when he saw that he was mocked of the wise men, was exceeding wroth, and sent forth, **and slew all the children that were in Bethlehem**, **and in all the coasts thereof**, **from two years old and under**, **according to the time which he had diligently enquired of the wise men**. Then was fulfilled that which was spoken by Jeremy the prophet, saying, In Rama was there a voice heard, lamentation, and weeping, and great mourning, **Rachel** {the wife of Jacob, the father of the tribes of Israel} **weeping for her children, and would not be comforted**, **because they are not**.'*

Mt. 2:16-18

~ Gee, I wonder who prodded Herod into killing all those babies; hum, could it have been Satan? ~

There's no question about it, and **Rev. 12:4** proves it! Satan tried to kill Jesus before Jesus could redeem the lost sheep of the House of Israel (*and all Gentiles as well*), but, of course, as we just read, God had already foretold that this would happen.[375] Therefore, Satan's evil attempt to end God's perfect plan for the salvation of the world before it even got off the ground was miraculously thwarted.

> *'. . . the angel of the Lord appeareth to Joseph in a dream, saying, Arise, and take the young child {Jesus} and his mother, and flee into Egypt,[376] and be thou there until I bring thee word: **for Herod will seek the young child to destroy him**.'*

Mt. 2:13

Rev. 12:5

> ***'And she brought forth a man child, who was to rule all nations with a rod of iron: and her child was caught up unto God, and to his throne.'***

[375] Jer. 31:15

[376] Hosea 11:1

We hardly need to comment on the preceding verse. Both it and the following Psalm clearly speak of Christ, revealing that when He returns He'll rule all nations with a rod of iron:

> *'I will declare the decree: the LORD hath said unto me,* ***Thou art my Son****;* ***this day have I begotten thee****. Ask of me, and I shall give thee the heathen for thine inheritance, and the uttermost parts of the earth for thy possession.* ***Thou shalt break them with a rod of iron****; thou shalt dash them in pieces like a potter's vessel.'*

Ps. 2:7-9

In the second half of **Rev. 12:5**, we find a clear reference to Christ's triumphant resurrection and return to Heaven. And, as is recorded in Scripture, after having failed to kill the infant Christ, Satan tried the next best thing; he tempted Jesus to sin.[377] Yet, as was to be expected, again, Satan failed miserably. Thus, after successfully fulfilling His earthly ministry as the *Pascal Lamb* and High Priest, and having, therefore, successfully paved a path of redemption for all who believe, Jesus returned to His former glorious existence in Heaven as the Creator of all things.

> *'God, who at sundry times and in divers manners spake in time past unto the fathers by the prophets,* ***Hath in these last days*** *spoken unto us by his Son, whom he hath appointed heir of all things,* ***by whom*** *{Jesus}* ***also he*** *{God the Father}* ***made the worlds****; Who being the brightness of his glory, and* ***the express image of his person****,* ***and upholding all things by the word of his power****, when he had by himself purged our sins, sat down on the right hand of the Majesty on high . . .'*

Heb. 1:1-3

This just can't be a coincidence!

The first five verses of John's vision of this woman wearing a crown with twelve stars (*representing the offspring of Jacob, from which the Messiah would descend*) is intended to cover a period spanning from the formation of the tribes of Israel, to the coming of the Messiah, and finally to Christ's resurrection and ascension to Heaven. Then, beginning with **Rev. 12:6**, we're about to read that John's vision of the women jumps ahead, to

[377] Mt. 4:1-11, Mk. 1:12-13, Luke 4:1-13

the end of the Church Age,[378] and begins to reveal what will happen during the first 3½ years of the seven-year tribulation period. Thus, John's vision in **Rev. 12:1-17** perfectly aligns with Daniel's foretelling that God has determined that there are to be 70 final weeks for the fulfillment of all prophesy,[379] and that just can't be a coincidence!

~ *Would you mind explaining that?* ~

In **Dan. 9:25-26** Daniel foretells of the coming of the Messiah; of His being ***'cut off** (sacrificially martyred), **but not for himself'***; of ***'the people of the prince'** (Titus' soldiers)* and their destruction of the Temple (*Herod's Temple in 70 AD*); and, finally, of the perpetual persecution of the Jews immediately following those events. Then, in the very next verse (*Dan. 9:27*), Daniel's prophecy skips ahead, roughly 2,000 years, just as does John's prophecy in **Rev. 12:6**, to the beginning of the seven-year tribulation period, and foretells of the signing of the seven-year covenant (*or treaty*), which will mark the beginning of that final seven-year period. But, like John, Daniel completely avoids any reference to the Church Age or how long the Church Age will last.

~ *So, why did both Daniel and John avoid prophesying about that roughly 2,000 year long period?* ~

Since Daniel's prophecy (*Dan. 9:24-25*) reveals specific events (*like Artaxerxes' {Cyrus the Great} giving the command to allow the exiled Jews to return and rebuild Jerusalem and the Temple—445 B.C.*) from which the exact emergence of the Messiah can be accurately calculated, it was necessary for the Lord to leave a gap (*the Church Age*) in His foretelling of 70 final weeks of prophecy, so as to prevent the Church from also being able to calculate precisely when the Rapture (*the catching-away*) of the Church would occur and the tribulation period would begin. As has been stated, Jesus made it clear that it is God's will that only He retain that specific knowledge.[380]

---

[378] The reference to the "Church Age" is a reference to the roughly 2,000 year historical period that began as Christ ascended to Heaven and the Church began to form and will end on the day of the Rapture (*1Th. 4:13-18*), the beginning of the seven year tribulation period.

[379] When reading Dan. 9:24-27, the 70 weeks is a reference to 70 *"periods"* of *"seven,"* which can be interpreted to indicate 490 years. The first 483 year portion of Daniel's prophecy began in about 445 BC and ended when Christ ascended to Heaven. The final 7 years (*or week*) will begin at the end of the *"Church Age"* when the saints are raptured and the tribulation period begins.

[380] Mt. 24:36, 25:13

Whether or not we can conclude that John was likewise shown nothing in the Chapter 12 portion of his vision regarding the Church Age for the same reason as was Daniel, I hesitate to presume; though, it does seem likely. We can be confident, however, that as we continue God's perfect, purposeful manner of revealing this vision to John and, by extension to the entire Church, will become evident. So let's keep moving, because what lies ahead will reveal a great deal!

A thousand two hundred and threescore days . . . .

Rev. 12:6

> ***'And the woman fled into the wilderness, where she hath a place prepared of God, that they should feed her there a thousand two hundred and threescore days*** *(which is 3½ years, the first half of the tribulation period).'*

It's important to note that John used the exact words in the preceding passage as he used to describe the length of the ministry of God's two witnesses back in **Rev. 11:3.** Had John not done this we might have missed the subtle significance of his words. Starting with the first half of the verse, John recorded that the woman will *"flee into the wilderness."* Before establishing why John used the word *"wilderness,"* we first need to understand just who or what the woman in this particular verse represents.

Since there's no scriptural evidence to even suggest that God will protect every descendant of Jacob (*every Jew, wherever they are around the world*) during any of the tribulation period, we can rule out the possibility of the woman in this particular verse being a representation of Jews in general. But, when we get to **Rev. 14:4**, we will see that the 144,000 will represent *"first-fruits"* of the descendants of Jacob to God. What's more, we know that God's two powerful prophets will dominate the earth during this first 3½ years (*'a thousand two hundred and threescore days'*) of the tribulation period, the precise amount of time indicated by the preceding verse.

Therefore, since, during that period, the 144,000 will represent the *"first-fruits"* of Jacob's descendants (*the twelve tribes of Israel*) and this verse is referring to that specific 3½ year period, it would not be illogical for us to consider the possibility that the woman in this particular verse may be a representation of the specially sealed and protected[381] 144,000 Jewish servants of God. As a matter of fact, just ahead, we're going to see irrefutable evidence to that effect.

[381] Rev. 7:2-4, 14:1

Protected in the Wilderness for 3½ years

Over the years I've heard many interpretations (*guesses really*) that have tried to explain John's use of the word "**wilderness**" in **Rev. 12:6**. Fortunately, we don't have to guess what John meant. If we take a quick look at verse 14, we will see that the woman will be given two wings with which to fly into the wilderness where she'll be nourished for ***'a time, and times, and half a time'*** (*3½ years*). Again, these are the same words used by John to describe the duration of the two witnesses' ministry. Thus, it seems pretty obvious that the two symbolic "**wings**," which will protect and nourish the woman (*the 144,000*) for 3½ years, will be God's two witnesses, and they'll do this while fulfilling their 3½ year ministry.

If we think back to our earlier study in **Rev. 6:9-11**, we talked about the unlikelihood and lack of any scriptural support for the 144,000 Jewish servants being evangelists. These verses support that position. In these verses we're being told that the woman wearing the crown with twelve stars will *"flee"* to a special place, where she'll be nourished during the first 3½ years of the tribulation period. That pretty much ends the discussion as to whether or not the 144,000 will be evangelists. According to this passage, the 144,000 will clearly stay in one specific location, where they'll be nourished and protected for 3½ years by God's two witnesses.[382] It really is that simple, and the rest of this chapter will bear this out.

~ *Aren't the prophets going to witness from Jerusalem?* ~

According to **Rev. 11:1-8**, God's two witnesses will be killed in the same city in which the Lord was crucified (*Jerusalem*); thus, it's likely their message will emanate from there. So the question is: *"What does Rev. 12:6 mean when it refers to a wilderness?"* Let's look to the Scriptures for clarification. With the following words about Satan's foolish rebellion, Isaiah gave us some insight into what will be the state and condition of the world during the tribulation period:

> *'How art thou fallen from heaven, O Lucifer, son of the morning! how art thou cut down to the ground,* ***which didst weaken the nations****! For thou hast said in thine heart, I will ascend into heaven, I will exalt my throne above the stars of God: I will sit also upon the mount of the congregation, in the sides of the north: I will ascend above the*

[382] During that 3½ year period, the 140,000 will restore true worship in Israel, thus fulfilling Jesus' words about the end-time return of Elijah — to *'restore all things'* – Mt. 17:11-12.

heights of the clouds; I will be like the most High. ***Yet thou shalt be brought down to hell, to the sides of the pit.*** *~*

{This reference to "the pit" [i.e., a waterless well, an inescapable hole in the earth, also interpreted as meaning: "prison, cell or dungeon"] is a clear reference to a spiritual/physical place of confinement, as is "the bottomless pit."}

~ They that see thee {Satan} shall narrowly look upon thee, and consider thee, saying, Is this the ***man*** *{i.e., male rather than female being} that made the earth to tremble, that did shake kingdoms;* ***That made the world as a wilderness,*** *{i.e., a wasteland}* ***and destroyed the cities thereof;*** *that opened not the house of his prisoners?'*

Isaiah 14:12-17

The *Hebrew* translation of the word *"wilderness"* in the preceding prophecy means precisely the same thing as does the *Greek* in **Rev. 12:6.** They both speak of the world as having become *"uninhabitable,"* a veritable *"wilderness,"* a complete *"wasteland."* So, when we read that the woman will *"flee into the wilderness,"* where she will be *"nourished for 3½ years,"* it isn't hard to recognize that Jesus' angel was, in fact, revealing that God will preserve His 144,000 Jewish servants, in Jerusalem, during the first half of the tribulation period. We know this because that's where God's two prophets will be. And that's where the new Third Temple will be built. Once the Holy Spirit is pulled back,[383] it won't be long before Jerusalem and the rest of the world will become a spiritual *"wilderness."* This will begin as the Rapture occurs, and, from that point on, conditions all over the world will only get worse with every passing day until the entire earth is almost totally laid waste!

~ So, how do we know if that's what these verses reveal? ~

To grasp the meaning of this portion of John's vision we merely need to assess what we've learned thus far. In **Rev. 7:1-8**, we learned that the 144,000 will be sealed immediately prior to the rapture of the Church. Next, we learned that the Rapture will kick-off the seven-year tribulation period. We also learned that God's two witnesses will descend at or near the same time as the Church will be raptured (*the beginning of this 3½ year period*). Now, in **Rev. 12:6-14**, John is telling us that the woman will

[383] 2Th. 2:7

be given two wings, which will enable her to *"flee into the wilderness,"* where she will be nourished for 3½ years. Therefore, since the prophets will be preaching in Jerusalem during that same 3½ year period, both 3½ year periods are in perfect alignment. This may (*though we don't know for certain*) indicate that God intends to have already assembled the 144,000 Jewish servants, in Israel, before He comes to catch-away the Church.[384]

Satan tries to prevent the Rapture of the Saints

Rev. 12:7-11

> ***'And there was war in heaven: Michael and his angels fought against the dragon; and the dragon fought and his angels, And prevailed not; neither was their place found any more in heaven.***
>
> ***And the great dragon was cast out, that old serpent, called the Devil, and Satan, which deceiveth the whole world: he was cast out into the earth, and his angels were cast out with him.***
>
> ***And I heard a loud voice saying in heaven, Now is come salvation, and strength, and the kingdom of our God, and the power of his Christ: for the accuser of our brethren*** *(Satan)* ***is cast down, which accused them before our God day and night.***
>
> ***And they overcame him by the blood of the Lamb, and by the word of their testimony; and they loved not their lives unto the death.'***

Through the Eyes of the Accuser

The Bible — God's infallible Word — serves to give us a vision of future events. We need this because, unlike Satan, we can't normally see into the spiritual world. When an angel is sent from Heaven to *"seal"* the 144,000 Jewish servants, just moments before the saints are raptured, Satan will be able to see that angel descend, but we (*the saints*) won't even know it's happening. However, immediately after that angel finishes sealing the last of those 144,000 special servants, the saints are going to instantly be caught-up into Heaven — to God's throne! Satan will see that too, and it's going to infuriate him! And why shouldn't it? From the first man Adam to this present generation, Satan has watched man presumptuously sin, repeatedly, century after century. Satan sinned just once and was cast out

[384] In the aftermath of the Rapture, travelling even short distances will prove to be extremely difficult. Airlines and railways will no longer be operational. Thus, overseas travel will be restricted to seafaring vessels, and, because of massive fuel shortages, that option will rapidly lessen with each passing day.

of Heaven forever. By his way of thinking that just isn't fair and he's right! Certainly none of us deserves to be redeemed. That's what makes God's grace and mercy so awesome. We don't deserve it, and we can't earn it.

When I examine myself, I don't have to look deep within to find countless reasons for the Lord to cast me out. I'm a sinner through and through. Therefore, if, like me, some Christians occasionally have a hard time understanding how God could love us, how could Satan grasp God's choosing to mercifully forgive even our presumptuous sins? I can certainly see why Satan would look at God's grace towards us and feel resentment.

Satan won't take the catching-away of the saints sitting down!

John's having witnessed a war between Satan and his fallen angels and Michael and God's heavenly host, in **Rev. 12:7-11**, is an indication of how Satan will react when God resurrects and catches away[385] all of His faithful and obedient children, which will include everyone from the creation of the first man (*Adam*) to the beginning of the tribulation period. Satan has been accusing us before God from the very beginning,[386] so he won't just stand there and watch as God mercifully resurrects and assembles us before His throne. As I've stated, Satan — "**our accuser**" — knows that each and every one of us deserves to suffer, just as he suffers; therefore, not being able to understand God's mercy toward the saints, Satan and all his fallen angels (*the powers of darkness*)[387] will aggressively pursue us when we're caught-up to Heaven and attempt to accuse us of sin. But, as **Rev. 12:7-11** reveals, before Satan can hurl a single accusatory word our way, Michael, the mighty Archangel, will lead God's heavenly army against him, swiftly casting Satan and all his fallen angels back down to earth!

~ How can we be sure of this interpretation? ~

This particular passage is filled with indicators that reveal its meaning. In fact, we're practically tripping over them as we read. Let's identify them, starting with what John wrote in **Rev. 12:9**. Notice the words, ***'that old serpent, called the Devil, and Satan, <u>which deceiveth the whole world</u>.'*** The underlined words prove that this is not a reference to Satan's first rebellion and expulsion from Heaven. When Satan was originally cast out of Heaven, after having drawn a third of the angels with him, he had only deceived those fallen angels. He had not, as of yet, deceived the whole world. Therefore, when we read the verse in context, it becomes clear that John's words can't be a reference to Satan's original expulsion.

---

385 1Th.4:13-18 and 5:1-3

386 Rev. 12:10

387 Eph. 6:12-16, Rev. 12:7-9

Furthermore, in verses **6** and **14**, John twice refers to a 3½ year period. Those references, we are learning, can only be interpreted as references to the first half of the seven-year tribulation period, because, only then (*during the tribulation period*), will a 3½ year period be significant. Consequently, in this Chapter 12 portion of his vision, John must have witnessed an allegorical representation of Satan's reaction to the future rapture of the Church, which will occur just a fraction of a second before that 3½ year period begins.

This explains why the woman, who, in this portion of Chapter 12 represents the 144,000, is seen *"fleeing into the wilderness to be nourished for 3½ years."* Since, only after the Rapture will a 3½ year period have prophetic significance, John's words must be interpreted as being a reference to that specific end-time period. And, since the woman in John's vision is clearly a representation of the tribes of Israel, and the 144,000 Jewish servants are intended to represent those twelve tribes, I can find no other more scripturally supportable interpretation of what John recorded witnessing in this passage.

Satan will only have seven years to build his Army

Rev. 12:12-14

> ***'Therefore rejoice, ye heavens, and ye that dwell in them. Woe to the inhabiters of the earth and of the sea! for the devil is come down unto you, having great wrath, because he knoweth that he hath but a short time.***
>
> ***And when the dragon saw that he was cast unto the earth, he persecuted the woman which brought forth the man child.***
>
> ***And to the woman were given two wings of a great eagle*** *(the two witnesses)*, ***that she might fly into the wilderness, into her place*** *(Jerusalem)*, ***where she is nourished for a time, and times, and half a time*** *(3½ years)*, ***from the face of the serpent.'***

The raptured saints are being told to rejoice; whereas, the inhabitants of the earth are being warned that Satan is coming down with great wrath! Knowing that time is running out, Satan (*through the son of perdition*) will vindictively persecute the Jews (*the woman which brought forth the man child*), wherever he can, in a violent attempt to kill every last descendant of Jacob. He won't, however, be successful. And, because God's two witnesses will be protecting them, Satan won't initially be able to kill God's 144,000 Jewish servants or overrun Jerusalem. However, as soon as he's permitted, Satan will gather the nations against Israel and attack Jerusalem, killing God's two witnesses and the 144,000 Jewish servants. Thus, he'll take half of Jerusalem's inhabitants into captivity,[388] and eventually kill every newly born-again child of God.

Eagles are mighty icons of supremacy and power; having wing spans spreading out to eight feet, powerfully lethal steely talons, and iron-like beaks, eagles are the uncontested lords of the sky. Thus, it's not hard to understand why God has chosen this particularly amazing creature to symbolize the powerful protection He'll provide through His two witnesses on behalf of the 144,000 Jewish servants. During the first half of the tribulation period, these two powerful prophets will rule the world, while being completely invulnerable to Satan's attacks. This will make it possible, amidst all the global anarchy, for the 144,000 to build the new Third Temple and commence worshipping God.

In the second half of verse **6**, John stated that the woman (*the 144,000*) will be nourished for 1,260 days (*3½ years*). Now, here, in verse **14**, John is telling us that the woman will be nourished in ***'her place'*** *(one location, not all over the world)*, ***'for a time, and times, and a half a time.'*** As I earlier stated, this is more proof that the 144,000 will not be evangelizing the world, but will, instead, stay together, in one place, for 3½ years, where they can be protected from ***'the face of the serpent'*** *(Satan and his false-prophets).* The next two verses will explain why this will be so important.

The earth saves the 144,000 from the Flood

Rev. 12:15-16

> ***'And the serpent cast out of his mouth water as a flood after the woman, <u>that he might cause her to be carried away of the flood</u>. And the earth helped the woman, and the earth opened her mouth, and swallowed up the flood which the dragon cast out of his mouth.'***

For years I believed these verses to be a reference to the nations of the world helping to save the Jews from total extinction during World War II. The Holocaust certainly would seem to fit this description of the dragon's casting out a deadly flood in his attempt to exterminate every descendant of Jacob. However, given that this attack will occur during the seven-year tribulation period, we know from the text that past events could not explain these prophetic passages. The fact is we just don't know what type of flood this portion of John's vision is indicating. It could symbolically represent just about any massive, spiritual and/or physical attack.

~ But could this attack actually be a flood? ~

---

[388] Zec. 14:2, Dan. 9:27, Mt. 24:15-24

Rev. 12:17

> ***'And the dragon*** *(Satan, the Devil and his demonic forces)* ***was wroth with the woman*** *(Either the 144,000 or Israel in general),* ***and went to make war with the remnant of her seed*** *(the "remnant" and the 144,000—Rev. 11:7-13),* ***which keep the commandments of God, and have the testimony of Jesus Christ.'***

We should start by noting that, since neither Israel nor Jews in general could be said to both *'keep the commandments of God'* and *'have the testimony of Jesus Christ,'* the preceding verse makes it clear that the woman, at least in this portion of **Rev. 12**, is a reference, not to the nation of Israel in general, but, rather, to the 144,000 Jewish servants (*who will repent and serve Christ*) and possibly also to "**the remnant**" — the very last saints to repent and be saved.

~ So, what about the possibility of an actual flood? ~

While it is true that Satan is said to be '***the prince of the power of the air'*** (*Eph. 2:2*) and, if God allowed, could easily cause a massive hurricane and tsunami to occur, since this chapter of John's vision is allegorical, we couldn't support a declaration that these verses indicate that Satan will produce an actual flood.[389] As I've stated, the word *"flood"* could simply be a reference to any type of overwhelming attack; therefore, I wouldn't be too quick to rule anything out.

Most likely . . . .

If the 144,000 are killed with the two witnesses, there's a good chance they'll also be instantly resurrected and caught-up to Heaven, at the same time as or soon after the witnesses ascend. We know this because, as we will soon discover in Chapter 14, the 144,000 will be immediately resurrected, either prior to or at the same time as the mark of the beast will begin to be imposed on the remaining Left-behinders. Therefore, when Satan sees that God has not only called His two prophets back to Heaven but has also resurrected and redeemed His 144,000 Jewish servants (*just as He will have done to the Church, 3½ years earlier*), he's going to, again, be furious! Hence, not being able to prevent the resurrection of God's two prophets or the 144,000, Satan will vindictively go all out, slaughtering every newly repentant believer in Christ. And make no mistake about it,

---

[389] Zechariah described such an attack (*Zec. 14:1-2*). What's more, Daniel's parallel prophecy about these events: the destruction of the Second Temple, the rise of the false-prophet (*the prince that shall come*), and the *abomination of desolation,* is worded very similarly to John's vision and includes a reference to a flood-like period of destruction;—see Daniel 9:26.

hiding won't help. The scriptures clearly state that Satan will easily find and kill every last believer on earth:

> *'And it was given unto him {the son of perdition, the false-prophet} to make war with the saints,* ***and to overcome them****:* ***and power was given him over all kindreds****,* ***and tongues****,* ***and nations****.'*
> *{This means that nobody will be beyond Satan's reach and authority!}*

Rev. 13:7

Daniel's following parallel prophecy further establishes this truth:

> *'I beheld, and the same horn {a reference to the false-prophet}* ***made war with the saints****,* ***and prevailed against them*** *. . .'*

Daniel 7:21

Chapter 31

Much More Than a Man

Rev. 13:1-2

> ***'And I stood upon the sand of the sea, and saw a beast rise up out of the sea, having seven heads and ten horns, and upon his horns ten crowns, and upon his heads the name of blasphemy.***
>
> ***And the beast which I saw was like unto a leopard, and his feet were as the feet of a bear, and his mouth as the mouth of a lion: and the dragon*** *(Satan)*[390] ***gave him his power, and his seat*** *(dominion)*, ***and great authority.'***

Where have we heard this before: *seven heads, ten horns, ten crowns, and the name of blasphemy on every head?* If you answered: *"Daniel Chapter 7,"* you were correct. Daniel's vision coupled with John's explanation of the seven-headed dragon in **Rev. 12:3-4** is the "**key**" to the Church's ability to understand this portion of John's vision. Without it we would have no way of properly interpreting much of what we consider to be "end-time scripture," so let's take a look at what Daniel recorded about his parallel vision.

Both Daniel and John saw their beasts rise up out of the Sea.

> *'Daniel spake and said, I saw in my vision by night, and, behold,* ***the four winds*** [391] *of the heaven strove upon the great sea. And* ***four great beasts came up from the sea****, diverse one from another. The first {beast} was like a* ***lion****, and had* ***eagle's wings****: I beheld till the wings thereof were plucked, and it was lifted up from the earth, and made stand upon the feet as a man,*

---

[390] Rev. 12:1-17

[391] Compare this verse to Rev. 7:1-3.

and a man's heart was given to it.' {*This first beast is a reference to the mighty king Nebuchadnezzar and the Babylonian Empire.*}

*'And behold another **beast**, a second, like to a **bear**, and it raised up itself on one side, and it had three ribs*[392] *in the mouth of it between the teeth of it: and they said thus unto it, Arise, devour much flesh.'* {*The bear symbolizes the Medo-Persian Empire, and its three canine teeth most likely represent its conquests of the Babylonian, Egyptian and Lydian Empires.*}

'After this I beheld, and lo another {*beast*}, ***like a leopard***, *which had upon the back of it four wings of a fowl; the **beast** had also **four heads**; and dominion was given to it.'* {*The leopard represents the speed with which "Alexander the Great" conquered the world. After doing so, in only ten years, Alexander died - 323 BC - leaving his kingdom to be divided among four of his surviving generals. This is indicated in Daniel's vision by the existence of the four-headed leopard. Four prominent generals or kings equal four heads.*}

Daniel 7:2-6

That's only six; aren't we missing a head?

So far, using Daniels vision, we've accounted for six of the seven heads on the beast John saw rising up out of the sea, but we're still missing a description of the most dreadful head of all. Thankfully, the following second half of Daniel's vision will reveal what that final terrible head represents.

*'After this I saw in the night visions, and behold a **fourth beast**, dreadful and terrible, **and strong exceedingly**; and it had great iron teeth: it devoured and brake in pieces, **and stamped the residue with the feet of it**: **and it was diverse from all the beasts that were before it**;* {*This beast with great iron teeth repre-*

[392] Some have interpreted this to indicate that the beast had three powerful canine teeth (*i.e., three powerful Persian kings—Dan. 11:2*). However, from my perspective, the wording just doesn't fit that interpretation. It seems more probable that the passage may simply be alluding to three specific conquests of the *Medo-Persian Empire* (*e.g., its conquests of Lydia, Babylon and Egypt*).

*sents the end-time kingdom of the "false-prophet."} and it had **ten horns**. I considered the horns, and, behold, there came up among them **another little horn**, before whom there were three of the first horns plucked up by the roots: and, behold, **in this horn were eyes like the eyes of man**, **and a mouth speaking great things**.' {This emerging little horn symbolizes the future power and might of the "false-prophet," the man to whom many refer, calling him the "anti-Christ." Thus, the "false-prophet," the "little horn," the "son of perdition" and the "anti-Christ" are all references to one evil, global dictator. This is absolutely provable as we will soon see.}*

Daniel 7:7-8

Daniel's fourth Beast

Although Daniel didn't live to actually see the rise of the Roman Empire or the blasphemous end-time kingdom of the false-prophet, he described the fourth beast in his vision (*the final evil kingdom to rule the earth*) as being exceedingly strong and dreadful. And, had he lived during the glorious apex of either the Roman Empire or the end-time kingdom of the son of perdition, I would imagine that he would have described those kingdoms in much the same way. With few exceptions, never before had the earth experienced such overwhelming, nearly global subjugation as was imposed by the Romans.

Having begun a slow rise to power between the 7th and 8th centuries BC and having ultimately ascended to rule the world for several centuries thereafter, some contend that the Roman Empire continued to exist, in one form or another, into as late as the 15th century.[393] Since the Roman Empire is considered to have slowly faded away, rather than having been outright conquered, many scholars believe that Daniel's fourth, dreadful, iron-toothed beast symbolizes not only the early rise of the Roman Empire but also an end-time reemergence of a revised Roman or Babylonian kingdom. We'll examine that possibility later, but before we do we need to acknowledge that a cohesive relationship between John's and Daniel's visions does exist. To help us do that, let's take a look at **Daniel 7:3-25** and **Revelation 13:1-5**, side by side. As we do, we'll see several pertinent parallels. Those amazingly similar parallels prove that John saw the same **four** beasts as did Daniel, but, since John's vision is a vision of end-time events, John saw the latter-day culmination of Daniel's four beasts and seven heads as **one** horrifically blasphemous beast!

---

[393] Some believe the Empire fell with Romulus Augustulus in September AD 476.

DANIEL 7:3-25	REV. 13:1-5
(7:3) 'And four great beasts came up from **the sea**, diverse one from another.' (7:4) 'The first was like a **lion** . . .' (7:5) 'And behold another beast, a second, like to a **bear** . . .'	(13:1) 'And saw a beast rise up out of **the sea** . . .' (13:2) '. . . his mouth was as the mouth of a **lion** . . .' (13:2) '. . . his feet were as the feet of a **bear** . . .'
(7:6) 'After this I beheld, and lo another, like a **leopard**, the beast had also **four heads**'	(13:2) 'And the beast which I saw was like unto a **leopard** . . .'
(7:7) 'behold a fourth beast, dreadful and terrible, and strong exceedingly; and it had great iron teeth... ...and it was diverse from all the beasts that were before it; and it had **ten horns**.'	(13:1) '. . . and saw a beast rise up out of the sea, having **seven heads** and **ten horns** . . .'{*Daniel's beasts also have a total of seven heads and ten horns*}
(7:8) '. . . behold, there came up among them another **little horn**, before whom there were three of the first horns plucked up by the roots: and behold, in this horn were eyes like the **eyes of a man**, and **a mouth speaking great things**.'	(13:5) 'And there was given unto him **a mouth speaking great things** and **blasphemies** . . .'
(7:21) 'I beheld, and the same horn made war with the saints and **prevailed against them** . . .'	(13:7) 'And it was given unto him to make war with the saints and to **overcome them** . . .'
(7:24) 'And the **ten horns** out of this kingdom are **ten kings** that **shall arise** . . .' *{Notice, these ten kings had not, as of yet, risen to power.}*	(17:12) 'And the **ten horns** which thou sawest are **ten kings**, **which have received no power as yet**; but receive power as kings **one hour** with the beast.' *{An hour indicates an unspecified period of time.}*
(7:25) 'And he shall speak great words against the most high, and shall wear out the saints of the most high, and think to change times and laws: and they shall be given into his hand until **a time and times and the dividing of time**.' *(3½ yrs.)*	(13:5) '. . . and power was given unto him to continue **forty and two months**.' *(3½ yrs.)*

Daniel's four Beasts have become John's end-time Beast

After seeing **Daniel 7:3-25** and **Rev. 13:1-5** side by side, recognizing that John's seven-headed beast is a clear latter-day culmination of Daniel's four individual beasts doesn't take a lot of imagination; it's obvious! Moreover, both Daniel's and John's visions indicate that the future false-prophet will be given the same final 3½ year period (*the second half of the tribulation period, which will begin with the abomination of desolation and the killing of the two witnesses*) to rule the earth.[394] And, since there's no record of that 3½ year reign having already occurred, both Daniel and John must have been referring to the same future 3½ year period.

So, what does John's seven-headed beast actually represent?

Just like Daniel's four separate beasts, which had a total of seven heads and ten horns and emerged from the "**sea**," this first beast in John's vision (*the first half of Rev. Chapter 13*) also was seen to have seven heads and ten horns and, likewise, ascended from the "**sea**," rather than the "**earth**." The word *"sea"* in these passages is most likely a reference to both *people* and *time*. Unfortunately, however, in **Daniel 7:3-25** and **Rev. 13:1-5**, neither Daniel nor John give us any direct clarification as to the meaning of the word, so we must look elsewhere in the Scriptures to gain insight.

*'And he saith unto me, **The waters which thou sawest**, where the whore sitteth, are peoples, and multitudes, and nations, and tongues.'*

Rev. 17:15

{We should note that the "whore" in the preceding verse and in the remainder of the passage is revealed to be a clear symbolic reference to the idolatrous influence that Satan and the "powers of darkness" ("the beast") have had and will continue to have on all the — 'peoples, and multitudes, and nations, and tongues' — of the world, starting with the first man Adam and continuing throughout the seven-year tribulation period.}

Later, when we examine the rest of this passage (*Rev. 17:1-18*), we're going to learn that John recorded seeing that the *"whore"* in the preceding verse was *'. . . **drunken with the blood of the saints and with the martyrs***

---

394 Both Daniel and John saw this man as a *"blasphemous mouth speaking great things"* during the seven year tribulation period. This is the same individual of whom Paul prophesied, calling him *"the son of perdition."* This man will rule the world and commit the *"abomination of desolation,"* declaring himself to be *"God in the flesh"*—2Th. 2:3-12, Rev. 13:1-10, 16:13 & 19:20.

of Jesus.' Those words define a period that reaches both backward and forward to include every person who will have lived and died having faith in God, beginning with the first man, Adam, and continuing through the seven-year tribulation period to include those who will die as a result of the Second Coming of Christ. Thus, John's vision of the whore being drunk with the blood of the saints[395] reveals two important facts: first, *"the whore"* and *"the seven-headed beast"* on which she sits have existed from the beginning of time, and, second, the word "**sea**" in **Daniel 7:3-25** and **Rev. 13:1-5** (*or "many waters" in Rev. 17:1-18*) is intended to metaphorically represent the many — *peoples, and multitudes, and nations, and tongues* — throughout the world, from the time of Adam to the end of the tribulation period. That being the case, it should now be quite clear that the *"seven-headed beast with ten horns"* that came out of the "**sea**" in John's vision and the *"four beasts with a total of seven heads and ten horns"* in Daniel's vision couldn't possibly be intended to represent a mere mortal!

Therefore, when we read a passage or verse that, on the surface, seems to be indicating that this *"purely wicked, seven-headed beast with ten horns and a mouth speaking great, blasphemous things"* is anything less than *"Satan and his timeless powers of darkness and their past, present and future affect on the inhabitants of the earth,"* we need to step-back, broaden our perspective, and allow "THE WHOLE OF SCRIPTURE" to reveal the much grander, wholly inclusive understanding of this allegorical "**beast**."

What we will see Emerge from the Text

Since it's been commonly taught that this *"seven-headed beast with ten horns"* will be a man, a world leader or dictator of sorts, it's been assumed that he and a false-prophet (*a subordinate spiritual leader*) will deceive and manipulate the world into submission. However, while this has been generally accepted, it warrants repeating that the Scriptures reveal that it will actually be just one notably powerful false-prophet who will be empowered for 3½ years to overcome the saints and rule the world.[396] This supremely wicked individual is clearly labeled in both Daniel's and John's visions as being a *"mouth speaking great, blasphemous things."* Thus, this powerful false-prophet will dominate and control ten subordinate kings, which is indicated by John's having seen *"ten horns"* on the seventh head of the seven-headed beast, which he saw come out of the sea. Those ten kings

---

395 Rev. 17:1-18

396 (*Dan. 7:19-26, Rev. 13:1-10, 2Th. 2:3-12*) Jesus warned that during the tribulation period there will be many *false Christs* and *false prophets* (*Mt. 24:11-24, Mk. 13:22*). In so doing, Jesus was revealing that the *son of perdition (the evil man who will deceive and rule the world*), will have many wicked subordinates, but he, alone, will enter the Temple and declare himself to be "God"—2Th. 2:3-12.

will initially have no choice but to resentfully[397] surrender their power and authority to this global dictator (*the false-prophet*). His plan will be to forcibly unite the world into one massive empire, and that empire will be divided into ten separate regions.

This explains why Daniel, Paul, and Jesus never taught, in any of their letters or discourses, that there will be both a tyrannical world leader and a false-prophet. Instead, they collectively taught that, during the tribulation period, there will be just one powerfully wicked ruler, and that ruler will be the false-prophet (*the son of perdition, Satan's puppet dictator*). Hence, by forcing every living soul to bear a mark of submission to his beastly kingdom, the false-prophet (*the mortal ruler of Satan's demonically inspired global kingdom*) will effectively be forcing the entire world to worship *"Satan and his powers of darkness"* — "**the beast**." Those who choose not to take that mark and submit will be killed.

The Challenge:

After we've finished exploring the rest of John's vision, try to forget everything you've read or heard taught about this subject and carefully study Daniel's, Paul's, Jesus,' and John's accounts[398] of this future wicked world leader — presupposing nothing! See if you can honestly prove, without reading anything into the text, that their teachings actually indicate the emergence of both a mortal world leader and a subordinate false-prophet. I've tried to prove that interpretation from virtually every perspective but have found it impossible to do so, without allowing for *presupposition, manipulation* and a *willful ignorance* of what is actually written in the text.[399]

Back to the beast from the Sea

The 13th chapter of John's book is divided into two distinctly different sections: **Rev. 13:1-10** and **Rev. 13:11-18**, and yet, it is still very easy to understand. Nonetheless, because so many continue to rigidly cling to what we will see amount to an illogical explanation of what the Scriptures clearly state about the continual existence of this seven-headed beast with ten horns, the proper interpretation of the text has continually eluded many knowledgeable students of eschatology. We'll soon see why.

---

[397] Rev. 17:12-18

[398] Dan. 7:1-27, 2Th. 2:3-12, Mt. 24:15-30, Mk. 13:14-26, Luke 21:20-24, Rev. 17:1-18

[399] We should acknowledge that, while prophesying of end-time events, Jesus warned that, during this final period, many false-prophets would arise, but Jesus never taught that a global dictator of sorts and a single, subordinate false-prophet would rule the world—Mt. 24:23-30.

Altogether, Daniel's four beasts have a total of:

- **Seven** heads, **six** *former kingdoms and* **one** *future end-time kingdom*
- **Ten** horns, *ten future tribulation period kings*
- And **one** notably stout — "**little-horn**" — *the false-prophet*

In Daniel's vision of this end-time kingdom (*Dan. 7:3-25*) Daniel witnessed an impressively *"stout, little-horn" (the false-prophet who will rule the world during the final 3½ years of the tribulation period)* arise from among ten individual horns (*kings or rulers*) after first subduing three. The difference between Daniel's and John's visions is that, since John was shown a vision of end-time events, on the seventh and most dreadful head of John's beast (*the head that was intended to represent the tribulation period kingdom of Satan and the false-prophet*), John saw ten horns wearing crowns. Those crowns symbolize the authority that those ten kings will possess while serving under the false-prophet's global dominion (*This will all be thoroughly confirmed as we move through Rev. 17 and 18*).

~ *Why didn't Daniel's ten horns have crowns?* ~

Daniel lived in Babylon during both the end of the *Babylonian Empire* and the emergence of the *Media-Persian Empire,* eventually living to serve under Darius the Mede. Thus, the 1st and 2nd kingdoms in Daniel's vision (*Babylon and Media-Persia*) had already come on the scene by the time Daniel experienced his vision of four great beasts emerging from the sea. The 3rd and 4th kingdoms (*the Grecian Empire and the final, end-time Babylonian Empire*),[400] however, had not yet assumed authority over the earth. Therefore, in Daniel's vision, the *"ten horns"* on his 4th and final *"beast"* (*Satan's tribulation period kingdom*) were not shown wearing crowns, because that end-time kingdom had not yet arisen.

Simply stated, in **Rev. 13:1-18**, John was shown all the kingdoms that Daniel saw in his Chapter 7:1-28 vision (*seven kingdoms in all*),[401] but John

---

[400] In Rev. 17, the angel speaking with John refers to the final tribulation period kingdom as: *"Mystery Babylon the Great."* Many, however, refer to that final kingdom, calling it: *"the Revised Roman Empire,"* because the fourth beast in Daniel's vision represented both the initial emergence of the original *Roman Empire* and a possible reemergence of a similar, globally dominant, latter-day *Roman Empire.*

[401] Remember, the Grecian Empire split into four separate kingdoms. This was represented by the 3rd beast in Daniel's vision having four heads. Thus, the four beasts in Daniel's vision had a total of seven heads (*individual kingdoms*). And the final head (*the future tribulation period kingdom*) was seen to have ten horns (*kings*), but Daniel recorded seeing the false-prophet (*an additional stout, "little-horn"*) emerge from among the other kings, subdue three, and rule the earth.

was shown those kingdoms together, as one powerful beast (*with seven heads and ten horns*). And, since John's beast is specifically intended to represent Satan's demonic influence on the entire world and its inhabitants during the earth's final seven years of "great tribulation," the ten horns on the seventh and most dreadful head of John's beast were seen wearing crowns, a sign that the end-time kingdom of the beast will have emerged. This explains why the symbolic dragon in Chapter 12 of John's vision (*a representation of the continual affect that Satan and his powers of darkness have had on the kingdoms of the earth*), which was said to have deceived the whole world,[402] also appeared having *"seven heads," "ten horns"* and *"seven crowns"* upon his heads.[403]

Do the Scriptures teach that Satan can raise the dead?

Rev. 13:3

> ***'And I saw one of his heads** (the seven-headed beast) **<u>as it were wounded to death</u>; and <u>his deadly wound was healed</u>: and all the world wondered after the beast.'***

The preceding verse has become a significant and continual stumbling-block in the middle of the Church's path of end-time understanding. For many years I've heard it taught that the false-prophet will rise from the dead during the tribulation period. That teaching is flat out wrong. Furthermore, it's a totally illogical interpretation of John's words and is in no way scripturally sound. Those of you who've believed and taught this over the years, please don't take offense. Instead, let's take a closer, more rational look at what the Scriptures actually teach.

~ Have we already forgotten about the 3½ years of unrelenting plagues and global devastation? ~

By the end of the first 3½ years of the seven-year tribulation period the earth will have become an absolute "**WASTELAND**," and I'm not being overly dramatic. If you doubt what I've just said, reread what we learned as we made our way through Revelation Chapters 8 and 9, and study the global effects that the plagues of God's two prophets will have had on the earth during that period.

When the false-prophet is finally allowed to begin his nearly unrestrained global reign of terror (*which will begin at the end of the first 3½ years—Rev. 13:5*), the odor of putrefying blood and decaying bodies will be

---

402 Rev. 12:9, Isaiah 14:16-17

403 The seven crowns on the seven heads of the Dragon represent Satan's influence on all past, present, and future kingdoms of the earth.

the predominant stench lingering in the heavily toxic, smoke-filled, barely breathable air around the world. This will largely be due to one-third of the oceans and seas having been turned into blood and the resulting dead, rotting fish and sea mammals washing up, with that blood, on the many shores around the world. As that blood washes up, it will slowly solidify and rot. And let's not forget that, during the thirteen months prior to the takeover of the false-prophet and his followers, one-third of the earth's population will have been slain by the 200 million killer-horsemen, and it's not likely that the survivors will be strong enough to burn or bury the many hundreds of millions of resulting corpses.

And, making things worse, God's two powerful prophets will likely have exercised their authority (*Rev. 11:6*) to shut-up the heavens. So the hydrologic cycle (*i.e., rain*), which would normally help to clean the air and land, will have offered little or no help. Thus, due to the massive amounts of stagnating blood, fish, and the hundreds of millions of dead and decomposing human and animal carcasses, the fly and insect population will have continued to thrive and increase to literally biblical proportions!

Imagine how the atmosphere around the world will look just a few days after the Rapture occurs, with hundreds of millions of automobiles, houses, industrial plants, and forests ablaze and out of control. Many of those fires will emit deadly smoke, teaming with chemicals and poisonous toxins. We're not even including the lethal nuclear fallout, which the multiple unmanned water reactors around the globe will have released into the air. And what about the sky after the first trumpet-plague has been released and one-third of the "**trees**" and "**all the green-grass**" have burnt to a cinder. Even if the prophets choose to shut-up the heavens and prevent it from raining for only part of that first 3½ year period, the death and devastation caused by their doing so will be astronomical!

From the very start of the tribulation period and throughout the first half, until the false-prophet can subjugate the remaining Left-behinders and begin to recreate a world economy, there will be no power, no running water, no active sewer systems, and at least one-third of the rivers, seas, lakes, and reservoirs will be "**bitter**" (*poisoned and undrinkable*). What's more, the *sun, moon,* and *stars* will give one-third less light; thus, the global climate will have drastically changed — killing many millions more.

All evidence indicates that more than half of the world's population will have died or been killed before the sixth trumpet-plague is over, and countless others will have already perished due to radiation poisoning, starvation, dehydration, various sicknesses, and exposure before that sixth trumpet-plague even begins. Furthermore, adding to the disastrous global effects of the Rapture and the two witnesses' plagues will be the destructive impact of 3½ years of wars and skirmishes. This will be the result of the false-prophet's having gone forth ***'conquering and to conquer'*** as Satan uses him to build his final global empire.

Will the earth be a "**WASTELAND**?" If we were here to experience the cold, dark, smoke filled skies, the ghastly cadaverous, global stench, the bloody ocean waters and coastal areas, the universal deaths, famine and, most of all, the palpably thick and dreary spiritual essence of pure hatred that will radiate from the heart of every still defiant Left-behinder, I doubt even one of us would find the term "**WASTELAND**" to be too strong a word for describing the earth's condition at the end of the first half of the tribulation period!

~ *Okay — so, what's the point?!* ~

The point is, as the first half of the tribulation period draws to a close and the false-prophet is allowed to kill God's two witnesses and take control, the entire earth will be in such utter shambles that nobody will believe it could ever be restored to a habitable state. The earth will appear to be dead! Hence, the dismal "**WASTELAND**" condition of the entire earth and its inhabitants will be that symbolic wounded head John saw in his vision of "**the beast**" (*Rev. 13:3*). This is why John recorded seeing only one of the beast's seven heads ***'as if it were wounded to death.'*** The other six heads on John's seven-headed beast serve only to represent past kingdoms. Thus, just the most dreadful head (*with the ten horns and iron teeth*) is a representation of Satan's final end-time kingdom. And, after 3½ years of plagues and death, that global kingdom will be an inhospitable "**WILDERNESS**" — an absolute "**WASTELAND**;" thus, it will appear to be dead!

And his Deadly wound was Healed

As seemingly irreparably devastated as the earth's ecosystem and global economy will be after 3½ years of wars, drought, and plagues, John did say that he saw this *"wounded unto death"* head of the beast healed. As the second half of **Rev. 13** will reveal, the false-prophet, with Satan's miraculous heavy-handed help, will eventually succeed at his attempt to fashion a functioning economy and social order out of that which will have appeared to be dead and beyond revival. Thus, the world economy will eventually stabilize, fostering a false atmosphere of validation, new hope and a sensation of global unity. This will only be enjoyed (*for want of a more appropriate word*) by those who'll have chosen to submit to the false-prophet's will by becoming part of his global empire. All others will be expeditiously put to death before the tribulation period draws to an end.

The false-prophet's ability to restore order to the earth and its inhabitants will be nothing short of miraculous! Thus, it's no surprise that John wrote: ***'. . . and all the world wondered after the beast.'*** The entire world will wonder in amazement when they witness the satanically empowered false-prophet bring to life the nearly dead, "**WASTELAND**" of an earth.

> *'I will tell thee the mystery of the woman, and of the beast that carrieth her, which hath the seven heads and ten horns. The beast that thou sawest* ***was****, and* ***is not****; and* ***shall ascend out of the bottomless pit****, and go into perdition:* ***and they that dwell on the earth shall wonder****, whose names were not written in the book of life from the foundation of the world, when they behold* ***the beast*** *that* ***was****, and* ***is not****, and* ***yet is****."*

Rev. 17:7-8

After reading the preceding verses in their proper context, it should be pretty obvious that the beast in John's vision is clearly not just a mortal being. For a man to fulfill the preceding prophecy, he would have to:

- have existed in the past (*prior to John's existence*), the beast that "**was**"
- re-emerge (*in the future and rule the earth*), the beast that "**is not**" (*i.e., has not, as of yet, re-emerged)*
- have been in existence (*when John received his vision*), the beast that "**yet is**"

Therefore, only a blending of the four beasts in Daniel's vision (*which represent the original Babylonian empire, the Media-Persia Empire, the divided Grecian Empire and the reemerged Babylonian empire—the end-time kingdom of the false-prophet*) coupled with Satan and the powers of darkness' influence on those kingdoms can completely live up to John's prophetic description of "**the beast**" in **Rev. 13:1-10**. We must remember that scripture, especially allegorically prophetic scripture, cannot be properly interpreted if we allow tunnel-vision to restrict our vision of the "COMPLETE IMAGE" that Scripture, "IN ITS ENTIRETY," is projecting.

Satan will ultimately Rule the Earth

With the Holy Spirit, the Church, and God's two tribulation prophets out of the way, [404] Satan will rule all the nations of the world, and his little *"puppet-leader"* (*the false-prophet*) will be at the helm. There won't be a

[404] When the Holy Spirit pulls back, these evil forces will powerfully emerge from the bottomless pit, precisely as both Paul and John stated—2Th. 2:7-8, Rev. 11:7, and 17:7-8.

single nation powerful enough to resist his will. Thus, just as John stated, all those who'll choose to reject Christ's final call to repent will marvel in awe at the uncontested power and might of this, soon to come, final evil empire: "THE GLOBAL KINGDOM OF THE BEAST!"

The Beast - the Mightiest Kingdom in History

Rev. 13:4

> ***'And they worshipped <u>the dragon</u>*** *(Satan and his powers of darkness)* ***which gave power unto the beast: and they worshipped the beast, saying, Who is like unto the beast? who is able to make war with him?'***

In Daniel's vision, he describes the head on the last of the four beasts as follows:

> *'Thus he {the angel speaking to Daniel} said,* ***<u>The fourth beast</u>*** *shall be* ***<u>the fourth kingdom</u>*** *upon earth, which shall be diverse from all kingdoms,* ***<u>and shall devour the whole earth</u>***, ***<u>and shall tread it down</u>***, ***<u>and break it in pieces</u>***. *'*

Daniel 7:23

The remainder of Daniel's vision (*Dan. 7:23-27*) continues to reveal this to be the kingdom that will precede the Lord's return to earth. Thus far, there has never been a kingdom of this magnitude. This evil empire, which Daniel's fourth beast symbolizes, will utterly engulf the earth and will be judged when Christ triumphantly returns.

Let's Sum Up

Daniel 7:19-27 clearly reveals that the last beast in Daniel's vision will be the final kingdom to rule the earth before the triumphant return of Christ at the end of the seven-year tribulation period. Thus, it will be the seemingly irreparable condition of the earth and the initial state of that global kingdom and all its citizens (*after having suffered through the aftermath of the Rapture, the ensuing 3½ years of God's two witnesses' horrific plagues, and countless wars and skirmishes*) that will appear to have been *"wounded unto death."* There's simply no other rational explanation for John's having seen only "**one**" of the heads on the "**seven-headed**" beast in his vision wounded unto death, and there's absolutely no scriptural evidence to indicate that God has given or will give Satan the power to raise the dead. Only God has power over life and death.

What's more, if we are to believe that the seven-headed beast in John's vision represents a single individual, who will be killed and miraculously rise again, then, for him to die, we would expect all seven heads on John's beast to be wounded unto death, not just one. That, however, is not what John recorded seeing. This is a straight forward, perfectly logical interpretation of these scriptures and, therefore, shouldn't be difficult to grasp.

~ So why do so many interpret these verses differently? ~

The difficulty lies in the sad reality that we have heard this taught incorrectly for many years, by many greatly loved and well respected leaders in the Church. That, however, is no reason to embrace that which is neither logical nor scripturally sound. We must not forget that, as we will see revealed in Rev. Chapter 17, the seven-headed beast in John's vision is a symbolic reference to the continued perverse affect that Satan and his fallen-angels have had and will continue to have on all the kingdoms and peoples of the earth, from early *Babel* (*Gen. 10 and 11*) to the end of the final *New-Babylonian Empire.*[405] The irrefutable evidence of this will continue to "self-emerge" throughout the remainder of John's vision.

The Dragon will be the Power behind this Evil Kingdom

When we made our way through **Rev. 12:1-17,** we learned that the dragon is symbolic for Satan and his continually evil influence on the earth. When John saw the great red dragon, it had seven heads, ten horns, and seven crowns upon its heads. In Daniel's vision, he also saw a total of seven heads (*without crowns*) but on four individual beasts, because, as we discovered earlier, at the time of Daniel's vision (*roughly 555 BC.*), only the Babylonian Empire had fully risen to dominate the earth. This is why Daniel's Chapter 7 vision is so miraculous; only God could have revealed the future emergence of what would become the most prominent global kingdoms to rule the earth.

> *'And the ten horns out of this kingdom are ten kings that shall arise: and another shall rise after them;* ***and he shall be diverse from the first, and he shall subdue three kings****.'*[406]

Daniel 7:24

[405] As I stated earlier, some refer to the final evil kingdom as being the *"Revised Roman Empire."* The angel who spoke with John, however, labeled it "BABYLON THE GREAT"—Rev. 14:8, 16:19, 17:5, 18:2, 10 and 21.
[406] During the tribulation period, the *"false-prophet"* will arise and subdue three of the original ten kings.

*'And he {the false-prophet} shall speak great words against the most High, and shall **wear out the saints of the most High**, and think to change times and laws: and they {probably a reference to all Left-behinders} **shall be given into his hand until a time and times and the dividing of time** {the last 3½ years of the tribulation period}.'*

Daniel 7:25

In the second half of this chapter (*Rev. 13:11-18*) we will read that the false-prophet will be allowed to kill every last saint, while speaking great words and blasphemies against God, but this final global empire will only last about 3½ years.

Satan's Kingdom and the big, blasphemous Mouth

Rev. 13:5-6

***'And there was given unto him** (the beastly seven-headed kingdom of the Dragon—Rev. 13:4) **a mouth speaking great things and blasphemies** (the false-prophet)**; and power was given unto him to continue forty and two months** (3½ years).*

***And he opened his mouth in blasphemy against God, to blaspheme his name, and his tabernacle, and them that dwell in heaven** (a reference to the abomination of desolation).'*

I find it interesting that in the following passage, Enoch, whom God later caught-up to Heaven, actually spoke prophetically in reference to the same blasphemous words and wicked speeches as did John:

*'And Enoch also, the seventh from Adam, prophesied of these, saying, Behold, **the Lord cometh with ten thousands of his saints, To execute judgment upon all**, and to convince all that are ungodly among them of all their ungodly deeds which they have ungodly committed, **and of all their hard speeches which ungodly sinners have spoken against him**. These are murmurers, complainers, walking after their own lusts; **and their mouth speaketh great swelling words**, having men's persons in admiration because of advantage.'*

{Enoch spoke these words between the years 633 and 987, dating forward from the week of creation.}

Jude 1:14-16

Those who wish to make the argument that Christianity's foundation of faith was laid as recently as the first century must contend with prophecies like the preceding prophecy from Enoch. Enoch was a seventh descendant of Adam, yet his prophetic words speak of Christ's returning to earth, with all His saints, at the end of the seven-year tribulation period. Thus, his divinely inspired words predate every religion and belief system on the planet, and that's not even the oldest Messianic prophecy in the Christian Bible![407] How's that for a sure foundation?

The false-prophet will be given Power to Overcome the Saints

Rev. 13:7-8

> ***'And it was given unto him to make war with the saints, and to overcome them: and power was given him over all kindreds, and tongues, and nations.***
>
> ***And all that dwell upon the earth shall worship him, whose names are not written in the book of life of the Lamb slain from the foundation of the world.'***

Once the dust settles, after God's two witnesses have been called back to Heaven and the Jerusalem earthquake (*which will kill 7,000 partying Left-hinders—Rev. 11:11-14*) has ended, the false-prophet's first order of business will be to hunt down and kill every newly repentant, truly born-again Left-behinder. That means "**the remnant**" better get ready to die for their faith.[408] As I stated earlier, we can forget the many books and movies that have mistakenly depicted repentant Left-behinders actually surviving the second half of the tribulation period, because that just isn't going to happen. John's words, in the preceding verses, make this fact perfectly clear! Frankly, I can't see how any true student of eschatology could arrive at any other conclusion then that the false-prophet will be given power to *"overcome"* (*kill*) all those who refuse to take the mark of the beast, especially after having read the preceding verses (*Rev. 13:7-8*).[409]

---

[407] God's prophetic conversation with Adam and Eve in the Garden of Eden, which also made reference to Christ, is the earliest prophecy known to man—Gen. 3:15.

[408] We read of these final saints getting saved just before the seventh angel sounded his trumpet, which signaled the end of the "Mystery of God" (*God's plan of salvation*) — Rev. 11:11-14, Rev. 10:1-7.

[409] As was stated earlier, Daniel's prophecy (*Dan. 7:21*), about this same end-time period, confirms this.

If neither Daniel's nor John's prophecies are enough to drive this point home, then **Rev. 13:5-8** should be the heavy scriptural mallet that gets the job done. In that passage John recorded having been told that all who dwell on the earth will be forced to worship the beast. Therefore, once the false-prophet has been given full power over the nations of the world, all newly repentant saints will be forced to die for their faith or submit to worshipping the image of the "**beast**" by receiving its mark. There's nothing ambiguous about that, and to eliminate any possible confusion, the Lord's angel made it clear that only those whose names **are not** written in the Lamb's book of Life will worship the beast (*Rev. 13:8*). Thus, once the false-prophet finishes killing the last of the newly repentant saints, only those who'll have received the damnable mark of the beast will remain.

Rev. 13:9-10

> ***'If any man have an ear, let him hear.*** [410] ***He that leadeth into captivity*** [411] ***shall go into captivity: he that killeth with the sword must be killed with the sword. Here is the patience and the faith of the saints.'***

Patience in death will equal Eternal Life

The word ***'captivity'*** in the preceding verse is used only one other time in Scripture, and, in both cases, it means *"captivity."* That was easy! The word ***'patience,'*** however, needs a little more clarification. From a purely biblical perspective, patience has to do with the enduring faith and perseverance of true Christians in the midst of severe trials, temptations, and most of all, imminent death. Therefore, the preceding verses powerfully warn all repentant Left-behinders — "**the remnant**" — to hold fast to their new faith. If they weaken and fearfully choose to forfeit their hope of salvation, not only will they have revealed their lack of true faith, but, by acquiescing and taking the mark of the beast, they too will become eternal spiritual captives of eternal damnation — "**death**!"

In your patience possess ye your souls . . .

We must consider that, while it's true that many will repent after watching the resurrection and ascension of God's two witnesses, just like today, during that end-time period, it may be possible that not all will have

---

[410] Jesus used these same words in His letters to the churches in Asia. They simply direct everyone who can understand to listen to what the Lord has to say while they still have the ability to do so.

[411] This is likely a reference to Zachariah's prophecy (*14:1-2*), which foretells of the nations attacking and leading the people of Jerusalem into captivity during the abomination of desolation.

completely surrendered their hearts and lives to Christ. Consequently, when those *"pseudo-Christians"* (*If there are any, and that's a big if!*) are faced with the prospect of suffering a terrifying and violent death for refusing to renounce their new faith in Christ, some may weaken, choosing instead to take the damnable *"mark of the beast."* Those who do so will suffer eternal damnation with no hope of ever being forgiven. Thus, they'll have to pay eternally for every sin they'll have committed and every idol word they'll have spoken, because their names will not be found written in ***'the book of life of the Lamb'*** (*Rev. 13:8*).

Chapter 32

A Lesser Beast Will Emerge From the Earth

In the first halves of their visions, both John and Daniel were shown allegorical images of vaguely describable "**beasts**," which represented kings and kingdoms. Then, in the second halves of their visions, the interpretations of what they had seen were revealed. Thus, both Daniel's and John's visions[412] were divided into two distinct halves: first, a vague allegory and, second, a more descriptive allegorical interpretation. This precise method of revelation has been consistently used throughout Scripture, and yet, sadly, the following second half of John's vision, which we will presently examine, has been repeatedly misinterpreted for centuries.

Regrettably, misinterpreting this "**key**" portion of John's vision has led to the erroneous teaching that, during the tribulation period, there will be two significant leaders: the *"anti-Christ"* or *"the beast"* (*whom some, despite all evidence to the contrary, believe to be represented by John's seven-headed beast—Rev. 13:1-10*) and a *"false-prophet"* (*whom some assume will be a spiritual leader of sorts*). This, we've discovered, can't logically be the case. Let's not forget that, since the seven-headed beast in John's vision has been proven to represent seven distinctly different kingdoms and periods (*six past and one future*),[413] it cannot also, at the same time, symbolize just one end-time individual. This lesser beast, however, whom John recorded having seen emerge from the "**earth**," rather than the "**sea**," can!

An Important Similarity between Daniel's and John's Visions

Because the initial portions of John's and Daniel's visions were allegorical, neither John nor Daniel could understand their meanings without God giving them further clarification. In the second half of Daniel's vision (*Dan. 7:15-16*), Daniel asked one of the heavenly beings to explain what he had just seen. As a result, Daniel was immediately given an explanation. John had a similar experience in **Rev. 13:11-18**; however, God didn't inspire John to ask for clarification, because God had already clarified the meaning

---

[412] Rev. 13 and Daniel 7

[413] According to Daniel 7:1-28, each of the heads on John's "seven-headed" beast (*which arose from the sea*) represents a different king/kingdom and dominion: (6) past kingdoms and (1) future.

of John's seven-headed beast through Daniel's prophecy (*Dan. 7:1-28*). Therefore, to help John and the Church understand the power and significance of the false-prophet who will rule the world, God just immediately followed up the first half of John's **Rev. 13:1-10** vision of the seven-headed beast with a second, more enlightening vision of a lesser beast. Thus, this second, inferior beast, of whom we are about to read, symbolizes the purely wicked nature and character of Satan's future false-prophet (*the son of perdition*) — the man whom Paul prophesied will claim to be God on earth.[414]

John Saw the False-Prophet Emerge as another Beast

Rev. 13:11

> ***'And I beheld another beast coming up out of the earth; and he had two horns like a lamb, and he spake as a dragon.'***

Because this son of perdition (*the false-prophet*) will be endued by Satan with greater powers of deception than any other human in history, in this second half of John's vision, this future evil dictator is also allegorically depicted as being a "**beast**." And, given that each "**king**" and "**kingdom**" in Daniel's Chapter 7 vision were likewise depicted as "**beasts**," this is precisely what we should expect.

As I stated, both Daniel and John recorded seeing this beastly figure (*the son of perdition, the false-prophet*) rise up out of the *"earth"*[415] rather than the *"sea."* In Daniel's case, he emerged as a powerful *"little horn"* from out of the head of the fourth and final beast in his vision.[416] That vision, we learned, after careful study, reveals that Daniel's fourth beast is a representation of the final evil kingdom to rule the earth (*Satan's demonically motivated, tribulation period empire*).[417]

Here, in the second half of **Rev. 13**, John saw the false-prophet (*this single headed, lesser beast*) emerging from the earth, having two horns (*like a gentle, nonthreatening lamb*), but he spake with the blasphemous words of a dragon (*Satan*). Since Jesus is the Lamb of God,[418] we should note that the two horns, ***'like a lamb,'*** which John saw on the head of this lesser

---

[414] 2Th. 2:3-12

[415] The false-prophet's emergence from the *earth*, rather than the *sea*, based on what we know about prophecy in general, is probably meant to indicate that he'll have come from a specific point in time, as opposed to having continually existed, (*as does Satan and his "powers of darkness"*) which John saw arising from the *sea* — representing a period that spans thousands of years—*Rev. 13:1*.

[416] Dan. 7:8 and 20, 21

[417] Dan. 7:17 and 23

[418] John 1:29,36, Rev. 5:6, 6:16, 7:17, 14:10, 15:3, 19:9, 21:22-23, 22:1-3

beastly creature, are probably an additional indication that this future evil dictator will be a false-prophet as well as being the leader of many subordinate false-prophets. Jesus sternly warned the world to beware of this very thing.[419]

> *'Then if any man shall say unto you, Lo, here is Christ, or there; believe it not.* ***For there shall arise false Christs, and false prophets, and shall shew great signs and wonders****; insomuch that, if it were possible, they shall deceive the very elect.'*
>
> **Matthew 24:23-24**

They'll believe the False-Prophet to be God

Rev. 13:12-14

> ***'And he*** *(this lesser beast from out of the earth)* ***exerciseth all the power of the first beast*** *(Satan and the powers of darkness)* ***before him, and causeth the earth and them which dwell therein to worship the first beast, whose deadly wound*** *(i.e., heavy affliction, plagues, global destruction)* ***was healed.***
>
> ***And he doeth great wonders, so that he maketh fire come down from heaven on the earth in the sight of men,***
>
> ***And deceiveth them that dwell on the earth by the means of those miracles which he had power to do in the sight of the beast; saying to them that dwell on the earth, that they should make an image to the beast, which had the wound by a sword*** *(His being wounded by a 'sword' is likely a reference to the Word of God, the powerful ministry of the two witnesses),* ***and did live.'***

These verses reveal how powerfully deceptive the false-prophet will be once all the powers of Hell (*which are represented by the seven-headed beast*) are working through him. Only "**the remnant**" (*those who will have repented after witnessing the ascension of the two prophets*) will be able to withstand this beastly tyrant's demonically inspired trickery. Both Jesus and Paul warned of this powerful deception.

> *'And then shall* ***that Wicked*** *{the false-prophet} be revealed, whom the Lord shall consume with the spirit of his mouth, and*

---

[419] Mt. 24:15, 21, 23-26

> *shall destroy with the brightness of his coming {read Rev. 19:20}: Even him,* ***whose coming is after*** *{i.e., in accordance or agreement with}* ***the working of Satan with all power and signs and lying wonders,***[420] *And with all deceivableness of unrighteousness in them that perish; because they received not the love of the truth, that they might be saved. And for this cause* ***God shall send them strong delusion,***[421] ***that they should believe a lie****: That they all might be damned who believed not the truth {the Gospel, the preaching of the two witnesses}, but had pleasure in unrighteousness.'*

2Th. 2:8-12

The beast will be wounded by the Sword - yet he'll live

John's vision reveals that the wounding of "**one**" (*not all seven*) of the heads on the beast will be caused by a ***'sword.'*** Given that the deadly wound will be inflicted during the first half of the tribulation period, as a result of the two prophets' preaching and plagues, I think we can safely say that the allegorical ***'sword,'*** to which the angel was alluding, is a reference to the *"sword of the Spirit" — "the Word of God!"*

> *'For* ***the word of God*** *is quick, and powerful,* ***and sharper than any two-edged sword****, piercing even to the dividing asunder of soul and spirit, and of the joints and marrow, and is a discerner of the thoughts and intents of the heart.'*

Heb. 4:12

> *'And take the helmet of salvation,* ***and the sword of the Spirit****,* ***which is the word of God*** *. . .'*

Eph. 6:17

As earlier stated, it will be the preaching of God's Word and the ensuing global plagues of God's two witnesses that will wound the earth and its inhabitants, rendering it a virtual "WASTELAND" after only 3½ years. John

---

420 All the *powers of darkness* will be exercised through this one wicked man.

421 Because they will not have listened to God's final warnings, God will shut the Door of Salvation and allow every continually defiant Left-behinder to be deceived. Only "the remnant" (*those who will have repented after seeing the ascension of God's two witnesses*) will be immune to this deception.

will see further affirmation of this towards the end of his vision, when he witnesses Jesus triumphantly return to judge the earth, having a mighty sword (*the Word of God*) protruding from His mouth (*Rev. 19:14-16*).

The Image of the Beast will speak

Rev. 13:15

> ***'And he** (the false-prophet) **had power to give life** [422] **unto the image of the beast, that the image of the beast should both speak, and cause that as many as would not worship the image of the beast should be killed.'***

We should note that this verse does seem to indicate that this lesser beast (*the false-prophet, the 'mouth speaking great things'—13:5*) will have the power to "**animate**" the image of the beast, so as to enable it to both speak and cause all who refuse to worship it to be killed. Through what means Satan will empower the false-prophet to do this, whether through *spiritual* or *mechanical* means, we just don't know. But, however he does it, the image will apparently not only speak but will also have the ability to kill, or at least "**cause to be killed**," every person who refuses to worship it by taking its damnable mark. The preceding verse makes that abundantly clear.

It certainly wouldn't be hard for Satan to design a simple, statuesque, mechanical image (*a symbol of his evil kingdom*), which could administer the *"mark of the beast"* and/or kill all who refuse to become part of his global empire. If that ends up being the case, as long as these beastly images are simply designed, they could easily be replicated and used, around the world, to administer the mark or kill all who resist receiving it.

On the other hand, since John was told that the false-prophet will have the power to give "**life**" to the image of the beast, we should acknowledge that (*in the Greek*) this word, *"life,"* means *spiritual* rather than *mechanical* life and can be used as a reference to either a good or evil spirit. This would open the door for the possibility that the image of the beast may actually be demonically manipulated or empowered. Now there's a terrify-

---

[422] More intimidating than Nebuchadnezzar's 90 feet tall golden statue (*Dan. 3*), the false-prophet will be able to make his *"image of the beast"* appear to live. The *Greek* word (*pneuma*) for *"life"* in this verse can be used to refer to the Holy Spirit or a demonic spirit. Scripturally speaking, Satan has never had power over life and death; therefore, however Satan will enable the false-prophet to spiritually (*demonically*) "animate" (*i.e., simulate life*) the life-like image of the beast, in reality, his doing so will be nothing more than an illusion — a miraculous deception.

ingly sober thought! Unfortunately, how all of this will be accomplished will remain a mystery until this prophecy is fulfilled.

~ Couldn't the image of the beast be computerized? ~

We need to be careful when speculating about these possibilities. The fact is we just don't know how this prophecy will be fulfilled. It would, however, be very difficult to make the case that, immediately following the horrifically devastating first half of the tribulation period, in the raw aftermath of the Rapture and 3½ years of immeasurably calamitous plagues and wars, the surviving Left-behinders will somehow be able to accomplish such a monumental task as repairing and restoring the global power grid. And that's precisely what would have to happen if the image of the beast is going to be some type of electronically powered computer or device.

That being said, it may be possible for generators to provide small amounts of localized energy, provided of course that gasoline and generators are still available. That extremely improbable scenario, however, would not enable a global network of satellites and computers to function, which is precisely what would be needed if computers will be used to continuously monitor the citizens of the new, one-world empire. This is why we're careful not to casually speculate. Speculating places us on a never-ending path of supposition, so let's stick to pure Scripture and logic.

His Mark, his Name or the Number of his Name

Rev. 13:16-17

> ***'And he causeth all, both small and great, rich and poor, free and bond*** *(i.e., everybody)*, ***to receive a mark in their right hand, or in their foreheads:***
>
> ***And that no man might buy or sell, save he that had the mark, or the name of the beast, or the number of his name.'***

In the past, like many others, I've been guilty of failing to recognize the simplicity of these two verses. The angel clearly told John that the false-prophet will force every Left-behinder, who wishes to buy or sell, to receive a ***'mark'*** *(the insignia of the beast)*, the ***'name'*** *(of the beast)* or the ***'number'*** of the beast's name. That means that the Left-behinders will either be given a choice as to which of the three marks of allegiance they wish to receive, or (*more likely*) they'll be "classified," by being forced to receive one of the three permanently affixed marks on either their right hand or their forehead.

Formerly, like many others, I presumed that the mark of the beast will be some type of tattooed identification number or a sophisticated implant of sorts. Now, after having properly taken into consideration the primitive, medieval-like state into which the world and its inhabitants will have been thrust by the time this mark of the beast will begin to be enforced, I've come to the logical realization that even the use of basic identification numbers would be absolutely impossible.

Without a universal power grid, power lines, or even functioning satellites (*which would be needed as soon as the false-prophet takes over in order to link and operate a global computer network and radio frequency systems*), neither microchip implants nor identification numbers could be used for citizenship monitoring and identification.

"Why do you say that?

According to John's vision, when the second half of the tribulation period begins, there could still be as many as a few billion Left-behinders who'll have chosen not to repent, and they'll all need to rapidly receive the *"mark of the beast."* Without a fully functioning global computer network, the newly formed, barely surviving one-world government would be forced to try and keep track of the identification numbers of billions of people on paper. If we really take the time to think through all the obstacles that would have to be overcome in order to create and keep a current manual system of that global magnitude universally up to date (*without the use of a global power grid, the internet or efficient international transportation*), it's pretty obvious how utterly impossible that would be. Just making and distributing the necessary paper on which to record the ever-changing data, under those medieval-like conditions, would prove to be an insurmountable task!

That brings us back to the feasibility of computers. In order to create a new universal society and functioning economy, the immediate need to establish global submission to Satan's new one-world government will be paramount. Hence, the only way identification numbers could be of use is if a global network of satellite-linked computers was already in place and capable of immediately monitoring the process of administering the mark of the beast as soon as the false-prophet assumes control. But, even if Satan miraculously assists the weak and weary surviving Left-behinders in their effort to restore what's left of the earth, that's just not going to be doable.

The staggering amount of restoration that will be needed in order to manufacture, install, and operate a functioning global network of power plants, transformer stations, power lines, satellites, control centers and a new global network of computers would be absolutely astounding! Even today, an undertaking of that size would require years of perfectly coordinated work, millions of healthy, skilled and experienced workers (*using modern tools and equipment*) and a vast array of readily available resources and raw materials. It certainly couldn't be accomplished within a few months or even years, and that's all the time they'll have.

Perhaps this is why the angel told John that all that will be required is for every individual to receive (***a***) *mark*, (**the**) *number*, or (***the***) *name of the beast* on their right hand or forehead. Since this mark will simply be some sort of insignia (*proof of submission to Satan's global tyranny*), it need not be an identification number. Thus, we should note that the scripture specifically says: "**the**" *number (signifying one specific number, i.e., the number of the beast),'* not "**a**" number, which, perhaps, could have been interpreted to indicated a personal identification number.

Therefore, a simple *"mark"* or *"brand"* (*more likely, burned into the skin*) could quickly and permanently be recognized in order to verify compliance. Hence, demanding the Left-behinders to receive one of three simple, identifiable marks would be a much faster and easier alternative for a nearly dead and *"struggling-to-rapidly-recover"* society to implement than would be an actual identification number, which would require a functioning and instantly updatable global monitoring system.

~ Okay - but why the right-hand or forehead? ~

Everyone has either a right-hand or a forehead on which to place the mark. Hence, the Left-behinders will probably be branded — "like cattle." That would be the fastest, simplest, most efficient method of enforcing the mark of the beast on the hundreds of millions of surviving inhabitants of the earth. And, though it may sound barbaric to us, it won't to Satan, and no one wishing to live will dare open their mouth against it!

The Number of his Name will be - 666

Rev. 13:18

> ***'Here is wisdom. Let him that hath understanding count the number of the beast: for it is the number of a man; and his number is Six hundred threescore and six.'***

We're not going to waste time guessing what this verse means, because it will most likely not be fully revealed until the *"mark of the beast"* is enforced. Any avid student of eschatology, who has been studying for ten years or more, will probably have heard just about every possible explanation for the use of the number **666**. Many of those guesses have to do with the unique, computer friendly quality of the invertible numbers **6** and **9**.

Computers, however, as we just discussed, will not be a viable option, and the other explanations for the number **666** are all over the map! The truth is, thus far, I've neither found nor heard any purely scriptural explanation for the significance of the number **666**, and the Scriptures don't seem to reveal (*at least not to my satisfaction*) the answer.

The number of the beast is the number of a man?

Sadly, because verse 18 reveals that the number **666** will correspond to the number of a man — most likely the false-prophet, who'll be claiming to be God — many have disregarded *"the whole of Scripture"* and jumped to the conclusion that John's seven-headed beast (*Rev. 13:1-10*) must also be a man. That, we've established, is impossible. This second, lesser beast, however, whom John saw emerge from the "**earth**" (*indicating that he'll emerge during a specific point in time*), is quite possibly the man to whom the preceding verse is referring. Since Paul taught that the son of perdition (*this lesser beast, the false-prophet*) will sit in the Temple and declare himself God,[423] his number (*however it will be determined*) will probably correspond with the *"image of the beast."* And, still, while that may prove to be the case, when asked about the origin or significance of the number of the beast, we're safer just admitting that we don't know.

The Remnant must choose to die or forever be damned

I can't imagine why any new believer, amidst such blatant evil and soul-grieving debauchery, would want to try and survive the second half of the tribulation period. During those final 3½ years, pure, unbridled wickedness will be unleashed on the earth as never before! Consequently, the 144,000 Jewish servants (*if they're still alive when the mark of the beast begins to be imposed*) and "**the remnant**" (*the very last saints to repent*) are going to have to prove their faith by refusing to receive the false-prophet's damnable mark. This, for most of those new brothers and sisters in Christ, will mean surrendering their lives to the sword and being beheaded. And, as we've learned, by the time Christ triumphantly returns to earth (*at the end of this seven-year period*), not a single saint will have survived.[424]

Those who take the mark will have been killed with Death!

Here's where we see the significance of the pale horse of hell and death from the middle of John's allegorical preview of tribulation events. The pale horse and rider (*which John saw as Jesus opened the fourth seal in Rev.*

---

[423] 2Th. 2:3-4

[424] Rev. 13:15

6:7-8) not only had the power to kill, he had the power to kill with "**death**." And, as we learned in that chapter, if any individual dies without having first received Christ or if they choose to take the damnable *"mark of the beast,"* in order to avoid being beheaded, they will have been eternally killed with "**death**." For those souls, there will be no hope of redemption!

> *'And I looked, and behold a pale horse: and his name that sat on him was* ***Death****,* ***and Hell followed with him****. And power was given unto them over the fourth part of the earth,* ***to kill with sword****,*[425] *and* ***with hunger****,* ***and with death****,* ***and with the beasts of the earth****.* '[426]

ꟷ **Rev. 6:8** ꟷ

---

[425] For hundreds of years, interpreters of John's Revelation vision have commonly suggested that a "guillotine" would be used to behead those who refuse to take the damnable mark of the beast. But now, in these latter-days, on an almost daily basis, we're hearing reports of Christian servants of God being brutally tortured and beheaded at the merciless hands of so called *"peace-loving"* Muslims. Thus, it's becoming clear why John was told that *"Death"* — the wicked rider of the *"pale horse"* — will use *"a sword"* (*not a guillotine*) to kill those who don't submit to his will during the tribulation period.

[426] This scripture reveals that the false-prophet will even be able to use the creatures of the earth to kill the newly repentant saints (*"the remnant"*), which will leave nowhere for those who'll refuse to take the damnable mark of the beast to hide. Hence, as I've stated, not a single believer in Christ will survive this evil period.

Chapter 33

First-fruits To God and the Lamb

Rev. 14:1

> ***'And I looked, and, lo, a Lamb stood on the mount Sion** (Zion), **and with him an hundred forty and four thousand, having his Father's name written in their foreheads.'***

As I formerly stated, I can't imagine God's 144,000 born-again Jewish servants hiding in fear from the future enforcers of the mark of the beast. Instead, they'll likely allow themselves to be led as lambs to the slaughter with the intent of setting a good example for their newly repentant brothers and sisters — "**the remnant**" — to follow.

Since, by this time, the seventh angel's trumpet will have already sounded (*which we've been told will signify the end of the Mystery of God, the sharing of the Gospel message—Rev. 10:7*) and the Door of Salvation will have permanently shut, no longer will an effort be made to call the inhabitants of the earth to repentance. Thus, those who'll have repented will have no reason to try and survive. God's gracious invitation to repent and be saved will have been withdrawn from the earth with the ascension of His two final witnesses — the prophets.

Therefore, if the 144,000 are not brutally slaughtered at the same time as or immediately after God's two witnesses are slain, they'll most likely be martyred as soon as the mark of the beast begins to be administered. Either way, the 144,000 will die for their testimony of having placed their faith in Christ and will be immediately resurrected and caught-up to Heaven. This is confirmed by what John recorded seeing in the allegorical preview portion of his vision, when Jesus opened the fifth seal:

> *'And when he had opened the fifth seal, I saw under the altar the souls of them that were slain for the word of God,* ***and for the testimony which they held****: And they* {the 144,000} *cried with a loud voice, saying, How long, O Lord, holy and true, dost thou not judge and avenge our blood on them that dwell on the*

earth? ***And white robes were given unto every one of them;*** *{the white-robes denote their having been resurrected and taken into Heaven—Rev. 14:1-5} and it was said unto them, that they should rest yet* ***for a little season, until their fellowservants also and their brethren*** *{"the remnant"},* ***that should be killed as they were,*** *{thus indication that the remnant will also be killed for holding their testimony}* ***should be fulfilled.*** *' {We'll see this fulfilled in the very next chapter of John's vision.}*

Rev. 6:9-11

While making our way through John's allegorical preview of tribulation events, in **Rev. 6:1-17**, the meaning of the preceding verses wasn't immediately apparent. However, now that we've entered the second half of John's vision and have witnessed the dramatic resurrection and ascension of God's two witnesses, the last minute repentance of "**the remnant**," and the glorious appearance of the 144,000 Jewish servants on Mount Zion (*in Heaven*), the significance of the preceding verses should be obvious.

Let's look at the Facts

In reference to what John saw as Jesus opened the fifth seal, back in **Rev. 6:9-11**, the only record of any saints being killed and resurrected immediately after the false-prophet is allowed to assume full control of the earth is found here, in **Rev. 14:1-5**. Thus, the martyred souls of the 144,000 are the only souls John could have witnessed *"crying out to be avenged"* after Jesus opened the fifth seal in **Rev. 6:9-11**. Hence, if we couple the information from **Rev. 6:9-11** with what John recorded seeing here, it's obvious that, sometime near the beginning of the second half of the tribulation period, the 144,000 servants of God will be slain, resurrected, arrayed in white robes, and gathered into Heaven.

Therefore, it makes perfect sense that, in these verses (*Rev. 14:1-5*), John recorded having seen the 144,000 Jewish servants standing on Mount Sion (*in white robes–Rev. 6:11*), with Christ Jesus — the Lamb of God.[427] Given that in the previous Chapter (*Rev. 13:12-18*) John recorded having witnessed the beginning of the administering of the mark of the beast, which will not commence until the first half of the tribulation period has ended, we should expect that the false-prophet's first order of business will be to kill God's special 144,000 Jewish Christian converts, if, of course, he hasn't already done so while desecrating the Temple.

[427] *Sion* - or - *Zion* - is a reference to the dwelling place of God – Heaven.

~ *Why do you say that?* ~

After surveying the entire first half of the seven-year tribulation period, the only evidence that anyone (*other than the 144,000*) will have repented was found in **Rev. 11:13**, where we read of "**the remnant**" repenting — *by giving glory to the God of heaven.*[428] Therefore, there are only two groups of saints who could be the souls John saw crying out for their deaths to be avenged in **Rev. 6:9-11**. Since we have no scriptural reason to believe that "**the remnant**" will be instantly martyred, only the 144,000 Jewish servants can be the souls John saw crying out to be avenged. What's more, if at this point in John's vision he had not witnessed the martyrdom and resurrection of the 144,000 Jewish servants, John would not have recorded (*in these verses—Rev. 14:1-5*) seeing them standing, with Christ, in Heaven.

~ *What exactly was said to the souls under the altar in John's allegorical preview of events - Rev. 6:9-11?* ~

While pleading to have their blood avenged, ***'the souls of them that were slain'*** (*the 144,000*) were given ***'white robes'*** (*obviously an symbolic reference to their having been resurrected*) and told to ***'rest yet a little season, until their fellowservants also and their brethren'*** (*"the remnant"*) are killed, as they (*the 144,000*) were. Since God will not begin to pour out His wrath on the wicked and rebellious kingdom of the beast until every last saint is safely before His throne, it makes perfect sense for John to have heard the martyred 144,000 being told to wait to be avenged until "**the remnant**" (*'their brethren'*) has also been martyred and resurrected. What's more, as we continue through the remainder of John's vision, we're going to see that immediately after "**the remnant**" is martyred they too will be resurrected and caught-up to Heaven. Thus, they'll be the final group of believers to be immortally resurrected.

How long will it take to kill the Remnant?

The 144,000 will be easy to kill, because, as we've learned, they'll stay in one location.[429] But it might take a while to hunt down and execute every newly born-again believer in Christ, because most of them will have

---

[428] John witnessed that corporate act of contrition occur immediately following the ascension of God's two witnesses and the subsequent Jerusalem earthquake, which killed 7,000 defiant followers of the false-prophet.

[429] The fact that John recorded seeing the 144,000 Jewish servants martyred and resurrected immediately after witnessing the abomination of desolation, affirms our earlier assertion that they, unlike *"the remnant,"* will have stayed in one location (*Jerusalem*), where they will have initially been protected by the two witnesses—Rev. 12:6 and 14.

either fled or chosen to stay away from Judea, just as God's two witnesses will have warned them to do. Thus, unlike the 144,000 Jewish servants, "**the remnant**" will likely be scattered all over the world, and John isn't told how long it will take to track them down. That, however, doesn't matter, because even if it takes two to three years, not a single drop of God's wrath will be poured out until "**the remnant**" has been resurrected and caught-up to His throne.[430] The Lord makes this perfectly clear in the chapters ahead.

First-Fruits to God and the Lamb

Rev. 14:2-5

> ***'And I heard a voice from heaven, as the voice of many waters, and as the voice of a great thunder: and I heard the voice of harpers harping with their harps:***
>
> ***And they sung as it were a new song before the throne, and before the four beasts, and the elders: and no man could learn that song but the hundred and forty and four thousand, which were redeemed from the earth.***
>
> ***These are they which were not defiled with women; for they are virgins. These are they which follow the Lamb whithersoever he goeth. These were redeemed from among men, being the firstfruits unto God and to the Lamb.***
>
> ***And in their mouth was found no guile: for they are without fault before the throne of God.'***

Since these verses are a clear reference to the 144,000, this passage is self-explanatory, with the possible exception of the term "**firstfruits.**" We don't want to digress into an exhaustive study regarding the significance and origin of the term, *"firstfruits,"*[431] so we'll just acknowledge that the *"Feast of Harvest"* and the *"Feast of Weeks"* (*Shavuot*) or what would later become known to the Church as *"Pentecost"* are all related to this term.

Since God originally promised that salvation would come to the Gentile world through the twelve tribes of Israel and, in order to accomplish that task, He had to allow Israel to become spiritually blind (*temporarily, while grafting the Gentiles into His plan*),[432] it's no surprise that God has seen fit

---

430 As we're about to read in Rev. 15:1-8, immediately before seeing the wrath of God poured out, John witnessed "the remnant" standing in white robes before the throne. That may indicate that it could take a couple of years to execute them.

431 Ex. 23:16-19, Lev. 2:12-14, 1Cor. 15:20-23, Jas. 1:18

432 Rom. 11:1-33

to reserve a special group of Jacob's descendants (*the 144,000 Jewish servants*) to be regarded as a type of *"firstfruits"* of His redemptive plan.

*'**For if the casting away of them be the reconciling of the world**, what shall the receiving of them be, but life from the dead?'*

Romans 11:15

*'I say then, Have they {Israel} stumbled that they should fall? God forbid: **but rather through their fall salvation is come unto the Gentiles**, for to provoke them {Israel} to jealousy.'*

Romans 11:11

*'**And they** {Israel} **also**, **if they abide not still in unbelief**, **shall be graffed in**: for God is able to graff them in again.*

Romans 11:23

Encouragement for those who must die . . . .

Rev. 14:6-7

'And I saw another angel fly in the midst of heaven, having the everlasting gospel to preach unto them that dwell on the earth, and to every nation, and kindred, and tongue, and people,

Saying with a loud voice, Fear God, and give glory to him; for the hour of his judgment is come: and worship him that made heaven, and earth, and the sea, and the fountains of waters.'

This angel can only be preaching to those (*all around the world*) who'll have already repented before the seventh angel sounded his trumpet, because, as we learned from **Rev. 10:1-7** and saw fulfilled in **Rev. 11:12-15**, as soon as "**the remnant**" repents and that seventh trumpet sounds, the "MYSTERY OF GOD" (*God's redemptive plan*) will be eternally finished. The Master of the house will have risen up and shut the Door of Salvation.[433] Therefore, as the second half of the seven-year tribulation period dawns, "**the remnant**," wherever they'll be all around the world, will need to heed the angel's warning and encourage each other to fear God, rather than the short-lived physical threats of the false-prophet. If they want to spend eternity in Heaven, they'll have to understand that, no matter how

[433] Luke 13:25

intimidating that wicked world leader may appear, he can only kill the body. He'll have no control over the souls of those who'll have put their trust in Christ.

> *'And fear not them which kill the body, but are not able to kill the soul: but rather **fear him which is able to destroy both soul and body in hell**.'*
>
> ℘ **Mt. 10:28** ℘

Babylon - the Great Spiritually-wicked City has fallen

Rev. 14:8

> ***'And there followed another angel, saying, Babylon is fallen, is fallen, that great city, because she made all nations drink of the wine of the wrath of her fornication.'***

At this point in John's vision the following will be true:

- Every child of God will have repented
- God will have permanently sealed the soul of every individual who'll spend eternity in His presence[434]
- And the Door of Salvation will have eternally shut

Thus, it should be clear to us that in the preceding verse the angel is making a proclamation about the ultimate fate of Satan's demonic reign over the kingdoms of the world. Hence, with this verse we begin to really see the long term allegorical significance of the spiritual city "MYSTERY BABYLON."[435] From a heavenly perspective, this wicked, powerfully seductive empire has been a spiritual "*harlot*," guilty of having continually seduced all the nations of the world, throughout time, into spiritual fornication against God. This is to what the angel was prophetically referring when John heard him declare: ***". . . Babylon is fallen, is fallen . . . ."***

In the preceding verses (*Rev. 14:7-8*), first, the angel prophesies of the future destruction of the false-prophet's beastly empire and, second, he

---

[434] The soul of every truly repentant, *"born-again"* believer in Christ is eternally *"sealed"* (*as with the signet-ring of God*) by the indwelling presence of the Holy Spirit. This is why true believers in Christ are referred to as *"saints"* — *"the true family of God"* — Eph. 1:13, 4:30.

[435] Rev. 17:5-6

warns the inhabitants of the earth not to take the damnable mark of the beast. We know that this is the intent of the angel's proclamation, because at this point in the tribulation period we've only just begun to enter the second half of the seven years. Thus, at this point in John's vision the false-prophet will have only just begun to miraculously build his magnificent new city from what's left of the barely salvageable wasteland of an earth. Consequently, "THE MYSTERY CITY BABYLON"[436] (*the future capital and spiritual hub of his global empire*) could not have already been physically destroyed, which is why we won't read of the fulfillment of the angel's proclamation until just prior to Christ's triumphant return to earth.

ꕥ REVELATION 14:9-13 ꕥ

A final warning to all surviving Left-behinders:

'And the third angel followed them, saying with a loud voice, ***<u>If any man worship the beast and his image</u>****,* ***<u>and receive his mark in his forehead</u>****,* ***<u>or in his hand</u>****,*

<u>The same shall drink of the wine of the wrath of God</u>*,* ***<u>which is poured out without mixture into the cup of his indignation</u>****; and he shall be tormented with fire and brimstone in the presence of the holy angels, and in the presence of the Lamb:*

And the smoke of their torment ascendeth up for ever: and they have no rest day nor night, who worship the beast and his image, and whosoever receiveth the mark of his name.

<u>Here is the patience of the saints</u>*:* ***<u>here are they that keep the commandments of God</u>****,* ***<u>and the faith of Jesus</u>****.*

And I heard a voice from heaven saying unto me, Write, ***<u>blessed are the dead which die in the Lord from henceforth</u>****: Yea, saith the Spirit, that they may rest from their labours; and their works do follow them.'*

[436] Rev. 17:5, 18:1-24

Chapter 34

Thrust in Thy Sickle and Reap

> ꕤ 'Be patient therefore, brethren, unto the coming of the Lord. Behold, the husbandman waitith for the precious fruit of the earth, and hath long patience for it, until he receive the early and latter rain.' ~ James 5:7 ꕤ

In the second half of Revelation Chapter 14, before being shown a vision of God's wrath being poured out on the perpetually rebellious cohorts of the false-prophet, John was shown the following allegorical depiction of Jesus, the Son of man, harvesting the saints from the earth.

Rev. 14:14-16

'And I looked, and behold a white cloud, and upon the cloud one sat like unto the Son of man,[437] having on his head a golden crown, and in his hand a sharp sickle.

And another angel came out of the temple, crying with a loud voice to him that sat on the cloud, Thrust in thy sickle, and reap: for the time is come for thee to reap; for the harvest of the earth is ripe.

And he that sat on the cloud** (Jesus) **thrust in his sickle on the earth; and the earth was reaped.'

The preceding allegorical verses seem to depict just one massive harvest of saints. In reality, however, when completed, the *"ingathering"* or *"harvesting"* of saints will actually include four mass-resurrections and one relatively minor resurrection.

---

[437] Because the passage says: '*. . . like unto the (rather than a) Son of man . . .* 'and is capitalized, we can be reasonably sure that this is a reference to Christ Jesus.

'And the graves were opened; and many {though, not all} bodies of the saints which slept {had passed away} arose, And came out of the graves ***after*** *his {Jesus'} resurrection, and went into the holy city, and appeared unto many.'*

Mt. 27:52-53

The preceding verses are a record of the first mass-resurrection, which eventually will have been the first of a total of four "**mass**" resurrections of the saints. Unfortunately, Matthew's Gospel doesn't reveal what happened to these saints after they were seen in Jerusalem. In fact, Matthew doesn't even reveal if those saints were resurrected as mortals (*as was Lazarus*)[438] or as immortals. Since, according to the Scriptures, Jesus is the *"first begotten from the dead"*[439] and He had already risen before these saints were resurrected, I suppose an argument could be made for their having been resurrected to immortality. If so, soon after making their appearance in Jerusalem they must have been taken into heaven. If not, like Lazarus, they simply lived out the rest of their mortal lives on earth. Either way, given that they were apparently recognized by the people of Jerusalem, the Lord must have resurrected them from among the recently deceased in the city. One thing's for sure, after being seen in Jerusalem, they certainly didn't return to their graves.

4 mass + 1 minor resurrections = God's Entire Family

Presently, the true Church is eagerly anticipating the long-awaited catching-away of the saints, which will immediately precede the formal[440] start of the tribulation period. When that extraordinary event suddenly takes place it will be the **2nd** resurrection of saints, and all God's faithful servants,[441] from the first man, "Adam," to the present, will instantly be gathered into Heaven. Therefore, since that single event will undoubtedly be the largest ingathering of saints of all time, many Christians recognize it to be the aforementioned *"early rain harvest"* — **Jas. 5:7**.

After the Rapture, the next resurrection will be that of God's two tribulation period witnesses — "the prophets." Their resurrection and ascension will occur in the middle of the tribulation period, just 3½ days after

---

438 John 11:1-44

439 1Cor. 15:20-23, Col. 1:18, Rev. 1:5

440 The Rapture will include the resurrection and/or redemption of all Old and New Testament saints and will occur just prior to the formal start (*Rev. 8:1-6*) of the seven year tribulation period—1Th. 4:13-18, Rev. 7:9-17.

441 Gen. 15:4-6, Hab. 2:4, Rom. 1:17, Eph. 1:12-14, Heb. 10:38

the abomination of desolation takes place. However, since only the two witnesses will be resurrected, it's not considered a "**mass**" resurrection.

The **3rd** mass-resurrection will be the resurrection of God's 144,000 Jewish servants. They will either be resurrected with the two witnesses or soon thereafter. It's doubtful, however, that God intends to resurrect the 144,000 Jewish servants at the same time as He resurrects His two witnesses, because, if that is to be the case, it probably would have been indicated in John's description of the witnesses' resurrection and ascension. Thus, it's more likely that the resurrection of the 144,000 will be a separate event (*just as Rev. 14:1-5 seems to indicate*). If so, it will be the **3rd** mass-resurrection of saints, and, as we just learned from **Rev. 14:1-5**, it will occur near the beginning of the second half of the tribulation period.

The **4th** and final mass-resurrection of saints will be the resurrection of "**the remnant**." We'll see John's record of having witnessed that resurrection very soon, and we'll learn that when it actually occurs it will take place just minutes before God's wrath begins to be poured out. We should note that, as we are about to learn, the necessity of the remnant's being resurrected prior to God taking vengeance on the lost will be the only thing restraining God from pouring out His wrath on the wicked inhabitants of the earth (*those who will be willful recipients of the damnable mark of the beast*).

~ So why, at this point, was John shown a vision of all the saints being gathered into Heaven? ~

The following Scriptures should help us answer the preceding question:

'. . . ***The Lord knoweth how to deliver the godly out of temptations***, *and to reserve the unjust unto the day of judgment to be punished . . .*'

℘ **2Pt. 2:9** ℘

'*For* ***God hath not appointed us to wrath***, *but to obtain salvation by our Lord Jesus Christ . . .*'

℘ **1Th. 5:9** ℘

If the previous vision of the *"Son of man"* (*Jesus*) gathering the harvest of the earth (*the saints*) into Heaven before casting the *"vine of the earth"* (*the still rebellious majority of Left-behinders*) into the great winepress of His wrath is meant to reveal anything, it's that the Lord will not allow even the least of His children to be punished with the wicked. Having clearly established that truth,[442] it's now time for the Lord to reveal what will happen to everyone who chooses to reject His final call to repent.

The Great Winepress of God's Wrath

Rev. 14:17-19

> ***'And another angel came out of the temple which is in heaven, he also having a sharp sickle.***
>
> ***And another angel came out from the altar, which had power over fire; and cried with a loud cry to him that had the sharp sickle, saying, Thrust in thy sharp sickle, and gather the clusters of the vine of the earth; for her grapes are fully ripe.***
>
> ***And the angel thrust in his sickle into the earth, and gathered the vine of the earth, and cast it into the great winepress of the wrath of God.'***

We'll see just exactly how the preceding verses will be fulfilled when we move into the next two chapters of John's vision.

One thousand and six hundred Furlongs of Blood

Rev. 14:20

> ***'And the winepress was trodden without the city, and blood came out of the winepress, even unto the horse bridles, by the space of a thousand and six hundred furlongs.'***

By some estimates, ***'a thousand and six hundred furlongs'*** is more than 180 miles. That's a lot of bloodshed no matter how we interpret these words, but, like the rest of this portion of John's vision, it's pretty obvious that this image of blood rising to the height of horse bridles is strictly allegorical. I mean, I certainly don't imagine that any of us actually expect an enormous winepress to be used for the dispensing of God's wrath! Therefore, both the winepress and the height of the blood it will yield are obviously allegorical and, as such, are meant only to indicate that a great deal of blood will be spilled when God's wrath is poured out on the wicked. And, while we know that the final *"battle of Armageddon"* will take place in the "*Valley of Megiddo*," since this bloodshed will be a direct result of God's wrath having been poured out and God's wrath will begin to be poured out long before the final battle of Armageddon begins, we shouldn't assume that all this blood will be shed as a result of that single, final event.

---

[442] John 3:36, Rom. 1:18 and 5:9, Eph. 5:6-7, 1Th. 1:10

Therefore, while this verse may or may not be a reference to a specific (*roughly 180 mile long*) battlefield or location, without having any solid scriptural evidence to support that position, once again, we're safer just moving on and seeing what we can learn from the remainder of John's vision.

Chapter 35

It's Nearly Time for Vengeance

Rev. 15:1

> ***'And I saw another sign in heaven, great and marvellous, seven angels having the seven last plagues; for in them is filled up the wrath of God.'***

The preceding verse is a clear declaration that God's wrath is about to be poured out. If any prior tribulation event had been a product of God's wrath, God certainly would have made sure John recorded that event as such. But nothing John witnessed, prior to the unleashing of these final seven plagues, with the possible exception of the Jerusalem earthquake,[443] can correctly be attributed to God's taking vengeance on the inhabitants of the earth. And yet, sadly, though the Scriptures clearly prove this to be true, many have mistakenly continued teaching otherwise, even without valid scriptural support.

~ *So, where, during the seven-year tribulation period, are we?* ~

Thus far, our end-time journey has led us from the Rapture (*the sudden catching-away of the saints, which launched us into the tribulation period*), through the two witnesses' 3½ years of preaching and plagues (*God's final attempt to reach the lost*), to here, where John is seeing God's wrath about to be poured out on all those who will have chosen to receive the eternally damnable *"mark of the beast."* Therefore, since God's wrath is about to be unleashed and God never punishes the righteous with the wicked, and since John was told that the false-prophet will be given power to kill everyone who refuses to receive the *"mark of the beast,"* we should expect to find evidence that, before the first of these seven angels begins to pour out his vile of wrath, every last saint will have been hunted down and killed for refusing to worship the image of the beast.[444] Well that's exactly what

---

[443] Exactly 7,000 rebellious Left-behinders will die during that event—Rev. 11:13.

[444] Apparently, most will be beheaded for refusing to take the mark—Rev. 13:15, 20:4.

we're about to read, but, since we don't know precisely how long it will take the false-prophet and the citizens of his beastly empire to hunt down and kill that last group of saints (*wherever they'll be all around the world*), there is really no way of knowing how much of the seven-year tribulation period will be left when God's wrath begins to be unleashed.

The "remnant" of saints is caught-up to Heaven!

The purposeful manner through which God revealed this final portion of the tribulation period to John shows how much it matters to our Creator that we understand how long-sufferingly He is holding back His vengeance and wrath on behalf of the saints. To begin with, John was shown seven angels standing in the Temple (*the Tabernacle in Heaven*), and each of those angels was holding a plague of wrath. Then, before seeing the angels pour out those plagues, John's focus was drawn to a *"sea of glass"* before God's throne. On that *"sea of glass,"* with harps in hands, stood the resurrected remnant of saints (*all the Left-behinders who will have wisely chosen to allow themselves to be martyred in order to retain their newly acquired hope of salvation through faith in Christ Jesus*). Hence, John watched as this final group of repentant souls, having become victorious over hell and death, triumphantly sang the song of Moses[445] and the song of the Lamb.

> *'And I saw as it were a sea of glass mingled with fire: and* ***them that had gotten the victory over the beast, and over his image, and over his mark, and over the number of his name, stand on the sea of glass****, having the harps of God. And they sing the song of Moses the servant of God, and the song of the Lamb, saying, Great and marvellous are thy works, Lord God Almighty; just and true are thy ways, thou King of saints. Who shall not fear thee, O Lord, and glorify thy name? for thou only art holy: for all nations shall come and worship before thee;* ***for thy judgments are made manifest****.'*

Revelation 15:2-4

[445] Though Moses and Miriam did sing a short celebratory song while exiting Egypt (*Ex. 15:1-19*), most scholars believe the preceding verses to be a reference to the song Moses recited to all the tribes of Israel just before his death. The lyrics of that particular prophetic song contain appropriate references to the coming of the Messiah and to His future judgment of all rebellious souls—Deut. 32:1-43.

How wonderfully infinite is God's Mercy

It would be criminal for us not to acknowledge what an extraordinary act of mercy and grace God's redemption of "**the remnant**" will be. While it's certainly true that not even the most diligent servant of the Lord can in anyway earn the right to eternal life, "**the remnant**" (*like the thief on the cross*) will not have had the opportunity to perform a single, so called, *"good-work"* before dying. Immediately after "**the remnant**" repents, the Door of Salvation will eternally shut, so they won't have the opportunity to witness to a single soul. And yet, just like all believers, every sincerely repentant Left-behinder will be welcomed into God's eternal family of saints, where they'll spend eternity basking in the immeasurable love and adoration of the one true God and Creator of all things!

~ How's that for divine mercy and grace?! ~

What's more, whether we choose to affirm this truth or not, God's grace in the lives of "**the remnant**" will have been no greater a miracle of mercy than that which is being extended to every believer in Christ today. Not even a thousand years of continual selfless suffering, hard work, and sincere servitude in the name of Christ could merit our spending even one second in the incomparably holy presence of God. If that doesn't demonstrate what an infinitely generous "free-gift"[446] God's offer of salvation to this lost and rebellious world is, then I don't know what will. And yet, many still pridefully choose to reject and deny the Lord and His goodness.

And the Temple in Heaven was opened . . .

Rev. 15:5-7

> ***'And after that I looked, and, behold, the temple of the tabernacle of the testimony in heaven was opened:*** [447]
>
> ***And the seven angels came out of the temple, having the seven plagues, clothed in pure and white linen, and having their breasts girded with golden girdles.***
>
> ***And one of the four beasts gave unto the seven angels seven golden vials full of the wrath of God,***[448] ***who liveth for ever and ever.'***

---

[446] Eph. 2:1-10

[447] The Temple is the inner most portion of the heavenly Tabernacle and surrounding courtyard, the *"Holy Place" and "Holy of Holies,"* where the *"Ark of the Covenant"* {*the testimony*} continually resides.

These verses are a little difficult to interpret, because John said he saw the seven angels come out of the heavenly Temple (*the tabernacle*) holding seven separate plagues. Then, he saw one of the four beasts from God's throne (*4:6-11*) give the seven angels seven "**vials**" (*bowls or shallow saucers*) full of the wrath of God. Given that the original Ark of the Covenant has never left Heaven[449] but, instead, has continually remained in the true Holy of Holies as a symbol of God's omnipotence, perhaps those seven plagues were intended to indicate that each of those angels will be given a specific measure of "**power**" and "**authority**" over something in Heaven and/or on earth. Thus, after having emerged from God's Temple, each angel was also given a "**vial**" containing a portion of God's wrath, apparently intending that God's wrath be mixed with the seven plagues and poured out on the earth and its inhabitants. This seems to be the most logical explanation for what John recorded seeing; however, since John didn't explain the significance of what he saw, we can't be sure.

Once again, God's Glory fills the Tabernacle

Rev. 15:8

> ***'And the temple was filled with smoke from the glory of God, and from his power; and no man was able to enter into the temple, till the seven plagues of the seven angels were fulfilled.'***

It will be just as it was on the day when Solomon dedicated the first fixed Temple in Jerusalem.[450] Once the Glory of God fills that heavenly Tabernacle and the angels begin to unleash God's plagues of wrath upon the inhabitants of the earth, no one will be able to enter the Temple until the very last plague has been poured out. What's more, in case you're wondering, it won't matter that we'll already have been transformed into perfectly holy, immortal beings. According to the angel speaking with John, we still won't presume to go near that Temple when this event occurs.

---

448 One of the four beasts gave the seven angels seven golden *"vials"* (*shallow bowls*), which contained wrath, and he did this after the angels had already emerged from the Temple with the seven plagues. The obvious question is: *"Since the angels already had possession of the seven plagues before they were given the seven vials of wrath, in what form or containers were the plagues?"* I guess it really doesn't matter, but I can't help wondering.

449 As has been stated, the Ark John recorded seeing here and in Rev. 11:19 is the original *"Ark of the Covenant."* That Ark and Tabernacle (*Temple*) has never left Heaven. God revealed it to Moses and instructed him to order the Hebrew exiles to make an exact duplicate of what he saw—Ex. 25:8-10, Heb. 8:1-6, Rev. 15:5.

450 2Chr. 5:3-14, 7:1-3

Will the surviving Left-behinders really deserve this?

If there's any question as to how righteous it will be for God and the Lamb (*Jesus*) to take vengeance on the hatefully blasphemous survivors of the tribulation period, we should revisit the aforementioned rhetorical question asked by Jesus:

"Nevertheless when the Son of man cometh, shall he find faith on the earth?"[451]

Luke 18:8

Once again, the answer to Jesus' question is an emphatic — "NO!" In fact, according to the following passage, there's solid scriptural evidence for believing that by the time Jesus returns to earth, at the end of the tribulation period, there won't be a single mortal on the planet who will not have willfully chosen to receive the damnable ***'mark,' 'number'*** or ***'name'*** of the beast!

'And he had power to give life unto the image of the beast, that the image of the beast should both speak, ***and cause that as many as would not worship the image of the beast should be killed****. And he causeth* ***all*** *{i.e., every living soul},* ***both small and great****,* ***rich and poor****,* ***free and bond****,* ***to receive a mark in their right hand****,* ***or in their foreheads****: And that no man might buy or sell, save he that had the* ***mark****, or the* ***name*** *of the beast, or the* ***number*** *of his name.*

Rev. 13:15-17

According to this passage, before Jesus returns to earth, every surviving Left-behinder will have chosen to receive the eternally damnable mark of the beast, and, sad and hard to fathom as that may be, there's just no other logical way to interpret the angel's words.

---

[451] Christ was referring to His gloriously triumphant return to earth at the end of the tribulation period.

Chapter 36

Seven Plagues of Wrath

As the seven-year tribulation period draws to a close, the citizens of Satan's beastly global empire will believe themselves to be beyond vulnerability. Confident in their new world leader (*the false prophet*), they'll be amazed that he'll have been able to bring about a functioning society out of what will have formerly been an absolute wasteland of an earth. Sadly, however, while their pride and misplaced feelings of vindication swell, in Heaven, a powerful voice from within the heavenly Tabernacle will order seven specific angels to begin pouring out the final plagues of the tribulation period — "GOD'S SEVEN POWERFUL PLAGUES OF WRATH!" Thus, one by one, seven mighty angels will empty God's horrifically potent vials of vengeance upon every wicked and arrogantly defiant inhabitant of the earth; all of whom will bear the eternally damnable *"mark of the beast."*

Basking blissfully in the Ignorance of Deceit

Rev. 16:1-2

> ***'And I heard a great voice out of the temple saying to the seven angels, Go your ways, and pour out the vials of the wrath of God upon the earth.***
>
> ***And the first went, and poured out his vial upon the earth; and there fell a noisome*** *(harmful, disgusting, odorous)* ***and grievous sore upon the men which had the mark of the beast, and upon them which worshipped his image.'***

Every surviving Left-behinder will have blatantly rejected God's grace, so, for the first time in history, Satan will totally rule the world. And, since Satan, through the false-prophet and his wicked army of followers, will have the power to enthusiastically kill every Left-behinder who refuses to submit to the authority of his global kingdom,[452] we can logically conclude that, when this plague is poured out, every person on the planet will bear Satan's damnable mark and will, thus, be affected. That's an important fact

---

[452] Rev. 6:8, 11:7, 13:5-7, 13:12-18, 14:9-13, 20:4, Dan. 7:19-21

to acknowledge, because there's absolutely no reason to assume, despite everything we've learned, that any of the surviving Left-behinders will have been able to resist being branded (*or otherwise marked*) with the damnable ***"mark,"*** ***"number"*** or ***"name"*** of the beast.

'. . . for it is written, Vengeance is mine; I will repay, saith the Lord.'

℘ Romans 12:19 ℘

Consequently, John watched, as the first angel poured out his vial, and every citizen and worshipper of the beast (*i.e., every person on earth*) was smitten with horrifically painful sores (*most likely skin ulcers, blisters and boils*). Hence, just when the unrepentant citizens of the earth will have begun to believe that they made the right choice, by choosing to worship the beastly image of Satan's blasphemous empire, the Lord will, once again, powerfully demonstrate that He alone is God!

The Second vial is poured out . . .

Rev. 16:3

> ***'And the second angel poured out his vial upon the sea; and it became as the blood of a dead man: and every living soul*** *(everything with the breath of life, both man and animal)* ***died in the sea.'***

When the second angel sounded his trumpet, back in **Rev. 8:8-9**, John saw one-third of the oceans and seas turn to blood and a third of all the creatures in the oceans and seas die. Now, with the pouring out of this second vial of actual "**wrath**," every living thing in the oceans and seas, all around the world, will die, as the wrath of God turns all the oceans and seas into, not just blood, but the blood of a dead man!

Let them drink blood, for blood they have shed!

Rev. 16:4-7

> ***'And the third angel poured out his vial upon the rivers and fountains of waters; and they became blood.***
>
> ***And I heard the angel of the waters say, Thou art righteous, O Lord, which art, and wast, and shalt be, because thou hast judged thus.***
>
> ***For they have shed the blood of saints and prophets, and thou hast given them blood to drink; for they are worthy.***
>
> ***And I heard another out of the altar say, Even so, Lord God Almighty, true and righteous are thy judgments.'***

It's impossible to even imagine the truly apocalyptic state into which the world will have been plunged after these first three plagues have been poured out, but, once this third angel finishes unleashing his plague, there won't be a fresh drop of water on the planet! Every river, stream, and natural spring on earth will have, like the oceans and seas, been turned into the blood of a dead man — "**martyr's blood**." God intends to avenge the shedding of the blood of all His faithful servants, including the 144,000 and "**the remnant**," and this will only be the beginning of His doing so.

Ghastly as it may be, I've read of desperate men bleeding and drinking the blood from their horses or camels, so as to keep from dying while being lost in the desert. And, while drinking the blood of a recently slain animal would be gruesome in the extreme, drinking the blood of a dead man, now that's taking it to an entirely different level of repugnancy!

What's more, these plagues aren't all going to happen in a single day, so, if they wish to stay alive, every citizen of the false-prophet's beastly kingdom will have no choice but to continue drinking this disgusting human blood, day after agonizing day! Moreover, bathing and washing clothes or the like will be out of the question, and, unlike contaminated water, boiling the blood won't help the situation. Imagine trying to take care of a sick loved one or a baby under these conditions, and the conditions are only going to get worse with every passing day. Later, while preparing for the great *"battle of Armageddon,"* these people will actually have no choice but to fill their water skins and canteens with this blood. That's almost poetic; don't you think?!

And yet, they'll continue to blaspheme the Name of God

Rev. 16:8-9

> ***'And the fourth angel poured out his vial upon the <u>sun</u>; and power was given unto him to <u>scorch men with fire</u>.***
>
> ***And men were scorched with great heat, <u>and blasphemed the name of God</u>, which hath power over these plagues: and <u>they repented not to give him glory</u>.'***

Unlike "**the remnant**," who humbly ***'gave glory to the God of heaven'*** after witnessing the ascension of God's two prophets, these boil-covered, blood-drinking, thoroughly wicked citizens of Satan's evil empire will hatefully blaspheme the name of the Lord, right to the end, and why not? They'll know full well that salvation and forgiveness will be eternally beyond the grasp of every fool who'll have willfully chosen to receive the damnable *"mark of the beast."* That means that even those whom God will allow to survive the *"Second Coming of Christ"* will have no hope of ever being forgiven for their sins, not even during the Millennial Period. Consequently, this fourth plague of wrath will give them even more reason to curse their Creator. And so, as only an angel could, the fourth vile will be poured out upon the sun. When that happens, fire, possibly (*we're not told*) in the form of large solar flares, will severely scorch the already blistered, boil-riddled and severely dehydrated bodies of the surviving inhabitants of the earth. Diving into the bloody oceans, seas, and lakes will be their only hope for relief — that's of course if the blood in those lakes and seas isn't too hot!

Breathing and swallowing will instantly become dreadfully agonizing. With each breath, the solar heated air will scorch their throats and lungs, causing their esophagi to dry-out and their tongues and chapped-lips to swell, split-open, and bleed. Can you imagine being terrified to simply breathe or swallow? And every day will be more excruciating than the day before. Hence, sleep will be practically impossible.

I realize how distressing the thought of all this is, but in reality we're only just scratching the surface. There's no way we could even come close to accurately assessing the full environmental or physiological impact of these seven dreadful plagues of wrath, and yet, these horrific effects will be an inescapable reality for every Left-behinder who survives to suffer the end of the tribulation period.

Darkness, like a blanket, will cover Satan's kingdom

Rev. 16:10-11

> ***'And the fifth angel poured out his vial upon the seat*** *(central hub or capital)* ***of the beast; and his kingdom was full of darkness; and they gnawed their tongues for pain,***
>
> ***And blasphemed the God of heaven because of their pains and their sores, and repented not of their deeds.'***

After having endured the scorching heat of the last plague, it would seem that this divinely inflicted darkness would offer some welcomed relief, but that just won't be the case. Instead, when this fifth plague is poured out on "THE MYSTERY CITY BABYLON" (*the spiritual hub of Satan's global empire*),[453] the false-prophet and all his subjects will instantly be plunged into total darkness!

Verses like this give rise to the belief that the beast will be a mere mortal, rather than an ever-present spiritual army of principalities and powers of darkness. Nonetheless, while that's an easy error to make, as we've learned and will confirm in the next two chapters of John's vision, drawing that conclusion would be a big mistake. Let's not forget that the beast was

---

[453] Rev. 18:1-10

seen to have seven heads and ten horns, and each of those seven heads is intended to represent a different kingdom and period of time (*beginning with the original Babylonian Empire and ending with this end-time beastly kingdom of Satan and the false-prophet*). Thus, as these scriptures have repeatedly affirmed, the beast can't logically be a mere mortal. Additionally, the ten horns John saw emerge from the final prominent head on the beast represent ten kings. Those kings will arise and serve as subordinate rulers to the false-prophet during the final 3½ years of the tribulation period. By now, this should be quite clear, and once we've finished examining Chapters 17 and 18 of John's vision, the figurative significance of John's seven-headed beast with ten horns should be even clearer.

How much of Satan's kingdom will be dark?

The question is: *"Since we just read that this fifth plague will be poured out on the "seat" or "central hub" of this final evil empire, how much of the earth will be affected by the darkness?"* Well, since we also read that the first plague will affect every person who bears the *"mark of the beast"* and each consecutive plague will do the same, it would not be illogical for us to consider the possibility that this darkness may begin at the residence of the false-prophet and spread out, until it eventually blankets the entire planet. Remember, this final kingdom will be global, which is evidenced by the fact that every living soul will be forced to take the *"mark of the beast"* or die. What's more, John's allegorical preview speaks of this same darkness blanketing the entire earth just prior to Jesus' triumphant return:

'And I beheld when he had opened the sixth seal, and, lo, there was a great earthquake; ***and the sun became black as sackcloth of hair****, and the moon became as blood . . .'*

Rev. 6:12

'But in those days, after that tribulation, ***the sun shall be darkened****,* ***and the moon shall not give her light****,* ***And the stars of heaven shall fall****, and the powers that are in heaven shall be shaken.'*

Mark 13:24-25

'The earth shall quake before them; the heavens shall tremble: ***the sun and the moon shall be dark****,* ***and the stars shall withdraw their shining*** *. . .'*

Joel 2:10

What's difficult to understand about this fifth plague of darkness is that John records that, apparently as a result of this darkness, the inhabitants of the earth will ***'gnaw their tongues for pain.'*** Perhaps that pain will just be residual pain, caused by the first four plagues, but, unfortunately, since John doesn't elaborate, we have no way of knowing. This pain could be the result of extreme cold or hunger due to less sunlight. Whatever the case, the wicked inhabitants of the earth (*Satan's entire global empire*) will just keep right on drinking blood, gnawing their swollen tongues, and defiantly blaspheming the blessed name of their Omnipotent Creator.

God will pave the way for the wicked Kings of the East

Rev. 16:12

> ***'And the sixth angel poured out his vial upon the great river Euphrates; and the water thereof was dried up, that the way of the kings of the east might be prepared.'***

It almost seems like God is *"spoilin"* for a fight with Satan, the false-prophet, and all the fallen-angels (*the beast*). I say that because by causing the mighty *Euphrates River* to dry-up God will essentially be leaving His back door open so the neighborhood thugs and thieves can attempt to ransack His house. That may sound funny, but we're about to see that that analogy isn't far from being spot-on.

If we were to look at the Middle East from the sky, we would see that the mighty *Euphrates* isn't the only obstacle with which the kings from the East will have to contend when they make their way down to the Megiddo Valley to participate in the battle of Armageddon. Presently, the *Tigris* is another mighty river and major barrier. That, however, may not be the case when the kings from the East begin their descent and attack on Israel.

By the way, we should note that, if we were to continue to look southward, towards the city of *Basra* in southern Iraq, we would find a massive confluence, where the *Tigris* and the *Euphrates* rivers meet. From that point of confluence southward, the river is called the *"Shatt al-Arab" (i.e., Stream of the Arabs)*, and it runs southeasterly for roughly 120 miles until it empties into the *Gulf of Persia.* It's possible that God will dry-up that river somewhere at its southern end, where the *Euphrates* and the *Tigris* converge. If so (*and we presently have no way of knowing if that will be the case*), this would clear the way for the kings to approach from the East.

It's also possible, even likely, that the pouring out of these final seven plagues of wrath will cause the entire river to dry-up, which, if that is to be the case, would open the door to a whole new set of possibilities. And, if the study of Scripture teaches us anything, it's that we should never paint God into a corner, especially while endeavoring to interpret prophecy. We need to consider the likelihood that, during the seven-year tribulation period, the topography of the Middle East and the rest of the earth will likely undergo radical change. Thus, it's very possible that, when the kings from the northern and eastern regions of the world are compelled to descend and assemble in the *Valley of Megiddo*, the mighty *Tigris River* may no longer even exist.

Three unclean spirits . . . .

Rev. 16:13

> ***'And I saw three unclean spirits like frogs come out of the mouth of the dragon, and out of the mouth of the beast, and out of the mouth of the false prophet.'***

Before examining the mission of these three unclean spirits, we should first take a close look at John's exact choice of words. John didn't say that he saw **one** unclean spirit come out of the mouth of the dragon, and **another** come out of the mouth of the beast, and still **another** come out of the mouth of the false-prophet, though John did speak of seeing three unclean spirits. If we must assume (*which we should be loathsome to do*), let's assume that John said what he said, the way he said it, with purpose, and for a specific reason. John could be telling us that he saw three unclean spirits, first, come out of the mouth of the "**dragon**" (*thus indicating that the three spirits were commissioned by Satan*), then, (*as a response to Satan's command*) come out of the mouth of "**the beast**" (*indicating that the three spirits are of the powers of darkness—demons*), and, finally, out of the mouth of the "**false-prophet**," as is depicted by the following illustration:

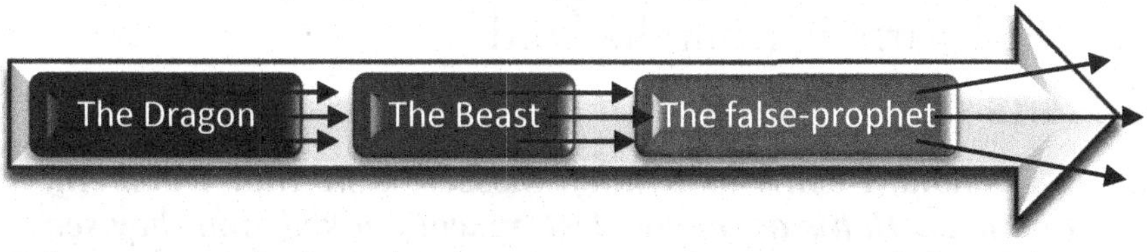

Either way we look at this event, since John witnessed these three unclean spirits emerge in unison, in order to do so, they must have first come from Satan — the ruler of the powers of darkness. Let's not forget what we learned a few chapters back:

> *'And there appeared another wonder in heaven;* ***and behold a great red dragon*** *{Satan}, having seven heads and ten horns, and seven crowns upon his heads.* ***And his tail drew the third part of the stars of heaven*** *{angels},* ***and did cast them to the earth*** *. . . '*

℘ Rev. 12:3-4 ℘

'And there was war in heaven: Michael and his angels fought against the dragon; ***and the dragon fought and his angels*** *. . .'*

'And the great dragon was cast out, that old serpent, called ***the Devil, and Satan****, which deceiveth the whole world:* ***he was cast out into the earth, and his angels were cast out with him****.'*

Rev. 12:7&9

These fallen-angels will continue to be subordinate to Satan, as part of his spiritually wicked empire, until the Lord returns and cast them into the eternal lake of fire, at the end of the tribulation period — **Rev. 19:20**.

Three miracle-working demons - sent by Satan

Rev. 16:14

'For they are the spirits of devils, working miracles, which go forth unto the kings of the earth and of the whole world, to gather them to the battle of that great day of God Almighty.'

After God dries-up the mighty *Euphrates,* Satan will unleash three miracle-working spirits from his army of fallen-angels. Subsequently, the false-prophet will be instrumental in either inspiring or provoking the kings of the earth to assemble in the great *Valley of Megiddo*. There, possibly intending to first attack the land of Israel,[454] the largest insidious gathering of men in the history of the world will prepare for battle.

One final warning from the Lord

Rev. 16:15

'Behold, I come as a thief. Blessed is he that watcheth, and keepeth his garments, lest he walk naked, and they see his shame.'

The preceding warning from the Lord — that He will come *"as a thief in the night"* — can only be intended as a pre-tribulation period warning (*a reference to the future rapture of the Church*), because it's not possible for the Lord's glorious *"Second Coming"* to be a complete surprise (*"like a thief in the night"*) to anybody, especially after the tribulation period has begun! It's commonly known, even among non-believers and skeptics, that the

[454] The ten subordinate kings will hate the authority of the false prophet, so they may forcibly descend with the intent of attacking his kingdom—Ezek. 38 & 39, Rev. 17:11-16-18.

tribulation period will last seven years and be climaxed by the Lord's triumphant return. Therefore, this warning must be intended for the Church (*pre-tribulation Christians*) and for non-believers today. We must remember that at the end of the tribulation period, which this portion of John's vision outlines, the following will be true:

- ❖ The "Door of Salvation" will have already eternally shut
- ❖ Everyone on earth will have willfully received the damnable "mark of the beast"
- ❖ And every saint will have already been resurrected and gathered into Heaven

Both Ezekiel and Zechariah prophesied of an Attack on Israel

Because Ezekiel's prophecies about this end-time period are subject to many credible, but varying, points of view,[455] we don't want to get side-tracked while endeavoring to accomplish a verse by verse interpretation. In his prophecies, Ezekiel refers to many *nations* and *peoples* having descended from four of Japheth's sons: *Gomer, Magog, Tubal* and *Meshech*. And, as have many others, I've lightly researched this topic for many years and am confident of only one thing: There's no way anyone can convince me that they can conclusively prove precisely how Japheth's descendants migrated and settled over the past forty-three hundred years! Therefore, from my perspective, we can't be absolutely certain just exactly who *"Gog"* and/or *"Magog"* are intended to represent in the following passage from Ezekiel. Frankly, I don't believe the Lord intended that we first understand the dynamics of the more than 4,300 year migration of Japheth's descendants before we can hope to understand the end-time relevance of Ezekiel's prophecies, so let's just stick to the basics. Let's stick to only that which is scripturally obvious. And, at this point, all we know for sure is that, whoever the people of *Gog* and *Magog* are, they'll descend into Judea from a land north and/or northeast of Israel.

When God sent an angel to give Ezekiel a vision of the future *"battle of Armageddon"* and the preceding events, the angel told Ezekiel the following:

> *'Therefore, son of man, prophesy and say unto Gog, Thus saith the Lord GOD; In that day when my people of Israel dwelleth* ***safely*** *{i.e., they'll be confident of their security but not in God}, shalt thou {Gog} not know it? {i.e., Gog will know it!} And thou shalt*

[455] Ez. 38 and 39

come from thy place ***out of the north parts****, thou,* ***and many people with thee****, all of them riding upon horses {The fact that John saw them riding horses indicates a post-Rapture, "medieval-like" state of existence.}, a great company, and a mighty army:* ***And thou shalt come up against my people of Israel****, as a cloud to cover the land;* ***it shall be in the latter days****,* ***and I will bring thee against my land****, that the heathen may know me, when I shall be sanctified in thee, O Gog, before their eyes.'*

ഗ **Ez. 38:14-16** ഗ

In **Ez. 38:1-9**, the Lord revealed that, in the latter days, He will put a hook in *Gog's* mouth, drawing *Magog, Persia, Ethiopia, Libya, Gomer, Togarmah* and *"many people with them"* down into the mountains of Israel.[456] Thus, the Lord revealed that — *"like a storm and a cloud for multitude"* — they will come up against the holy land (*Israel*). We should note that, when this event actually occurs, even though every single inhabitant of Israel will have chosen to rebel against God by receiving the damnable mark of the beast, God still refers to the descendants of Jacob by saying: "*My people of Israel."* God will certainly punish Israel for their obstinacy and rejection of Christ, but He'll never disown them. Despite their continued defiance, Israel will always be the apple of God's eye.[457]

Doesn't this attack from the north precede the Rapture?

For decades it has been taught, by many, that this massive attack from the north, against the land of Israel, will trigger the start of the tribulation period. That, I can confidently say, is scripturally impossible, and the following is just one of many reasons why:

'But as the days of Noe {Noah} were, so shall also the coming of the Son of man {Jesus} be. For as in the days that were before the flood they were eating and drinking, marrying and giving in marriage, ***until the day that Noe entered into the ark****,* ***And knew not until the flood came****,* ***and took them all away****;* ***so shall also the coming of the Son of man be****. Then*

[456] It is most commonly accepted that this reference to *Gog* is a reference to the leader of the descendants of *Magog, Japheth's* second son (*Gen. 10:2*). Many believe *Magog's* descendants to include a multitude of different groups of people, including those in various portions of the Asian continent—1Chr. 5:4.
[457] Zec. 2:8

> *shall two be in the field; the one shall be taken, and the other left. Two women shall be grinding at the mill; the one shall be taken, and the other left.* ***Watch therefore: for ye know not what hour your Lord doth come.***
>
> ☙ **Mt. 24:37-42** ❧

Though some have failed to recognize it, with the preceding words, Jesus was definitely not warning of His triumphant return at the end of the tribulation period. Instead, He was warning us to be ready for the catching-away of the Church — the Rapture.[458] A careful, all inclusive study of Jesus' words will make this point quite clear. Consider the following:

> If massive armies, from the most powerful nations around the world, began ascending and descending on the nation of Israel, over hundreds of miles and from every direction, precisely as Ezekiel prophesied they will, is it logical to believe that Christians everywhere wouldn't begin to wonder if the catching-away of the saints {*the Rapture*} and the beginning of the seven-year tribulation period was about occur? I think not!

It wouldn't take a Christian to see the writing on the wall

If the preceding scenario were to actually occur, even those who don't believe in Christ would soon realize what was about to happen. Thus, if the preceding situation is to be the case, the Rapture certainly would not occur ***'like a thief in the night,'*** as Jesus clearly warned it will but, instead, would be like the thief sending a singing telegram to announce his intent to ransack your house!

When the attack described by Ezekiel (*Ez. 38:14-16*) occurs, it will take time to move such an enormous army, ***'from many nations,'*** into Judea. Thus, the population of the earth (*especially the Church*) would easily see that coming. Moreover, there's just no way we would be standing idly by, ***'eating, drinking, marrying and giving in marriage,'*** if something that monumental were on the rise. No way! We would definitely be expecting either the catching-away of the Church or the beginning of a third world war. Therefore, this vast attack from the north (*and from the south and*

[458] 1 Th. 4:13-18

west—Ez. 38:4-6), of which Ezekiel prophesied, must occur sometime near or at the end of the tribulation period, just prior to Christ's triumphant return. Fortunately for us Ezekiel's prophecy, combined with John's Revelation vision, further proves this point beyond any reasonable doubt, and we're about to see how.

One final bit of Information from within the Text

John's Revelation vision includes the following extremely revealing and helpful words about the three unclean spirits:

> *'For they are the spirits of devils, working miracles, which go forth unto* ***the kings of the earth and of the whole world****, to gather them to the battle of that great day of God Almighty.'*
> *{John couldn't be clearer! Every nation-state on earth will assemble for this final battle, not just Gog and those from the north.}*

Rev. 16:14

The preceding words are extremely important, because, although most scholars seem to focus on *Gog's* massive attack (*the attack from the armies that will descend from the north and east*), Ezekiel, Zechariah and John[459] clearly state that every nation on earth, even those from the far northwest and south, will be involved in this final battle. We'll see just how much this will affect Jerusalem and the people of Israel later, when we examine Zechariah's prophecy.

---

459 (*Ez. 38 and 39, Rev. 6:12-17 and 16:14*) We need to keep in mind that Zachariah's prophecy (*Zec.14:1-5*) likely includes a reference to the false-prophet's initial attack on Israel during the middle of the tribulation period — *"the abomination of desolation."*

Chapter 37

It Is Done

A Gathering of Fools

Rev. 16:16

> *'**And he** (the false-prophet) **gathered them** (the kings of the earth—16:14) **together into a place called in the Hebrew tongue Armageddon.**'*[460]

What could these people be thinking? I don't care how many impressive and seemingly impossible miracles or inexplicable wonders will have been performed by the false-prophet, once the tribulation period begins to draw to a close, these foolish citizens of Satan's beastly kingdom will have to be plumb out of their minds to believe that they can stand up against Christ at His return! **Heb. 7:1-28** reveals that Jesus, "KING OF KINGS AND LORD OF LORDS," is also referred to in Scripture as being Melchisedec (*i.e., King of Righteousness*), and is, therefore, the original King of the city of Salem (*i.e., the City of Peace*). Today, we refer to that city as Jerusalem. Thus, when these nations violently come against Jerusalem, they'll actually be attacking a kingdom of which Jesus has been the King from the beginning of time.

John's vision doesn't reveal whether or not these wicked individuals will gather having had a clear understanding that they're doing so for the purpose of directly confronting Christ. But, whatever ends up being the case, although Satan and the false-prophet will believe themselves to be controlling this event, according to Ezekiel's prophecies, God will actually be the one in control. Thus, using Satan's little *"puppet-leader"* (*the false-prophet*) to draw the masses into the *Valley of Megiddo* from every nation

---

[460] The word *Armageddon* comes from the Hebrew: *"Har"* {*i.e., a mountain, probably a reference to Mt. Carmel*} and *"Megiddo"* {*a mound created by many peoples or tribes having settled in that location*}; thus, *Armageddon* is a reference found only in the book of Revelation, which likely refers to the large, fertile valley in Galilee, commonly known as *the Jezreel Valley* or *the Plain of Esdraelon.*

on earth, God will essentially be casting the multitudes — "*the vine of the earth*"[461] — into the great winepress of His wrath. Thus, the whole world, along with the people of Israel, will be severely punished for having polluted His Holy City and for having chosen to worship the beast and his image, rather than the one true God. Both Ezekiel and John were shown visions of this universally massive end-time event:

> *'And it shall come to pass at the same time* ***when Gog shall come against the land of Israel****, saith the Lord GOD, that my fury shall come up in my face. For* ***in my jealousy*** *{The Lord will be jealous, because the children of Israel will worship the false-prophet—Ez. 39:7} and* ***in the fire of my wrath*** *have I spoken, Surely in that day* ***there shall be a great shaking in the land of Israel****; So that the fishes of the sea, and the fowls of the heaven, and the beasts of the field, and all creeping things that creep upon the earth, and* ***all the men that are upon the face of the earth****, {That means this earthquake will affect the entire earth.} shall shake at my presence,* ***and the mountains shall be thrown down****,* ***and the steep places shall fall****,* ***and every wall shall fall to the ground****.*
>
> *And I will call for a sword against him throughout all my mountains {Ez. 39:1-4}, saith the Lord GOD:* ***every man's sword shall be against his brother****. And I will plead against him with* ***pestilence*** *{plagues} and with* ***blood****; {This is a clear reference to the plagues of wrath John witnessed in Rev. 16:2-21.} and I will rain upon him, and upon his bands, and upon* ***the many people that are with him****, an overflowing rain, and great hailstones, *fire, and brimstone.'*
>
> {Ez. *39:6, Rev. 14:10, *16:8-9}

Ez. 38:18-22

John witnessed these events earlier, in **Rev. 6:12-17**, as Jesus opened the sixth seal of the allegorical preview of events. Now, in **Rev. 16:1-21**, John is being shown a more detailed version of those same events.

> *'And the seventh angel poured out his vial into the air; and there came a great voice out of the temple of heaven, from the throne, say-*

[461] Rev. 14:18-19

ing, ***It is done*** {See also Ez. 39:7-8}*. And there were voices, and thunders, and lightnings; and* ***there was a great earthquake****,* ***such as was not since men were upon the earth****,* {These words prove this to be the same earthquake John witnessed in Rev. 6:12-17 and 16:17-21} ***so mighty an earthquake****,* ***and so great****.* ***And the great city*** {Babylon, the kingdom of the beast} ***was divided into three parts****,* ***and the cities of the nations fell****: and great Babylon came in remembrance before God, to give unto her the cup of the wine of the fierceness of his wrath.* ***And every island fled away****,* ***and the mountains were not found****.* {These verses and the preceding verses (Ez. 38:18-22) mean exactly what they say and no less. When this earthquake ends, as amazing as the thought of it may be, the mountains will no longer exist! We'll see why that's so relevant later.}

And ***there fell upon men a great hail out of heaven****, every stone about the weight of a* ***talent:***[462] *and men blasphemed God because of the plague of the hail; for the plague thereof was exceeding great.'*

℘ Rev. 16:17-21 ℘

Everything we've just read is in perfect alignment with what John witnessed in his allegorical preview of the tribulation period (*Rev. 6:1-17*). What's more, the similarities between Ezekiel's and John's prophecies prove beyond any reasonable doubt that they were both shown the same event. They both witnessed God dispense His judgment and wrath on all the nations of the world. And, since both Ezekiel's and John's prophecies describe an earthquake that will be so universally powerful that it is said to occur only once, they must have witnessed the same earthquake. In fact, as we earlier established, the following words from John's detailed prophecy make this very clear:

'. . . and there was a great earthquake, ***such as was not since men were upon the earth*** *. . .'*

℘ Rev. 16:18 ℘

This earthquake will cause every mountain and steep place on earth to be thrown down (*Ez. 38:18-22*), every island to be moved out of its place,

---

[462] These hail stones will weigh roughly 75 to 100 lbs.

and every wall to fall to the ground. And, as has been stated, when this occurs it will never have occurred before and will never occur again. What's more, this massive earthquake will occur just moments prior to Christ's return, and both Ezekiel and John mentioned seeing great hail stones with fire and brimstone descending from the heavens during its occurrence. This will all coincide with Christ's triumphant return to earth.

In the following passage from the tribulation preview in **Rev. 6:12-17**, we learned that after Jesus opened the sixth seal John witnessed a vision of Christ's return to earth. That vision combined all the effects of the seven plagues of wrath and ended with Christ's vengeful return to earth. Let's take another quick look at the end of that allegorical passage.

> *'And I beheld when he had opened the sixth seal, and, lo,* ***there was a great earthquake****;* ***and the sun became black as sackcloth of hair****,* ***and the moon became as blood****;* ***And the stars of heaven fell unto the earth****, even as a fig tree casteth her untimely figs, when she is shaken of a mighty wind.* ***And the heaven departed as a scroll when it is rolled together****; {How could this be anything other than Christ's triumphant return with the saints and angels?}* ***and every mountain and island were moved out of their places****.*
>
> *And the kings of the earth, and the great men, and the rich men, and the chief captains, and the mighty men,* ***and every bondman****,* ***and every free man****, {Doesn't this clearly include every person on earth?} hid themselves in the dens and in the rocks of the mountains; And said to the mountains and rocks, Fall on us, and* ***hide us from the face of him that sitteth on the throne****,* ***and from the wrath of the Lamb****: For the great day of his* ***wrath*** *is come; and who shall be able to stand?' {That's a very good question!?}*

Rev. 6:12-17

There is nothing ambiguous about the preceding verses. John clearly witnessed the sky roll back, as the Lamb of God (*Jesus Christ*) returned to exact His vengeance and wrath upon every living soul.

Jesus prophesied of His Return

Before we move into Chapters 17 and 18, let's take a quick look at what Jesus said will happen when He returns to earth at the end of the tribulation period.

'For as the lightning cometh out of the east, and shineth even unto the west; ***so shall also the coming of the Son of man be****. {Since Christ will not be seen by those on earth when He raptures the saints, this can only be a reference to His triumphant return!} For* ***wheresoever the carcase is****,* ***there will the eagles be gathered together****. {Jesus is referring to the fact that, after the battle of Armageddon, the birds will eat the remains of the dead—Rev. 19:17-18.}*

Immediately after the tribulation of those days shall ***the sun be darkened****,* ***and the moon shall not give her light****,* ***and the stars shall fall from heaven****,* ***and the powers of the heavens shall be shaken****: And then shall appear the sign of the Son of man in heaven: and then shall all the tribes of the earth mourn,* ***and they shall see the Son of man coming in the clouds of heaven with power and great glory****.*

{Compare this passage with John's visions of the same event—Rev. 6:12-17 and 16: 8-20. Jesus was undoubtedly describing His Second Coming.}

Mt. 24:27-30

Let's Sum Up:

As we've made our way through these seven mighty plagues of wrath, we've learned that God will begin severely punishing Israel and the rest of the world even before Jesus triumphantly returns to finish the job. And, while (*at the end of the first 3½ years*) the earth will nearly be a total wasteland, it will still have been a veritable paradise compared to the blood drenched global pile of rubble that will exist after God's angels finish dishing out the Lord's seven mighty plagues of wrath!

How so? Consider the following:

- All oceans, seas, lakes, streams, and reservoirs will have been turned into the '**blood of a dead man.**' Even the moon will initially appear to have turned to blood before being totally blacked-out.
- The sun will become **black** (*as sackcloth of hair*), and the stars will have fallen from the sky (*At least that's how it will appear when those 75 lb. flaming hailstones start raining down and the stars disappear.*

- Every person on the planet will be covered with skin ulcers, boils, blisters, and burns. Hence, in the total darkness that will blanket the entire earth, they'll '**gnaw their tongues for pain**' and curse the Almighty God — their Creator.

Consequently, every hate inspired Left-behinder will somehow muster the strength to assemble, with sword in hand, mindlessly prepared to confront the Lord in the *Valley of Megiddo* for the final – "GREAT BATTLE OF ARMAGEDDON." Then, just moments before the Lord peels back the sky to reveal the glorious majesty of His vengeful return to earth, the final seventh angel will pour out his dreadful vial of wrath into the air. This will trigger an earthquake of truly biblical proportions, bringing every mountain and wall to the ground and moving every island out of its place!

At this point, the Lord will not have even begun to Fight!

As unimaginably horrific as these descriptions of life on earth just prior to the Second Coming of Christ have been, when it comes to thoroughly examining all that John was shown about Christ's triumphant return to earth, we've only just scratched the surface. God gave Ezekiel, Daniel, Zachariah, and John incredibly detailed visions of that event. So, after we quickly uncover the mysteriously enlightening significance of the next two chapters of John's vision (*Chapters 17 and 18*), we'll move speedily into the exhilarating climax of the seven-year tribulation period, precisely as it was revealed through the prophets.

Chapter 38

Thou Shalt Have No Other Gods before Me

(Chapters 17 and 18 of John's Vision)

> ꕥ 'I am the LORD thy God, which have brought thee out of the land of Egypt, out of the house of bondage. Thou shalt have no other gods before me. Thou shalt not make unto thee any graven image, or any likeness of any thing that is in heaven above, or that is in the earth beneath, or that is in the water under the earth: Thou shalt not bow down thyself to them, nor serve them: for I the LORD thy God am a jealous God . . . .'[463]

When God first thundered these words, He had recently performed several truly spectacular miracles on behalf of Jacob's descendants, while leading more than two million Hebrew children out of what would have been a lifetime of severely intolerable bondage and eventual death in Egypt. Thus, standing at the base of Mount Sinai, freed from oppression but still quivering in terror at the sound of the Creator's voice, the former Hebrew slaves witnessed the preceding proclamation of terms for their future reverent worship and faithful obedience to the one true God. That same commanding voice had spoken the universe into existence in just one day (*Gen. 1:14-18*), so it's no wonder Jacob's descendants feared for their lives as the Spirit of God descended upon the mountaintop (*in the form of thunder, lightning, fire, and thick, dark smoke*) and began openly laying the ten foundation stones of His law, "THE TEN COMMANDMENTS." Those laws were intended to teach every one of us how desperately we need God's mercy and grace. Sadly, however, despite His continual attempts to extend His loving, redemptive hand to this lost and sinful world, just as Jesus warned would be the case, most of mankind has irreverently turned a deaf ear and defiant heart toward God.[464]

---

[463] Ex. 20:1-5

[464] Mt. 7:14, 20:16, 22:14, Luke 13:18-30

More than 3,500 hundred years have passed since that gloriously magnificent day when God's children heard His audible voice while standing at the base of that mountain, and from that day forward the heart of man has grown ever colder. Most of the world still abides in faithless rejection of its Creator. Even so, as spiritually desolate as this world may presently seem, by the end of the seven-year tribulation period, with all the foolish inhabitants of the earth having willfully chosen to worship Satan and his beastly kingdom, more than ever before, the world will be a total wilderness of lost and desperate souls.

The Allegory of Idolatry

Rev. 17:1-2

> ***'And there came one of the seven angels which had the seven vials** (of wrath)**, and talked with me, saying unto me, Come hither; I will shew unto thee the judgment of <u>the great whore that sitteth upon many waters</u>:***
>
> ***With whom the kings of the earth have committed <u>fornication</u>, and the inhabitants of the earth have been made drunk with the wine of her fornication.'***

While it may be tempting to immediately begin forming an opinion as to the allegorical significance of the preceding verses, we won't actually be able to properly interpret them without having first read all of Revelation Chapters 17 and 18, so you may wish to take a minute and do so. Then, rather than assessing those chapters verse by verse, as we have while interpreting previous chapters, we'll assess both chapters at the same time, just as was intended.

The woman and the Scarlet colored Beast

Rev. 17:3

> ***'So he carried me away in the spirit into <u>the wilderness</u>: and I saw a woman sit upon a <u>scarlet coloured beast</u>, full of names of blasphemy, <u>having seven heads and ten horns</u>.'***

Once again we find the word *"wilderness"* being used to depict a spiritually desolate place or state of being, just as we did earlier, in **Rev. 12:14**. Here, in Chapter 17, John records having seen a vision of a ***'great whore'*** sitting upon ***'many waters.'*** Those waters, according to verse 15, represent the woman's influence over ***'peoples, and multitudes, and nations and tongues.'*** Thus, when we take into account the significance of the seven-headed beast on which the whore sits and acknowledge that each of the beast's seven heads represents an individual kingdom and period of time, we begin to understand that this ***'whore,'*** like the beast on which she sits, has been around for thousands of years.

To fully grasp this, we must remember what we learned earlier, which was that Daniel saw five of the seven heads of this scarlet colored beast as individual kingdoms, prior to their having risen to power. Only the *Babylonian* and *Medo-Persian* empires (*the first and second of the seven heads*) had, at that time, emerged to dominate the kingdoms of the world. It's interesting to note that the first head Daniel saw in his vision represented the height of the *Babylonian Empire,* prior to its being overthrown by the *Media-Persian Empire.* I say this because, in John's end-time vision, written on the forehead of this ***'great whore,'*** John saw the name:

'MYSTERY, BABYLON THE GREAT, THE MOTHER OF HARLOTS AND ABOMINATIONS OF THE EARTH'

Why is this interesting? It's interesting because early *Babylon* is said to have been originally founded as the kingdom of Babel,[465] from whence God forced the dispersing of Noah's descendants by confusing their languages. As time progressed and pagan forms of worship began to take root among the peoples of the earth (*thanks to Satan and his army of demons—'the beast'*), the early Babylonians began to practice a form of idolatry known as *"The Mysteries."* From that time forward, idolatry (*pagan worship and religion — the "great whore" in John's vision*), in one form or another, has continually pervaded every kingdom and nation on the planet without exception, including Israel, God's chosen people. Thus, this *"great whore"* has provided the excuse (*through past and present forms of pagan religion*) that every obstinately rebellious soul, from one generation to the next, has sought to embrace. By pridefully clinging to the futile rituals of religion, tradition, and blatant pagan idolatry, one generation of mankind after another has repeatedly sidestepped God's true path of salvation — a path of sincere, obedient submission to God through faith in Christ alone.

The great whore, "IDOLATRY," still wields her bloody Sword

Rev. 17:6

Earlier (*as we made our way through Rev. 7:14*), I made mention of the horrific trials and tribulations that many of our brothers and sisters in Christ are enduring as part of their day to day profession of faith in the various anti-Christian countries around the world. John said he saw this great whore ***'drunk'*** with the blood of the martyrs of Christ. This should come as no surprise to any well informed Christian.

[465] Gen. 10:8-10, 11:1-9

At the start of 2012, according to a list of the ten most Christian intolerant countries on earth, one country was predominantly *Buddhist*, another was *Atheist* (*in this case, communist*) and the other eight were more than 99% *Islamic*. In those countries and in many countries like them, Christians are still being killed for their faith in Christ. And yet, regardless of what many believe, Jesus (*the Messiah*) is still the world's only hope for salvation. If we follow the teachings of Christ[466] and judge many of those who practice *Buddhism*, *Islam* or *Atheism* only by the fruit of their religion, it's pretty hard to see how they can honestly claim to be propagating or inspiring peace, tolerance or unity.

Of course this is nothing new. The prophets of old regularly endured persecution and/or death at the hands of Godless kings — often for having done nothing more than speak the oracles of God. Thus, beginning with the crucifixion of Christ and continuing to the present, Christians have been tortured and killed while professing their faith to followers of non-Christian (*pagan and idolatrous*) religions. Sadly, as we've learned (*thanks to John's vision*), that's not going to change until the very last saint has been slaughtered and the light of the Gospel of Christ has been temporarily snuffed out.[467]

The whore, Religion and Pomp

John saw this woman — ***'the great whore'*** — spectacularly adorned with gold, precious stones, and pearls, and wearing royal colors — ***purple and scarlet***. Even today, if we were to honestly evaluate the most prominent religious groups and the religious attire of those in leadership, we would sadly see the same opulent, spiritually meaningless garments being ritually worn. Some of these groups questionably claim Christ to be the center of their faith. It doesn't seem to matter that Jesus openly spoke in clear opposition to the sumptuous apparel and arrogant conduct of the established religious leaders of His day, and those religious leaders were claiming to be conducting themselves in accordance with God's Law!

After all, by washing the disciples' feet, just prior to His death, wasn't Jesus setting a standard of meekness and modest servitude for all believers to follow, especially those who consider themselves to be ministers, called to devote their lives to serving the body of Christ — the Church? Speaking in reference to religious leaders, Jesus said the following:

> *'But all their works they do for to be seen of men: they make broad their phylacteries, and enlarge the borders of their gar-*

466 Mt. 7:15-23

467 Rev. 18:23-24

ments, And love the uppermost rooms at feasts, and the chief seats in the synagogues, And greetings in the markets, and to be called of men, Rabbi, Rabbi {teacher or master}. But be not ye called Rabbi: for one is your Master, even Christ; ***and all ye are brethren*** *{whether clergy or layperson, male or female, we are all brothers and sisters, equal in Christ}.* ***And call no man your father upon the earth*** *{Jesus is speaking against referring to any man as a "spiritual father" rather than a "paternal father."}* ***for one is your Father*** *{God the Father},* ***which is in heaven****.'*

'. . . ***But he that is greatest among you shall be your servant****. And whosoever shall exalt himself {in any way} shall be abased; and he that shall humble himself shall be exalted.'*

Mt. 23:5-12

How could so many religious groups get this so terribly wrong? Holiness can't be attained or declared through the donning of lavishly ornate ritual apparel. It just doesn't come that easily. As ministers we can't simply pull holiness out of our closets and put it on in the morning, only to take it back off and hang it up at the end of the day. Our hope of eternal sanctification (*true holiness*) was purchased through the supreme suffering and death of our Savior. Thus, true, eternal sanctification can only be attained through deep, introspective, soul surrendering contrition, which always leads to placing one's hope and faith in Christ. Holiness is a free-gift from God[468] that is birthed in our soul the very moment we truly surrender our life and will (*our earthly plans and ambitions*) to God in the name of Jesus Christ our Savior. Jesus described this true conversion experience as being "born-again."[469]

When we are truly "born-again," a spiritual re-birth evokes in us an unnatural (*divinely inspired*) recognition that we've been called to humbly serve the Lord and one another rather than ourselves. Thus, it's from this new, inner humility that the true image of Christ begins to emerge in our lives. Christ "**in-us**" (*the Holy Spirit within*)[470] does not engender a desire to be exalted or admired; although, our *"old-nature"* (*i.e., our carnal, fleshly, prideful nature*) will certainly continue seeking to attain that unmerited worldly respect. Instead, as the Holy Spirit and love of God enters our soul,

---

468 Rom. 5:15-18, Eph. 2:4-10
469 Jn. 3:1-10
470 Col. 1:25-29, Jn. 3:3-21, Heb. 10:16-31

He evokes a modest, love motivated desire to prefer, encourage, and strengthen others in Christ's stead.

~ *So what's the point?* ~

The point is, only *"false-religion"* (*which is idolatry*) needs to cloak itself with opulent attire and enigmatically complicated rituals that worshippers don't truly understand. This is the allegorical significance of the sumptuously attired *"great whore"* John saw riding the *"seven-headed beast."* Her mysterious opulence is part of her *"allure"* — *"her power to seduce."* That's precisely what idolatry and false religion is to our soul, a means of temporarily suppressing the true, divinely inspired conviction of the Holy Spirit. False religion (*i.e., idolatry*) seduces us to choose a different path from that which God has already perfectly preordained and established for our salvation. There is, however, only one very simple and straight forward path of truth, and that path leads directly to a humble acknowledgment of Christ.[471] All else is mere idolatry: ***"the seduction of the great whore."***

Therefore, any religion, philosophy, scientific theory, hobby, or way of life that seduces us away from submitting to God's preordained path of salvation can simply be categorized as one of many forms of idolatry, and no complicated religious rituals, traditions, seemingly deep philosophies, or pseudo-scientific teachings can change that fact!

Unfortunately, despite that truth, from one generation to the next, billions of people have pridefully rejected God's free-gift of salvation, foolishly choosing, instead, to climb into bed with this *"great whore upon the beast,"* whom the angel speaking with John labeled:

> 'MYSTERY, BABYLON THE GREAT, THE MOTHER OF HARLOTS AND ABOMINATIONS OF THE EARTH'

John wondered at the woman and the beast . . .

As John wondered in amazement at the opulence of the great whore straddling the seven-headed beast, the angel began to explain the significance of that beast:

> *'The beast that thou sawest **was**, and **is not**; {This means the beast existed in the past and will also exist in the future.} and **shall ascend out of the bottomless pit**, and go into perdition: {When the Holy Spirit is pulled back, Satan's demonic forces will powerfully emerge as*

[471] John 14:6

*never before—2Th. 2:3-12.} **and they that dwell on the earth**[472] **shall wonder** {be amazed and deceived}, whose names were **not** written in the book of life[473] from the foundation of the world, when they behold the beast that **was**, and **is not**, and **yet is**.'*

☙ Rev. 17:8 ❧

By stating that the names of those who will *"wonder when they behold the beast"* (*i.e., to admire the beast—Rev. 17:8*) were not written in the book of Life, the angel revealed that only the eternally lost will ultimately be deceived by the beast.[474] As has been stated, the beast in John's vision represents Satan's powers of darkness and their influence on the kingdoms of the world from the beginning of man's existence to the end of the final evil kingdom of the false-prophet. This is why the angel explained that the beast — "**was**" (*an obvious reference to Satan's influence on past generations*), and — "**is not**" (*indicating that, during John's life, the final, future evil kingdom had not yet arisen*), and that he (*the beast*) — "**yet is**" (*i.e., Satan's powers of darkness continue to exist in the present, influencing every kingdom on earth*).

By now it should be pretty clear that the seven-headed beast and the woman (*the whore, who was seen riding that beast and represents Satan's continuous idolatrous affect on the kingdoms and peoples of the earth*) have actually been inseparable. We learned earlier that Satan is the dragon that controls the beast (*the fallen angels—Rev. 12:1-9*) and that Satan has been at work, deceiving the nations of the world, since the fall of man (*which explains why the dragon in Rev. 12 was seen wearing seven crowns upon his heads*),[475] but the degree to which Satan has been able to do so is presently being restrained by the powerful presence of the Holy Spirit on earth.[476] This explains why the angel told John that, during the tribulation period

---

[472] This is a reference to every person on the planet at the end of the tribulation period. How do we know this? We know this because every Left-behinder who will have refused to take the mark of the beast will have already been resurrected before even one drop of God's wrath will have been poured out—Rev. 15:1-8.

[473] The angel speaking to John is stating that those left on earth at the end of the tribulation period will not have their names written in the Book of Life. Instead, they'll all have been eternally doomed for having received the damnable mark of the beast.

[474] 2Th. 2:8-12

[475] Given that the seven heads on the dragon are intended to allegorically represent the same seven kingdoms as are represented by the seven heads on the beast, the crowns on the dragon's heads are clearly intended to reveal Satan's evil influence on all past, present, and future kingdoms of the world.

[476] Rev. 12:9, 13:4

(*when the Holy Spirit is pulled back and Satan and his powers of darkness are allowed to vicariously rule the world through the false-prophet*),[477] the beast (*the powers of darkness*) will powerfully ascend from the bottomless pit. If the beast were merely a man, the angel's words would make no sense. But it makes a great deal of sense for the Lord's angel to have told John that the soon to be unfettered principalities and powers of darkness, through which Satan and the false-prophet will mightily establish their evil end-time empire, will eventually ascend out of the bottomless pit.

The question we must ask, if we wish to understand the angel's explanation of the beast, is: *"When we read John's account of his having seen the vision of the beast in Rev. 13:1-10, was one of its heads a representation of the final evil kingdom to rule the earth?"* And, of course, as we thoroughly covered while going over those scriptures, the answer to that question is clearly, *"Yes!"* In fact, if one of the beast's heads does not represent that final tribulation period kingdom, then the beast John saw would have only had six heads. Thus, Daniel's prophecy reveals the significance of each of those seven heads. And the seventh, most dreadfully significant head on John's beast (*which was Daniel's fourth and final beast with great iron teeth—Dan. 7:7-8 and 7:19-27*) is a clear representation of the final evil kingdom to rule earth. Therefore, the angel's words clearly indicate that the source of this final evil kingdom's unfettered power will undoubtedly emerge from the depths of the bottomless pit!

~ *Does that mean that Satan and his fallen-angels are not currently at work?* ~

In the next verse we will see evidence that will indicate that Satan and his army of fallen-angels are always at work, but that doesn't mean that God has continually allowed Satan to totally dominate the inhabitants of the earth by vicariously ruling global empires. Still, we must acknowledge that the first six heads on John's beast do represent kingdoms that almost totally ruled the earth during their existence, and the seventh head (*Satan's global kingdom*) will be the first kingdom to succeed in forcing "every living soul" to submit to its authority. Again, the angel indicated this by stating that the names of those who will admire the beast (*every citizen of Satan's global empire*) were not found written in the Lamb's book of Life.

We should note that, today, the earth is ruled by many individual kingdoms (*nations*), but clearly none of them could accurately be said to presently represent the final global kingdom that both Daniel and John saw rule the earth.

---

[477] 2Th. 2:3-12

'And here is the mind which hath wisdom. ***The seven heads are seven mountains****, on which the woman* ***sitteth****.'*

☙ Rev. 17:9 ❧

The last word in the preceding verse (*"sitteth"— present tense*) should give serious pause to any staunch believer that the ***'seven mountains,'*** of which John wrote, are a sure reference to a specific future location of Satan's global kingdom. John was told that the seven heads of the beast are ***'seven mountains'*** on which ***'the woman sitteth'*** (*present, not future tense*). That means that this *"great whore"* was already sitting on the beast when John received this Revelation vision. This is confirmation of our earlier assertion that *"the beast," "the dragon" (from Rev. 12:1-17)*, and *"the whore"* have harmoniously existed over thousands of years.

~ So, what about the seven mountains? ~

We wouldn't be wise to spend a great deal of time trying to figure out what these seven mountains represent, because what really matters is what we can scripturally prove, not what we presume or what we've heard suggested. It's commonly taught that the former *Roman Empire* was referred to as *"the City on Seven Hills."* Unfortunately, the list of other cities that are also said to have been built on seven hills is enormous! As a matter of fact, our beloved City Jerusalem has similarly been referred to as, *"the City of Seven Hills."* Thus, we need to be careful not to rush to a conclusion about John's reference to seven mountains in these verses.

Thanks to Daniel's vision, we do know that each of the seven heads on John's beast represents a past or future *"kingdom"* and/or *"period of time."* We also know that six of those kingdoms were not located in precisely the same place. In fact, they each covered many hills, not just seven. Since verses 17:10-11 speak of the *past, present* and *future* existence of seven different *kings* and *kingdoms*, the mountains to which verse 17:9 may be referring could simply be (*though we can't be sure*) a reference to seven different periods of time, rather than a specific, geographic location.

'And there are seven kings: ***five are fallen****, and* ***one is****, and the other is* ***not yet come****; and when* ***he*** *{the false-prophet and global kingdom of the beast} cometh, he must continue a short space {seven years}. And the beast that* ***was****, and* ***is not****, even* ***he is the eighth, and is of the seven****, and goeth into perdition.' {We need to remember that the Scriptures often refer to both kings and kingdoms as one entity.}*

☙ Rev. 17:10-11 ❧

~ Wait a minute! Could you please explain John's reference to an eighth kingdom? ~

The only entity that fits the angel's description of a symbolic *"eighth kingdom"* (*which is said to have existed during each of these seven kingdoms and periods of time*) is, *"the beast"* — *"the powers of darkness."*

> *'And there appeared another wonder in heaven; and behold a great red dragon {Satan}, having* ***seven heads*** *and* ***ten horns****,* ***and seven crowns upon his heads****. And his tail drew the third part of the stars of heaven {fallen-angels}, and did cast them to the earth . . .'*

Rev. 12:3-4

Though some kingdoms and nations, through their submission to God, have experienced prolonged periods of great spiritual growth and prosperity, the truth is, through his continual manipulation of these principalities and powers of darkness,[478] Satan has eventually managed to adversely affect and corrupt every kingdom on earth, and he'll continue doing so right up to the end. God's having chosen to nearly exterminate mankind by flooding the earth after only 1,656 years of man's existence was our first evidence of this truth. Just look at the world today. Even countries that once stood as great bastions of faith and obedience to God have now, in this morally degenerate world, completely caved, choosing to give way to the incessant pressure of the pagan, atheistic, anti-Christian, politically-correct (*though extremely offensive to God*) "**majority**." Of course, Jesus warned that this would eventually happen:

> *'And* ***because iniquity shall abound****,* ***the love of many shall wax cold*** *{i.e., man's reverence and love for God will greatly diminish}. But he that shall endure {i.e., those who retain their faith in Christ} unto the end, the same shall be saved. And this gospel of the kingdom shall be preached in all the world for a witness unto all nations; and then shall the end come.'*

Mt. 24:12-14

In the following passage (*which we earlier assessed*), Paul also warned of an end-time global apostasy:

---

[478] Rev. 12:3-9, Eph. 2:1-3, 6:12-18

> '. . . *for that day {Paul is referring to the Second Coming of Christ, not the Rapture.) shall not come,* ***except there come a falling away first*** *{a falling away from faith in God and Christ, an apostasy}, and that man of sin be revealed, the son of perdition . . . .*'

2Th. 2:3-4

"Was" and "Is not" and "Is" of the Seven

The angel told John that ***'the beast that was and is not, even he is the eighth*** *(kingdom)* ***and is of the seven'***. A thorough study of both Daniel's and John's visions, coupled with an understanding of the original *Hebrew* and *Greek* manuscripts, will reveal that the words *king* and *kingdom* in Daniel's and John's visions are nearly transposable. In other words, in **Rev. 17** and in **Dan. 7**, when it comes to their interpretation, *king* and *kingdom* both refer to the *"foundation of power"* of each individual kingdom and are, therefore, basically interchangeable. Thus, the seven heads on both Daniel's and John's beasts represent both *kings* and *kingdoms* at the same time.

This knowledge should help us grasp how this *"eighth kingdom,"* which the angel said ***'is of the seven,'*** must be a spiritual kingdom. If that were not true, it couldn't consist of each consecutive kingdom, starting with the *Babylonian Empire* and ending with the final evil kingdom of the false-prophet. There doesn't seem to be any other logical way to interpret the angel's words, and Chapter 18 of John's vision further affirms that conclusion.

Think "New World Order" or even worse!

Rev. 17:12

> ***'And the ten horns which thou sawest are ten kings, which have received no kingdom as yet; but receive power as kings one hour*** *(i.e., an unspecified period of time)* ***with the beast.'***

The angel told John that these ten future leaders (*kings*) had received no kingdom as yet. That, however, was true in John's lifetime. They may very well be in positions of power and authority today, though presently we have no way of knowing. Whether they're currently in power or not, once the false-prophet establishes his global kingdom, these ten leaders will be forced to worship and totally submit all authority and control of their respective kingdoms to him. Daniel's following prophecy clearly details this truth:

'Thus he said, The fourth beast shall be the fourth kingdom upon earth, which shall be diverse from all kingdoms, ***and shall devour the whole earth****,* ***and shall tread it down****,* ***and break it in pieces****.* *{Daniel's fourth beast, the seventh head in his vision, represents the final, evil kingdom to rule the earth. Never before has a kingdom this destructive and of this magnitude existed!} And the* ***ten horns*** *out of this kingdom are* ***ten kings*** *that shall arise:* ***and another shall rise after them****;* *{This makes it clear that the ten leaders will already be in power, before the false-prophet assumes full control; although, that doesn't necessarily indicate they'll have been in power at the start of the tribulation period.}* ***and he*** *{the false prophet}* ***shall be diverse from the first****,*[479] ***and he shall subdue three kings****.* '[480]

Dan. 7:23-24

The Ten Kings will hate the Beast

Most of us are acquainted with the term, *"New World Order,"* and, while the very thought of living under that type of heavy-handed, spiritually oppressive, one-world government is terrifying in the extreme, it in no way compares to the exceedingly intolerant religious tyranny that will be enforced during the final evil kingdom of "**the beast**!" As has been true of all autocratic and communistic societies, the idea of communism may sound plausible and look doable on paper but when put into practice it's an absolute "train-wreck" for every individual who doesn't happen to be at the top of the social pyramid. Daniel made it clear that this will also be true of the false-prophet's beastly kingdom. In fact, as we just read,[481] Daniel prophesied that, before the Lord returns to judge the earth, the beast and

[479] The *"son of perdition"* (*the "false-prophet" or "anti-Christ"*) will be diverse from the other ten kings; now there's the understatement of the century! The word diverse, in this instance, means: *to be altered, changed* or *different.* Unlike the other ten kings, the false-prophet will be directly empowered and controlled by Satan and his army of demons—*the beast.*

[480] Dan. 7:8 makes it quite clear that this last powerful king (*the false-prophet*) will pluck three of the first ten kings up by the root. This explains why, at the beginning of the tribulation period (*Rev. 6:1-2*), John saw this leader going forth *'conquering and to conquer.'* Hence, these three kings may very well be three of his first victims. However, since John was told that ten kings will rule under this false-prophet for 3½ years, those three kings will obviously be replaced.

[481] Dan. 7:23

its evil dictator will completely devour the earth, tread it down, and break it in pieces!

The citizens of Satan's beastly kingdom will be as expendably worthless to Satan as would be a painfully embedded pebble in the inner sole of his shoe. Thus, after having recently endured at least 3½ years of humiliating submission under the false-prophet's global tyranny, the angel told John that these ten subordinate kings will passionately hate having to worship the kingdom of the beast. Hence, as soon as they can, they'll pridefully seek to be freed from the degrading spiritual oppression of Satan's beastly, global kingdom.

*'And the ten horns {ten kings} which thou sawest upon the beast, **these shall hate the whore**, and shall make her desolate and naked, and shall eat her flesh, and burn her with fire.*[482] *For God hath put in their hearts to fulfil his will, and to agree, and give their kingdom unto the beast, until the words of God shall be fulfilled.'*

Rev. 17:16-17

It's not perfectly clear just how these verses will be fulfilled, but it's obvious that the citizens of this final evil empire will no longer be happily worshipping their new world leader when the tribulation period draws to a close. A comprehensive study through **Ezekiel 38** and **39** — two chapters that speak prophetically about the days that will precede Christ's return to earth — will reveal that a state of *"total, global volatility and extreme unrest"* will exist before the great battle of Armageddon begins. Nonetheless, though many brilliant minds have chosen to offer their expert opinions as to precisely how all this turmoil will play out, when we get right down to it, only the Lord knows exactly what will happen and when.

*'And the woman which thou sawest is that great city, **which reigneth** {present tense} **over the kings of the earth**.'*

Rev. 17:18

[482] The hatred of these ten subordinate kings will apparently be directed at *"the great whore"* (*spiritual oppression*) rather than at the physical kingdom. This would seem to indicate that their hatred will be a result of having to worship Satan through their submission to his beastly kingdom. *Gee, what a shock! You mean the Left-behinders who will have chosen to worship pure-evil aren't going to be happy doing so? Who'd a thunk it?!*

The preceding verse is the straight forward confirmation for which we've patiently waited. Without mincing words, the angel told John that the woman he saw sitting on the beast "**is**" that "GREAT CITY BABYLON" of which he spoke. She is the demonic kingdom that has adversely impacted every kingdom, from the beginning of man's existence, and will continue to do so until the Lord returns at the end of the tribulation period.

The Prophesied Collapse of Satan's Demonic Empire

> *'And after these things I saw another angel come down from heaven, having great power; and the earth was lightened with his glory. And he cried mightily with a strong voice, saying, **Babylon the great is fallen**, **is fallen**, **and is become the habitation of devils**, **and the hold of every foul spirit**, and a cage of every unclean and hateful bird.'*

℘ Rev. 18:1-2 ℘

Having just witnessed (*in the preceding portion of his vision—Rev. 16*) the unleashing of the powerfully destructive seven plagues of God's wrath upon the surviving citizens of this future evil "GREAT CITY BABYLON," the next thing John witnessed was this prophetic depiction of the wicked city's inevitable collapse. And, again, we must acknowledge that everything John recorded seeing in this portion of his vision (*Rev. 17 and 18*) is metaphorical and must, therefore, be interpreted with appreciation for its obvious symbolic significance.

Idolatry, the very Bricks and Mortar of this Evil City

The symbolic ***'great whore that sitteth on many waters'*** (*who was found to be drunk with the blood of apostles, prophets, and saints*) is intended to reveal that the degrading, adulterous affect that Satan and his rulers of darkness have continually had on the many ***'peoples, and multitudes, and nations and tongues'*** of this world is the very mortar and bricks with which this spiritual "MYSTERY CITY BABYLON" was built.

> *'And there followed another angel, saying, Babylon is fallen, is fallen, that great city, **because she made all nations drink of the wine of the wrath of her fornication**.'*

℘ Rev. 14:8 ℘

Starting in **Rev. 12:9** and continuing through **Rev. 19**, the angel speaking to John repeatedly refers to this spiritually ageless city as *"a woman,"* *"a harlot,"* or *"a whore."* Throughout each consecutive generation, from the Garden of Eden to the present, this spiritual "MOTHER OF HARLOTS" has managed to allure and seduce leaders from virtually every tribe, empire, and nation on the planet to climb into bed with her and commit spiritual adultery against God. Thus, by casting his perfectly aimed darts at the soft underbelly of man's physical and spiritual vulnerabilities, Satan has skillfully exploited man's natural, carnal weaknesses and insatiable desire to sin. This is the affect that Satan and his army of demons (*the beast on which this mother of harlots sits*) have had on the inhabitants of the earth, throughout man's existence.

One final suggestion:

If you haven't already ventured through Chapter 18 of John's vision, when you take a few minutes to do so, it's important to pay close attention to important clues, like verses **18:20-24**. Those verses refer to *past, present* and/or *future* events that prove the current, continued existence of this spiritually wicked city of darkness — "MYSTERY BABYLON." We should note, however, that, while this mystery city is indeed an allegorical reference to Satan's and his army of fallen angels' incessant evil work on earth, it is still true that, in these last days, there will arise a mighty physical manifestation of this tyrannical empire, which will be ruled by Satan, through a *"puppet leader" (an anti-Christ) — "the false-prophet."* Satan will consider that future city to be his ultimate victory over God and mankind. But, fortunately, as we just read and are about to see fulfilled, that victory will be very short lived!

Chapter 39

The Triumphant Return of the Lord

Rev. 19:1-3

'And after these things I heard a great voice of much people in heaven, saying, Alleluia; Salvation, and glory, and honour, and power, unto the Lord our God:

For true and righteous are his judgments: for he hath judged the great whore, which did corrupt the earth with her fornication, and hath avenged the blood of his servants at her hand.

And again they said, Alleluia. And her smoke rose up for ever and ever.'

While moving through the first fifteen chapters of John's vision, we learned that God revealed to John that He will not allow a single drop of His wrath to be poured out on the perpetually wicked inhabitants of the earth until every member of His eternal family — *"the bride of Christ"* — has been safely gathered into His presence. Thus, in Rev. Chapter 15, John recorded having witnessed the very last of the saints (*the resurrected "remnant"*) standing before God's throne, on a sea of glass, and singing a song of thanksgiving to God and the Lamb.[483] Then, in Chapter 16, one by one we saw seven horrific plagues of wrath being poured out on the remaining inhabitants of the earth, but we were not shown how the seventh and final plague (*the global, unprecedentedly powerful earthquake*) will coincide with Christ's triumphant return to earth. So, since we've reached that earth-shaking end of the seven-year tribulation period, in this nineteenth chapter of John's book, we're going to see precisely how everything John was shown, in both the allegorical and the interpretive portions of his vision, serves to create one clear picture of what will happen on earth when the seventh and final plague is poured out and the Lord mightily

---

[483] John saw all those who had been martyred for having refused to take the mark of the beast (*the remnant*) standing on a sea of glass before any of the plagues of wrath had been poured out—Rev. 15:1-8.

returns to finish the job of avenging the deaths of all His faithful martyred servants — "**the saints**."

The long awaited Marriage Supper of the Lamb

'And the four and twenty elders and the four beasts fell down and Worshipped God that sat on the throne, saying, Amen; Alleluia. And a voice came out of the throne, saying, Praise our God, all ye his servants, and ye that fear him, both small and great. And I heard as it were the voice of a great multitude, and as the voice of many waters, and as the voice of mighty thunderings, saying, Alleluia: for the Lord God omnipotent reigneth. Let us be glad and rejoice, and give honour to him: ***for the marriage of the Lamb is come, and his wife hath made herself ready****. And to her was granted that she should be arrayed in fine linen, clean and white: for the fine linen is the righteousness of saints. And he saith unto me, Write,* ***Blessed are they which are called unto the marriage supper of the Lamb****. And he saith unto me, These are the true sayings of God.'*

Rev. 19:4-9

There's more mystery about this blessed future event than revelation. And, while that's true, in light of the staggering amount of teaching that's been done on the subject, you wouldn't believe that to be the case. I've frequently heard it taught that the *Marriage Supper of the Lamb* will immediately follow the rapture of the Church. Yet, having read the preceding passage, it should be quite clear why that couldn't possibly be the case. Metaphorically speaking, Jesus certainly doesn't intend to allow His long awaited marriage supper celebration to begin without the bride, and, until every sanctified and redeemed soul is assembled before His throne, the bride of Christ won't be entirely present![484]

Gracious and Merciful beyond Words

The preceding passage states that Christ's wife ***'hath made herself ready.'*** From my perspective the Lord's assessment of the situation is

[484] The bride of Christ won't be fully assembled before God until the end of the seven-year tribulation period, when the last of the saints are resurrected (*Rev. 15:1-6*), just moments before the plagues of wrath begin to be poured out.

incredibly generous. Every member of the body of Christ (*i.e., every saint*) is guilty of sin and, therefore, deserves to be adorned in crimson red, not white.

'Come now, and let us reason together, saith the LORD:
though your sins be as scarlet, they shall be as white as snow;
though they be red like crimson, they shall be as wool.'

Isaiah 1:18

Despite our continual mortal proclivity to sin, on the glorious day of the Lord's triumphant return to earth, He will graciously declare that we, His wife, ***'hath made herself ready,'*** even though we could never be credited with having sanctified ourselves. We'll have done nothing but choose to receive His free-gift[485] of eternal life, and, still, He'll consider us ready to be clothed in His righteousness. What's more, the inescapable reality of this truth will powerfully come to light when, on the glorious day of His return, by clothing every saint in pure white raiment, the Lord will be boldly declaring the righteousness of His *"bride"* to our accuser (*Satan*) and to all those who will have chosen to reject His free-gift of eternal sanctification through faith.

Now that we've final got all the pieces . . . .

It's time to put all the pertinent scriptures together so we can see the completed picture of the Second Coming of Christ and the unprecedentedly massive earthquake that will coincide with His return.

Rev. 19:11-14

'And I saw heaven opened, and behold a white horse; and he that sat upon him was called Faithful and True, and in righteousness he doth judge and make war.'

'His eyes were as a flame of fire, and on his head were many crowns; and he had a name written, that no man knew, but he himself.

And he was clothed with a vesture dipped in blood: and his name is called The Word of God.

And the armies which were in heaven followed him upon white horses, clothed in fine linen, white and clean.'

---

485 The greatest gift of all is *"the gift of God"* — *"eternal life through Christ,"* and, as is true of all gifts, it can't be earned—Eph. 2:1-10, John 15.

If we think back to the beginning of our journey, we'll remember that the preceding verses don't represent the first time John recorded having seen the universe peal back to reveal the dwelling place of God. The first time John saw this happen is recorded in the following verses, which affirm our earlier assertion that everything John recorded seeing in **Rev. 6:1-17** (*the opening of the first six seals*) was intended to serve as nothing more than an allegorical preview of the seven-year tribulation period.

'And I beheld when he had opened the sixth seal, and, lo, ***there was a great earthquake*** *and the sun became black as sack-cloth of hair, and the moon became as blood; And the stars of heaven fell unto the earth, even as a fig tree casteth her untimely figs, when she is shaken of a mighty wind.*

And the heaven departed as a scroll when it is rolled together; ***and every mountain and island were moved out of their places***.

And the kings of the earth, and the great men, and the rich men, and the chief captains, and the mighty men, and every bondman, and every free man {That means everybody!}, hid themselves in the dens and in the rocks of the mountains; And said to the mountains and rocks, Fall on us, ***and hide us from the face of him that sitteth on the throne***, ***and from the wrath of the Lamb***: ***For the great day of his wrath is come; and who shall be able to stand***?'

Rev. 6:12-17

When we couple everything we've learned thus far about the unprecedentedly destructive earthquake that will coincide with Jesus' triumphant return to earth with the following prophecy from **Zec. 14:3-4**, which is a depiction of the same event, we get a clear and complete picture of Christ's glorious Second Coming.

'Then shall the LORD go forth, and fight against those nations, as when he fought in the day of battle. ***And his feet shall stand in that day upon the mount of Olives****, Which is before Jerusalem on the east,* ***and the mount of Olives shall cleave in the midst thereof toward the east and toward the west***, ***and there***

shall be a very great valley *{Just think how large this future valley will have to be in order to be considered a very great valley! We'll cover this more just ahead.};* ***and half of the mountain shall remove toward the north, and half of it toward the south.'***

Zec. 14:3-4

It's hard to imagine even the staunchest haters of God being so foolish as to assemble with the intent of challenging the Lord at His return. And yet, as the tribulation period draws to a close, like a tidal wave of lost and desperate souls, the barely surviving Left-behinders will begin pouring into the vast Megiddo Valley[486] with the idiotically suicidal goal of waging war against Christ and His army of angels and saints! Even more unimaginable is the fact that, while those lost souls are busy stumbling around in the non-existent light of a blacked out sun, the ground will be violently shaking beneath their feet. Then, in an instant, all their prideful arrogance and pomp will turn to mush as the eerily thick, dark sky overhead suddenly rolls open like a scroll and a glorious light, clearer and brighter than any star, mightily breaks through upon them. As it does, the citizens of Satan's beastly global kingdom, which will be every person on the planet, will terrifyingly find themselves staring straight up and into Heaven at the radiantly majestic face of the one true God on His throne! [487]

Instantly, whatever confidence they'll have had in their earthly leader and in his limited authority over the powers of darkness will vanish! No force or fear on earth could compare to the holy terror they'll experience when ***'great hailstones, fire and brimstone'*** are sent crashing down upon them.[488]

Like millions of cockroaches suddenly exposed to a loud noise and bright light, the horror-stricken inhabitants of the earth will violently spill each other's blood, trampling and slashing at one another, as they pointlessly rush in every direction, futilely attempting to escape the refining, radiant majesty and wrath of the Lamb of God! They'll be so terrifyingly exposed to the Lord's omnipotent presence that they'll hysterically cry-out to the mountains and rocks:

> ***"Fall on us and hide us, from the face of him that sitteth on the throne, and from the wrath of the Lamb; For the great day of His wrath is come; and who shall be able to stand?"*** [489]

---

[486] Zec. 14:1-13, Rev. 6:12-17, 16:1-16, Ez. 38:21
[487] Rev. 6:14-17
[488] Isa. 30:27-30, Ez. 38:22, Rev. 16:21
[489] Rev. 6:15-17

The Armies of the Lord

Just precisely to whom John was referring when he recorded having seen the armies in heaven following the Lord on white horses as He triumphantly returned to earth is exciting to contemplate, because before the occurrence of this future event no saints (*of whom I am familiar*) will have ever been included within the ranks of the heavenly armies of the Lord. However, as we're about to see (*thanks to our big brother Enoch, who lived long before the flood of Noah's day*), though only angels have served in that holy capacity in the past, it has always been the Lord's intent to adopt and enlist the saints into His heavenly army. Hence, more than 5,000 years ago Enoch prophesied as follows:

'Behold, the Lord cometh ***with ten thousands of his saints****,*
To execute judgment upon all . . .'

ꟼ Jude 14 ꟼ

Also speaking of Christ's triumphant return, Zechariah prophesied:

'. . . the LORD my God shall come, ***and all the saints with thee****.'*

Zec. 14:5

If we were to draw a conclusion as to who the armies of the Lord will comprise based solely on the preceding scriptures we could mistakenly conclude that only the saints will take part in the Lord's triumphant return to earth. That, however, as the following prophecy reveals, would be a mistake:

'. . . And to you who are troubled rest with us, ***when the Lord Jesus shall be revealed from heaven with his mighty angels****, In flaming fire taking vengeance on them that know not God, and that obey not the gospel of our Lord Jesus Christ . . .'*

2Th. 1:7-8

The Lamb of God will not be returning like a Lamb

It's true that both angels and saints will accompany the Lord upon white horses when He returns to earth, but the fiery-eyed Lamb of God, whom John saw clothed ***'in a vesture dipped in blood,'*** will certainly need no help from us when carrying out His vengeance. And, while this is certainly true, our Savior, the Omnipotent Creator of all things, has affectionately decided to allow those who'll have chosen to embrace His will to share the spotlight during His gloriously triumphant return to declare His authority to rule the earth. His return will be an event unparalleled by any past act of God. There's just no way we can truly imagine what it will be like for those who'll have been left-behind when they suddenly look up to see billions[490] of angels and saints descending from Heaven upon white horses, with Christ Jesus, "KING OF KINGS AND LORD OF LORDS," leading the way!

Rev. 19:15

> ***'And out of his mouth goeth a sharp <u>sword</u>, that <u>with it he should smite the nations</u>: and he shall rule them with a rod of iron: and he treadeth the winepress of the fierceness and wrath of Almighty God.'***

Since God our Savior simply spoke the word and the universe was formed, how terrified do you suppose the inhabitants of the earth should be when the entire universe actually peels back to reveal its divine Creator, "THE WORD OF GOD," returning with a symbolic two-edged sword fiercely protruding from His mouth? That sword (*the Word*) and the Son of God are inseparable. The first chapter of John's Gospel makes this perfectly clear, declaring Christ Jesus to be *"the Creator of all things," "God in the flesh" — "the Word."*[491] Thus, when Jesus returns, He won't be returning as the willfully vulnerable sacrificial *"Lamb of God"* or *"Son of man."* He'll be returning as "ALMIGHTY GOD THE SON," in all His glory, to execute judgment on the rebellious inhabitants of the earth! In short, He'll be coming to carry out His "WORD," which is precisely what the two-edged sword John saw protruding from His mouth represents:[492]

> *'. . . the LORD shall utter his voice before his army: for his camp is very great: **<u>for he is strong that executeth his word</u>**: for the day of the LORD is great and very terrible; and who can abide it?'*

℘ Joel 2:11 ℘

> *'Repent; or else I will come unto thee quickly, and will fight against them **<u>with the sword of my mouth</u>**.'*

℘ Rev. 2:16 ℘

---

[490] We'll discuss the likelihood of there being many billions of angels and saints in the ensuing chapters.
[491] John 1:1-14, Col. 1:15-19, Heb. 1:1-14
[492] Heb. 4:12, Rev. 1:16, 2:12, 2:16

A Feast for Fowls

Rev. 19:16-18

> ***'And he hath on his vesture and on his thigh a name written, KING OF KINGS, AND LORD OF LORDS.***
>
> ***And I saw an angel standing in the sun; and he cried with a loud voice, saying to all the fowls that fly in the midst of heaven, Come and gather yourselves together unto the supper of the great God;***
>
> ***That ye may eat the flesh of kings, and the flesh of captains, and the flesh of mighty men, and the flesh of horses, and of them that sit on them, and the flesh of all men, both free and bond, both small and great.'***

Now let's read Zechariah's chilling prophetic description of what will actually happen to the surviving inhabitants of the earth on the day of the Lord's return and see if we can still imagine any flesh being left for those fowls to eat!

'And it shall come to pass in that day, that the light shall not be clear, Nor dark: But it shall be one day which shall be known to the LORD, not day, nor night: but it shall come to pass, that at evening time it shall be light.' ~ 'And this shall be the plague wherewith the LORD will smite ***all the people that have fought against Jerusalem*** *{This plague will be specifically directed at those who'll have attacked Jerusalem.}; Their flesh shall consume away while they stand upon their feet, and their eyes shall consume away in their holes, and their tongue shall consume away in their mouth. And it shall come to pass in that day, that a great tumult from the LORD shall be among them;* ***and they shall lay hold every one on the hand of his neighbor****' {Severely panicked and terrified, they'll kill each other trying to escape the wrath of the Lamb.}* [493]

℘ Zec. 14:6-7 & 12, 13 ℘

The preceding prophecy has obviously not been fulfilled, but it paints a disturbingly vivid picture, much like that of humans being exposed to a nuclear blast. Nonetheless, while that may be true, Zechariah was clearly

---

[493] Ez. 38:21, Rev. 6:12-17

not prophesying of a future nuclear exchange. Instead, he was describing something far more powerful. He was describing the horrifically devastating effect that the unveiled radiant-majesty of the Lord will have on all those who'll have fought against Jerusalem and all who will have foolishly gathered to resist the Lord when He triumphantly returns to earth. A thorough study of **Zec. 14:1-15**, combined with everything we've learned thus far, should make this abundantly clear.

~ So, what about the feast for fowls? ~

Zechariah specified that only the flesh of those who will have fought against Jerusalem will ***'consume away while they stand on their feet.'*** That means that not every citizen of Satan's beastly empire will be instantly incinerated when the Lord returns, only those who will have fought against Jerusalem. That leaves several millions who will have been killed by the global earthquake and by panic-stricken Left-behinders trying to hide from the fearsome presence of the Lord, who will not have been instantly incinerated. Hence, it's in reference to the carcasses of those individuals that, in **Rev. 19:17-18**, John recorded seeing the angel beckoning all the fowls of the air to come and engorge themselves on the flesh of:

> ***'kings, and the flesh of captains, and the flesh of mighty men, and the flesh of horses, and of them that sit on them, and the flesh of all men, both free and bond, both small and great.'***

While examining Jesus' prophecy about His future return to earth, we learned that He also referred to this event:

> *'For as the lightning cometh out of the east, and shineth even unto the west; so shall also the coming of the Son of man be.* ***For wheresoever the carcase is, there will the eagles be gathered together****.'*

Mt. 24:28

Jesus' words reveal two significant facts. First, when Jesus returns it won't be in secret, but, rather, it will be like an electrical storm, ***'every eye shall see him.'*** [494] And, second, the fowls will gather to eat the carcasses of the dead. Jesus' reference to the eagles (*i.e., eagles, vultures, hawks and the like*) being gathered at His return irrefutably ties this prophecy to what John recorded seeing in **Rev. 19:17-18**. Thus, when we put together all that we've learned, it becomes clear that, upon His return, the Lord intends

---

[494] Rev. 1:7, 6:12-17

to use the ***'fowls of the air'*** and the ***'beasts of the field'*** to cleanse the post-tribulation period earth of all remaining dead and putrefying flesh.

'Thou {Gog} shalt fall upon the mountains of Israel, thou,
and all thy bands, and the people that is with thee:
I will give thee unto the ravenous birds of every sort,
And to the beasts of the field to be devoured.'

℘ Ez. 39:4 ℘

No time for formalities . . . .

Rev. 19:19-21

'And I saw the beast *(all the fallen-angels)*, ***and the kings of the earth, and their armies, gathered together to make war against him that sat on the horse*** *(Christ Jesus)*, ***and against his army.***

And the beast was taken, and with him the false prophet that wrought miracles before him, with which he *(the false prophet)* ***deceived them that had received the mark of the beast, and them that worshipped his image. These both were cast alive into a lake of fire burning with brimstone.'***

'And the remnant *(those in the Valley of Megiddo who will not be instantly cast into the lake of fire)* ***were slain with the sword of him that sat upon the horse*** *(Jesus)*, ***which sword proceeded out of his mouth: and all the fowls were filled with their flesh.'***

Since the Lord certainly will not allow hundreds of millions of demons to roam the earth during His millennial reign, according to John's vision, when Jesus triumphantly returns to begin His thousand year reign on the earth, He will immediately cast *"the beast"* (*all the fallen angels*) and *"the false-prophet"* (*"Satan's global dictator," "the anti-Christ," "the blasphemous mouth of the beast"*)[495] headlong into the eternal lake of fire.[496] Their judgment will be so swift that they won't even be allowed to stand before the Great White Throne and be judged! Thus, of the powers of darkness, only Satan will be left, and we're about to read that he will be bound in the

[495] Dan. 7:20-27, Rev. 13:5
[496] *"Outer darkness"* and the *"Lake of Fire"* are references to the same eternally destitute, physically and spiritually dark place, a place of eternal suffering and damnation—Mt. 8:12, 22:13 and 25:30.

bottomless pit throughout Christ's thousand year reign on earth. There's just no other logical interpretation for what John recorded in the preceding verses, and I'll explain why.

If the preceding verses (*Rev. 19:19-21*) are not a prophetic record of God's final judgment of both Satan's demonic army of fallen angels (*"the beast"*)[497] and also of that wicked false-prophet (*the man of sin, the son of perdition—2Th. 2:3-12*), then, as was stated earlier, the Scriptures give no clear explanation as to the eternal fate of all of those hundreds of millions of evil, spiritual beings (*the fallen angels*). That's a big deal, because we're about to learn that there is no scriptural indication that those demonic beings will be bound in the bottomless pit, with Satan, during that Millennial Period. What's more, as we've learned and will continue to learn while moving ahead through the final chapters of John's vision, the Scriptures give a clear accounting of the eternal fates of all spiritual beings (*angels as well as humans*), without leaving anything to our imagination or supposition. So, if these verses are not a record of God's final judgment and punishment of Satan's army of fallen angels (*the powers of darkness, the beast*) then no record exists, and we're left wondering or guessing as to what their eternal fate will be. That unlikely possibility would be utterly contrary to how God has revealed the other details of His perfect plan thus far.

~ *So, why has this always been so hard to understand?* ~

Since both Daniel's and John's end-time visions[498] allegorically allude to the kingdoms of this earth and to Satan's *past, present,* and *future* demonic influence on them by simply referring to those kingdoms as either four individual *"beasts"* (*as in Daniel's case*) or as one seven-headed *"beast"* (*as in John's case*), it's easy to understand how these verses could frequently be misinterpreted. Even so, as we've firmly established, it's not possible for the beast with seven heads in John's vision to be a mere mortal.

By now it should be quite clear that it could not be said of a man that he has existed in the *past*, and in the *present*, and will also exist in the *future* (*Rev. 17:1-11*), or that he will one day emerge from the depths of the bottomless pit. What's more, the beast is said to currently be the *"eighth kingdom"* and to be ***'<u>of the seven</u>*** *(kingdoms)* ***and goeth into perdition'*** *(17:11)*. Only an army of supernatural beings (*fallen angels, the powers of darkness*) could exist in the *past, present,* and *future* and more powerfully emerge (*in the later-days*) from the spiritual recesses of the bottomless pit and vicariously rule the world through a subordinate leader — *"a false-prophet."*

---

[497] 2Pt. 2:4, Jude 6, Rev. 12:4 and <u>7-9</u>
[498] Dan. 7, Rev. 13,14,15,16 and 17

Therefore, based on a straightforward, logical assessment of everything we've learned from Scripture – "AS A WHOLE" – it should be quite clear that *"the beast"* John saw being cast into the lake of fire with the *"false-prophet"* (*Rev. 19:20*) is the same *"seven-headed beast"* on which John had seen *"the whore"* (*idolatry*) in **Rev. 17:1-6** sit. And that symbolic *"whore"* is intended to represent the incessant, evil influence that Satan and the powers of darkness (*the fallen angels*) have had on all past and present kingdoms of the earth. This is why she (*the whore, who was seen seated on the seven-headed beast*) was said to be:

> ***'. . . drunken with the blood of the saints, and with the blood of the martyrs of Jesus . . . .'***

The following scriptures give us a little additional insight as to the existence and ultimate judgment of all those fallen angels:

*'For if God spared not the angels that sinned, but cast them down to hell, and delivered them into chains of darkness, **to be reserved unto judgment** . . . .'*

꧁ 2Pt. 2:4 ꧂

*'And the angels which kept not their first estate, but left their own habitation, he hath reserved in everlasting chains under darkness unto **the judgment of the great day**.'*

꧁ Jude 6 ꧂

Jesus' gloriously triumphant return to earth, at the end of this horrific seven year period, with all His angels and saints, will be that great and dreadful day of judgment for Satan's entire army of fallen-angels, the powers of darkness, the beast!

*'For **the great day of his wrath is come**; and who shall be able to stand?'*

꧁ Rev. 6:17 ꧂

Chapter 40

The Thousand Year Reign of Christ

At this point in John's vision *"the beast"* (*all the fallen-angels*) and the false-prophet (*the anti-Christ or son of perdition*) will have already been cast ***'alive into the lake of fire.'*** [499] That means that only Satan will be left to deceive the surviving mortal inhabitants of the earth, but he won't get the chance — at least not until the end of Christ's thousand year reign on earth.

Bound for a thousand years . . . .

Rev. 20:1-3

> ***'And I saw an angel come down from heaven, having the key of the bottomless pit and a great chain in his hand.***
>
> ***And he laid hold on the dragon, that old serpent, which is the Devil, and Satan, and bound him a thousand years,***
>
> ***And cast him into the bottomless pit, and shut him up, and set a seal upon him, that he should deceive the nations no more, till the thousand years should be fulfilled: and after that he*** *(he alone)* ***must be loosed a little season.'***

While it may be hard to imagine an actual bottomless pit opening in the crest of the earth, I'm not prepared to label this passage purely allegorical. Let's not forget the fifth trumpet-plague of locusts. After that fifth angel sounded his trumpet, John recorded seeing ***'a star'*** (*an angel*) fall from heaven, who, likewise, was given a key to the bottomless pit. With that key, John saw the angel release countless locusts, which, as we've learned, will cover the earth and torment the Left-behinders for five agonizing months during the first half of the tribulation period. Those locusts will be both physically and spiritually real beings, and, as John was told, they'll emerge from somewhere deep within ***'the bottomless pit.'*** [500] Therefore, an actual hole or opening in the crust of the earth isn't entirely out of the question.

---

[499] Rev. 17:1-8, 19:19-20

[500] Rev. 9:1-11

As a matter of fact, it's possible that after seeing Jesus cast *"the beast"* and the *"false-prophet"* alive into the lake of fire, John next saw that same angel, who had earlier released the plague of scorpion-tailed locusts, descend, once more, with ***'a great chain,'*** and bind Satan to the side wall of that same bottomless pit. Perhaps this is to what Isaiah was referring when he prophesied the following:

> *'How art thou fallen from heaven, O Lucifer, son of the morning! how art thou cut down to the ground,* ***which didst weaken the nations****! For thou hast said in thine heart, I will ascend into heaven, I will exalt my throne above the stars of God {*the Heavenly host, angels*}: I will sit also upon the mount of the congregation, in the sides of the north: I will ascend above the heights of the clouds; I will be like the most High.* ***Yet thou shalt be brought down to hell****,* ***to the sides of the pit****. They that see thee shall narrowly look upon thee, and consider thee, saying,* ***Is this the man that made the earth to tremble****,* ***that did shake kingdoms****;* ***That made the world as a wilderness****, and destroyed the cities thereof; that opened not the house of his prisoners?*

Isaiah 14:12-17

Whether we lean towards believing in a literal interpretation of the bottomless pit or not, it wouldn't be wise to take too firm a stance while attempting to interpret these prophecies, because until they're actually fulfilled we just won't know how much (*if any*) of what John witnessed in this part of his vision was allegorical. What's important to note is that the whole world will enjoy one thousand years of complete freedom from the effects of Satan — *"the prince of the power of the air"* [501] — and all his evil principalities and powers of darkness. The question I have is:

> Since Jesus is going to cast all the fallen angels and the false-prophet into the lake of fire the very instant He returns to judge the earth, why isn't He going to do the same to Satan, instead of just temporarily binding him to the inside of the bottomless pit?

The answer to that question — and it's a very good question — is likely the same as the answer to the following question: *"Why did God let Satan*

[501] Eph. 2:1-10, 6:12

enter the Garden of Eden and allow him to tempt Adam and Eve into rebelling against His direct command?" Before we've finished this portion of John's vision, the answers to these questions will likely emerge.

The Lamb of God will finally Rule the Earth

> *'When the Son of man shall come in his glory,* ***and all the holy angels with him, then shall he sit upon the throne of his glory:***[502] *And before him shall be gathered all nations: and he shall separate them one from another, as a shepherd divideth his sheep from the goats:* ***And he shall set the sheep on his right hand, but the goats on the left.***[503] *Then shall the King say unto them on his right hand, Come, ye blessed of my Father, inherit the kingdom prepared for you from the foundation of the world . . .'*

Mt. 25:31-34

The preceding verses are only the first half of Jesus' message, yet it's easy to see that the Lord intends His millennial kingdom to be inherited only by those who'll have clung to the hope of salvation through faithfully surrendering their lives to His will. The following second half of Jesus' message bears this out. Speaking first to the righteous (*the saints*), Jesus said the following:

> *'. . . For I was an hungred, and ye gave me meat: I was thirsty, and ye gave me drink: I was a stranger, and ye took me in: Naked, and ye clothed me: I was sick, and ye visited me: I was in prison, and ye came unto me. Then shall the righteous answer him, saying, Lord, when saw we thee an hungred, and fed thee? or thirsty, and gave thee drink . . .' 'And the King shall answer and say unto them, Verily I say unto you,* ***Inasmuch as ye have done it unto one of the least of these my brethren, ye have done***

---

[502] Christ Jesus will sit on the throne of His glory when He returns to rule the earth during the Millennial Period. As we learned in the previous chapter, both saints and angels will triumphantly return with Christ to earth.

[503] Those who return with Christ will be *"the sheep."* All the inhabitants of the earth who survive Christ's return will have already chosen to receive the *"damnable mark of the beast."* Thus, they'll be *"the goats,"* and, as we'll sadly see, they'll have no hope of salvation.

__it unto me__.' 'Then shall he say also unto them on the left hand, __Depart from me__, __ye cursed__, __into everlasting fire__, __prepared for the devil and his angels__: For I was an hungred, and ye gave me no meat: I was thirsty, and ye gave me no drink . . . '[504]

℘ **Mt. 25:35-37** & **40-42** ℘

The First Resurrection

There will be mortal survivors of the tribulation period who will succeed in totally repopulating the earth, but they'll all bear the damnable mark of the beast.[505] That being the case, it should be obvious that Christ's Millennial Period Kingdom will not have been prepared as a reward for those who survive the tribulation period nor for their descendants, and the following verse makes that truth painfully clear.

Rev. 20:4

'And I saw thrones, and they sat upon them, and judgment was given unto them: and <u>I saw the souls of them that were beheaded for the witness of Jesus</u>, <u>and for the word of God</u>, and which had not worshipped the beast, neither his image, <u>neither had received his mark upon their foreheads</u>, <u>or in their hands</u>; and they lived and reigned with Christ a thousand years.'

The preceding verse is merely a confirmation that *"the remnant"* (*those who will refuse to take the mark of the beast and, instead, choose to hold on to their new found hope of salvation through Christ*), will live and reign with the rest of the saints for a thousand years. Unfortunately, however, many have mistakenly taught that the resurrection of those saints will occur at the end of the tribulation period, when Jesus returns to earth. Nonetheless, as we made our way through **Rev. 15:1-8**, we learned that those saints will be martyred and resurrected long before the tribulation period ends. In those verses, the angel of the Lord was careful to make it clear to John that all who get the victory over the beast (*by refusing to take his damnable mark*), will be resurrected before a single drop of God's wrath is poured out! This will happen before Jesus returns to earth, and when those souls

---

[504] We all know the rest of the passage. When Jesus finished, He explained that all those on His left will go away into everlasting punishment. The resurrection of those souls will not occur until the end of the Millennial Period and will be the final resurrection, a resurrection unto death — *"the second death"* (*Rev. 20:6-14*). The righteous, however — those on His right — will inherit eternal life.

[505] Rev. 13:14-17

are resurrected, at that moment, for the very first time the entire family of God will be together in Heaven.[506]

Thus, the resurrection of *"the remnant"* will complete what is referred to in the next few verses as: ***'the first resurrection.'*** Only those who will have been resurrected or raptured prior to Christ's return to earth (*His Second Coming*) will be considered part of that ***'first resurrection'*** and, therefore, live and reign with Christ in new immortal bodies[507] — not only throughout the Millennial Period but for all eternity as well.[508] This makes perfect sense, because, when Jesus returns to judge the earth, He'll be returning triumphantly, with His *"bride"* (*which includes all saints*) and all the angels to begin His eternal reign.[509]

Rev. 20:5-6

> ***'But the rest of the dead lived not again until the thousand years were finished. <u>This is the first resurrection</u>.***
>
> ***<u>Blessed and holy is he that hath part in the first resurrection</u>: on such the second death hath no power, but they shall be priests of God and of Christ, <u>and shall reign with him a thousand years</u>.'***

The clear implication from the preceding verses is that *"the second death"* (*eternal damnation*) "**will**" have power over all those who are not part of *"the first resurrection"* (*i.e., all those who will not have returned to earth with Christ at the end of the tribulation period*). To briefly recap, over the course of our end-time journey, we've learned that, in this passage, when John wrote of ***'the first resurrection,'*** he was actually referring to a combination of <u>four</u> separate, mass-resurrections. The first of which was recorded by Matthew and occurred sometime soon after Christ's resurrection.[510] The second mass-resurrection (*the Rapture*) will be the largest of the four and will include the resurrection and catching away of all Old and New Testament saints, from the creation of Adam to the beginning of the

---

506 Rev. 13:15-17, 15:1-7, 20:4

507 1Cor. 15:42-54, Rev. 15:1-7

508 This is why the angel told John in the next verse that only those who return with Christ {*'the first resurrection'*} will be immune to eternal damnation—*"the second death."* The revelation of this is just ahead.

509 Jude 14-15, Joel 2:1-11

510 It's possible that those who were part of that particular resurrection may not have been resurrected to immortality; thus, they may have lived out the remainder of their lives and died, as did Lazarus. If that's the case, those souls will be resurrected with the rest of us when the Church is raptured, as will Lazarus. The Scriptures just aren't clear on this point—Mt. 27:52-53

tribulation period (*1Th. 4:13-17*). Next, 3½ days after the abomination of desolation takes place, God's two witnesses will be resurrected. Their resurrection will not, however, be a mass-resurrection. The third mass-resurrection will be that of the 144,000 Jewish servants,[511] which (*as we've established*) will most likely occur at the same time as or very soon after God's two witnesses are martyred and resurrected. And, lastly, precisely as John recorded witnessing, just moments before God's wrath begins to be poured out, all those who will have been martyred for refusing to take the mark of the beast will be resurrected and caught-up to Heaven.[512] That means that every saint (*everyone who will spend eternity in the kingdom of God*) will be resurrected before the seven-year tribulation period ends, as part of "THE RESURRECTION OF LIFE" — "THE FIRST RESURRECTION."

> *'**Blessed and holy is he that hath part in the first resurrection**: on such the **second death** {eternal damnation} hath no power, but they shall be priests of God and of Christ, and shall reign with him a thousand years.'*

Rev. 20:6

> *'Marvel not at this: for the hour is coming, in the which all that are in the graves shall hear his voice, And shall come forth; **they that have done good**, **unto the resurrection of life** {the first resurrection}; and they that have done evil, unto the resurrection of damnation {the second death}.'*

John 5:28-29

Therefore, just as we earlier read (*Rev. 19:4-14*), the entire family of God (*i.e., the saints, the bride of Christ*)[513] will participate in Jesus' gloriously triumphant return to earth and in the subsequent *"Marriage Supper of the Lamb."*[514] What's more, we're about to learn that all those saints will continue reigning as kings and priests with God the Father, God the Son and God the Holy Spirit, not just during the afore mentioned Millennial Period, but also throughout all eternity as well!

---

511 Rev. 14:1-5
512 Rev. 15:1-8
513 Eph. 5:25-27, Rev. 19:7-9
514 Rev. 19:7-9

The Glorious Mountain of the Lord

The Lord's severely destructive return to earth will serve at least three purposes. First, it will eliminate all those who will have been foolish enough to think they could actually oppose Jesus' divine authority. Second, it will completely churn-up and recontour the earth's surface, so dramatically that Jerusalem will apparently become the highest elevation on the planet![515] And, third, it will reduce the desecrated tribulation period Temple (*the Third Temple*) to rubble, if it's still standing. I realize that this may sound too incredible to believe; even so, after we examine a few pertinent prophecies, we'll see that this is precisely what the Scriptures reveal.

> *'For, behold, I create* ***new heavens and a new earth****: and the former shall not be remembered, nor come into mind. But be ye glad and rejoice for ever in that which I create: for, behold, I create Jerusalem a rejoicing, and her people a joy.'*
>
> **Isaiah 65:17-18**

Because the preceding passage from Isaiah speaks of new heavens and a new earth, it has frequently been misinterpreted to be a reference to the future "NEW JERUSALEM," which will descend from Heaven (*after the Great White Throne Judgment has ended*) and eternally exist on a completely new planet.[516] However, a thorough study of Isaiah's entire message will reveal that Isaiah was not prophesying about that eternal city.[517]

~ So what's with the reference to new heavens and a new earth? ~

Let's start with the new heavens. In **Rev. 6:12-17**, John recorded a vision of Christ's future triumphant return to earth. Through that vision the angel revealed that during the end of the tribulation period the sun will become black, the moon will become as blood, and the stars will fall from the sky (*i.e., they'll cease to exist)*.[518] What's more, in their end-time visions, both John and Isaiah actually saw the sky roll together like a scroll.[519] That means that, immediately after Jesus returns to earth, the sun, moon, and

---

[515] We'll get to those Scriptures just ahead.

[516] 2Pt. 3:7-10, Rev. 20:11, 21:1

[517] Isa. 65:1-25

[518] During Christ's return to earth, not only will a global earthquake completely reshape the surface of the earth, but great hailstones (*each weighing about 75 to 100 lbs.*) will fall from the sky. During John's time, this would be understood as stars falling to the earth—Ez. 38:20, Mark 13:25, Rev. 6:1-17, 16:21.

[519] Isa. 34:4

all the stars (*i.e., the entire universe as we know it*) are going to be in serious need of God's creative handiwork. In short, the earth is going to need a completely new atmosphere.[520]

Now let's deal with Ezekiel's reference to a New Earth

Prophesying about the Lord's return to judge the earth, Ezekiel wrote that there will be ***"a great shaking in the land of Israel,"*** such a mighty shaking that:

> *'. . . the fishes of the sea, and the fowls of the heaven, and the beasts of the field, and all creeping things that creep upon the earth, and all the men that are upon the face of the earth, shall shake at my {*the Lord's*} presence, **and the mountains shall be thrown down, and the steep places shall fall, and every wall shall fall to the ground**.'*

Ez. 38:20

Ezekiel's prophecy clearly includes every mountain and steep place on earth and every creeping thing (*including every man on the planet*) — not solely those in Israel. Therefore, without a scriptural reason for doing so, we shouldn't assume that Ezekiel's words only indicate a local, Judea-centric, event. We should also note that Ezekiel having thus prophesied that ***'every wall will fall to the ground'*** does not exclude the Third Temple in Jerusalem. According to the Hebrew text and several other end-time scriptures, the translators of Ezekiel's prophecy got it right. This global earthquake will be so powerful that ***"every mountain"*** — all around the world — and every single wall will be brought down! Furthermore, as we read earlier, Zechariah prophesied that when the Lord returns to earth . . .

> *'. . . his feet shall stand in that day upon the mount of Olives, Which is before Jerusalem on the east, and the mount of Olives shall cleave in the midst thereof toward the east and toward the west, **and there shall be a very great valley**; and half of the mountain shall remove toward the north, and half of it toward the south.'*

Zec. 14:4

---

520 Let's keep in mind that many of what we refer to as being *"stars"* are, in fact, distant galaxies. Thus, the universe will no longer exist as it does today.

Hence, the earthquake will be so powerful that the whole mountain will split in two and become separated by several miles of valley, which will be lifted up to create the new mountain plain of Jerusalem (*Zec. 14:10-11*). Imagine how massive this earthquake will have to be in order to have this effect! Zechariah continued, explaining that Jerusalem and a massive portion of the land around it will be "*lifted up*" so as to become one enormous plateau.[521] That plateau is where the new fourth and final Temple will be built.[522] This will be necessary because, according to Ezekiel 40 thru 47, this Millennial Period Temple will be significantly larger than any previous Temple. What's more, specific portions of that structure will actually be three stories high![523]

> *'But in the last days it shall come to pass, that **the mountain of the house of the LORD shall be established in the top of the mountains**, and **it shall be exalted above the hills**; and people shall flow unto it. And many nations shall come, and say, Come, and **let us go up to the mountain of the LORD**,[524] and to the house of the God of Jacob; and he will teach us of his ways, and we will walk in his paths: for the law shall go forth of Zion, and the word of the LORD from Jerusalem.'*

Micah 4:1-2

Though it may seem possible that only the mountains in and around Israel will be made lower than the future plateau of Jerusalem, since this earthquake will be globally devastating, it's more reasonable to take the scriptures at face value and conclude that every mountain on earth will be lowered — just as Micah, Zechariah, Ezekiel and John prophesied.[525]

But - "No Mountains!" - Really?!

Thus far, the mountain ranges around the globe have served as national security barriers, and in some cases they've even served to minimize the effects of severe weather. During the Millennial Period, however, under a universal atmosphere of peace, mountain barriers will no longer be needed. In fact, large mountain ranges would actually be a hindrance to the

---

[521] Zec. 14:9-11, Mic. 4:1-2
[522] Ez. 40 thru 47
[523] Ez. 41:6
[524] Incidentally, this prophecy from Micah is almost identical to Isaiah 2:2-4. To fully grasp this, it's important to thoroughly study Zechariah 14:1-11.
[525] Mic. 4:1-2, Zec. 14:3-21, Ez. 38:20-22, Rev. 6:12-17, 16:17-21.

inhabitants of the earth, who will immediately begin to reshape the earth into vast farming and grazing lands and will need to make regular ascents to the new Mount Jerusalem in order to observe mandatory holy convocations.[526] What's more, because illness and infant death will become nearly nonexistent, the global population will soar to formerly unthinkable numbers, eventually requiring a great deal more habitable land.[527]

The Lord will need to Sanctify the surface of the Earth

Currently, the earth is covered with many blasphemous edifices, including: idols, pagan temples, shrines, brothels, and all manner of pornographic and cultic materials, and that's only going to be worsened by the reign of the false-prophet. Thus, this massive, global earthquake will be necessary in order to facilitate the complete "sanctification by demolition" of every structure through tectonically "churning-up" the surface of the earth and burying every abominable creation of man. In essence, this earthquake will cleanse the earth of man's massive sinful footprint, thus, preparing it for habitation by the Ever-Holy — "KING OF KINGS AND LORD OF LORDS."

Additionally, from a geologic and agricultural perspective, the crust of the earth is currently divided into about twelve major and three minor tectonic plates. The constant movement of those plates (*more recently referred to as "Plate Tectonic Recycling"*), combined with God's amazingly effective *"Hydrologic Cycle"* — serves to re-fertilize and enrich the soil and surface of the earth, including all the oceans and seas. Consequently, an earthquake of this global magnitude would greatly aid in the rejuvenation and restoration of the new millennial kingdom of Christ.

The healing waters of the Lord will heal the Earth

*'And it shall be in that day, that **living waters shall go out from Jerusalem**; half of them toward the former sea, and half of them toward the hinder sea: in summer and in winter shall it be. **And the LORD shall be king over all the earth**: in that day shall there be one LORD, and his name one.'*

Zec.14:8-9

---

[526] Supporting Scriptures: Isa. 2:2-4, Jer. 3:16-17, Joel 3:9-21, Zec. 8:3-7, 14:9-16.

[527] It's estimated that from the time of Christ until now, more than 100 billion people have populated the earth. During the Millennial Period (*with people living much, much longer—Isaiah 65:20*), amazingly, that number could double or even triple! Thus, by eliminating mountain ranges and re-contouring the earths' surface, a great deal more fertile, habitable land will be created.

Since, in the preceding passage, the word *"day"* could be interpreted to mean: *"period"* (*thus indicating an unspecified length of time*), it's a little hard to tell whether the healing waters of the Lord will begin to surge as soon as Jesus descends upon the Mount of Olives (*causing it to split in two*) or if the waters will begin to flow after the new Millennial Period Temple has been built.[528] Whichever the case, once the Lord establishes His permanent Temple on the top of that newly raised plain of Jerusalem (*which will be a massive plateau*),[529] according to Ezekiel (*Ez. 47:1-12 and Zec. 14:8*), healing waters will begin to flow both eastward and westward from under the eastern threshold of the enormous fourth and final Temple. The easterly flowing waters will run down the mountain and into the desert (*a place formerly known as Shittim and currently considered to be located just north of the Dead Sea*); then they'll continue southwardly until they reach the sea. Thus, the *Dead Sea* will be healed, and, apparently for the first time, that formerly lifeless sea will abound with a great multitude of fish.[530] The westward flowing waters will make their way down the new Mountain of the Lord and into the *Mediterranean Sea,* thus, healing it as well.

'And it shall come to pass, that every thing that liveth, which moveth, whithersoever the rivers shall come, shall live . . .'

Ez. 47:9

The Hebrew text indicates the previous passage to include both animal and plant life; therefore, apparently everywhere these waters flow, healing will take place. Since, presently, the *Dead Sea* is the lowest elevation on the planet and only microbial fungi and assorted forms of bacteria have been able to survive in its salty waters, and, given that **Ezekiel 47:8-10** tells us that after being healed the *Dead Sea* will team with multitudes of fish, it would seem that either the sea will need to be stocked with new fish or the Lord intends to miraculously furnish the sea with fish when He heals it.

Just a Thought:

When the healing waters reach the *Mediterranean Sea,* it's possible that they'll continue flowing westward, across the sea, through the *Strait of*

---

528 Considering that the entire planet will be in an unspeakably dreadful bloody, smelly state when the Lord returns to earth, I can't imagine the Lord not immediately beginning the process of miraculously cleansing the planet so as to make it fit for habitation. That, however, is just my opinion. It's not provable, but it may explain the need for a global earthquake coinciding with Jesus' return.

529 Zec. 14:7-11

530 Ez. 47:8-12

Gibraltar and out to the *North Atlantic Ocean.* From there, the waters could easily reach virtually every major body of water on the planet. And, thanks to God's awesome global hydrologic cycle, the healing waters in the seas and oceans could easily be converted into vapor and released as rain over all the earth. This would immediately facilitate the regeneration of both animal and plant life, which may (*and, perhaps it's a big "may"*) at least partially explain how the bloody ocean waters, beaches, lakes, reservoirs, and chard forests, all around the world, will be healed (*Rev. 16:3-7*). We should also take into consideration the fact that the Second Coming earthquake will be so globally devastating that the Lord will have to preserve both human and animal life so as to prevent total annihilation of both man and beast. Therefore, we can safely conclude that the contours of the land, the oceans, and all seas will radically change throughout the earth.

Some very Special Trees

Not only will the waters of the *Dead Sea* be healed and the sea life commence to flourish, but new, very special fruit bearing trees of various sorts will begin to grow all along the banks of the healing waters river.

> *'And by the river upon the bank thereof, on this side and on that side,* ***shall grow all trees for meat*** *{all fruit bearing trees}, whose leaf shall not fade {the leaves will not change color, fade or fall to the ground}, neither shall the fruit thereof be consumed: it shall bring forth new fruit according to his months,* ***because their waters they issued out of the sanctuary****: and the fruit thereof shall be for meat, and the leaf thereof for medicine.'*
>
> **Ez. 47:12**

The leaves of these special[531] trees will never die nor fall to the ground. Instead, they'll be used medicinally, by the mortals, to promote healing. The saints won't need healing. What's more, the trees will beautifully adorn the banks of the river, both eastward and westward, and will produce new, edible fruit every month.

The Repulsive Valley of Hamongog

After the Lord returns and avenges the shed blood of the saints and the descendants of Jacob, the former mountain and valley areas of Israel will

---

[531] Ezekiel's prophecy seems to indicate the possibility that the trees will only be special because they'll have been affected by the healing waters of the Lord—Ez 47:12 (*see the underlined portion of the above scripture*).

be littered with the decaying carcasses of *"Gog"* and all the other nations that will have foolishly followed him into the Valley of Megiddo (*Ez. 39:3-7*). Birds, feasting on the rotting flesh, will remove most of the fleshly remains, but the earth will still be an absolute mess! So, before any worship can begin, the land of Israel will need to be cleansed. To accomplish this, the Lord will direct the surviving descendants of Jacob to bury the remnants of the dead in the future *"Valley of Hamongog,"* which means: *"the multitude of Gog."* By this time, the earth will have changed so much that we can't really be certain just precisely where this valley graveyard will be, but it's presently considered to be located somewhere to the east of the *Dead Sea*.

According to **Ez. 39:11-16**, after the Lord triumphantly returns to judge the earth, the initial task of burying the dead will take seven months, and the stench of that valley (*Hamongog*) will be so pungent that those who pass by will plug their noses. At the end of that initial seven month period, Israelite men (*mortals, not saints*) will be commissioned to wander about the land in search of any remaining fragments of bone. When found, the bones will be buried. Additionally, those who dwell in the land and those passing through will be instructed to erect a stone or monument of some kind if they should happen upon a previously undiscovered bone. This will make it possible for the searchers to find the bone and bury it with the others. Thus, the land of Israel will be thoroughly cleansed.

That's a Lot of Weapons

> *'And they that dwell in the cities of Israel shall go forth, and shall set on fire and burn the weapons,* ***both the shields and the bucklers, the bows and the arrows, and the handstaves, and the spears****, and they shall burn them with fire seven years . . .'*
>
> ℘ **Ez. 39:9** ℘

Because so many weapons of war will be leftover from the battle of Armageddon, the people of Israel won't need to gather any wood or cut down any trees. In fact, for seven full years, city dwellers will use only the remnants of those weapons for fire wood (*Ez. 39:10*), which brings to mind an important point. Most modern weapons are fabricated using various metals and composites; thus, burning them would be toxic. That won't be the case with the rudimentary, medieval-style, mostly wooded weapons that will be fabricated during the tribulation period. This may serve to confirm our earlier assertion, which suggested that immediately after the tribulation period begins the world will be thrust into what will soon become a perpetually primitive state of existence, during which fabricating new, modern weapons of war will become impossible. Thus, as Ezekiel's prophecy reveals, during that period it will only be practical to fabricate simple, medieval, mostly wood and metal base weapons (*like, e.g., bows, arrows, hand staves, swords, shields, and spears*), which will not need precision, powder–actuated ammunition.

Who will be seated on Thrones during the Millennial Period?

As we earlier read, Jesus indicated that, during His millennial reign, He will sit on His throne of glory.[532] Unfortunately, after reading the following prophecy about the future Millennial Period Temple and the glory of God, the physical and spiritual significance of the Lord sitting on His throne of glory is a little hard to grasp:

> *'Afterward he brought me to the gate {the gate of the Millennial Period Temple}, even the gate that looketh toward the east: And, behold, the glory of the God of Israel came from the way of the east:* ***and his voice was like a noise of many waters****:* ***and the earth shined with his glory****.'*[533] ~ *'So the spirit took me up, and brought me into the inner court;* ***and****,* ***behold****,* ***the glory of the LORD filled the house****.'*

℘ Ez. 43:1, 2 & 5 ℘

The preceding verses certainly seem to be speaking of the Holy Spirit rather than the physical presence of Christ. However, let's take a look at another verse from a little further along in the same passage:

> *'And he said unto me, Son of man, the place of my throne,* ***and the place of the soles of my feet****, where I will dwell in the midst of the children of Israel for ever, and my holy name, shall the house of Israel no more defile . . .'*

℘ Ez. 43:7 ℘

---

[532] Mt. 19:28, 25:31-34

[533] Could this prophecy be referring to Jesus as the glory of the God of Israel, or will it be as it was when the Spirit of the Lord filled the Holy of Holies during the dedication of Solomon's temple? Either way, this prophecy does align with Zechariah's prophecy—Zec. 14:6-7. Zechariah wrote that, when the Lord returns with all the saints, *'the light shall not be clear, nor dark.'* Zechariah prophesied that during the evening it will be light.

'At that time ***they shall call Jerusalem the throne of the LORD****; and all the nations shall be gathered unto it, to the name of the LORD, to Jerusalem . . .'*

Jer. 3:17

The preceding two passages seem to indicate that the Lord will physically sit on a throne and dwell in the midst of the children of Israel; however, I doubt the Lord will do nothing more than sit on a throne inside the Holy of Holies. Let's not forget that Jesus is capable of being everywhere, at the same time, both physically and spiritually.

Rev. 20:4 *~ continued*

'And I saw thrones, and they sat upon them, and judgment was given unto them . . . .'

From both Rev. 20:4 and Mt. 19:28, we can infer that, during His millennial reign, at least twelve of Jesus' disciples will sit on subordinate thrones administering the Lord's authority over the twelve tribes of Israel:

'And Jesus said unto them {His disciples}, Verily I say unto you, That ye which have followed me, in the regeneration[534] when the Son of man shall sit in the throne of his glory, ***ye also shall sit upon twelve thrones****, judging the twelve tribes of Israel.'*

Mt. 19:28

The fact that Jesus' disciple will sit on twelve thrones judging the twelve tribes of Israel does not preclude other saints and patriarchs, like, for example, King David from being honored in the same way. According to **Ez. 47:13** thru **48:35**, during the Millennial Period the land of Israel will again be divided among the twelve tribes of Israel. At that time, David (*who is scripturally referred to as "the prince"*)[535] will rule over the entire nation of Israel as a type of *"prince-regent."* He'll do this under the authority of Christ, who, as we just read, will be seated[536] (*either physically, spiritually, or both*) in Jerusalem, on His throne of glory (*Mt. 19:28, 25:31-34*).

We should note that many brilliant theologians have varying views as to who will sit on the chief throne in Jerusalem during Christ's thousand year reign. Personally, after exhaustively studying all pertinent scripture, I believe Christ Jesus will rule the entire earth, while David will rule under

---

534 The regeneration is a reference to Christ's millennial reign.
535 We'll cover this as we continue—Ez. 37:25, 45:16-22, 46:2-18, 48:21-22.
536 Ez. 43:4-7

Christ, over the apostles and all Israel. Listed below is a wealth of scripture on the subject, which, without proper prayerful evaluation, could be interpreted to support either point of view:

Isa. 2:2-4, 9:6-7, 11:1-12, 65:17-25, Jer. 23:3-8, 30:7-9, Ez. 34:23-24, 37:24-28, Dan. 2:44-45, Has. 3:4-5, Mic. 4:1-3, Zec. 8:3-7, 14:6-2, Mt. 19:28, 25:31-34, Luke 1:32-33, Rev. 2:26, 20:4-10

~ So, who will survive to repopulate the earth? ~

Now that's a good question! Having studied everything the Scriptures reveal about the Lord's vengeful return to earth, it doesn't seem possible that anyone could survive and begin the process of repopulating the planet. Nonetheless, speaking of that calamitous end-time period of wrath being poured out on the earth, Jesus revealed the following:

> *'And* ***<u>except that the Lord had shortened those days</u>****,* ***<u>no flesh should be saved</u>****:* ***<u>but for the elect's sake</u>****, whom he hath chosen,* ***<u>he hath shortened the days</u>****.' {Given that John's vision clearly reveals that only those bearing the damnable mark of the beast will be on earth when Christ triumphantly returns, this is likely an indication that the Lord will shorten the tribulation period and the longevity of His plagues of wrath so as to enable a predetermined number of Left-behinders to survive.}*

Mark 13:20

We're learning from **Rev. 20:4-6** that only those who return to earth with Christ at the beginning of the Millennial Period (*the participants of what the angel speaking with John referred to as — 'the first resurrection' — Rev. 20:5-6*) can be considered to be ***'the elect.'*** It will be for those faithful saints that Jesus will allow various groups of Left-behinders to survive and repopulate the earth. Therefore, since the Lord has promised us a place in His Millennial Kingdom,[537] during which He will righteously rule the entire planet (*as the following scripture indicates*), we can logically conclude that at least a portion of the Left-behinders will survive Christ's violent return and, subsequently, repopulate the newly renovated earth.

But who will they be? Fortunately, it seems that the Lord may have given our big brother Ezekiel a vision that might give us some insight as to which group of Left-behinders will end up being the most prominent during that thousand year period.

[537] Dan. 7:13, 14 and 26, 27, Mt. 19:28, 25:31-34

'Thus saith the Lord GOD; Behold, I am against thee, O Gog, the chief prince of Meshech and Tubal:[538] *And I will turn thee back, {God will pull Gog back, towards the mountains of Israel.}* ***and leave but the sixth part of thee, and will cause thee to come up from the north parts, and will bring thee upon the mountains of Israel*** *. . .' {God will begin doing this sometime before the final battle of Armageddon begins.}*

ꟸ Ez. 39:1-2 ꟹ

Thanks to Ezekiel's prophecy, we know that God will preserve one out of six of the surviving descendants of Japheth (*specifically the descendants of Gog, Meshech and Tubal*) for the purpose of replenishing the earth during the Millennial Period. John confirms this interpretation in **Rev. 20:8** by referring to all those who will have repopulated the earth at the end of the Millennial Period as being ***'Gog and Magog.'*** This doesn't mean, however, that only Japheth's descendants will survive to repopulate the earth. In fact, there are many powerful prophecies that speak of the Lord gathering the descendants of Jacob back to Israel during the Millennial Period from all around the world.[539]

'And it shall come to pass in that day, that the Lord shall set his hand again the second time to recover the remnant of his people, which shall be left, from Assyria, and from Egypt, and from Pathros, and from Cush, and from Elam, and from Shinar, and from Hamath, and from the islands of the sea {in other words, the Lord will gather the descendants of Jacob from all over the world into the land of Israel}. And he shall set up an ensign {i.e., a banner of sorts} for the nations, ***and shall assemble the outcasts of Israel, and gather together the dispersed of Judah from the four corners of the earth****.'*

ꟸ Isaiah 11:11-12 ꟹ

{The preceding prophecy is just one of many such prophecies regarding the regathering of the descendants of Jacob back into Israel during the Millennial Period.}

---

538 As I've stated, I don't currently believe it can be conclusively proven that—*Gog, Meshech and Tubal*—is a reference to any specific nation or group of people. That being said, we can scripturally deduce that, whoever these people are, they're currently flourishing somewhere in a land north of Israel—Ez. 38 & 39.

539 Isa. 11:11-16, Jer. 23:3-8, Has. 3:4-5, Zec. 8:4-6

Chapter 41

A Final Magnificent Fourth Temple?

As I mentioned earlier, while Jesus sits on the throne of His glory, David will be established as a servant king — a "**prince-regent**" of sorts — over the twelve tribes of Israel:[540]

> *'And **David my servant shall be king over them**; and they all shall have one shepherd: they shall also walk in my judgments, and observe my {*the Lord's*} statutes, and do them.'*
>
> ꧁ **Ez. 37:24** ꧂

During his former earthly reign, David served only as King of Israel. When he returns with Christ at the start of the Millennial Period, however, Ezekiel prophesied that David (*'the prince'*) will serve as both king and priest.

> *'And **it shall be the prince's part** [541] to give burnt offerings, and meat offerings, and drink offerings, in the feasts, and in the new moons, and in the sabbaths, in all solemnities of the house of Israel: **he shall prepare the sin offering**, **and the meat offering**, **and the burnt offering**, **and the peace offerings**, to make reconciliation for the house of Israel.'*
>
> ꧁ **Ez. 45:17** ꧂

Obviously, the sin offerings won't need to be offered on behalf of the saints (*those who will have returned to earth with Christ*), who, unlike the mortals, will have already been transformed into eternally sinless beings.

---

[540] Ez. 37:25-28, Has. 3:4-5, Mt. 19.28, 25:31-34

[541] Ezekiel 34:23-28 and 37:24-25 specifically identify David as being the future *"prince"* and *"king"* over the house of Israel. Jeremiah 23:4-8 and 30:7-9 may also be helpful references.

However, according to **Zec. 14:16-21** and **Ez. 34:23-26**, all mortal survivors of the battle of Armageddon, from every nation (*each bearing the damnable mark of the beast*), will be required to annually go up the mountain of the Lord (*the new plateau of Jerusalem*) ***'to worship the King, the LORD of hosts'*** (*Jesus, not David*) and to keep *"the Feast of Tabernacles"* (*Sukkot, "the Feast of Booths"*). Those who fail to do so will initially have no rain in their land or on their crops. And, if a severe case of drought isn't enough to inspire the openly rebellious inhabitants of the earth to submit to the Lord's mandate, the Lord will ultimately respond to their open rebellion by smiting them with *"plague,"* which in this case means death!

That's right! Just as one would expect, some of the formerly God hating inhabitants of the earth, who will have chosen to receive the damnable mark of the beast rather than serve God, are going to be so eager to worship the Lord that the Lord will deem it necessary to impose an ultimatum (*a covenant of peace*) on them and on their offspring in order to force them to submit to worship. We'll address the dark reality of that later, but before we move on we need to address the following obvious question:

"Why will animal sacrifices need to be offered during the Millennial Kingdom of Christ, and for whom will they need to be offered?"

This is a much bigger, more spiritually significant question than it appears. In truth, it exposes such a sensitive subject that in order to do it justice I'd much rather address it prayerfully, on a *one-on-one* basis. Why do I say this? I say this because most of us have listened to a sermon or read a book, happily agreeing with the pastor or author nearly to the end, then, just when we thought all was well, the author threw out what we believed to be a truly *"off-the-wall"* theory or opinion that left us suddenly deflated and questioning the author's actual knowledge of the entire subject! Attempting to answer the question as to why there will be the need for animal sacrifices during the Millennial Period honestly and with complete scriptural integrity could evoke that same skepticism.

Unfortunately, in order to properly address this question, we are also forced to tackle the question of whether or not those who will be born during that period will have the opportunity to become saints. And that's where our ability to truly trust in God's unfailing righteousness will be put to the test. Nonetheless, if we're going to continue on our present course, claiming to totally trust in the righteousness of God and interpreting God's Word precisely as written (*even when we may not fully understand*), there's really no way to avoid recognizing some clearly established scriptural truths. So, rather than making a case for any particular perspective, I'll try (*although I'm not sure it's possible*) to continue doing as I've done thus far and objectively lay out just the relevant scriptural facts. However, if we're going to truly trust God, we must acknowledge the following:

~ *The Lord always does that which is holy and just, even though we may not fully comprehend the righteousness of His actions.* ~

Let's face it, while it's true that many of us have accepted Christ and are considered by God to be *"saints,"* we are still mortals; thus, we're limited to a *"mortal/spiritual"* way of thinking. I realize this sounds a little "science-fictionish," but we're still only carnal beings. That means we have limited knowledge and are, as of yet, incapable of fully understanding the depths of God's righteousness and mercy. Because Paul understood this, he wrote the following:

'***For now we see through a glass***, ***darkly***; *but then face to face:* ***now I know in part***; *but then shall I know even as also I am known.*'

1Cor. 13:12

Only after being resurrected anew will we be able to begin comprehending the full measure of God's unmerited mercy and grace toward the saints — *"the elect of God."* With this in mind, Paul also wrote:

'For who hath known the mind of the Lord that he may instruct Him . . .'

1Cor. 2:16

Sadly, over the years I've observed that many Christians unintentionally interpret Scripture based on their *"emotional assessment"* of the text, regardless of the facts. When we make that mistake we're revealing our inability to truly trust in the immutable holiness and righteousness of our Creator.

> 'For my thoughts are not your thoughts, neither are your ways my ways, saith the Lord. For as the heavens are higher than the earth, so are my ways higher than your ways, and my thoughts than your thoughts. - **Isaiah 55:8 and 9**

~ *Okay; so why the need for animal sacrifices?* ~

The author of Hebrews made it perfectly clear that sprinkling ***'the unclean'*** (*mortal beings*) with the sacrificial blood of bulls and goats does, in fact, ***'sanctifieth to the purifying of the flesh'*** (*Heb. 9:13*). In other words, properly offered animal sacrifices do serve to temporarily sanctify the flesh of sinful man. That, however, doesn't save or sanctify the inner man, the soul or spirit. Therefore, we must ask the question: *"During the Millennial Period, for whom and for what purpose will the animal sacrifices be offered?"* Animal sacrifices certainly won't need to be offered on behalf of the saints, and there is no logical scriptural explanation for them being offered on behalf of any newly born-again Christians (*assuming there will be any, which I'm not*).

Jesus made Full Atonement for all Sin

As was earlier stated, on the glorious day when Jesus (*our eternal High Priest*) made atonement for all the sin of the world by suffering a humiliating death on the cross, the massive veil in the inner Temple was ripped from top to bottom. That incredible event signified that full atonement had been made for all sin and that a new covenant of faith and trust in Christ had been established.[542] Thus, having firmly established a ***'new and living way'*** (*through the veil of His flesh*), our Savior made it possible for all who seek to be freely justified to boldly enter the throne room of grace (*the true Holy of Holies in Heaven*), through prayer, and be eternally forgiven.[543] Hence, thanks to Jesus' sacrificial life, death, and resurrection, no longer was there any need to offer animal sacrifice, which, as the author of Hebrews clearly stated,[544] only served to ceremonially sanctify *"the flesh"* but could never sanctify (*make holy*) the *"inner-man"* (*the soul or spirit*).

> *'For the law having a shadow of good things to come, and not the very image of the things,* ***can never with those sacrifices which they offered year by year continually make the comers thereunto perfect****. For then would they not have ceased to be offered?* ***because that the worshippers once purged should have had no more conscience of sins*** *{i.e., if they could permanently sanctify the soul, animal sacrifices would have only had to be offered once}.'*

Hebrews 10:1-2

Therefore, if Jesus' death and atonement somehow failed to thoroughly and eternally sanctify all believers in Christ and animal sacrifice is still necessary in order to complete our sanctification, we can be certain that both Christ and the apostles would have instructed the early Church to continue in that practice. But that's not what happened. Instead, the apos-

542 Mt. 27:51, Heb. 8 thru 10
543 Ex. 25:8-9, Heb. 8:1-5, 10:10-23, Rev. 11:19
544 Heb. 9:1-14

tles taught quite the opposite. Paul, writing to the Christians at Galatia, admonished the early church with the following words:

> *'Knowing that a man is not justified by the works of the law, but by the faith of Jesus Christ, even we {the Jews} have believed in Jesus Christ,* ***that we might be justified by the faith of Christ****, and not by the works of the law:* ***for by the works of the law shall no flesh be justified****.'*

℘ Gal. 2:16 ☙

Observance of animal sacrifice and strict adherence to the law cannot justify the soul. If it could, there would have been no need for Christ to offer Himself as the atonement for all sin. In truth, Jesus' blood so completely satisfied the law of God that no other form of sacrifice will ever be needed. Jesus openly signified this eternal truth just before dying by uttering the words: "*... **It is finished** ...*"[545] And, as was stated earlier, God the Father powerfully confirmed this truth by ripping that massive, more than four inch thick,[546] veil barrier in the Temple in half!

There's still so much to Learn

Although many teach about the Millennial Period with great confidence and claim to have a firm grasp on its full spiritual significance, for most honest eschatologists (*me included*), the Millennial Period leaves a lot of questions unanswered. For instance, if, as some assert, the mortals who will repopulate the earth will be able to truly repent and be born-again, why will it be necessary for all mortals to continually observe annual animal sacrificial worship during the Millennial Period? If full justification and complete forgiveness of sin (*eternal salvation*) will be extended to the Millennials,[547] thus inspiring some to repent, won't they also instantly be filled with the Holy Spirit, as are those who repent and receive Christ today? And, if so, won't they also be instantly and completely sanctified, as are all truly born-again believers in Christ? And, if that's the case, since Jesus has already made full atonement for all sin, thereby forever sanctifying all who believe, why will it be necessary to offer animal sacrifices? Could it be (*as some may presume*) because the repentant mortals (*assuming there will be any*) will still be in carnal bodies and will, therefore, need

---

[545] John 19:30

[546] Some believe that veil to have been nearly 60 to 80 feet tall and as many as 12 inches thick!

[547] Hard as it may be to comprehend, all scriptural evidence indicates that that will not be the case.

to offer atonement for the sins of the flesh? If so, the same rationale would apply today, which would mean that those of us who've placed our faith in the blood atonement of Christ have not, as of yet, been thoroughly sanctified in the sight of God. Hence, if that were true, how could the Holy Spirit dwell within us, and why aren't we still offering animal sacrifices for our flesh?

I can't imagine a single Christian, after thoroughly studying Hebrews 8 thru 10, concluding that animal sacrifice on behalf of the saints will still (*in any way*) be necessary for their sanctification. Moreover, as I've stated, if a mortal were to be "born-again" during the Millennial Period, he or she would instantly be sanctified by the blood of Christ and the indwelling presence of the Holy Spirit. Thus, offering an animal sacrifice on their behalf would, in no way, serve to further their sanctification. If I'm mistaken, what then was the spiritual significance of God's having dramatically ripped the massive veil in the Holy of Holies from top to bottom after Christ finished making atonement for <u>all</u> sin? If having faith in the atonement of Christ so thoroughly sanctifies the soul of the believer in the sight of God that the Holy Spirit (*the Spirit of Holiness*) can instantly dwell within that soul, how could anything add to that sanctification?

~ So, what's the verdict? ~

Based on everything we've learned about the atoning blood of Christ, it's pretty obvious that the animal sacrifices, during the Millennial Period, will not be performed for the purpose of further sanctifying newly repentant Millennials (*should there be any, which I doubt*)[548] or the already immortal saints, who will have returned to earth with Christ and will be adorned in white raiment — the very symbol of the pure righteousness they'll have freely attained by trusting in the blood atonement of Christ.

That leaves only one logical, scripturally supportable explanation for the need to offer animal sacrifices during the Millennial Period. Animal sacrifices will serve to do precisely what they've always done; they'll temporarily sanctify the flesh of the Millennial Period mortals, so as to make it possible for them to participate in the observance of mandatory holy convocations and feasts. So much for my having maintained objectivity, right?

A truly sad state of Affairs

> *'And it shall come to pass, that every one that is left of all the nations* ***<u>which came against Jerusalem</u>*** *shall even go up from*

[548] You'll see why I doubt this before we finish this chapter of John's vision.

year to year to worship the King, the LORD of hosts, and ***to keep the feast of tabernacles****. And it shall be, that whoso will not come up of all the families of the earth unto Jerusalem to worship the King, the LORD of hosts,* ***even upon them shall be no rain****. {Although, initially, most mortals will willingly submit to worshipping Christ, this passage certainly doesn't give the impression that the mortals will continue to do so, does it?}*[549] *And if the family of Egypt go not up, and come not, that have no rain;* ***there shall be the plague, wherewith the LORD will smite the heathen that come not up to keep the feast of tabernacles****. This {death by plague} shall be the punishment of Egypt,* ***and the punishment of all nations that come not up to keep the feast of tabernacles****.'*

Zec. 14:16-19

According to Zechariah, the naturally rebellious mortals are going to be so eager to worship the Lord that at least some of them will have to be threatened with death to get them to do it! In the preceding passage that's precisely what *"plague"* means.

~ *But I thought the Millennial Period was going to be like Heaven!* ~

The Old Testament is filled with many wonderful prophecies about the Millennial Period, which on the surface could easily be interpreted to suggest that the world will experience an almost universal obeisance toward Christ and His divine authority. And, while those prophecies certainly seem to indicate a prolonged paradisiacal period, many of those prophecies have dual meanings, which have partially already been fulfilled or will be fulfilled by a combination of both tribulation period and Millennial Period events.

While this may be hard to comprehend, the truth is, if we suppress our emotions and allow the Bible to speak for itself, only a weak, scripturally constricted argument can be made to support the assertion that, during the Millennial Period, mortals will repent and be born into the eternal kingdom of God. In other words, there's absolutely no solid scriptural

549 Some believe the *"Feast of Tabernacles"* or *"Feast of Ingathering"* will be celebrated in recognition of the great harvests of souls, *'the first resurrection,'* — the resurrection of the saints. And, as we've learned, that resurrection will have concluded before the Millennial Period even begins—Rev. 20:6.

proof, not a single verse, that (*when properly interpreted*) irrefutably states that any of the Millennials will actually become saints.[550] What's more, if we were to try and make that argument, we would be forced to completely ignore all the scriptures we've already studied, which clearly reveal that, before the Millennial Period even begins, the Door of Salvation will have already eternally shut.[551] And, while this is certainly hard to comprehend, it's still true.

If we think back to the middle of John's vision, just prior to his witnessing the sounding of the seventh and final trumpet,[552] John heard a mighty angel[553] declare the following:

> ***"But in the days of the voice of the seventh angel, when he shall <u>begin</u> to sound, <u>the mystery of God should be finished</u>. . . ."***

While surveying that portion of John's vision, we learned that the mighty angel's proclamation is intended to reveal precisely when, during the tribulation period, the Lord's symbolic Door of Salvation will be eternally shut. Furthermore, we learned that if that isn't the purpose of the mighty angel's proclamation, then the angel's proclamation actually has no apparent significance at all! That fact just can't be ignored.

Consequently, in **Rev. 11:13-15**, John recorded hearing the seventh angel sound his trumpet immediately after seeing the last of the saints (*"the remnant"*) repent, *"giving glory to the God in heaven."* This coincided with the resurrection and ascension of God's two witnesses, which marked the end of the preaching of *"the Gospel"* — *"the Mystery of God."* Thus, when this actually happens, the revealing of God's formerly mysterious plan of salvation will be over. No one will ever preach the Gospel again! That's why, immediately after having witnessed *"the remnant"* repent, John heard the seventh angel sound his trumpet, thus signifying the fateful closing of the symbolic "Door of Salvation" — the end of the "Mystery of God." That's not an opinion. It's precisely what the mighty angel in John's vision proclaimed (*Rev. 10:1-7*), and there's simply no other scripturally supportable way to interpret the angel's words.

Furthermore, while making our way through John's vision, from the sounding of that seventh trumpet until now, we've found no scriptural evidence that could be interpreted or even manipulated into suggesting that the Door of Salvation will ever reopen. That's because, as Jesus taught, once closed, that door will never open again. In fact, if it were to open, it

---

[550] If this isn't clear, it would probably be helpful to review our assessments of Revelation 10 and 11

[551] Luke 13:23-28, Mt. 8:11-12

[552] Rev. 11:15-19

[553] Rev. 10:1-7

would make the mighty angel's proclamation false and Jesus a liar. And, as sad and hard to understand as this may be, we can't just choose to interpret these scriptures to suit our emotional needs. Moreover, the fact that animal sacrifices will need to be offered during the Millennial Period further confirms this truth. God's plan is perfectly righteous, whether we mortals are able to understand it or not! Let's not forget that the inhabitants of the earth, who will survive the tribulation period and fulfill the following prophecy from Isaiah, will all bear the damnable mark of the beast and will, therefore, have no hope of being forgiven for their sins:[554]

'And it shall come to pass in the last days, that ***the mountain of the LORD'S house shall be established in the top of the mountains and shall be exalted above the hills****;*[555] *and all nations shall flow unto it.*

And many people shall go and say, Come ye, and ***let us go up to the mountain of the LORD****, to the house of the God of Jacob; and he will teach us of his ways, and we will walk in his paths: for out of Zion shall go forth the law, and the word of the LORD from Jerusalem.*

And he shall judge among the nations, and shall rebuke many people: ***and they shall beat their swords into plowshares****,* ***and their spears into pruninghooks****: nation shall not lift up sword against nation, neither shall they learn war any more.'*

Isaiah 2:2-4

~ But, how do we know that the people in the preceding prophecy are not a future Millennial Period generation, who will not bear the damnable mark of the beast? ~

That's a good question! Both Micah (*Mic. 4:1-3*) and Isaiah prophesied about this initial phase of the Millennial Period, stating that these same individuals (*the survivors of the tribulation period*) will, ***'beat their swords into plowshares, and their spears into pruninghooks.'*** Those words

[554] Rev. 14:8-12

[555] These verses further establish the fact that the *"Mountain of the Lord"* will be the highest elevation on earth during the Millennial Period, and all the nations of the earth will regularly be required to ascend that mountain to worship—Mic. 4:1-3, Zec. 14:3-11.

clearly distinguish these individuals from all future generations of Millennial Period mortals (*whom we'll refer to as Millennials*), because (*precisely as Ezekiel prophesied—39:8-10*) only the first generation of Millennials (*those who will have survived the tribulation period and Second Coming of Christ*) will participate in the seven year process of burning and destroying the countless weapons of war.

THE PERPETUALLY SINFUL STATE OF MAN

As we're about to read, the Millennials (*who will completely repopulate the earth*) will have a limited measure of free will. And, even after having lived for a thousand years in perfect peace and prosperity, as soon as those mortal inhabitants of the earth are tempted to do so, they'll prove themselves to be no better than all those who died the last time God destroyed every thoroughly rebellious soul on the planet by flooding the earth.

> *'God saw that the wickedness of man was great in the earth, and that every* ***imagination of the thoughts of his heart was only evil continually****. And it repented the LORD that he had made man on the earth, and it grieved him at his heart. And the LORD said, I will destroy man whom I have created from the face of the earth . . . .'*

Genesis 6:5-7

The very instant Satan is released from the bottomless pit (*at the end of the thousand years*) he'll go up on the breadth of the earth and do just as he did to Adam and Eve when they lived in perfect peace and righteousness in the Garden of Eden. He'll convince every mortal on the planet (*and all estimates suggest that there will likely be many billions*) to rebel against the "KING OF KINGS AND LORD OF LORDS" and all the saints.

Rev. 20:7-9

> ***'And when the thousand years are expired, Satan shall be loosed out of his prison,***
>
> ***And shall go out to deceive the nations which are in the four quarters of the earth*** *(that means everybody)*, ***Gog and Magog,***[556] ***to gather them together to battle: the number of whom is as the sand of the sea .'***[557]

---

[556] Ez. 39:1-6

[557] John's words seem to suggest total complicity, not just a few insurgents.

> ***And they*** *(all the mortals from all over the world)* ***went up on the breadth of the earth, and compassed the camp of the saints about,***[558] ***and the beloved city: and fire came down from God out of heaven, and devoured them.***

For those of us who have a difficult time embracing the countless scriptures that clearly indicate that salvation will not be accessible during the Millennial Period, we must ask ourselves the following question:

"Can we honestly say that the preceding verses depict a global population of billions of adoring worshippers of Christ?"

For that matter, is it possible for us to extract from John's words even the "slightest hint" that any of the Millennials will refuse to participate in this global uprising? If this brazen act of unified, global rebellion and hatred towards God and the saints doesn't reveal how thoroughly prideful and rebellious man is when allowed to fully exercise "free-will," then I don't know what could![559] Without the Holy Spirit directly intervening in the lives of those who will repopulate the earth (*as He currently does in the lives of God's elect*),[560] the Millennials will eventually reveal their true, thoroughly sinful nature by following the same evil path of depravity and pride as did those who populated the earth during the Antediluvian Age.[561]

~ But what possible reason could the Millennials have for choosing to rebel? ~

During the beginning of Christ's one thousand year reign on earth, those who will have survived to repopulate the earth will have suffered through God's seven plagues of wrath and the powerfully destructive return of Christ. Prior to that, they'll have endured the heavy handed rule of the false-prophet and his beastly, global empire, an empire they will have grown to violently hate (*Rev. 17:15-17*). Therefore, at least initially, the mortals who survive that period will probably be happy, even grateful for the chance to live in and be a part of the new global kingdom of Christ. And why not?! During that one thousand year period, the earth, in many

558 The camp of the saints will consist of billions and will, therefore, be hundreds of miles in circumference. That means it will take a much larger army of mortals (*countless billions strong*) to encompass it.

559 Rom. 3:10-18, Mt. 19:17, Gen. 6:5-7

560 Ro. 8:14-17, Jn. 6:36, 37, 44, 64 and 65, Eph. 1:4, 2:8-10, Gal. 4:1-6, Mt. 16:17

561 This is a reference to the 1,656 year period prior to Noah's flood, though we probably shouldn't refer to the *"world-wide flood"* as being *"Noah's flood."* I mean, it isn't like Noah caused the flood by accidently leaving his garden hose running or something!

ways, will become, to the mortals who'll repopulate it, almost exactly what the Garden of Eden originally was to Adam and Eve — an absolute paradise! Both animal and man will live in harmony. Even a child wandering into a pack of wolves or putting his or her hand in a snake's den will have nothing to fear:

'And ***the sucking child shall play on the hole of the asp****, and the weaned child shall put his hand on the cockatrice' den.'*

℘ Isa. 11:8 ℘

'And I will make with them a covenant of peace, ***and will cause the evil beasts to cease out of the land****: and they {the inhabitants of the earth} shall dwell safely in the wilderness, and sleep in the woods.'*

℘ Ez. 34:25 ℘

'The wolf and the lamb shall feed together, and the lion shall eat straw like the bullock: and dust shall be the serpent's meat. They shall not hurt nor destroy in all my holy mountain, saith the LORD.'

℘ Isa. 65:25 ℘

Therefore, for those who survive the hellish existence of the tribulation period and the wrath of God, being governed by the Lord and His saints during the initial phase of the Millennial Period will be a welcome relief, which explains the reason for the many pleasant scriptural references to mortal life during Christ's one thousand year reign on earth. But eventually, as new generations of Millennials populate the earth and the tribulation period survivors die-off, the world will fall into the same sinful cycle as did Israel prior to the coming of Christ, when the tribes of Israel were governed by judges, prophets and kings:

- First, the people of Israel would reject God's laws and fall into sin
- Next, God would punish them with drought, famine, captivity and the like
- Then, after a period of prolonged suffering, fervent crying-out to God, and sincere repentance, the Lord would mercifully respond, reestablishing Israel to a right relationship with Him and each other
- Finally, the people would enjoy a period of willful submission to God, peace, and prosperity

❖ But, eventually, that generation would die off; the next generation would emerge; and the whole sinful cycle would begin again

Consequently, by the end of the Millennial Period, those who populate the earth won't have the slightest clue how good they've got it or how fierce the anger and vengeance of the Lord can be. So, when they are forced to leave their crops, businesses, and homes behind so they can make regular pilgrimages to the mountain of the Lord in Jerusalem, where sacrificial worship will be offered for the sanctification of their flesh,[562] they'll resent it! What's more, they'll want to sin and live as they please!

~ But, if Satan will be bound, why would the mortals still Sin? ~

In his letter to the Christians in Rome, Paul stated: '*. . . by the offense of one (Adam) judgment came upon all men to condemnation . . . .*'[563] That means that Adam's sinful nature will continue being carried down into every new-born child until the Millennial Period is over. Therefore, even without Satan's constant tempting, since the mortal citizens of the earth will physically be no different than all previous mortals, their irresistibly carnal nature and pride will eventually cause them to sin.[564] That's going to present a problem, because during the Millennial Period the Lord will not allow the citizens of His global kingdom to blatantly sin as did those who died in the flood. So, unless they're willing to face immediate punishment for their offenses,[565] the mortals will have to suppress those sinful desires. That's not going to be easy, and it certainly isn't going to inspire the mortals to love and adore the Lord and His saints, who'll be ruling the nations with a rod of iron.[566]

Thus, after a thousand years of forcibly submitting to the holy statutes of the Lord, the mortals will have completely forgotten the horrors of the tribulation period, and will probably be aching to get out from under the restrictive, watchful eye of the Lord so they can begin living as uninhibitedly as they wish. In order to do that, however, they'll first have to overthrow the Lord and His kingdom of angels and saints.

But, hey, if they'll have been sincerely worshipping Christ Jesus for a thousand years (*as some would have us believe*), how could they possibly be motivated to try and kill the Lord, their beloved "KING OF KINGS," the

---

562 Ez. 34:23-26, 37:24-28, 45:17, Heb. 9:1-14

563 Ro. 5:18

564 Ro. 3:10-18, 1Cor. 2:14, 3:3

565 Zec. 14:16-19, Isa. 2:1-5, 9:7, Rev. 2:26-27, Ps. 2:8-9

566 Rev. 2:26-27, Ps. 2:7-9

very object of their adoration? Perhaps the answer to that question is tied to the answer to our earlier question: *"Why, when Jesus returns to earth, won't He just immediately cast Satan into the lake of fire with all the other fallen angels and the false prophet?"*

Let's see if we can logically answer that Question.

When God allowed Satan to enter the Garden of Eden, by using nothing more than a few twisted words of deception, Satan was able to successfully expose man's greatest area of vulnerability — "PRIDE." After that, man's rapid descent from his original perfect state of being was inevitable. During the Millennial Period nothing will have changed. While Satan is bound (*for a thousand years*) in the bottomless pit, the mortals will recognize their inability to resist the divine power of God and will, therefore, either continue worshipping and paying lip-service to God (*in order to be recipients of rain and avoid being punished*)[567] or they'll rebel and be exterminated. But, just as John witnessed in his vision, the very instant Satan is released from the bottomless pit he'll aggressively rush about the earth tempting man to once again rebel against his Creator. Hence, one last time, the Lord will use Satan to reveal the truly evil heart of man.

> *'. . . for we have before proved both Jews and Gentiles, that they are all under sin; As it is written,* ***There is none righteous, no, not one****:* ***There is none that understandeth, there is none that seeketh after God****.*
>
> *They are all gone out of the way, they are together become unprofitable;* ***there is none that doeth good, no, not one****. Their throat is an open sepulchre; with their tongues they have used deceit; the poison of asps is under their lips:*
>
> *Whose mouth is full of cursing and bitterness:* ***Their feet are swift to shed blood****:* ***Destruction and misery are in their ways****:* ***And the way of peace have they not known****:* ***There is no fear of God before their eyes****.'*

℘ Romans 3:9-18 ℘

The preceding words reveal the thoroughly sinful nature of every mortal man. This is why Paul wrote that flesh and blood cannot inherit the

[567] Zec. 14:16-19

kingdom of God.[568] Without God's gracious intervention and sanctification, mortal beings are simply too wicked to enter the refiningly holy presence of the Lord. Perhaps (*and we won't know until the proper time*) the Millennial Period is God's way of revealing to the saints just how amazingly gracious His mercy towards those who receive it is!?

How could the mortals be so foolish?

There's no reason to believe that any of the survivors of Christ's powerful return to earth will still be alive when Satan is released from the bottomless pit at the end of the Millennial Period. Therefore, it's likely that the mortal inhabitants of the earth will have nothing more than a *"word of mouth"* knowledge of how terrifyingly destructive the righteous arm of the Lord can be. And, though fundamentally *"the curse"* will still be in effect throughout the entire Millennial Period,[569] the mortals will have enjoyed a thousand years of total, global peace, prosperity, and safety.

Therefore, just as John's vision reveals, despite having lived their entire lives under the peaceful, protective umbrella of the Lord, as soon as Satan is released from the bottomless pit and begins exercising his great power to tempt and deceive mortal man, the discontented mortal inhabitants of the earth, as one massive army of Millennials, will ferociously rebel! Thus, as we just read, like a wild pack of ravenous dogs, they'll viciously surround the camp of the saints, intending to attack.

JUST A QUICK THOUGHT:

John's having indicated that Satan and the Millennials will surround the camp of the saints and the beloved city doesn't necessarily indicate that the saints will perpetually reside around the base of the new "MOUNT JERUSALEM"[570] and the Temple. It's much more likely (*though not provable*) that the saints will gather in Jerusalem from all the regions of the earth and encamp around the Temple Mount as part of a massive, holy convocation. Hence, Satan and his vast army of Millennials will probably just take advantage of the saints' apparent vulnerability and surround their encampment. I say probably, because, thus far, I have found no further scriptural clarification. Whatever the case may be, I can't imagine that the saints will be oblivious to Satan's nefarious plans.

---

[568] 1Cor. 15:50

[569] Gen. 3:14 -19, Rev. 22:3

[570] Isa. 2:2-4, Jo. 3:15-18, Mic. 4:1-2, Zec. 14:4, 9-11, 16-17

Satan finally gets his just Reward

Rev. 20:9-10

> ***'And they** (all the mortals) **went up on the breadth of the earth, and compassed the camp of the saints about, and the beloved city: and fire came down from God out of heaven, and devoured them.***
>
> ***And the devil that deceived them was cast into the lake of fire and brimstone, where the beast and the false prophet are, and shall be tormented day and night for ever and ever.'***

The preceding verses bring to mind an important point of fact. Since this passage gives us absolutely no reason to believe or assume that any of the mortal inhabitants of the earth will choose not to participate in Satan's final act of rebellion, if (*as some suggest*) a significant number of mortals will have become heirs of salvation during the Millennial Period, how come we don't find any evidence of even a single mortal refusing to rebel? Instead, John and everything we've learned thus far seems to indicate that Satan will achieve total complicity among all the nations of the earth; so much so, in fact, that God the Father will have to send fire down from Heaven to completely dissolve the earth (*2Pt. 3:7-11, Rev. 20:11*) in order to exterminate this innumerable number of murderous insurgents!

Before moving on, we should acknowledge that the preceding verses make no mention of Satan's army of fallen-angels also being cast into the lake of fire, with Satan, when these events occur or of those fallen-angels emerging, with Satan, at the end of the thousand years. This is important to acknowledge, because, as was earlier stated in our discussion of **Rev. 19:19-20**, the very moment John witnessed the Lord return to earth (*at the beginning of the Millennial Period*), he saw *"the beast"* and the *"false-prophet"* being cast, live, into the eternal lake of fire. Then, John saw an angel bind Satan to the bottomless pit for a thousand years. Therefore, we must logically ask:

> "If the beast John witnessed being cast into the lake of fire when the Lord returned to earth is not an allegorical representation of Satan's immense army of fallen angels instantly being judged, where in Scripture do we find a clear, irrefutable account of that monumentally important event, and why are those fallen-angels not mentioned as being participants in this final, global act of rebellion?"

Chapter 42

The Great White Throne Judgment

> 'And I saw a great white throne, and him that sat on it, from whose face the earth and the heaven fled away; and there was found no place for them.' - **Revelation 20:11**

Though some surprisingly teach that when Christ's one thousand year reign on earth dramatically ends the earth will simply suffer a surface burn and be rejuvenated, Peter's following prophecy, like the preceding prophecy, clearly indicates that the heavens and the earth will be completely dissolved.[571] That means they'll no longer exist.

'But the heavens and the earth, which are now, by the same word are kept in store, reserved unto fire against the day of judgment and perdition of ungodly men.'

2 Peter 3:7

*'. . . **the day of the Lord**[572] **will come as a thief in the night**; in the which the heavens shall pass away with a great noise,[573] and the elements shall melt with fervent heat, the earth also and the works that are therein shall be burned up.'*

2Pet. 3:10

---

571 Rev. 21:4-5

572 As was earlier explained, *"the Day of the Lord"* will actually last about 1,007 years. How so? Only the rapture of the Church will come *'as a thief in the night.'* All other end-time events will be scripturally predictable. Therefore, according to 2Pt. 3:10 *"the Day of the Lord"* will commence with the instantaneous and unexpected rapture of the Church and end with *"the Great White Throne Judgment."*

573 Peter's reference to the heavens passing away with a great noise is likely a reference to the universe, including the earth, ceasing to exist. And, as we're about to see, God plans on making all things new.

No more 24 hour days

At this point in John's vision, the Millennial Kingdom of Christ will have ended, the heavens and the earth will have been dissolved, and Satan will have finally been cast into the eternal lake of fire. Thus, it will be time for all those who will not have been resurrected as part of the "**resurrection of life**" (*the first resurrection*)[574] to be resurrected. Hence when all of this actually occurs, it will do so very quickly, and it will mark the end of the final 24 hour day and the beginning of eternity. That means that it will be time to judge and eternally punish all lost and rebellious souls.

> *'And I saw the dead, small and great, stand before God; and **the books were opened**: **and another book was opened, which is the book of life**: and **the dead** {not the saints} **were judged out of those things which were written in the books**, according to their works. And the sea gave up the dead which were in it; and death and hell {a reference to earthly graves} delivered up the dead which were in them: and they were judged every man according to their works. **And death and hell** {all rebellious souls} **were cast into the lake of fire**. **This is the second death**. And whosoever was not found written in the book of life was cast into the lake of fire.'*

Revelation 20:12-15

This might take awhile

All those who choose not to humbly repent and receive Christ's free-gift of eternal life will have to give account for every sin they'll have committed, which Jesus said will include every idol word.[575] According to the preceding scripture, an accurate record of each of those sins, in book form, is currently being kept in Heaven, and all who've rejected Christ (*i.e., those whose names will not be found written in the Lamb's book of Life*) will be judged according to what is written in those books. That being the case, since God certainly isn't likely to suffer memory loss or any form of dementia, it's obvious that He's keeping a physical account of those sins so as to have a tangible record from which to adjudicate all rebellious souls on the day of judgment — not for His benefit, of course, but for theirs.

---

574 John 5:29, Rev. 20:4-6
575 Mt. 12:36

We're talking about a lot of books!

Stop for a minute and imagine how many thousands of books it would take just to create an accurate record of every sin you've committed. And, keep in mind, God's record of our sin would begin at our birth and be far more accurate than ours; thus, it would require many more volumes of books than we would likely imagine. Now imagine how many books it would take to record all the sins of every person in your immediate community, your state, your country. Starting to get the idea? If we extrapolate that out to every person on earth and multiply that many times to include everyone who has ever lived, from the time of Adam until the present, we're talking about an absolutely unfathomable number of books! All that to say, the Great White Throne Judgment is going to be no small event!

Terrified and Reverently Silent before the Throne

If you've done much witnessing, you've probably encountered at least one resentfully irreverent soul who, despite your affectionate attempts to reach them for Christ, arrogantly blathered something like: *"Oh Yah; well, when I see God, He's going to have to explain . . . !"* I'll bet most of you could complete the rest of that sentence using your own memories of sad attempts to reach the lost. The truth is, when the eternally lost are resurrected and placed before the judgment seat of Christ,[576] they won't be wearing white robes, as will the saints.[577] In all probability they'll be naked, thoroughly ashamed, and lying prostrate in the presence of pure holiness, justice, and truth, having no hope of covering their guilt. I can't prove it, but I'll bet most of you will agree that, if being in the presence of an angel can cause a strong man to instantly collapse, it's highly unlikely that even the boldest individual will utter a single word, while lying prostrate before the mighty throne of Jesus Christ, our Omnipotent Creator!

Moreover, since all the powers of darkness will have already been cast into the eternal lake of fire, deception will no longer exist. Thus, nothing but pure, unadulterated truth and clarity will fill the minds of the lost as they terrifyingly tremble in the very presence of Almighty God, waiting to be judged. That means that God won't have to explain a single thing! Every lost soul awaiting judgment before the throne will know full well why they're being eternally condemned to death. Hence, having repeatedly rejected Christ's gracious, merciful offer of eternal atonement and sanctification through faith alone, they'll have no hope of avoiding judgment and the interminable finality of the "**second death**" (*eternal damnation*). Thus, having no covering for their sins, they'll remain tight lipped, unjustified

---

[576] John 5:22-29, Mt. 12:18, 2Cor. 5:10
[577] Rev. 6:11, 7:9-14, 19:6-8

and totally exposed before the judgment seat of Christ, while they hopelessly await their imminent doom. And so, every unrepentant mortal who's ever lived will tremble uncontrollably, dreading the fateful moment when a commanding voice from the throne will call their name and they too will be judged and inescapably cast – "**live**" – into the eternal lake of fire! I can't say for sure, but I'll bet what will cause every eternally lost soul the greatest agony and regret will be the memories they'll have of every time a child of God lovingly reached out to them, while attempting to extend God's gracious invitation of salvation, only to be verbally slapped across the face for having done so!

"Hell . . . a party for sinners?" – I think not!

Let me assure every reader of the following inescapable truth: Hell, also referred to by Christ as "**outer darkness**,"[578] contrary to the staggering amount of idiotic rhetoric we hear being ignorantly churned out by fools on a daily basis (*as if they were never going to be held accountable for their foolishness*), is not going to be one giant party for sinners! The truth is in the *"lake of fire"* Satan will be just another fool who'll be suffering right along with every other fool who'll have chosen, of their own free-will, not to submit to the authority and righteousness of God their Creator. While describing *"outer darkness,"* Jesus warned that it will be a spiritually dark place of incessant ***'weeping and gnashing of teeth,'*** where death will never end and the fire will never cease. Try putting that description on a party flyer and see how many attend! When we couple Jesus' descriptive words with John's having foretold of the countless billions who'll be judged and eternally cast into the *"lake of fire,"* the truth of how ghastly this time of final judgment will be and the ultimate reality of eternal damnation should present a painfully disquieting mental image for all those who ceaselessly endeavor to reach the lost.

~ But aren't the Saints also going to be judged? ~

Over the years I've talked with a few truly wonderful brothers and sisters in Christ, who, probably because of their religious upbringing, believe that even Christians will have to answer for their idle words and the areas of their lives in which they've failed to please God. While that is a genuinely contrite perspective and usually reveals a thoroughly humble heart, it isn't a scripturally sound position to take; what's more, it doesn't properly reflect an accurate knowledge of the infinite grace and mercy of God Sadly, some passages, like the following message from Paul, have inad-

[578] Mt. 8:12, 22:13, 25:30, Mk. 9:44-48, Rev. 19:20, 20:10-15

vertently been misinterpreted and have, therefore, added to the inability of some to more fully understand God's boundless grace toward the saints.

> '. . . *for we shall* ***all*** *stand before the judgment seat of Christ. For it is written, As I live, saith the Lord, every knee shall bow to me, and every tongue shall confess to God. So then every one of us shall give account of himself to God.'*

Romans 14:10-12

The previous verse clearly confirms that at some point in time every individual will reverently bow the knee and confess their sins to God. And, while I can't point to any particular scripture for confirmation, I'm confident that throughout eternity the saints will continue to adoringly bow their knees in worship and thanksgiving to the Triune God. But the question we should be asking is: *"Does the preceding verse indicate that even the saints will be required to re-confess at least some of their sins and shortcomings after having been resurrected as immortal beings?"* For the answer to that question, let's take a quick look at a few very insightful passages.

> '***Some men's sins are open beforehand***, ***going before to judgment***; *and some men {the sins of those who reject Christ}* ***they follow after***. *Likewise also the good works of some {the saints} are manifest beforehand;* ***and they that are otherwise*** *{the sinful lives of the lost}* ***cannot be hid***.

1 Tim. 5:24

John 3:18-21, **5:24**, **1Cor**. 11:31, **2Cor**. 5:10 and **Mt**. 12:36-37

In the preceding verse, Paul explained that those of us who've truly repented and fully embraced the hope of salvation through Christ have already chosen to openly confess our sins directly to God, in the name of Christ, before we die. Having done so, our sinful lives and every sin we'll ever commit have already gone before us to the judgment and have, therefore, been covered by the blood atonement of Christ Jesus, our Messiah. Therefore, from God's timeless perspective, our old, sinful nature is already dead, crucified, and resurrected in Christ. That's precisely what water baptism (*of adults, not infants*) symbolizes.[579] As born again believers in Christ, our lives are eternally hidden, with Christ, in God.[580] So, as far

[579] Rom. 6:1-11, Heb. 2:11
[580] Col. 3:3

as God is concerned, we no longer live; instead, Christ lives in us.[581] This being the case, Paul really drove this point home in the following passage:

> *'What shall we then say to these things? If God be for us, who can be against us? He that spared not his own Son, but delivered him up for us all, how shall he not with him also freely give us all things?* ***Who shall lay any thing to the charge of God's elect****?* ***It is God that justifieth****. Who is he that condemneth? It is Christ that died, yea rather, that is risen again* {we, who believe, are risen with Christ}*, who is even at the right hand of God, who also maketh intercession for us.*

Romans 8:31-34

> *'Verily, verily, I say unto you, He that heareth my word, and believeth on him that sent me,* ***hath*** *{has already attained} everlasting life,* ***and shall not come into condemnation****; but* ***is passed*** *{present tense, not future tense} from death unto life.'*

John 5:24

A logical point worthy of Consideration

For those who still believe that the resurrected saints will have to give an account sometime in the future for their shortcomings, it might be helpful to actually imagine how this supposed admonition could physically fit into God's perfect plan and still align with everything we've learned about the grace of God and end-time prophecy. First of all, our names will only be written in the *Lamb's book of Life*, not the other books, which contain a record of the sins of the dead (*unredeemed souls, not saints*).[582] Thus, while God is keeping an accurate record of the sins of the lost, He's not keeping a record of the offenses of His saints. Those sins are eternally covered, blotted-out (*i.e., obliterated, washed away*) and atoned for by the blood of Christ.[583] Secondly, John recorded seeing all the saints clothed in white robes and returning triumphantly with Christ at the end of the tribulation period.[584] If God does intend to force even the saints to give an

---

[581] Gal. 2:19-20, 5:24, Jn. 6:53-58

[582] Rev. 20:12-15

[583] Isa. 43:25, 44:22, Acts 3:19

[584] Of Course, we're still sinful, but one day soon we'll shed these corruptible sinful bodies and be eternally clothed with new, holy, spiritual bodies—1Cor 15:42-54, John 3:1-5 and 31, Rev. 19:7-14.

account for every shortcoming, are we to believe that after resurrecting all the saints as new immortal, spiritually holy beings and clothing each of us with white robes (*the very symbol of His having made us righteous through Christ*), God's next move will be to verbally upbraid or physically punish and shame every already repentant and remorseful saint?! If so, so much for God's promise of forever wiping away our tears when we're resurrected![585] I guess, instead, we can plan on seeing millions of bloodshot eyes and sad, droopy faces during the blessed *"Marriage Supper of the Lamb."*[586]

Lastly, with regard to the possibility of the saints being judged at the *"White Throne Judgment,"* let's not forget that by that time the saints will have already been sinlessly ruling and reigning on earth, as ***'kings and priests'*** with Christ for a thousand years.[587] Can you imagine hundreds of millions of kings and priests being punished or reprimanded, in even the slightest way, for sins they committed in their former mortal bodies, after having lived a new, totally sinless existence in the presence of Christ for more than a thousand years? That scenario simply does not align with what we read in the entirety of God's Word.

Jesus warned that if we want to be forgiven for all our trespasses we must first be willing to fully and continually forgive all those who, even repeatedly, trespass against us.[588] Could it be that we're somehow expected to be more merciful and forgiving than God? I think not!

Therefore - in Conclusion

We can rest in the following glorious truth about God's immeasurable grace toward the saints:

*'For ye are dead, **and your life is hid with Christ in God**.*
When Christ, who is our life, shall appear, then shall ye also
*appear with him **in glory** {not shame—1John 2:28}.'*

Col. 3:3-4

Since our lives are hidden in Christ, God no longer sees us as sinners. As a matter of fact, being the truly merciful and loving Father He is, God has chosen to eternally forget our transgressions, so as to prevent us from having to re-live the inherent shame of our constant offenses and temporarily mortal, sinful nature.

---

585 Rev. 7:17, Isa. 25:8, 65:19
586 Rev. 19:4-14
587 Rev. 1:6, 5:10, 1Pt. 2:5-9
588 Mt. 18:21-35

'As far as the east is from the west, So far hath he removed our transgressions from us.'

ꕥ Psalms 103:12 ꕥ

*'I, even I, am he that **blotteth out thy transgressions for mine own sake**, **and will not remember thy sins**.'*

ꕥ Isaiah 43:25 ꕥ

According to Scripture, the Lord's greatest joy is extending mercy and grace to those who revere Him and strive to live in accordance to His will. Thus, blotting-out His children's transgressions and granting them full unmerited pardon is our Merciful Creator's greatest delight.[589] Because this is true, God's righteousness, in the ultimate judging and condemning of those who choose to reject His offer of mercy and forgiveness, is firmly established.

The eternal significance of our completely unmerited sanctification through Christ's atonement can't be overstated. Amazingly, however, if we were to take the time to digress and further explore this topic, we would soon find ourselves running through every book of the Bible. Instead, let's just gratefully embrace the following words of our Savior and move on to John's exciting vision of Heaven and the new earth.

*'Verily, verily {truly, truly}, I say unto you, He that heareth my word, and believeth on him that sent me, **hath** {has already attained} **everlasting life**, **and shall not come into condemnation**; **but is** {presently} **passed from death unto life**.'*

ꕥ John 5:24 ꕥ

ꕥ **1Jn.** 1:7-9, 2:28, **Rom.** 9:33, 10:11 and **Col.** 1:20-22 ꕥ

[589] Psalm 103:8-18, Micah 7:18-19

Chapter 43

Death Is Swallowed Up In Victory

> ‘And I saw a new heaven and a new earth: for the first heaven and the first earth were passed away; and there was no more sea.’ - **Revelation 21:1**

After John witnessed the final rebellious soul being violently hurled into the eternal lake of fire, the dreaded "Great White Throne Judgment" came to an end. That means that when that actually happens all that is evil and dark will have finally been eternally cast into outer darkness, far away from the presence of God and His entire heavenly family of angels and saints. That's a big deal, because from that point on, throughout all eternity, all that is impure, dark, and evil will have been irrevocably separated from all that is holy, righteous, and good! That total separation of "GOOD" and "EVIL" is the ultimate purpose of God's eternal plan, and, when His plan is concluded, just as the prophet said, death will have been swallowed up in "**VICTORY**!"[590] Of course it's impossible to know just how we'll feel at that moment, but I would imagine that the heart of every saint will swell with unspeakable gratitude and love for God our Savior, as the glorious promise of our being allowed to spend eternity in His presence joyfully becomes a reality!

How spiritually significant is Jerusalem to God?

As soon as the "Great White Throne Judgment" ended, John saw something truly spectacular. Gloriously, the "NEW JERUSALEM" (*God's eternal city*) descended from Heaven, ***'prepared as a bride adorned for her husband.'*** Earlier, we learned that, after being resurrected, every saint will be given a new name. Even Jesus will have a new name,[591] which at least

[590] Isa. 25:8-9, 1Cor. 15:54-55
[591] Rev. 2:17, 19:12

initially only He will know. The name of God's holy city, however, "NEW JERUSALEM," will never change.

God, Himself, shall be with them and be their God

After seeing "NEW JERUSALEM" descend, John heard a great voice from Heaven say:

> ***"The tabernacle of God is with men, and He will dwell with them, and they shall be His people, and God himself shall be with them, and be their God."***

If ever a verse merited being ended with an exclamation point, the preceding verse is it! And, if the thought of our Omnipotent Creator actually dwelling on a new earth, directly in our midst, doesn't absolutely thrill you to the core, it might be advisable to give yourself a massive shot of adrenaline!

How awesome will the reality of the infinitely powerful God dwelling in our midst be? Consider this: Conservatively speaking there are an estimated 70×10^{21} (*70 x 100 billion x 100 billion*) stars in the universe. Many of those stars are several hundred times larger and more powerful than our sun. Our sun (*perhaps an average star*), in just one second, gives off enough energy (*roughly 3.8 - 4.0 x 10^{21} watts/sec.*) to sustain our current global civilization and it's modern way of life for hundreds of thousands of years, and that's just one second of power from an average star.

Now let's broaden our scope to include not only our own Milky Way galaxy but the rest of the universe as well. As I stated, there are approximately 60 to 70 sextillion stars in the universe. That's an extraordinarily large number (*70 x 10^{21} or 70 with 21 zeroes after it*). In an attempt to wrap our minds around this number (*and a futile attempt it will be*), let's imagine scooping up a large handful of sand, pouring it out onto a smooth surface, and carefully counting every individual grain. How arduous a task do you suppose that would be?! With this in mind, let's pretend that all those grains of sand are actually stars and each of those stars are at least as large as our sun. Now, let's imagine that every grain of sand on our favorite beach is a star. That would be an unbelievable amount of stars, wouldn't it? Okay, now let's imagine that every grain of sand on every beach on the planet is a star. Have we got it? Good! But hold on; we're not even close to being finished. Let's combine all those grains of sand, from all the beaches on earth, with all the grains of sand from all the deserts on earth as well. Now we're finally starting to grasp how extraordinarily large the number 70 sextillion is!

But, honestly, if truth be told, could any human actually envision all those individual grains of sand as being stars? Of course not! And, amazingly, we've still only just begun. With everything we've just envisioned in mind, let's continue visualizing all those grains of sand, plus all the grains of sand from ten more identical planet Earths. That's roughly how many stars are estimated to exist. If we can visualize that and at the same time imagine that each of those grains of sand is actually a "**star**," miraculously capable of continually producing energy at a rate comparable to detonating about a trillion 1 megaton bombs every second, then we're beginning to understand how utterly impossible it is to grasp the truly unlimited power and majesty of our gloriously omnipotent Creator!

According to Scripture, Jesus merely *"spoke"* all this power into existence. What's more, simply by the word of His power,[592] all those trillions upon trillions of stars have continued, year after year, radiating this incalculable amount of energy, and they do this simply because, on day four of the week of creation, the Lord commanded them to do so. And, beyond our comprehension is the fact that, from God's omnipotent perspective, His creating this awe-inspiring universe required so little effort that He simply inspired Moses to record the event by writing: ***'. . . he created the stars also.'***[593]

It's been suggested that early Greek philosophers had a far more logical perspective of the omnipotent nature of God than do the majority of Christians today. As philosophers they apparently had a problem, not with the ability of an omnipotent God to create the earth, the universe, and everything else in a six day period, but, rather, with the prospect of it taking an all-powerful Creator six days to do it! Now that's a proper perspective of our Almighty God! So, with that in mind, I ask once more: *"How awesome will the reality of the infinitely powerful God actually dwelling in our midst be?"* I doubt mere words could ever adequately address such a question.

'But as it is written, Eye hath not seen, nor ear heard, neither have entered into the heart of man, the things which God hath prepared for them that love him.'

1Cor. 2:9

Jesus promised us a place in Heaven

When most Christians ponder the promise of their future eternal heavenly habitation with God, one particular, very special passage usually takes center stage in their minds. It comes from a message Jesus gave just moments before surrendering His sinless life to the agony of the cross. Lov-

592 Heb. 1:3, Isa. 45:5-7, Jn. 1:1-3, Col. 1:16-17

593 Gen. 1:14-19

ingly thinking of us first, as Jesus always does, and selflessly choosing to push the fear of His imminent suffering aside,[594] Jesus comforted His disciples and, by extension, all future believers with the following words:

> *'Let not your heart be troubled: ye believe in God, believe also in me.* ***In my Father's house are many mansions****: If it were not so, I would have told you. I go to prepare a place for you. And if I go and prepare a place for you, I will come again, and receive you unto myself; that where I am, there ye may be also.'*

℘ John 14:1-3 ℘

We probably won't be confident of our interpretation of Jesus' promise until we actually participate in its fulfillment. I say this because there are differences of opinion as to the correct interpretation of the word *"mansions."* The Lord may be preparing hundreds of millions, even billions, of beautiful, stately mansions in the New Jerusalem for some of His most subservient and deserving children or even, perhaps, for every child of God, but the word *"mansions,"* as used in this verse, could be argued to be correctly interpreted as meaning: *"dwellings"* or *"abodes."*

The saints are referred to as *"the Children of God"* because, together, we constitute a family. Thus, it's possible that, like a family, we will all live together with God. However, as we move a little further into this chapter, we'll see that **Rev. 21:24-27** suggests that there will be *"nations of saints"* in the new earth, which will bring their glory and honor into God's holy city. Therefore, from my perspective, an even better scriptural argument could be made for the possibility of the new earth being filled with vast, glorious cities and agricultural areas. That's an exciting thought; isn't it?

It is done!

Rev. 21:5-7

> ***'And he that sat upon the throne said, Behold, I make all things new. And he said unto me, Write: for these words are true and faithful.***
>
> ***And he said unto me, It is done. I am Alpha and Omega, the beginning and the end. I will give unto him that is athirst of the fountain of the water of life freely.***
>
> ***He that overcometh shall inherit all things; and I will be his God, and he shall be my son.'***

---

[594] Heb. 5:1-8, 2:9-11

After hearing the Lord make the preceding proclamation, one of the seven angels who had participated in the dispensing of God's seven plagues of wrath carried John, in the spirit, to a great and high mountain and showed him ***'that great city, the holy Jerusalem, descending out of heaven from God, Having the glory of God: and her light*** *(her brightness, not the city itself)*[595] ***was like unto a stone most precious, even like a jasper stone, clear as crystal....'***

Before revealing this to John, the angel told John that he was going to show him the bride of Christ — the Lamb's wife. Then, the angel immediately showed John the New Jerusalem as it descended from Heaven. Thus, it would seem that, when the "Great White Throne Judgment" ends, since the saints will already be in Heaven, the Lord may simply usher them directly into the New Jerusalem, before it descends and becomes permanently affixed on the new earth.

A massive Jasper wall will surround the Great City

The New Jerusalem will lie ***'foursquare'***[596] and have a perimeter wall ***'great and high'*** surrounding it, with twelve gates. Three of those gates will face east, three north, three south, and three west. It seems criminal, however, to simply state that this jasper wall, which will surround the entire city, will have twelve gates, because these gates are sure to be absolute wonders of God's creative beauty!

To begin with, each gate or *"gateway"* will have been sculpted from a single, massive pearl, one pearl per gate (*or gateway*). And, considering that the angel told John that the height of the wall will be ***'an hundred and forty and four cubits,'*** which is somewhere between 216 to 264 feet high (*depending on the length of the cubit*), in order for these gates to be proportionately sized to the height of the jasper wall, they're going to have to be remarkably tall, very wide, and extraordinarily thick. How exciting!

---

[595] Jasper can be nearly colorless and clear as crystal, or its color can range from purple to bronze. So it's fortunate that John clarified what he saw by telling us that the *'light'* of the city {*the luminosity, not the city itself*} was crystal clear. It's important that we don't make the mistake of confusing this *'crystal clear,'* radiant light of the city with the apparently darker - *jasper* - color of the city's 216-264 ft. tall perimeter wall with pearly gates.

[596] At this point, John is only telling us that the city will lie *'foursquare.'* That information alone does not indicate that the city will be a cube; in fact, it's being foursquare simply indicates that the city will be *"quadrangular" (a rectangle or a square)*. In this case, however, John is going to be told that the footprint of the outer wall (*the perimeter Jasper wall*) of the city will have four equal sides and angles, thus, making its base a square but not necessarily indicating that the actual city within the wall will be a cube. We'll cover this in detail very soon.

Of course we really have no way of knowing, but let's suppose the Lord intends these massive pearly gates (*which will likely be double-hung*) to be just one-third the height of the city's more than 200 feet tall perimeter wall (*the jasper wall—Rev. 21:17-19*). Even at that disproportionately small size, it would mean that each pearly gateway would be at least 70 feet high and somewhere between 70 to 120 feet wide. On the other hand, it certainly wouldn't be beyond the realm of possibility for God to make these gates as tall as or even taller than the 200 feet high perimeter wall.

Just for fun

The next time you're in the city, find a twenty story building. Stand beside it, and imagine you're standing in the opening of one of the gateways of this massive perimeter wall. Then imagine that that 20 story building is the jasper wall that will completely encompass the outer courtyard of the golden city, "NEW JERUSALEM." But remember, this 20 story high wall is just the perimeter wall of the city, not the actual city wall, which will be 1,500 miles (*not feet*) high! Next, imagine that the wall continues running, in both directions, much farther than your eyes can see, for hundreds and hundreds of miles! Look up. Can you envision standing next to a set of pearly white gates that are intricately carved, measure more than two hundred feet high, are at least ten feet thick, and are two to three hundred feet wide? That's the length of a football field!

Will gatekeepers, in God's holy city, really be necessary?

Though the apostle Peter is jokingly regarded as being the keeper of Heaven's pearly gates, as we just learned, in reality, there will be twelve entrances to the outer courtyard of the holy city, and according to **Rev. 21:12**, an angel, not Peter, will be posted at each entrance. However, since all evil will have already been eternally cast into outer darkness, what possible reason could there be for posting angels at the entrances to God's holy city? It's not like a murderer or a thief could somehow escape the eternal bondage of outer darkness and slyly sneak into God's holy Kingdom.[597] So, rather than acting as guardians, perhaps these angels will serve some other useful purpose.

Logically, if these gates are going to be as impressive as John indicates (*and they'll definitely be at least that impressive*), then it stands to reason that the Lord will post an equally impressive and probably very large angel at each of the twelve gates. Imagine that! The Scriptures don't tell us, but, since John was told that the gates of the city will never close (*Rev. 21:25*), these angels won't be posted there for the purpose of opening and

[597] Rev. 21:27

closing gates. Thus, perhaps these angels will be distinctively large, physically imposing beings, who'll be positioned at the gateways for the purpose of doing nothing more than majestically adorning the entrances to the city, while watching the saints go in and out. How exciting will the sight of that be?!

Each Gate will bear a Special Name

Rev. 21:12-14

Either on the gates themselves, on the mantles of the gates, or possibly on massive gemstone placards[598] above each gateway will be inscribed the names of the original twelve tribes of Israel. Precisely how this will be done isn't clear, but each gate will bear the name of one of the original tribes of Israel. However, since these gates will never be shut, placing placards, bearing the names of the twelve original tribes, above or on the permanently opened gates does seem logical. And, although the tribe of Dan will not be counted as one of the tribes from which the 144,000 Jewish servants will be sealed (*Rev. 7:4-8*), according to **Ez. 48:30-35**, Dan will likely be recognized on one of these twelve massive gateways to the city.

The Foundation Stones will also be engraved

Not only will the perimeter wall[599] have twelve massive gates, it will also sit upon twelve colossally large foundation stones, each of which will be precious (*a gem stone*) and will be engraved with the name of one of the twelve apostles. That's fitting, considering that most of the apostles helped to lay the foundation of the Church by surrendering their lives to the point of death for the furtherance of the Gospel of Christ. The question is: *"Which apostle will be honored in place of Judas Iscariot?"* Certainly, no other apostle has suffered more or done as much to further the Gospel message as has Paul.[600] And yet, as was earlier mentioned, it was Matthias who was

598 I mention the possibility (*and it's just a possibility*) of the tribal names being inscribed on twelve massive gemstone placards because of the historical significance of the golden ephod (*the breastplate*), which the high priest wore while serving in the tabernacle. On the high priest's ephod, twelve different precious stones were inscribed and set. Each stone bore the name of one of the original twelve tribes of Israel, and each tribe had its own unique, corresponding stone. In this way, all the original tribes of Israel were represented before the Lord—Ex. 28:15-29.

599 The reason for my referring to the more than 200 feet tall jasper wall as being a perimeter wall will be explained as we continue through the remainder of this portion of John's vision.

600 1Cor. 15:10, 2Cor. 11:17-28

ordained for the purpose of replacing Judas Iscariot.[601] I guess this mystery won't be revealed until we're there and can actually read the names on those foundation stones for ourselves.

12,000 furlongs, that's a lot of furlongs; - isn't it?

Rev. 21:12-21

Most scholars seem to agree that a furlong is about 660 feet. Therefore, since the angel measured the city — which would include the footprint of its massive, more than 200 feet tall, perimeter wall — and declared it to lie ***'foursquare,'*** with its length, breadth, and height each stretching 12,000 furlongs, we can safely conclude that the city will measure 1,500 miles square and 1,500 miles high. Unfortunately, from this point on, interpretations as to the shape of the holy city differ, and it's been my experience that most Christians, whether well read or not, have great difficulty being truly open minded when considering the possible veracity of alternate interpretations. So, before we examine John's description of this city any further, let's acknowledge that when we actually see the New Jerusalem our current opinions will no longer matter. We can be confident that however God has chosen to make that holy city it's going to be awesome! Therefore, since we're all fallible, let's humbly open our minds and see what additional "**facts**" can be gleaned from the remainder of the text.

What, if anything, have we assumed?

Of course I can only speak for myself, but early on, like many other students of eschatology, I likened the 10 cubit square by 10 cubit high (*15 ft. x 15 ft. x 15 ft.*) Holy of Holies[602] (*the heart of the Tabernacle*) to God's eternal city — "NEW JERUSALEM." Everything I read about the Holy of Holies seemed to insist that its 15 feet cubed design was intended to be a shadow (*a physical representation*) of the future New Jerusalem, the eternal dwelling place of God. That, however, may or may not prove to be the case. At the present, though some would disagree with my saying so, we simply don't know. Nonetheless, for years, because of that possibility, I repeatedly misinterpreted the word ***'foursquare'*** (*in Rev. 21:16*), presuming it to mean: *cubed*. This led to my concluding that the New Jerusalem, like the Holy of Holies, must also be a cube. That was a presumptuous mistake on my part. As we earlier established, John's use of the word ***'foursquare*** actually means: *quadrangular* (*not cubular*), which simply indicates that the *"foot print"* or *"total acreage"* of the future city (*which would include everything within its outer courtyard and perimeter walls*) will be as long

---

601 Acts 1:15-26, see also - 1Cor. 15:8-9

602 Ex. 26:15-25

(*from front to back*) as it will be wide (*from side to side*). Thus, the fact that the angel stated that the city will be quadrangular in no way can be said to prove that the city will be a cube. Once I understood that I had been allowing my assumption that the city would be a cube to skew my interpretation of John's vision, other equally valid interpretations began to naturally emerge from the text (*Rev. 21 and 22*).

Additionally, because I had prematurely concluded that the New Jerusalem could only be a cube, I also mistakenly envisioned the 1,500 mile high city structure to be mostly solid from top to bottom and positioned directly over the jasper wall and pearly gates. It simply never occurred to me that the city could just as easily be 1,500 miles high (*in the center*), without being a cube, and still be a perfectly accurate representation of John's vision. So, with this in mind, let's look at the possibilities.

1,500 miles by 1,500 miles by 1,500 miles

To most, since the angel declared the future city to be as high as it will be deep and wide, there's simply no room for alternate views; therefore, for those individuals, the city must be a "**cube**." Arriving at that conclusion, however, is, in itself, a supposition. Regardless of what some may think, as the following side-view illustration reveals (Fig. 1), a pyramid can be 1,500 miles deep and wide, while still being 1,500 miles high. As a matter of fact, any structure matching those dimensions would actually be much stronger than a cube of the same height.

Figure 1

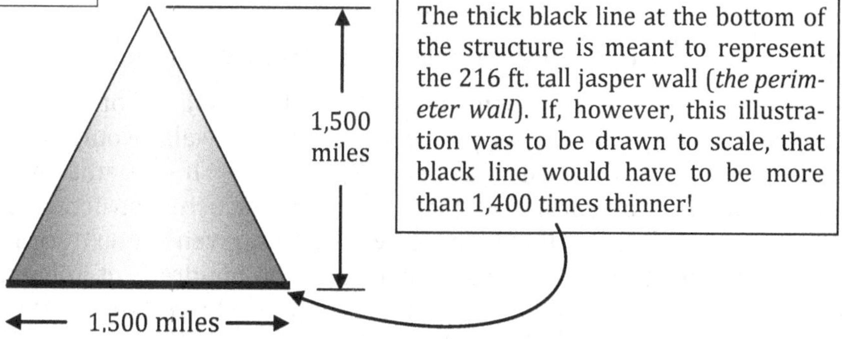

1,500
miles
The thick black line at the bottom of the structure is meant to represent the 216 ft. tall jasper wall (*the perimeter wall*). If, however, this illustration was to be drawn to scale, that black line would have to be more than 1,400 times thinner!
1,500 miles

We need to consider that, in order for a pyramid to be as tall as it is wide, it will have to be very steep. We should also note that walled cities are most commonly measured by the square miles within their perimeter walls.[603] Therefore, if the New Jerusalem's

---

603 Jericho was one type of *"walled city."* In the case of cities like Jericho, the actual structure and living quarters of the city were designed to create a thick and tall

more than 216 feet tall perimeter wall (*the jasper wall*) is not positioned directly beneath the golden city, as **Fig. 1** depicts, the city will have to be even steeper, which is depicted by the image in **Fig. 2**.

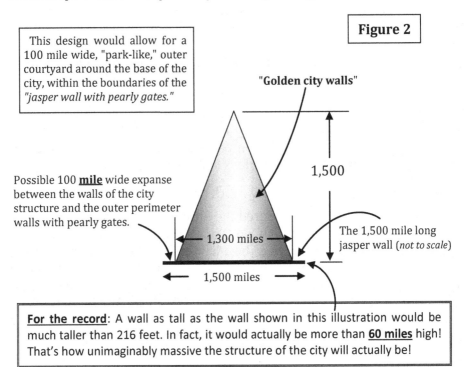

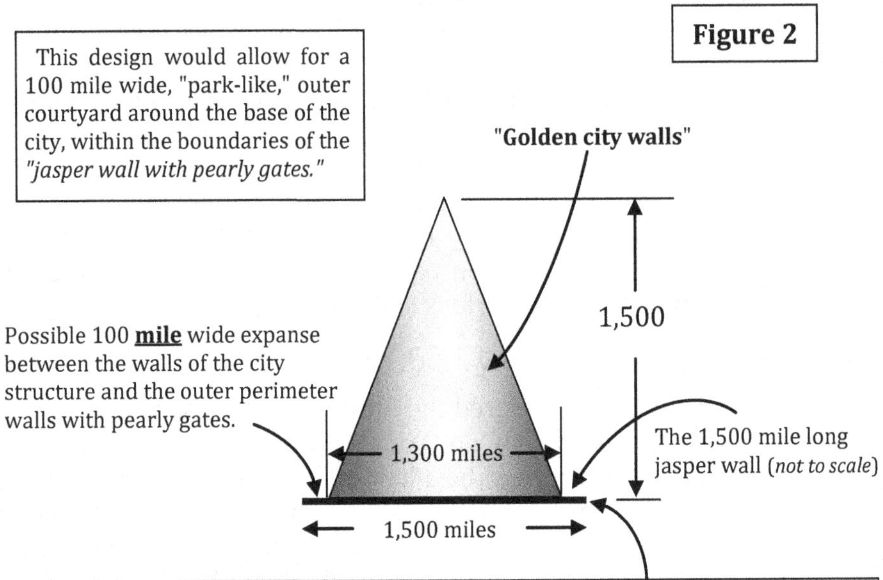

For the record: A wall as tall as the wall shown in this illustration would be much taller than 216 feet. In fact, it would actually be more than **60 miles** high! That's how unimaginably massive the structure of the city will actually be!

So how will the New Jerusalem be shaped?

Whether the New Jerusalem is revealed to be a pyramid or a cube (*and I suppose both options are scripturally possible*), its walls would likely be built like those of the former ancient city Jericho.[604] If so, gathering halls and dwellings of all sorts would logically form the actual structure of the massive, 1,500 mile high golden city walls. This, given the extraordinary height of those walls, could mean that they'll be hundreds of miles thick. Isn't that an exciting thought?! That option would certainly create an enormous amount of individual and communal living area within the

---

perimeter wall, which was intended to be occupied by its inhabitants; thus, with that design, there would be no need for a separate, additional perimeter wall. In other words, Jericho would have no need of an off-set, perimeter jasper wall, like the wall John described seeing around the base of the New Jerusalem.

[604] Jos. 2:15

actual golden walls of the city, while still allowing for hundreds of miles of totally open space inside the overall city structure (*see Figures 3 and 4*).

Figure 3 **Figure 4**

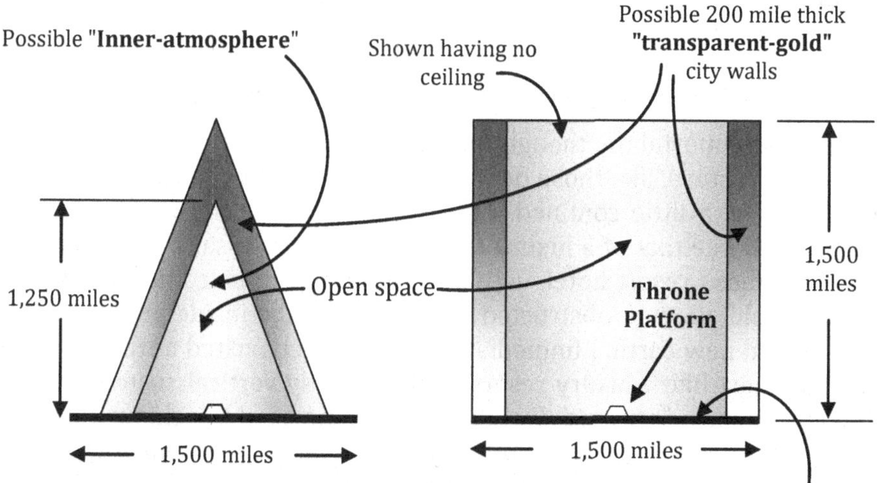

> **Note**: If the city is to be a 1,500 mile cube, the jasper wall will have to be positioned directly beneath it. Therefore, since the jasper wall in this illustration is shown at more than 1,400 times its true height, from this perspective, it would actually be impossible to see the wall or any of its pearly gates.

As shown, the atmosphere inside the New Jerusalem, whether shaped like a cube or a pyramid,[605] could still be several hundred miles higher than the current atmosphere on Earth.[606] And, again, so that the more than 216 feet tall perimeter wall (*Rev. 21:17-19*) will be visible in the illustration, it's shown at the extremely exaggerated height of 60 miles tall, more than 1,400 times taller than it will actually be! That should help us get an idea of the immense size of God's future eternal kingdom. If that doesn't do it, take a look at the little white throne platform shown at ground level in the middle of the structures. The Bible doesn't tell us how large God's

---

605 In contrast to a pyramid, a cube shaped design would have three times the amount of space.

606 Currently, the earth's total atmosphere extends outward for about 280-300 miles from the earth's surface, but only about 10,000 feet — *or about a mile and a half of that atmosphere* — is conducive to prolonged periods of healthy breathing.

throne platform will be; only that it will be positioned within the holy city. But Mount Everest — the tallest mountain in the world — is more than five miles high. So, to get an idea of how large this city will be, in order for God's throne platform to be even close to the size of the little white platform in the illustration, it would have to be about 20 times larger than Mount Everest! This is why the more than 200 feet tall perimeter wall in the illustrations is shown at such an exaggerated size. Like the throne platform, if the perimeter wall were drawn to scale it would be far too small to be seen.

The Jasper wall may just be the key to Understanding this City

As a mere mortal the thought of dwelling within the confines of a massive city structure, like those depicted in the preceding illustrations, causes me to feel a little confined. But if I imagine that city as having been constructed like that of a luxury cruise ship or a colossally large and brilliantly terraced resort hotel, with giant openings to balconies and patios, which would allow unobstructed views of both the inside and outside of the city and new earth, I immediately begin to get excited at the possibilities! And, just like a luxury resort, both a strictly vertical structure and a steeply terraced, *"pyramid-like"* design could be used to achieve this goal. The question is: *"Based solely on the facts within the text, which of the two shapes emerges as the most logical, scripturally accurate option?"*

Let's first consider the Cube option

A cube shaped New Jerusalem is by far the most commonly accepted interpretation of John's vision, but if the city ends up being a cube, it would mean that, in order for the city and its jasper wall to measure out at exactly 1,500 miles square and 1,500 miles high (*as the angel stated it will—Rev. 21:15-16*), the jasper wall could not be a perimeter wall at all.[607] Instead, it would have to be part of the city's foundation. Therefore, it would have to be positioned directly under the city, like an above ground footing.[608] And, while God certainly can do anything, that option just doesn't seem to make a lot of sense. Why do I say this? It's actually pretty simple. The problem is with the wall's size. Although the jasper wall will appear to be colossally large to those who'll pass through its gigantic pearly gates (*again, think*

607 Perimeter walls typically surround a city; they're not positioned under the actual city. So, if this Jasper wall is to be positioned beneath the 1,500 mile high city frame, why did the angel bother telling us that the Jasper wall will be more than 200 feet tall? In this case, its height would, of necessity, be measured integrally with the golden city walls.

608 See Figure 4, but remember that the height of the perimeter wall in the illustration is extremely exaggerated.

twenty story building), the truth is any structural engineer would tell us that a wall of that size would still be woefully inadequate and ridiculously disproportionately sized to serve as a foundation for a city with walls reaching 1,500 miles high!

Looking at it from a more Relatable Perspective

If we were standing next to this massive city, "NEW JERUSALEM," while the international space station passed overhead, we wouldn't be able to hear or see it happen, but the space station would crash into the lower, one-sixth portion of the city. In other words, in order for the space station to clear the holy city while in orbit, it would have to establish a new orbit seven times higher. That's a big city! And a city of that magnitude will certainly rest upon foundation stones much larger than the 200 feet tall perimeter wall!

Most of us have seen cubular shaped illustrations of the New Jerusalem, and nearly all of them include a foundation or base that is intended to represent these 216 feet tall jasper walls with pearly gates. That's the problem; though most of those illustrations don't state it, they're all drawn drastically out of scale. I certainly don't wish to hurt anybody's feelings, but if we hope to begin to grasp how massive the New Jerusalem will be, we must first envision the true size of these jasper walls and compare them to the extraordinarily larger size of the 1,500 mile high walls of the transparent golden city.

The True Size of the Holy City

To help us understand how disproportionately small a roughly 216 feet high base structure (*above ground footing or foundation*) would be if positioned under a city as unbelievably immense as will be the future New Jerusalem, let's imagine drawing (*with an ordinary pen*) a 24 inch x 24 inch square on a large piece of butcher paper. After having done so, that thin horizontal line at the bottom of our square would accurately represent the length and height of our more than 200 feet tall jasper wall. And somewhere along that 1,500 mile long wall would be three massive pearly gateways. That means that the jasper wall will be so long that if we were able to see the entire length of one of its four sides, neither the wall nor the three massive pearly gateways on that side of the city would be visible.

That's how small the jasper wall will be in comparison to the immense size of the 1,500 mile high and wide golden city. And yet, even though these scaled dimensions are accurate, thus far, I've been unsuccessful in finding a single illustration that even comes close to accurately depicting the truly enormous size of God's future city. With this in mind, it should quickly become apparent that, in order for the massive size of the jasper wall to be seen as being impressive, it would have to be positioned a great distance away from the gigantic, 1,500 mile high, golden walls of the city structure.

~ Why would a wall that's designed to be part of the city's foundation have its own foundation stones? ~

That's a good question! It's important to note that in **Rev. 21:12-14** the angel told John that the jasper wall will have its own foundation stones and will support twelve massive gates (*or gateways*). Therefore, if (*as some propose*) the jasper wall will not be a perimeter wall and will not be positioned out and away from the city's base, why did the angel bother telling John (*in verse 21:18*) that the wall will be constructed of *"jasper stone,"* instead of pure transparent gold, as will the walls of the New Jerusalem? Moreover, if the jasper wall will not stand alone, creating a perimeter around the city (*rather than under it*), why did the angel even bother telling John the height of the wall? If the wall is to be positioned underneath the 1,500 mile high city, as some have assumed, wouldn't its actual height be integrally measured as part of the height of the 1,500 mile high city? If not, the city will not actually measure out to be 1,500 miles long, wide and high.[609] At the moment this may seem trivial, but its significance will soon come to light.

What if?

If the golden city ends up taking the shape of a 1,500 mile high, steeply terraced building, rather than a cube, it could be positioned within the boundaries of a more than 200 feet tall, 1,500 mile wide, by 1,500 mile long perimeter wall (*made of "jasper"*), just as the angel stated. This would allow for the actual walls of the golden city to be set back, perhaps a hundred miles or so, so as to create a gap (*like a park*) between the inside of its *"off-set"* perimeter wall (*the jasper wall*) and the actual base of the golden city structure. In this way, whether one was heading toward the golden city from out in the new earth or making their way out of the city to go exploring all of God's creation, the sight of that massive, 200 feet tall perimeter wall, with its enormous pearly gates, would be truly impressive!

---

[609] If the city ends up being positioned <u>within</u> a 1,500 mile square perimeter wall and garden area, the city structure will not be a cube. Since the angel indicated that the Jasper wall will lie 1,500 miles *'foursquare'* (square), the actual walls of the city structure could not also lie 1,500 miles - *square* - and still be set-back from the perimeter Jasper Wall. Thus, the actual "transparent gold city" would create a smaller footprint (*less than 1,500 miles*), which would mean the city would fit the description given to John but would not be a 1,500 mile high cube.

Moreover, if the perimeter wall ends up being positioned out and away from the golden city, it would create a space for stunningly beautiful botanical gardens and pathways all around the outside of the city's base. Thus, a vast garden paradise of sorts, many miles deep and hundreds of miles wide, all around the entire base of the city, could provide a visual buffer. This would minimize the otherwise disproportionately huge size of the golden city, and prevent it from detracting from the likewise impressive height of the massive, 20 story high jasper wall with pearly gateways.

What a view!

Try and visualize being able to walk out onto a lavishly designed balcony built hundreds of miles high into the side of a steeply terraced, 200 to 300 mile thick, golden city wall.[610] That city wall will actually be so large that, if you were on a balcony in the middle of it, it would be impossible to see (*whether looking up, down or side to side*) where the city begins or ends. If you can imagine that, try to picture yourself looking out from that balcony and seeing an absolutely breathtaking view of God's vast garden paradise — "THE NEW EARTH." Now envision looking in every direction and seeing countless other saints enjoying the same unobstructed view, from hundreds of millions of other extravagantly designed balconies and patios, also built directly into the colossally large walls of the golden city. Having the very plushest of presidential suites on the highest floor of the most magnificent Swiss chalet, built way high up in the Alps, wouldn't even come close to comparing to the experience!

What's more, since the inside of the city, whether a pyramid or a cube, will most logically have its own atmosphere (*as Figs. 3 and 4 indicate*), it could have hundreds of thousands of square miles of open space for majestic garden pathways, enormously spacious amphitheaters, gloriously ornate dome-covered pavilions, magnificent forests with all manner of towering trees, and velvety green rolling hills with beautiful flowering plants and shrubs. Imagine yourself on the inside of the city walls and being able to lean out and look over a pearly guardrail to peer hundreds of miles down and inward at all the unspeakably awesome sights, sounds, and beckoning fragrances of God's fabulously designed Golden City, not to mention the majesty of His magnificent throne pavilion and crystal-clear river of water of life!

To Sum-up:

After having spent a great deal of time, over many years, attempting to gain a firmer understanding of just what John's vision reveals about the shape of God's eternal holy city, I've arrived at the following conclusion:

---

[10] Rev. 21:18

~ I don't think it can be irrefutably proven just how God's holy city will be shaped! ~

Therefore, we shouldn't allow this mystery to become a bone of contention. No matter how God does it, when we finally see it we're all going to agree that nothing mankind has ever built or imagined could, in any way, compare to the splendor of that heavenly structure!

~ So what do we know about the new earth? ~

Unfortunately, John's vision gives us little in the way of details with regard to the actual size or even the general topography of the new earth God's going to create, and we certainly don't want to reach beyond the boundaries of pure Scripture in our attempt to formulate an accurate mental picture of Heaven.

~ So, just what does John's vision reveal? ~

It's estimated that roughly 70% of our current planet is covered with water (*97% of which is salt water*). In **Rev. 21:1**, John wrote that the new earth will have no sea, which means it won't be covered with water. That fact alone will significantly set the new earth apart from our present earth. However, we must remember that just because the new earth will have no "**sea**" (*i.e., oceans*) doesn't necessarily mean it will have no streams, rivers, lakes, ponds, or natural springs. In fact, in just a minute, we're going to learn about a very special river that will flow directly from the throne of God.

~ Should we expect an all-powerful God to spend eternity on a relatively tiny Earth? ~

I can't imagine any astronomer comparing our present earth to the countless other much larger celestial bodies in the universe and saying:

"Wow, our planet is unbelievably huge!"

That's not a criticism of our current Planet Earth. We all know that size is relative. But, seeing that our earth could easily fit inside the sun more than a million times, and considering that (*as I earlier stated*) our sun is, by some estimates, just an average size star and there are countless trillions of stars out there that are several hundred times larger than ours, the earth is, by no means, a massive planet!

~ Okay, so what's the point? ~

I once preached a sermon with the intent of helping a congregation understand just how massive the holy city New Jerusalem will be. Sadly, that particular body of believers had been taught that this earth will eternally exist and eventually be reutilized as the foundation for God's future, heavenly kingdom. So, to help that congregation begin to appreciate the implausibility of such a notion, I placed a standard classroom size globe on the pulpit. Then, I commenced my message by placing a sugar cube on top of that globe and telling the congregation that it represented the holy city, "NEW JERUSALEM." After the *"oohing"* and *"ahhing"* ceased, I replaced the sugar cube with an even larger cube and continued doing so until I had finally placed a proportionately sized cube (*about 2 inches square*) to that of the future holy city atop the global. You should have heard the bewildered congregation's stunned response. That properly scaled cube rocked like a *"teeter-totter"* on the top of that globe, and its disproportionate size looked absolutely ridiculous! I probably don't need to say it, but after that sermon the congregation no longer believed in the prospect of a rejuvenated planet earth continuing throughout eternity.

The New Earth will likely be immeasurably massive!

To get an idea of how large the new earth will need to be in order for it to properly accommodate the unprecedentedly enormous size of God's future city – "NEW JERUSALEM," consider the following:

> If a grading contractor were to prepare a level area on the surface of this planet large enough to accommodate the massive 1,500 mile square floor plan of the holy city "New Jerusalem," that contractor would have to excavate to a depth of nearly **100 miles**. At that depth, he will have broken through the earth's crust and into its "upper mantle" by as much as 80 miles! Thus, the holy city would need to be both impervious to heat and able to float; as it would be resting on molten rock!

I make the preceding point, not to remake a case for a new earth,[611] but instead to help us comprehend how large the new earth will need to be in order for it to be proportionately sized to God's eternal holy city. Looking at it logically, since God made the Universe as incalculably large as it is, even though He knew it would only exist for about seven thousand years, how immense should we expect God to make the new earth, which we've

[611] Rev. 20:11, 21:1-5, 2Pt. 23:7-10

been assured will last forever? My guess, and it's nothing more than a guess, would be that God will make the new eternal earth unprecedentedly larger and far more spectacular than anything He's ever made — including the Universe! And why wouldn't He? After we've spent hundreds of trillions of years exploring the new earth's many splendid intricacies (*which will only be a vapor of time when compared to eternity*), we'll still have only just begun. So why not make the new earth nearly infinitely large? It's just a thought, but it certainly wouldn't be hard for God to do it. What's more, it's definitely a logical possibility and fun to imagine!

John sees the New Jerusalem

> *'And I saw no temple therein: for the Lord God Almighty and the Lamb are the temple of it. And the city had no need of the sun, neither the moon, to shine in it:* ***for the glory of God did lighten it****, and the Lamb is the light thereof. And the nations of them which are saved shall walk in the light of it:* ***and the kings of the earth do bring their glory and honour into it****. And the gates of it shall not be shut at all by day: for there shall be no night there.* ***And they shall bring the glory and honour of the nations into it****.*[612] *And there shall in no wise enter into it any thing that defileth, neither whatsoever worketh abomination, or maketh a lie: but they which are written in the Lamb's book of life.*

Revelation 21:22-27

> Since the glory of the Lord will magnificently illuminate all of God's new creation, once we're there do you suppose we'll ever see another shadow?

612 These words may indicate that the new earth, out and around the New Jerusalem, may be filled with other glorious cities, governed by saintly kings (*and probably queens*), but without a clear scriptural description of that possibility we're safer not expounding on this passage.

Chapter 44

The Curse Ends and Eternity Begins

Having reached the end of John's written account of what was undoubtedly the most fascinating revelation of end-time events any human has ever experienced, we've already examined everything John's vision reveals about the outside of God's transparent-gold city. Now, these final verses of John's book are going to let us take a quick peek at the inside of that 1,500 mile high structure, the golden City of God, "NEW JERUSALEM."

> 'And he shewed me a pure river of water of life, clear as crystal, proceeding out of the throne of God and of the Lamb. In the midst of the street of it, and on either side of the river, was there the tree of life, which bare twelve manner of fruits, and yielded her fruit every month: and the leaves of the tree were for the healing of the nations.' ~ **Rev. 22:1-2**

A New Throne for a New, Eternal Kingdom

When the Lord told John: *"... Behold, I make all things new,"*[613] He could have simply been referring to His creation of the new heaven and earth. However, since God's eternal place of dwelling will be with all of His children, in the midst of the New Jerusalem, on an entirely new earth, it's clear that what we currently refer to as "Heaven" (*God's present place of dwelling*) will no longer exist. Thus, while making a new heaven and earth, God may also choose to create an entirely new, even more spectacular throne, a throne of unspeakable splendor, a throne worthy of being prominently positioned as part of the focal point of His holy city, most importantly, a throne that will evoke no remembrance of the "Great White Throne Judgment" — an event that will have proven to be the second most horrific event in all eternity (*the brutal crucifying of our Creator being the first*).

---

[613] Rev. 21:5-6

The pure, crystal-clear River of Water of Life

In **Rev. 21:6**, the Lord promised to ***'give unto him that is athirst of the fountain of the water of life freely.'*** That promise is only directed at the saints. They'll be the only resurrected beings to have access to the river of water of life, which John recorded *(in Rev. 22:1)* seeing proceed directly from God's throne and out into the holy city. This incredible river will be ***'clear as crystal'*** and will run right down the middle of what is sure to be an unprecedentedly wide and impressive street. Evidently, that street will be a sort of "Main Street" in the New Jerusalem and will lead to and from God's throne, which will be the very heart of God's eternal kingdom.

Streets of gold - imagine that!

Because gold is Earth's most malleable element, it's possible to hammer or role it until it becomes transparent. However, in order to do that, the gold would become unworkably thin and fragile; it certainly couldn't be used to pave a street. Normally, on this present earth, we mortals make streets out of the least expensive, most durable products possible, and we wouldn't think of covering them with gold. Things in Heaven, however, will be much different. Thus, after having seen the New Jerusalem's Main Street and pure river of water of life, John described that street as being made of such pure gold that it had the appearance of being fabricated of gold-tinted, transparent glass.[614] So, since the Main Street and overall structure of the heavenly city are going to be made of pure, transparent gold, how incredible do you suppose the rest of the New Jerusalem will be?

'In the midst of the street of it . . . .'

If we look carefully at John's preceding choice of words (*Rev. 22:1-2*), we can logically conclude that John is describing an unspeakably beautiful, crystal-clear river running right down the middle of what will be the most prominent street in God's holy city. Hence, considering the immense size of the New Jerusalem and the fact that even its perimeter wall (*the boundary wall around the city*) will be constructed of pure jasper stone and stand at least as tall as a twenty story building, it certainly wouldn't be wildly presumptuous of us to imagine that this Main Street could be far wider and more impressive than any previous street or avenue conceived by man! What's more, given that as a family of many billions of saints and angels we're likely to regularly use this golden Main Street as a means of joyfully making our way toward God's throne (*to participate in corporate praise and worship*), I wouldn't be surprised if in addition to the massive Main Street the Lord doesn't also create an enormously vast and gloriously

[614] Rev. 21:18-21

ornate courtyard around His throne — a courtyard designed to accommodate a gathering of many billions of saints and angels all at the same time. I make this point because I seriously doubt the saints will have to gather around God's throne in shifts, for lack of space!

Today, when we see an image of just a million or so people gathered in one place we're amazed by the size of the crowd. So, to help us broaden our thinking and enable us to lightly grasp the unfathomable size of God's future, eternal kingdom and how incredibly vast a paved gathering area around the throne will have to be if God intends us all to assemble as one enormous family of saints and angels, consider the following:

> According to most estimates, in just the past 2,000 years, more than 100 billion people have populated the earth. So, just for fun, let's very conservatively estimate that only two to three percent of that 100 billion (*from the birth of Christ to the present*) will end up in Heaven. We won't even attempt to guess how many saints will ultimately be redeemed from among those who lived during the first 4,000 year period, prior to the birth of Christ; which means that the actual number of saints, who will ultimately spend eternity with God, will likely be significantly larger than our estimate.
>
> So, if we allow for just enough space on the courtyard around God's throne to enable just 2 to 3 billion saints to corporately assemble, without bumping into each other, that courtyard will have to be roughly **40** to **50** miles in diameter!

Stop for just a minute. Go outside and imagine a sea of smiling saints, in brilliant white robes, covering every square foot of land, far beyond what you can see in every direction. Now, try and imagine how much larger the courtyard around God's throne will have to be once we've allowed for the hundreds of millions of angels who will also be there!

With that in mind . . . .

If God does intend to create a massive gathering area surrounding His throne (*Unfortunately John's vision doesn't reveal any details.*), then the *"pure river of water of life,"* which will proceed directly out of God's throne, will undoubtedly run right through the center of that courtyard, continue straight down the middle of the massive golden Main Street, and outward, into the rest of the city. What's more, given that this miraculous river will be a life-giving river, and the new earth will, no doubt, be bursting with all manner of never before seen plants, animals, and flora, it certainly seems likely that this river will continue flowing all the way out of the golden city and into the new earth. I don't believe it can be proven, but, given the divine nature and origin of this miraculous river, I doubt it will ever end!

Can't you just see it?

To envision what John described, let's imagine that this tremendously wide and gloriously ornate golden "Main Street" will start at the edge of the vast courtyard around God's throne and continue outward, throughout the city, and further onward, toward the new earth. Now, let's envision the crystal-clear *"pure river of water of life"* running right down the middle of this vast golden street, dividing it into two immensely wide, parallel avenues. Before we continue, let's not forget that the open area inside the New Jerusalem could logically be several hundreds of miles long, wide and high! That means that this transparent gold street and the river of water of life could also be several hundreds of miles long and unprecedentedly wide, so wide, in fact, that, if we were standing on one side of the golden street, we would likely have to strain our eyes (*if we were still mortals*) to see across the river and its botanically ornate tree, shrub, and grass-covered banks to the enormous golden parallel avenue on the other side!

The Tree of Life will adorn the Banks of the River

John doesn't attempt to describe the unspeakable beauty he saw in the New Jerusalem and the new earth, but we can imagine this crystal-clear river of water of life and its banks having spacious green grassy lawns, and plush splendidly fragrant planter areas, with breathtakingly beautiful, never before seen, flowering trees, plants, and shrubs.

Rev. 22:3

> ***'And <u>there shall be no more curse</u>: but the throne of God and of the Lamb shall be in it*** (the city) . . .'

For just a very short time Adam and Eve experienced life without *"the curse,"* but even they have no idea how eternally blissful a continually immortal existence of basking in God's blessings, rather than the shame of His curse, will be. Never again will we – "the saints" – be reminded of our past shortcomings and failures. Hence, possibly as a perpetual reminder that there shall be no more "curse,"[615] all along the banks of the pure river

[615] Thanks to Ez. 47:12, we learned that, during the Millennial Period, all along the *"healing waters river"* will grow trees that will be very similar to the trees that will grow along the banks of the river of life in the New Jerusalem. However, although the trees of which Ezekiel spoke will also yield new fruit each month and their leaves will not fade, Ezekiel never referred to those trees as *"trees of life."* There

of water of life, God will plant the tree of life. That's right! Throughout all eternity, the tree of life will majestically adorn the banks of that life giving river and stand as a perpetual symbol of God's infinite, loving grace toward the saints. What's more, the leaves of those miraculous trees of life will be for the healing of the nations; thus, they'll never wilt nor fade. Plus, those particular trees have been designed to bare a different type of fruit every month.[616] We shouldn't, however, be thinking of mere apples, oranges or pomegranates, because these very special trees are sure to bare twelve totally unique and excitingly different fruits!

How can we help but to wonder?

Throughout our extensive examination of end-time prophecy, my unremitting conviction to adhere to a strictly straight forward interpretation of Scripture, free of supposition, should have become clearly apparent. I firmly believe that if a thought or theory hasn't "**self-emerged**" from the text we shouldn't embrace it or teach it as though it were fact. Only through this discipline can Christians properly submit to a divinely inspired interpretation of God's Holy Word and, thereby, ensure our credibility and sound foundation for faith among skeptics.

Having hopefully made that clear, you may have noticed that while surveying these final scriptures, which reveal the New Jerusalem and new earth, I've chosen to exercise a little less restraint in the hopes of enabling us to imagine just how awesome this future eternal kingdom of God will be. Personally, I can't see the Lord not expecting us to do so. How could we help but to try and envision the actual fulfillment of John's description of Heaven? Revealing these few specific details regarding the building materials and dimensions of our future place of eternal residence (*as the Lord has chosen to do through John's vision*) and expecting us not to allow our imaginations to explore the glorious possibilities of this wonderful city's

---

fore, we shouldn't make the mistake of assuming that those trees will be the same as the trees in the New Jerusalem. Let's not forget that, during the Millennial Period, *"the curse"* will still be in effect, and sinful mortals will still inhabit the earth. Therefore, *"the curse"* won't actually end until the New Jerusalem begins—Rev. 22:3. Thus, it's a little hard to understand why John was told that the leaves on the *"trees of life"* will be for the healing of the nations, because by that time we'll all have been immortally resurrected and will all be dwelling in God's eternal city. We should acknowledge, however, that the word *healing* in that passage can be translated as meaning *therapy,* and I would imagine that just seeing those *"trees of life"* is going to be extremely therapeutic for us all.

[616] Given that, throughout eternity, there will no longer be a moon (*Rev. 21:23*), we're forced to presume that John is being told that these trees will bare new fruit "seasonally." Now we only need to figure out what "seasonally" will mean on the new earth. *Hey, good luck with that!*

design would be like placing a tasty morsel of beef on the tip of a dog's nose and forbidding him to eat it! Our God isn't cruel; He would never do such a thing. However, though I do believe that God expects us to joyfully anticipate and try to imagine the realization of these scriptures, while openly doing so, my intent is to always make it perfectly clear when my musings are merely *"free-thinking"* rather than fact.

Foreheads like billboards?

That's a pretty strange thought—isn't it? Nonetheless, if we're meant to couple Jesus' words from **Rev. 3:12** with the following passage and interpret them literally, rather than allegorically, then God must intend to extensively tattoo or permanently mark in some way the foreheads of the saints. Having told John that throughout eternity the curse will no longer be in effect, the angel continued by explaining that the citizens of the holy city will forever serve God and the Lamb:

> '. . . *And they shall see His* {the Triune God's} *face; and* ***His name shall be in their foreheads****. And there shall be no night there; and they need no candle, neither light of the sun; for the Lord God giveth them light: and they shall reign for ever and ever.*'

℘ Rev. 22:3-5 ℘

Most of us have seen at least a few flamboyant souls, who of their own freewill have chosen to decorate their foreheads with some sort of permanent tattoo, but if you're anything like me you probably cringe at the mere thought of doing so. Nonetheless, if we reflect back to the close of Jesus' letter to Christians at Philadelphia, Jesus promised to write ***'the name of His God, the name of the city of His God and His new name'*** upon the forehead of every overcomer. That seems like a lot of writing; doesn't it? Just before having said this, however, and in the same sentence, Jesus also promised to make every overcomer a *"pillar"* in the Temple of God. Thus, since I doubt the Lord would expect any of us to be excited at the prospect of becoming an eternally fixed *"column"* (*pillar*) in His golden city, perhaps we should consider the possibility of an allegorical, rather than literal, interpretation of the text.

According to **Rev. 21:22**, there will be no Temple in the New Jerusalem, for the Lord God Almighty and the Lamb will be the Temple thereof. Therefore, Jesus' promise of making every overcomer a pillar in the Temple of the Lord was clearly intended to assure every saint of their future permanent status and unrestricted access to the eternal kingdom and throne of God. But does that necessarily mean that nothing Jesus said in His entire discourse was intended to be taken literally? Let's see.

'And I looked, and, lo, a Lamb stood on the mount Sion, and with him an hundred forty and four thousand, ***having his Father's name written in their foreheads****.'*

Rev. 14:1

What John expressed seeing in the preceding passage will take place precisely as John described. Hence, there's absolutely no logical reason for our assuming that the foreheads of the resurrected 144,000 Jewish servants will not literally bear the name of God; thus, we have a solid precedent for God's name being written on the forehead of at least some of the saints. Therefore, since everything the angel told John in **Rev. 22:1-6** is intended to be taken literally, there's a good chance that throughout all eternity the foreheads of each and every saint will proudly bear the name of God and the Lamb.

The time is at hand . . .

Rev. 22:7

'Behold, I come quickly: blessed is he that keepeth the sayings of the prophecy of this book.'

When John's revelation of end-time events drew to a close, as is often the case when mortals interact with heavenly beings, John couldn't help but to fall down and begin to worship the angel (*messenger*) through whom the Lord had revealed this incredible vision. However, as John began to do so, the angel swiftly responded with the following words:

'See thou do it not: for ***I am thy fellowservant****,* ***and of thy brethren the prophets****, and of them which keep the sayings of the prophecy of this book:* ***worship God****.'*

Rev. 22:9

The angel, being of divine origin,[617] was not likely declaring his humani-y (*although that is a possibility*). Instead, it seems more logical to conclude hat he was merely explaining that he, like John and every other prophet, s only a messenger (*a servant of God*) and, therefore, not an object of

[6]17 Rev. 21:9

adoration. God alone is worthy of our worship and adoration. Thus, after making it perfectly clear that he, like all angels and saints, is merely a servant of God, the angel further instructed John as follows: ***"Seal not the sayings of the prophecy of this book: for the time is at hand."*** Since the angel made this declaration nearly 2,000 years ago, just as Peter's following prophecy foretells, many scoffers (*during these final days before the Lord triumphantly returns to earth*) have made the foolish mistake of presuming this warning to be nothing more than a myth.

*'. . . there shall come **in the last days scoffers**, walking after their own lusts, **And saying**, **Where is the promise of his coming**? for since the fathers fell asleep, all things continue as they were from the beginning of the creation.'*

2 Peter 3:3-4

Sadly, this seems to be the haughtily faithless state of most of the world today, both Jews and Gentiles alike. I've even had defiantly spiteful individuals, to whom I had been witnessing, respond by saying:

"I can't wait for the time to come when Christians will have to humbly admit that they were fools for having warned the world of Christ's imminent return to judge the earth!"

Nonetheless, Jesus is not slack concerning His promises. Instead, as Peter further prophesied, Jesus is mercifully long suffering:

'The Lord is not slack concerning his promise, as some men count slackness; but is longsuffering to us-ward, not willing that any should perish, but that all should come to repentance.'

2 Peter 3:9

'He that is unjust, let him be unjust still: and he that is filthy, let him be filthy still: and he that is righteous, let him be righteous still: and he that is holy, let him be holy still. And, behold I come quickly; and my reward is with me, to give unto every man according as his work shall be. I am "**Alpha**" and "**Omega**," the beginning and the end, the first and the last. - **Rev. 22:11-12**

Once eternity begins, whatever you are - forever you will be!

Though the mercy of God is measureless, God is righteous. That means that there must come a time when it will be eternally "too-late" to respond to the Lord's call to repent. When that fateful moment arrives, every soul will forever exist in whatsoever state it is, whether justified and made holy through faith in Christ, or filthy and defiled for having lived a life of self-willed obstinacy — ever failing to truly submit to the Lord's will. So, before delivering what is possibly the most terrifying warning in all of Scripture, Jesus offers one last invitation to all unrepentant souls:

> *'And the Spirit and the bride {the Holy Spirit and all the redeemed of Christ} say Come. And let him that heareth say, Come. And let him that is athirst come. and whosoever will, let him take of the water of life freely.'*
>
> **Rev. 22:17**

The preceding message is a clear reference to the Holy Spirit and the true Church's current, continual preaching of the Gospel. Jesus is not only instructing all who hear the Gospel message to repent, but to also testify of that which they've heard and believed. It's not enough to simply harbor the truth. For if we are ashamed to openly testify of our faith in Christ's atonement for our sin, Jesus, likewise, will be ashamed to testify on our behalf before the Father.[618]

One Final, very powerful word of Warning

For several years I've heard many well-intentioned Christians mistakenly apply the following warning to the entire Bible:

Rev. 22:18-19

> ***'For I testify unto every man that heareth the words of the prophecy of <u>this book</u>, If any man shall add unto <u>these things</u>, God shall add unto him the plagues <u>that are written in this book</u>:***
>
> ***And if any man shall take away from the words <u>of the book of this prophecy</u>, God shall take away his part out of the book of life, and out of the holy city, and from the things <u>which are written in this book</u>.'***

---

[18] Luke 9:26

While I would personally expect a lightning bolt, a meteor, or possibly even a satellite to come crashing down on my head were I to intentionally misrepresent a single word of Scripture, the preceding passage was expressly intended to warn against willful perversion of John's prophetic record of end-time events. There's little doubt that any individual who would willfully choose to corrupt or misrepresent any book or letter of Scripture will eventually find themselves answering to God for having done so; that's a given! Nonetheless, we don't want to detract from the intended severity of Christ's warning by generalizing it and blanketly applying it to the entire Bible. Let's not forget that at the beginning of John's vision he was specifically told to write everything he was about to see in a book and send it to the seven churches, which, at that time, existed in Asia Minor.[619] That book — the book of Revelation (*mostly because of its date of origin and prophetic end-time content*) — was selected to be the final book in the modern Bible. Good choice! Thus, since Jesus repeatedly referred to ***'this book'*** in the preceding warning, we can be confident that His warning was specifically directed to those with knowledge of John's end-time vision.

John's Closing Salutation

Unlike some of the earlier prophets,[620] John gives no indication of having felt sick or weary after having received his Revelation vision. Instead, John simply relays Christ's final words, ***'Surely I come quickly.'*** Then, he affirms his vision with a quick ***'A'- men,'*** expresses a wish for Christ's rapid return, and ends his book with the following words: ***'The grace of our Lord Jesus Christ be with you all. A'-men.'***

The body of Christ (*the true Church*) has come a long way since John received this end-time vision and even further since Daniel, Ezekiel and Zechariah received theirs. Hence, all that remains is for believers in Christ to continue in faith, diligently persevering until the Lord returns, which can't be far off! Thus, our big brother Paul extends the following words of admonition, encouraging us to do precisely that:

'Be not deceived; God is not mocked: for whatsoever a man soweth, that shall he reap. For he that soweth to his flesh shall of the flesh reap corruption; but he that soweth to the Spirit shall of the Spirit reap life everlasting. And let us not be weary in well doing: for in due season we shall reap, if we faint not.'

Gal. 6:7-9

---

[619] Rev. 1:11

[620] Dan. 8:27, Hab. 3:16

DON'T GET COMFORTABLE; IT'S JUST A TEMPORARY DEPOT, NOT A PERMANENT DWELLING!

This brilliantly designed earth and all its splendor was created to be little more than a transition area of sorts — "**just a temporary depot**." God never intended us to consider our existence here to be our final destination. In fact, God's plans for our eternal existence are so fantastic and beyond anything we could ever hope to experience in this world that, while we're still in these mortal bodies, we could never begin to comprehend their wondrous fulfillment!

Sure, as far as depots go this earth is quite large, and for the lucky few the benches are sheltered and reasonably comfortable. But it's not the Lord's will that we let our relatively short lives in this metaphorical train station or our prideful need to have the very best seat in this waiting area ultimately distract us from what should be our only goal here on earth. And that goal is to be ready to get on the train when — *"in a flash" - "in just the twinkle of an eye"* — it unexpectedly comes roaring into the station.

So, before we even spend a single second surveying the waiting area for a comfortable seat, we first need to humbly approach the ticket window and lay claim to that *"free ticket"* Jesus so lovingly purchased and left in will-call for our retrieval. Because when that train does suddenly rush into the station there will have been no warning prior to its arrival, and when it stops it will only be for a fraction of a second. In that instant, only those who are already waiting on the platform — "**with ticket in hand**" — will be allowed to board. All others will sadly be left-behind!

'Behold, I stand at the door, and knock: if any man hear my voice, and open the door, I will come in to him, and will sup with him, and he with me.'

Rev. 22:17

Until our Savior returns and our toils end, may the grace of God be with you all - Amen.

Isaiah 1:18

Maranatha